Never Feel A Stranger

Peter Biddlecombe

ABACUS

An *Abacus* Book
First published in Great Britain in 2001
by Abacus

A CIP catalogue record for this book
is available from the British Library.

ISBN 0 349 11448 X

Typeset in Galliard by M Rules
Printed and bound in Great Britain
by Clays Ltd, St Ives plc

Abacus
A Division of
Little, Brown and Company (UK)
Brettenham House
Lancaster Place
London WC2E 7EN

Contents

*Expenses; I Came, I Saw, I Lost My Luggage;
Now Change Me Back Again; Faster, They're Gaining* and *A
Nice Time Being Had By All*, all of which are available from
Abacus Travel.

He is the first travel writer to have visited and written
about over 160 different countries.

Introduction

I'm lucky. Unlike most people I know, who go abroad just to
avoid mowing the lawn or spending yet another weekend
with the in-laws, I've been forced to travel so much in life just
to earn a crust that nowadays I never feel a stranger to whatever they throw at me. In fact, I travel so much that whenever
I use my credit cards in the UK they always ring me up to
check they haven't been stolen. Even that doesn't faze me.

Reluctance, indifference, a total lack of concern – I've had
them all. And that's usually just getting my foreign currency.
Or trying to.

I call NatWest at 208 Piccadilly. This is not what you are
supposed to do. You are supposed to dial their superefficient
Customer Call Centre. But because I have dialled their superefficient Customer Call Centre so many times in the past,
and complained like mad because I've had to call them a million times before they answer the phone, wait for a lifetime
before they put me through to somebody who can help me,
and then they've either given me the wrong amount of the
wrong currency or, worse still, nothing at all, the bank, in its

wisdom, told me, 'Forget our superefficient Customer Call Centre. Call the branch direct.'

What happens when I call the branch direct? I'll tell you exactly what happens. In fact, I'll tell you exactly what happens to me on Thursday 3 June 1999.

09.15: Call branch number. Phone rings for five minutes. No reply.

10.15: Call branch number. Phone rings for five minutes. No reply.

11.15: Call branch number. Phone rings for five minutes. No reply.

12.15: Call branch number. Phone rings for five minutes. No reply.

13.55: Call branch number. Phone rings for five minutes. No reply.

To think these guys told me to ring the branch number direct because they were going to offer me a better service.

14.00: Call superefficient NatWest Customer Call Centre. Machine answers. Wait. Wait. Wait.

14.07: Superefficient Call Centre girl says, 'Hang on, I'll put you through to your local branch.'

I say, 'I've been trying to call them since nine-fifteen. They're not answering. Can I order some US dollars?'

'No. You have to order them from the branch.'

'But I was told I had to order them from you. It was only because you were so inefficient that the branch told me—'

I am put on hold.

I hang on and hang on.

Girl comes back.

'Name,' she barks. 'Address. Postcode. Name of account. Account number. Date account was opened.'

Date account was opened? Good God in heaven. I begin to explode. 'How the hell can I . . . Look, all I want is to order some—'

'It's Data Protection. If you can't tell me, I can't—'

'Look, all I want is—'

She cuts me off. For crying out loud, the great NatWest, which has been quite happy to have its hands in my pockets for fifty years, which charges me for just breathing when I walk past its doorway, which is supposed to pride itself on offering a service to its customers, has put the phone down on me. I begin to go ballistic. But what can I do? I need my US dollars.

14.13: I call the branch again. No reply.

14.18: I call the so-called superefficient NatWest Call Centre again. Machine answers.

14.37: I finally get to talk to a so-called superefficient Call Centre tofu. 'I need some US dollars,' I say.

'I'll put you through to your local branch.'

'I don't want . . . All I want is to order some US dollars. Since nine-fifteen this morning—'

'I'll call you back,' screeches the voice.

'I don't want you to call me back. All I want is—'

She puts the phone down on me. A second so-called super-efficient Call Centre yooha . . . The great and glorious NatWest, which has been taking money out of my . . . It's now nearly three o'clock in the afternoon, and I still haven't got my US dollars.

15.57: Yet again I call the so-called superefficient NatWest Customer Call Centre. Machine answers.

16.12: A so-called NatWest superefficient Call Centre yak deigns to come on the line.

I am, I'll admit, beginning to lose my cool. 'I want some US dollars. Twice you guys have put the phone down—'

'I'll put you through to your branch.'

'I don't want—'

I am put on hold.

16.16: The girl comes back. 'The line is still engaged. You'll have to wait until they're—'

'Why the hell should I wait?' I scream. 'I've been trying to order some US dollars since nine-fifteen . . . I've made . . . Twice . . . All I want is . . . What do I have to do to . . .'

'Well, you'll have to wait,' barks the superefficient yak. 'They're dealing with a customer.'

'Well, tell them I'm a customer and I've been trying—'

'Yes. But they're dealing with a customer who's taken the trouble to go into the branch.'

'Taken the trouble? What the hell do you think I've been doing?'

'You'll just have to wait.'

Now another voice comes on the line.

'Yes?' she says in that smarmy tone they're taught to use with unreasonable customers who are getting angry just because they've been trying to order some US dollars for seven hours. 'Yes? Can I help you?'

'Yes,' I whimper. 'Seven hours . . . Ten calls . . . Twice . . . US dollars... Three thousand pounds' worth.'

'Yes,' she oozes. 'Certainly. Thank you.'

Obviously a prime candidate for the NatWest Lifetime Achievement Award for Putting up with Customers.

On Monday 7 June they ring me back.

'What did you say your account number was?'

'My account . . . ? I've told you a million . . . I've been a customer at your branch for . . . All you've got to do is . . .'

I'm a nervous wreck.

Then there's agony, heartache, misery – terminal misery. Terminals are no strangers to me, either, thanks to the fact that I'm forced to fritter away my life in airports all over the world. I say airports. They're more shopping malls and fast-food operations with runways attached.

I hate them. Hate everything to do with them. I hate the knuckleheads who don't know what they're doing, where they're going or what flights they are supposed to be getting. I hate the big, beefy, burly, superfit yahoos who look as though they're on thrice-daily injections of steroids, who are so strong and fit and healthy that they can't carry their little designer suitcases a mere twenty yards. Instead they have to daintily pull them along behind them on those little wheels, blocking up all the walkways and swerving into everyone in sight.

I hate the wazzocks who take up all the seats at the bar, drink nothing but yucky glasses of mineral water and go on and on about how, if the number on your British Airways Executive Club card begins with a 7, you're automatically entitled to any upgrades going.

And am I the only one getting tired of all the old Granny, don't do this, don't do that signs like:

'DANGER! MAN-EATING CROCODILE BEHIND THIS DOOR'

'DANGER! NO ENTRY. 500 MILLION VOLTS'

that they keep plastering up all over the place?

I hate all those recorded voices. 'You are approaching the end of the travelator. Start walking now.' My God. We spend more money on education now than we have ever done in the history of the world; more people have degrees, play with computers and watch *Who Wants to be a Millionaire?* This might come as a shock to airport managers, but people can tell when the travelator is coming to an end and they have to start walking.

In the old days I used to believe in travelling early and drinking late. Now, is it any wonder, I believe in drinking early and travelling late.

Then there are my other friends: shame, humiliation and pointless, mind-numbing, jaw-dropping stupidity. In other words, the check-in. To think that when I first started dragging myself around the world, my biggest headache was what the old dumper behind the counter was going to think of my non-matching suitcases. Now checking in is about as many laughs as fighting your way into a coil of razor wire.

Take the queues. What's the point in airlines forcing me to buy my ticket on-line to save their time and make them more money if, when I turn up at the airport, I have to spend three days queuing to be wrongly checked in for a flight which is going to be overbooked? Don't they realise the longer I have to queue, the more time I have not only to read my airline ticket but to read between the airlines as well?

Name. Now this is not, of course, your real name, but the airlines' idea of your name, and how they feel it should be spelled.

Passenger ticket and baggage check. This is to remind them to allocate the wrong passenger to the wrong suitcase. You think I'm kidding? Look at the airline quality ratings. They reckon that something like three out of four suitcases go missing on national or international flights. I'm vague about it because I had the full report in my suitcase, and my suitcase went missing. All congratulations, however, to the Indian government. At least they're honest about it. Coming in to land at Bombay once, I was given a disembarkation card that read, in big bold type, 'Passengers expecting mishandled baggage later should obtain landing certificate from customs.'

Origin/Destination. Have they made certain that not only have they allocated the wrong passenger to the wrong baggage, but have put them both on the wrong flights?

Booking reference. Have they put down the wrong reference so that when all hell breaks loose nobody can find anybody?

XO. This tells you how long or how short a time you can spend in the place you're trying to get to if, of course, you ever get there. X means there is no limit on the time you can stay in any place. O means if you decide to stay there, there's nothing there.

Carrier. This lists the diseases carried by the aircraft and the ones you could carry back home.

Flight. The flight the disease arrived on.

Class. This indicates the quality of staff wot are on yer flite. Check any number of tickets for any flight anywhere and you will see the airlines' own admission that they have very few first-class staff on board. B means Bloody awful. Y means too Young to do the job, but that's all they could get. V means they were so bad they even got fired by Virgin. X means I'd make a will if I were you.

Status. OK or KK means your booking has been 100 per cent accepted by the airline, confirmed and underlined three times. It is indisputable proof that you will get on the flight. Probably. WI means you're entitled to all the wine you can drink so long as it's in I (International airspace). RQ means they've got you down as a Raving Queen. If they ever did that to me, air rage or no air rage, I'd tear the plane apart.

Fare basis. The most unfair part of the ticket: how much they overcharged you for it. QL means Quite a Lot. HO means Heavily Overcharged. HOX means not only Heavily Overcharged but Heavily Overcharged Xceedingly. H23W means Heavily Overcharged and it should take you at least twenty-three weeks to pay for it.

Consumer protection? You've got to be joking. You read the small print. The passenger is merely an irritant to be shunted and shuffled around and then disposed of at will. If we force the airline to cancel the flight – it's never their fault – they might just, if we tear the place apart, consider giving us an alternative flight this side of the next millennium. There is no mention of the cost of keeping secretaries waiting, the extra night in an hotel, the caviar, the champagne, rearranging meetings, the inconvenience, or of the physical and mental cost of trying to convince the wife that the flight really was cancelled and it wasn't your fault you had to spend an extra week in the south of France holed up in an apartment in the Negresco with half a dozen air stewardesses because it was the only room left in town.

Having read and studied as many airline tickets as I have in my time, I now try, for the sake of my health, to avoid queuing altogether, by either turning up very early (in the old days you could get somebody else to turn up early and check in on your behalf, which was a million times better), or very, very late when – I know it's unfair – I will be rushed immediately to the head of the queue. Well, other people do it all the time, so why can't I?

If I can't help arriving in between very early and very late, I try to use one of the following tricks to avoid the queues.

Electronic check-in
Will someone please tell me why, if I check in at the desk, I get all the damn fool questions about who packed my luggage, but if I check in electronically I go straight through, no questions asked?

Club check-in
I pretend the office made a mistake. Oh hell. I asked them to book one Club, but, goodness me, is that really a horrible tourist ticket? I do apologise. But now that I'm here, I wonder . . .

The ticket counters
I pretend I've got a query on my ticket. I ask a lot of stupid questions, then, just to get rid of me, they check me in.

Boarding gate

This is easy in the States, but risky in the UK and Europe. On the other hand, I'll take any risks to bypass a queue.

Some airlines have roaming check-ins. In the US I've noticed that Alaska Airlines have check-in staff wandering around the terminals on dog sledges equipped with hand-held computers. They're a great help. If, of course, you're travelling on Alaska Airlines and you've had your tetanus jab. Swissair have the best system I've come across. Walk through passport control at Zurich, and they give you your boarding card. The first time it happened to me I thought I was being deported.

But, whatever options you try, sooner or later, one way or another, you're face to face with disgust, revulsion, bitterness, ridicule. Yawning in your face. Raging tempers. In other words, the check-in desk. My God, where do they find these bozos? The nonsense they come out with. No wonder they all look as if they're in the middle of some kind of psychic breakdown.

'Did you pack your luggage?' Who the hell else is going to pack my luggage? In any case, what's the point of asking me if I packed my luggage or not if you have no way of checking whether whatever I say is true?

'Did anyone put anything in your bag without your knowledge?' Good God Almighty. If anyone had put anything in my baggage without my knowledge, how the hell would I know? Don't these dorks listen to the rubbish they spout again and again and again?

Now there's the question of the luggage itself. Does it meet their impossible regulations – which must have been drawn up by some prehistoric lump of Samsonite – or does it not? Just think for a moment. If the problem is weight, then surely they shouldn't just check the size and weight of the baggage, but the size and weight of the baggage and passenger combined. Why should I, a svelte, athletic 150-pounder with a briefcase that is a mere 0.0001 of a kilo over their arbitrary limit for hand luggage be bounced all over the place while some 27-stone anally retentive scumbag paying the same fare as me is given two seats and allowed to take on maximum luggage and maximum hand luggage? The whole thing is a nonsense.

I know some guys who travel so light they take only a toothbrush with them which they use for everything from brushing their hair and getting the blonde hairs off their jackets to gouging out whatever they find living between their toes. I don't travel quite that light. I always take a briefcase.

You can only take 1.17 kilos, they say. Who says? Why not 1.18½ kilos? You can't take 1.19 kilos, they say. It could fall out of the overhead compartment and injure passengers. OK, so fix the overhead compartments so that it can't fall out. What is this? The most difficult problem in the world? Lots of people with lots of carry-ons delay the plane from taking off on schedule, they say. OK, so bring forward the time of boarding.

The thing I don't understand is why they make all the fuss about carry-ons but nobody says a word about the booze. According to the rules – something else I read while queuing up – anything that is highly inflammable is not allowed on board. Booze that is 140 degrees proof is highly inflammable, but that's allowed on board. How come? Why don't they check every bottle that comes on board? Why don't they ban airport duty-frees from selling anything over 140 degrees proof?

My solution, which is so sensible, fair and honest it will naturally be completely ignored, is to take the airlines at their word and base everything on weight. So much for passengers occupying one seat. So much more for passengers occupying one seat with six inches of legroom. Double for passengers occupying two seats. So much more for hand luggage. So much more still for checked-in luggage. That way svelte, athletic types like me with only a briefcase to their name would pay far, far less than 27-stone dinks with hand luggage the size of a cheap Spanish *hacienda*.

But why stop there? I'd be happy to pay even more to sit in a peanut-free zone as far away as possible from smelly old women with dogs, vegetarians, tut-tutting non-drinkers and howling kids. And what wouldn't anyone pay for their luggage to be delivered to the same continent in the same week/month/year as their flight?

Finally, if you haven't been totally crushed by all the shame, humiliation and pointless, mind-numbing, jaw-dropping stupidity, the clouds will part, there will be a distant sound of trumpets and you will be handed your ticket and boarding pass. Not that, in the wonderful world of airlines, it means a thing. Whatever bit of paper you've got, whatever it says, they can do whatever the hell they like. You can, for example, buy from them one day a perfectly legal back-to-back ticket, which is cheaper than buying a standard-fare ticket, and the next day, for reasons of their own, they can refuse to accept it. You can one day buy from them a perfectly legal throwaway for a series of trips such as London–Delhi–London–Larnaca, which for some strange reason is cheaper than the straight London–Delhi–London ticket, and just not use the final London–Larnaca sector. The next day, unaccountably, they can refuse to accept it. Then, even if you've got a valid booking, even if the airline has confirmed your booking, even if you've checked in, even though they're for ever telling you they love you and that, as far as they're concerned, you're the only person in the world, you can still be thrown off the flight. Not because of any mistake you've made, but because they overbooked. Be warned. Most airlines now overbook by at least 10 per cent. Lufthansa go for 12 per cent, while Air France, that most devoted-to-its-customers airline, goes for 20 per cent. *Bon chance*, as they say.

Now, as if that were not more than enough for a single lifetime, comes arrogance, pretence, bombast, bluster and a whole wide world of little Adolfs. In other words, security.

First things first. What's the point of subjecting passengers to security check after security check if there are no controls on people wandering all over the airport itself? Take, for example, Sheremetyevo Airport in Moscow, which you would think was as secure as they come. No way. It has so many holes in its perimeter fencing it looks like one of their nuclear submarines. Some of the gaps are big enough to drive a NATO truck through if they could afford the price of the petrol. As for security patrols, even the Russians themselves admit they have only one car and two guards to patrol the whole 15-kilometre boundary fence.

Then, in virtually any airport in which you are wasting your life away, I guarantee that, wherever you turn, there are planes left unlocked and unattended for hours on end.

But the biggest laugh of all are the X-ray machines. After years of getting past X-ray machines in jewellery and precious-metal companies all over the world which are a million times more powerful, not to mention more efficient than those in airports, I can get past practically any security arch or X-ray machine anywhere in the world. I reckon even your typical Virgin passenger would have no problem staggering through an airport X-ray machine with armloads of plastic explosives. Don't tell anyone I told you, but only eighty airports in the security-obsessed US have the magic CTX 5000 CAT-scan machine that can detect plastic explosives. As they cost a good few hundred thousand dollars a time, you can imagine how few other airports elsewhere in the world have them.

If the X-ray machines are Mickey Mouse, what about the security staff, most of whom look as if they couldn't recognise a stick of Semtex if it was stuck up their nose? With all due respect, even if they have had two and a half hours of in-depth training and have given up a career at McDonald's to do the job for an unbelievable US$7.50 an hour, can you really say you are happy to put your life in the hands of such a bunch of knuckleheads, failures, perverts and freemasons, albeit de-aproned and de-fanged? Remind me, by the way, not to open any envelopes for the next month. Or at least, any envelopes with my name scrawled in green ink in KAPTAL LETUCE.

You don't believe the security checks are as bad as I say? So what about the number of guns and fake bombs, complete with battery wires and timers, carried through by various security inspectors? Still don't believe me? OK, test them for yourself. Next time you're going on a trip, strap a gun to the small of your back before you go through the arch. The bells will ring like mad. Some security scumbag, if he's not asleep or deep in some highly complicated picture crossword, will shuffle up to you and give you the magic-wand treatment. Stand with your arms to your sides and the gun will set it off. If you stand with your arms outstretched, the jacket will pull away from your back and the gun will go undetected.

Finally, I'm through security. Is that the end of all the nonsense? Of course not. Now there are the loudspeaker announcements from Planet Stupid. 'Attention passenger Kim Jong-il. Will you please come to Gate 357H, where we are now in the process of unloading yourself and your nuclear missile from this flight.'

'Passengers on flight AB123, will you please make your way to Gate 85A, where the flight is now closed.'

I tell you, being forced to travel the world for a living you never feel a stranger to anything.

And I haven't even been bounced off the plane yet.

Passenger name: BIDLECOM/PYTR
Booking reference: DODGI
Destination: ᴎꞱꓷꓷ∩ꟺᗡᎈ∩ᴎꓤꓤꓖ

Peshawar

Talk about the Great Game.

There I was, 3,500 feet up in the Khyber Pass, one of the most spectacular passes I think it has ever been my privilege to see, apart from the one in that pub in Nottingham all those years ago, which I'll tell you about some other time. If I ever get my breath back.

There it was. Thirty-five miles long and 25 miles wide, although at one point two camels could hardly pass each other without getting the hump. Through here, raping and pillaging, came all the gentle, civilising giants of history: Mahmud of Ghazni, Alexander the Great, Sabuktigin, Darius, Tamurlane, or rather, Timur the Lame, Genghis Khan, the Emperor Babur, Nadir Shah, Ahmad Shah Abdali and, of course, the British, although it took them no fewer than forty goes in forty-four years to finally make it, maybe because they enjoyed the raping and pillaging more than all the others. Who knows?

Now, on a blisteringly hot Sunday morning, it was my turn. To experience the Khyber Pass, that is. The rest would have to wait. Especially as it was a Sunday.

In front of me, way down in the valley, veiled in the mist, was the border with Afghanistan. But then, thanks to the Taleban, practically everything in Afghanistan is veiled one way or another. I could just about make out a couple of squat, boring buildings which looked like public libraries, although at one time one had been a motel and the other a restaurant, and I swear that was Osama bin Laden waving at some US space satellite way overhead and then climbing into a rickety old taxi and heading back to the mountains.

Once this was a favourite stopping point and picnic site for people crossing backwards and forwards over the frontier, not to mention the scene of many bitter battles:

'I think I'll have another drink.'

'No, you can't, you're driving.'

'But Vienna is a long way off.'

'That's the trouble with you, Genghis, you never know when to stop. Just once more, and I warn you I shall go home to Mother.'

All around the border, the so-called Durand Line drawn up by the British way back in 1893 to separate British India from Afghanistan, were all kinds of barricades and booby traps, tank traps and every kind of tourist trap you could think of. Including, no doubt, some guy selling cans of Coke at US$10 a throw.

Way beyond, you could just about see the outline of a ninth-century fort, the scene of one of the last battles between the British and the Afghans in 1919. It's an outline because practically anything worth anything in Afghanistan has been wrapped in straw and newspapers, packed in gun-metal boxes, labelled 'handicrafts of no commercial value' and flown out from remote airstrips to art dealers all over the world. But nobody anywhere knows anything about it. *Comme d'habitude*, as the art dealers say, although which country they come from I have no idea.

On my right, going down towards the border, was a non-stop stream of battered cars, smashed-up vans and huge, colourful, madly decorated psychedelic trucks loaded not just with your usual tea, soap, batteries and tyres, but also (I could tell by reading the outside of the boxes – another trick I learned during the Great Game) Sony video disk-players, Panasonic TVs, Compaq computers, a case of Patek Philippe watches, spare parts for a Ferrari, a couple of goats, an ox and, of course, the odd donkey which didn't know which way to turn. And it hadn't even got to the border yet.

Twisting and turning its way up from the border was a similar non-stop stream of battered cars, smashed-up old vans and huge psychedelic trucks bringing with them all the necessities of life: pistols, machine-guns, laser-sighted automatic rocket-launchers, SAM missiles, probably even the occasional Russian-made nuclear warhead, a couple of goats, an ox and of course, the odd donkey.

Weaving in between the cars and vans and trucks were millions of funny-looking three-in-one bicycles: the one the rider was on, with the front wheels of two others strapped either side of his back wheel. Ride them all the way from Kabul, across the border and through the Khyber Pass into Pakistan proper and sell all three, which is not too difficult, and you can look after your family for at least a couple of weeks. Unless, of course, your leg muscles can't take it: it's no Sunday school outing, even if you have been out on the kid's mountain bike a couple of times during school term. Then the family has to look after you for much longer.

But most of the stuff, whether it be a nuclear warhead or a bicycle, is not being smuggled across the frontier, you'll be pleased to hear. As befits a Muslim country with a strict moral code, an unshakeable allegiance to the very highest ethical standards and more Taleban white flags than is good for its health, it is being smuggled-smuggled across. Or, to use a technical term, double smuggled. Because Pakistan insists on charging huge tariffs on practically every consumer item you can think of, the clever guys bring shiploads of everything into Karachi tax-free because, they say, it is not for Pakistan, but for poor, landlocked Afghanistan. Then they load it all on to enormous trucks, drive them the length of the country, take them into Afghanistan, pay the much, much lower rates there, and then bribe Pakistani border officials with a big smile and a small brown envelope to allow them to bring them back into Pakistan, where everything can be sold at a huge profit.

Way over there in the distance are the vast Plains of Jalalabad and the Hindu Kush that Eric Newby made such a fuss about, and just down there – can you see them, by that big rock? – picking their way carefully up the hillside, the most modern and up-to date and swinging end of the Pakistani–Afghan cross-border trade: a long, straggling line of moth-eaten old camels. Inside each sack they are carrying is raw opium straight from the poppy fields of Afghanistan, the biggest poppy fields in the world. Two thousand five hundred tons of raw opium, don't forget, can be refined down to 250 tons of heroin, more than enough to keep the discreet, intimate parlours of Long Island, New York, Newport, Rhode Island and Greenwich, Connecticut echoing to aimless laughter for a couple of seasons. In any case it makes a change from methadone, or the even more deadly mix of 80 milligrams of straight Lithium Prozac they tend to take whenever they can't get hold of the real stuff. Or, if you really want to hit the high spots, a mixture of eggs and sage baked in the oven until it's as tough as old boots, mashed and then dried which, I'm reliably informed, looks and tastes more like the real thing than the real thing, and costs nothing at all. On the other hand, 250 tons of heroin, you don't need me to remind you, has a street value of around US$2.5 to $3 billion. So these moth-eaten old camels probably do more business in a single trip than all the cars and vans and trucks do in a year.

The big laugh is that all the weapons the mighty United States shipped to Afghanistan in 1979 to help them fight off the Soviets ended up in the hands of the big drug dealers who, while the Taleban still can't make up their minds whether growing opium is banned by the Koran or not, still use them even today to protect not only their supply routes but their growing fields as well. Clever guys, the Americans. Helping to wreak havoc on their own cities and to destroy their own people. But then, I suppose the Americans have always done more damage to themselves, their friends and their allies than they ever did to their enemies. Incidentally, the Chinese, who poured just as much arms and ammunition into Afghanistan to help the mujahidin, at least sent in over 300 military officers as well to make certain everything got through, was not side-tracked and was not used for any other purposes. But then, they are just a bunch of peasants.

Behind me, apart from half a million kids all trying to sell me second-hand chewing gum, were 15 million of the most gentle, peace-loving, violent, aggressive, most heavily armed, wheeler-dealing, smuggling, gun-making, gun-running, land-grabbing tribesmen in the world: the Pathan. Every single one of them was fingering a Kalashnikov underneath his cloak and wondering why the hell he should let me off when over the years they've thought nothing of cutting down thousands of British soldiers for half the price of a pint of camel's milk.

You haven't forgotten what Mahbub told Kim at Lucknow railway station, have you?

'Trust a snake before a harlot and a harlot before a Pathan.'

The Pathan have not mellowed in any way at all over the years. Just a few days before I got to the Khyber Pass, I was told, two local Pathan families had started arguing over a bunch of dead animals. Seven people ended up dead and four injured.

Was I worried? No way. Because I had with me my very own personal bodyguard. Well, I say bodyguard. He was about five foot nothing, as thin as a rake and wearing the regulation four-inch beard, a filthy pair of *shalwar qamiz*, the brother-in-law baggy pants, and the long, flowing shirt everybody wears so you can't see how much money they've got hidden in their pockets. But he did have an AK47 over his shoulder with what looked like a hundred-round banana clip. Oh yes, and he said he was not only prepared to guard my body, but to die for me as well.

Let me tell you, nobody has ever before in my life even pretended that I rated anything higher with them than a monthly pay cheque or a brown envelope on the corner of a desk. Not, I hasten to add, that the bodyguard was my idea. He was one of the conditions that the form-filling, time-consuming, rubber-stamping authorities way back in Peshawar, the one-time glorious winter capital of the Kushans, whose empire once rivalled that of Rome, and now the terrorist capital of the world, had insisted on before giving me permission to make my way up to the border with Afghanistan. At the time the Khyber Pass and the whole mountainous, craggy, lawless North-West Frontier Province, which runs for 700 kilometres along the border with Afghanistan, was definitely not, they kept insisting, the place to be. The Taleban were going bananas. Refugees were pouring out of the place like the blood out of a stone used to kill some poor guy for even thinking of saying good morning to his sister-in-law. Practically wherever you went this side of the border there were refugees everywhere: in proper official camps, in single tents tucked away behind a village in the middle of nowhere, or playing polo with a goat's carcass on a spare patch of dust surrounded by a million supporters.

At the same time the non-fighting Taleban and their super-fundamentalist teaching and customs were pushing their way deeper and deeper into northern Pakistan. 'Stay on the road, you're safe. Go off the road, you're dead,' I was told by one Pakistani soldier.

'No in between?'

'No in between.'

And he wasn't joking.

As soon as I started heading north to Peshawar and the Khyber Pass on the old Imperial Highway, which is now more of a dirt track, a country lane and a dual carriageway all rolled into one, I could see what he meant. It was about the riskiest thing I've ever done, apart from drinking that can of Coke in Belize City. The signs of the Taleban were everywhere. No kite-flying. No paper bags. No football shorts. The regulation four-inch beard. And, of course, the most obvious sign of all, the *burqa*, the virtual head-to-toe wigwam with what looks like a built-in metal grille in front of the eyes.

The ordinary veil, or even the *chador*, I think is a great idea for most women. I know many it would serve only to flatter. But these things, even I will admit, are going a bit too far.

'We want it for women. With *burqa*, women will be safe from our eyes,' an old man who appeared to be as blind as a bat kept telling me as I was wandering around looking at some huge fish tank near the Sikh temple just outside Hasan Abdal. Good old Jahangir, a friendly local despot, used to spend days on end here catching the big mahseer fish in order to put precious pearls in their mouths and then throw them back in the river again. Their descendants, it is said, are in the tank. With or without the precious pearls I couldn't tell.

By Attock, where the Kabul River meets up with the Indus, and which has been a garrison town for about as long as any-body can remember, the country was practically smothered in them. The odd one or two women who were not wearing the *burqa* were wearing veils of one sort or another. In fact the only female I saw not wearing some kind of veil was an old mare pulling a decrepit old cart pulling a broken-down Pakistani army Land Rover. Which must mean something or other.

The veil apart, the almost total separation of men and women was quite apparent. Not only is all music and dancing banned, but people are forbidden to sing or even whistle. All pictures and photographs are against the law. If a woman clicks her high heels under her *burqa* she is taken away and beaten.

Finally there were the mosques. Not just the number of mosques, but the amount of business they were doing, and the number of guys shuffling in and out of them. This was no Church of England Sunday-morning service attendance. This was more St Peter's Square on Easter Sunday morning. And it wasn't even Friday.

'Sharia is very strict law. Good people have no problems with Sharia. Only bad people. Only bad people and corrupt people against Sharia,' an eager young mullah with a white turban told me.

'But Sharia is cruel. It means they cut . . .' I began.

'Not a problem for good people. Good people not have to worry. Only bad people have to worry. Sharia law is very good.'

Another mullah joined us. He also had a white turban.

'Sharia makes bad people good people. Sharia very good,' he said.

On the other hand, it's not surprising they all agree with each other. Whichever side of the border they're on, they are all Pathans. They have the same history, the same traditions, the same customs, the same religion. Well, almost the same. Afghanistan and the Taleban are Sunni. Pakistan is Sunni with, admittedly, a Shia minority. But it's the Sunnis who run the place. Especially today.

Finally of course, Taleban or no Taleban, Sunni or no Sunni, everyone, not just the kids with the chewing gum, was desperate to do business. The war and the flood of refugees had thrown everything up in the air. All the old, established contacts had broken down. Anyone with two bits of coloured glass could do business – and they were. It's hardly surprising, therefore, that whatever the West had to say or quietly threaten, Pakistan was one of the first and one of the very few countries in the world to recognise the Taleban as the official government of Afghanistan.

As for Peshawar, which is an old Pakistani word for 'whatever you do, don't look round or you'll get a bullet in your back', I'm not saying it's crawling with terrorists, former CIA agents (or operations executives, as they like to call themselves today) and ex-Russian spies, it's just that the place is bursting with Afghans. Some say over 2 million of them are now packed into a city which at one time had a population of only around half a million. As a result, wherever you turn there are Afghan houses, Afghan hotels, Afghan hospitals, Afghan schools, Afghan universities, Afghan companies, especially transport companies, and, would you believe, Afghan volleyball and football teams. No shorts allowed. So far there are no Afghan cricket teams, but apparently they are working on it. Well, why shouldn't they encourage yet another country to beat England at the game at which we are supposed to be the best in the world?

At the same time it is also, inevitably, very Taleban. It's virtually surrounded by Taleban training camps – I was told the guys who let off the bombs in the US Embassy in Saudi Arabia were trained here. There's an official Taleban office in town, the hotels all have signs outside saying, 'Gunmen are required to deposit their weapons with hotel security', and whoever you meet is up to something or other. Like the Irishman I ran into in the jewellery bazaar, who kept advising me, for my own safety, to prepone, as opposed to postpone, any meeting I arranged. It was, he said, 'the need of the hour'.

A camp outside of town run by an organisation called Harkat-ul-Mujahidin, one of the most militant, hard-line

Islamic groups in the country (they were behind the hijacking of the Indian Airlines plane at the end of 1999) was, I heard, always open to the demands of the consumer. They ran free bus services from the middle of Karachi for would-be terrorists and assassins. Fancy joining them? If so, on the third Thursday of every month, be at the secret rendezvous near the port in Karachi and a bus will take you and twenty or thirty other young fanatics 600 miles north, where you can take a forty-day course in anything from beating up old ladies because they crossed the road with their husbands to hijacking planes, negotiating a handsome fee for the release of prisoners and escaping into the bush without any interference from the police or military. All for free.

One evening I was dodging the rickshaws and bullock carts in the old city when I stumbled across a bunch of guys who even to my untrained eye, did not look like Pakistanis. They weren't. They were Sri Lankans. They told me they were being trained not by the Taleban, but by Pakistani military in the big fort which dominates the town.

'You mean you're Tamil Tigers?' I hesitated.

They grinned. We all shook hands and I headed for my car as casually as possible.

It was then that I noticed we'd been standing outside a building announcing itself as the Army Squash Complex, which at the time sounded pretty ominous.

As well as being the terrorist capital of the world, Peshawar is probably also the smuggling capital of the world. Whatever Afghanistan needs, Afghanistan gets. Via somebody in Peshawar. Everything from videos to Marks & Spencer sweaters, from Nike shoes to the odd camel or, I suppose, packet of Camels. Not to mention a huge slice of the illegal imports pouring into Iran.

The most famous shopping street of all is, of course, Qissa Khawani Bazaar, Kipling's (yawn) Street of a Million Street

Stories, or whatever, which is nothing like it was in his day. It looks about 500 years older. Old Kippers went on about it being romantic, dangerous, a gathering point for fierce and sullen tribesmen, their eyes smouldering with burning light from the North-West Frontier. Nonsense. It's a place where a bunch of scruffy old men in greasy nightshirts come to do their shopping.

Romantic? There's not a woman in sight or, at least, not anything that looks like a woman. Unless, of course, after all that time in the Khyber Pass, you're attracted to sheep or even camels. Dangerous? It is if you step into the road without looking. You're likely to be run over by a donkey. Fierce and sullen tribesmen? They're like a bunch of pansies arguing about the price of a single tomato down at the local deli. Ask yourself, if these guys were fierce and sullen and had eyes smouldering with burning light, would they really spend all day long doing the shopping while the wife did nothing but hang around the house, eating chocolates by the containerload and moaning because she's got nowhere to go? Of course not.

As for the stories that old Kippers went on about, the only ones they seemed able to tell me involved all kinds of reasons why the price of everything they were selling 'thereabouts hithertofore', as one old shopkeeper put it, was so high. And of course, I believed them. Well, they could have turned romantic and dangerous, couldn't they?

The place to go today is the Hayatabad Bazaar, a massive, sprawling football stadium of a market with over, I would guess, 5,000 different stalls and shacks and shops. It must be the biggest smugglers' paradise in the world. Turnover is said to be around US$1.5 to $2 billion a year, give or take a couple of containers of AK47s. The bazaar didn't seem particularly romantic or dangerous to me. And I didn't see any fierce and sullen tribesmen, with or without their eyes smouldering with burning light. What I did see were a million wheeler-dealers, 2 million calculators, 3 million bicycle tyres from China, 4 million cans of goodness knows what and lots of rusty gunmetal boxes half hidden under piles of papers.

What is still pure Kipling, however, is not what people say but the way that they say it. It's as if they swallowed *Kim* for breakfast. Which most of them look as though they would have done, given half a chance.

They're never, for example, pleased to see you. They're 'greating to meet you'. Or at any rate, they say they are. If you're having a meeting they will 'evince a keen interest' in what you're going to 'speak your heart out' over and promise to come 'right way' even if it is in the 'wee hours'. But be warned, they won't offer you a chair. They will declaim: 'On backside sit. Very good, sir.' Instead of explaining, they 'dilate'. People do not make mistakes, they are 'being misbehaved with'. They don't steal, they 'decamp with', because they are 'aspiring for even higher avenues'. Bombs are never planted in cars. They're planted to a car. When they go off they don't explode, they 'press the road making it a hollow space'. The lucky ones are then carted away not in a police van but in a 'mobile'. The unlucky ones are eventually taken to hospital not to be treated, but to be 'entertained'. As for the road, it isn't resurfaced, it's 'recarpeted'. What am I saying? I don't think a road anywhere in Pakistan has been recarpeted for years.

But whoever you are, businessman, colleague, thief or aspirer for even higher avenues, everyone stops for a tiffin. Terribly 'Herbert Spencerian', as Kim's protector, the fat old buffer Hurvee Babu, would say.

What is also still pure Kipling is the border crossing to the North-West Frontier itself. It's like something out of a B-movie. Huge towers made of rough stonework and covered with mud on either side of the road. Big gates. Military, or rather army men all over the place, every one of them desperate to shoot anything that moves. Then all around the military your rough, tough Pathans. Dozy. Sleepy. Indifferent. Then to the left and right of the gate, stretching way into the distance, rows and rows of tents. One of the army men, who was either a genuine bluff old colonel or an ordinary soldier taking the mick out of a bluff old English colonel, told me the frontier was home to over 2 million Afghan refugees from Ningarhar, Laghman, Kunar, Herat and all points north of Kabul. Which, to be honest, I very much doubt. To me it looked like home to about three or four refugees and 1,999,995 arms dealers from Ningarhar, Laghman, Kunar, Herat and all points north of Kabul.

I was OK, though. I had a stackful of official passes and authorisations. I had my bodyguard, his AK47, his hundred-round banana clip. I also had my driver, an old soldier who, whenever I even thought of saying something to him, would immediately spring to attention, give me a high-precision, quivering salute and bark at the top of his voice, 'Pakistani army driver. Wagah Division. At your service. Saaaaaah.'

As a result I was through in no time at all. On the other side, however, everything suddenly changed. The military became dozy, sleepy, indifferent, while the Pathans were all desperate to shoot anything that moved.

For this is their country, not Pakistan's. They run the place, not Pakistan. Their law prevails, not Pakistan's. Abide by their law – trust only members of your own family, nobody else – and you're a Pathan. Don't, and you're dead. And that includes the kids, and I mean kids, who seemed to be carrying as many guns and as many knives stuck in their belts as the grown-ups did, if not more. Give most people a gun and you tell them to be careful with it. Not the Pathans. Even today they still give guns to their kids practically as soon as they can walk from one side of an ammunition dump to the other and tell them, 'Please God, one day you will kill a man with it.'

The landscape also changes. It is like being on the moon. Wherever you look there is nothing but dirty grey slate. Dirty grey slate soil. Dirty grey slate tracks and roadways. Dirty grey slate valleys stretching for miles ahead of you. Dirty grey slate hills and mountains all around. Then, very quickly, our first dirty grey slate hairpin.

'No problem, sir. Pakistani army driver. Wagah Division. Saaaaaah!' shrieked the driver as we careered straight up it at about a million miles an hour.

But it was worth it. First because it proved that I did at least have a drop of Pathan blood in me. I didn't scream, even though a number of times I thought we were going to . . . we were going to . . . going to . . . Second, because from the top you could see what it was all about. In front of you was the Khyber, corkscrewing its way through the mountains. Over there was what remains of the old Khyber Railway, built by the British in the 1920s. At one time, because it travelled so slowly through some of the most dangerous country in the world, it was the most looted train in history. Not any more. That honour now belongs to the 7.32 from Buxted to Victoria, at least, it does if the fares they charge are anything to go by. Today the Khyber Railway lines are twisted and buckled or even missing altogether. I saw only one stretch where the lines were all intact. It was the soil underneath that was missing. The lines were just swinging backwards and forwards in mid-air.

Now came something even more terrifying than the climb to the top. The descent the other side.

'No problem, sir. Pakistani army driver. Wagah Division. Saaaaaah!' shrieked the driver as we hurtled . . . as we . . . as . . . down to the floor of the valley.

My next memory is of a small green mosque and the Ali Masjid Fort, or rather, when I opened my eyes, there in front of me was a small green mosque and the Ali Masjid Fort that commands the pass at its narrowest point. There was also a small cemetery for all the British soldiers who fought and died during the second Afghan War. Though, to be honest, I was amazed it wasn't bigger and there weren't more of them killed, because, let's face it, they were sitting ducks. All the Pathans had to do was pick them off one by one. Then when the British fought back they just melted into the hills. It was a classic guerrilla campaign.

As we drove further into the pass, on the hillsides were the huge, colourful regimental badges of the British regiments who fought and died there: the South Wales Borderers, the York and Lancasters, the Cheshires, Gordon Highlanders, the Essex Regiment, the Royal Sussex Regiment. They looked more like a series of enormous macabre recruiting posters for the British Army than a tribute to the bravery of those soldiers.

As the grey slate began to give way to a green, fertile valley, we came across a funeral procession. At least, I think it was a funeral procession. A bunch of guys were running and slipping and sliding along a narrow hillside path carrying on their shoulders what looked like a bed covered in sheets with Arabic writing and flowers all over them. All I can say is that if the guy wasn't dead when they started out he would have been by the end of it.

In the valley proper, dotted all over are forts, most of them huge, impregnable mud-and-brick fortresses with massive wooden gates, armed sentries and walls three to four feet thick with narrow slits in them. There are probably enough guns, pistols, rifles and rocket-propelled grenades inside to start World War Three.

Secure within these forts, as in similar forts all over Balochistan and Sindh provinces, are the chiefs, or feudals, as they are known, who are far more than just lords and masters of all they survey and of all the people who live in their territory. They have their own courts, their own legal systems, their own prisons, their own executioners. They decide whether they want schools or not. Most don't. Education they see as a threat. They decide whether they want to build roads through their territory. Most don't. It would make it easier for people to start moving in and causing trouble. It would also make it easier for their loving subjects to escape. Most important of all, they can decide whether they want anything to do with Pakistan or not. Most decide – guess what? – that they don't. The feudals themselves, however, are anything but feudal. They are definitely twenty-first century. One of them, I was told, was on trial in the United States, accused of being some big drugs baron.

At Zarai, the regimental headquarters of the Khyber Rifles, I was checking out a second-century Buddhist *stupa* when I met a Pakistani doctor who had trained in France. What he told me about life among the feudals and the Pathans was unbelievable, I mean *incroyable*. If they are shot or injured they are expected to get on with it. If an arm or leg gets chopped off they carry it around with them until the day they die so that they can be buried whole. As for the women, don't ask. Not even other women are required to help them. Not even when they are giving birth. They are expected to shuffle off to some hole somewhere, have their baby and then get back to work. The reason for this is that, according to age-old Pathan tradition, if somebody else is present – a friend, a relative or even a doctor – and they help, and in spite of their help the person dies, they must die as well.

If that is not logical enough for you, why do you think they want to keep the *burqa*, the veil? Because of the British. I couldn't believe that was our fault as well.

'If the Pathans find out their wives play games, they cut their noses off, right?' said the good doctor.

'Right? I mean, are you kidding? Is that what they do?'

'Of course. It is tradition.'

'But how are the British to blame?'

'Because a businessman in Banna has started importing British noses by air mail to replace the bits that have been cut off.'

'British noses? How does he import British noses?' That's me. For ever the innocent.

'From dead bodies. He has arrangement with undertakers in England. Pakistani undertakers. They sell them to him at ten, twenty US dollars a time. But the British have white noses. White noses look funny on black faces. So women have to wear the veil or people laugh at them.'

Well, that's what he told me, although he could have been a French agent sent there to cause trouble. The Great Game and all that.

More twisting and turning and shrieks of 'No problem, sir. Pakistani army driver, Wagah Division. Saaaaaah!' and we were out of Kipling country and into Landi Kotal, a rough, scruffy, dangerous pile of a place which was, at one time, they say, the contraband capital of the world.

As soon as we pulled up in the main street, or rather, as soon as we skidded to a halt in a cloud of dust, I could tell the place was dangerous. My own personal bodyguard, the guy who had pledged his life to guarding my body, promptly announced that he was going off to visit a friend and – zonk – he was gone. So was his AK47 and his hundred-round banana clip. So much for loyalty. If Kipling had still been going strong, he would no doubt have turned the thing into half a dozen short stories, a couple of dozen roistering poems and a full-length novel. As for my Pakistani army driver, Wagah Division, he . . . Wait a minute. He was here a minute ago. Where's he gone?

Experiencing the same kind of thrill you get when you walk into a room knowing you're going to make everyone redundant or, worse still, cancel their annual bonuses, I

clambered out of the car. I could feel a million and one eyes
upon me. The one was looking at me through the sights of
his Kalashnikov.

As it happened – if you're anything like my wife this will disappoint you – I not only survived, I had a great time. Not that
Landi Kotal is one of the great cities of the world. It's more of
a dustbin that's been strewn over a hillside. The buildings are
filthy and the streets, or rather dusty tracks, are choked by
fumes, by ancient ponies with huge sores all over them pulling
wooden carts left behind by Alexander the Great, and by fragile, even more decrepit little donkeys pulling even older carts.
The city was chock-a-block with every type of baggy pants and
shirts and slippers and turbans, including the black and white
plumed turbans of the Taleban militia. For the life of me –
well, it was my life now that my bodyguard had left me – I
couldn't tell who was genuine, who was a spy, who was selling
drugs, who was selling arms, who had a gun, who had a knife
or who had been hired by my wife to keep an eye on me to
make sure I didn't get up to any mischief. But as for wigwams,
or rather women, there wasn't a single one in sight.

I stopped in the centre of the dustbin, I mean town. Turn
left and you head back through the pass to Pakistan. I turned
right, down a pile of rough rocks towards what was either a
huge open sewer or a maze of tiny shops. Or maybe it was
both. It was like going back to the days of the Old Testament,
oops I mean, Koran. Everyone was selling something. Meat
that looked so heavily spiced it could almost kill the bacteria
crawling all over it. Nans so old they were more like great-
great-grandnans. Peppers. Onions. Chillies. Every kind of
cloth you can imagine. Rugs. Jewellery. Bottles of all sorts of
colours and smells capable of curing everything from a broken
leg to a multiple heart attack and about as many hookahs as
you'd find in Frankfurt during the International Book Fair.
Or any fair, come to that.

One poor old man sitting picking his toes in a carpet shop turned out to be worth millions. He had a company and a house in Chicago and another company and house in Miami. He bought carpets in Iran and Azerbaijan for next to nothing and sold them for a fortune in the States.

'Pakistani carpets, sir. I don't touch them,' he told me between dealing with his toes. 'They are not carpets. They are floor coverings.

'I tell you how I make my real money, sir,' he went on. He threw back one of the carpets, I mean floor coverings, hanging on the wall. Behind it was a huge cupboard. He opened the door. Inside was a mass of Buddhist statues, tiny paintings, manuscripts, plaques, coins, tiles, jewellery and silver daggers. They had all been lifted from museums and temples across the border in Afghanistan.

'This, sir,' he said, 'is how I make my real money. I buy them cheap. I sell them in America for fifty thousand, a hundred thousand dollars, even more. It depends on the customer. Of course, it's all illegal. But,' he shrugged his shoulders, 'this is Pakistan.'

'If it's illegal, how do you get it out of the country?'

I had to ask him, didn't I?

'Easy. Big statues we cut up into different pieces, ship each piece out separately then reassemble them afterwards. Smaller pieces, no problem. In Pakistan everything is possible.'

While we were talking a guy with a turban on the point of collapsing, a greasy nightshirt and a fancy waistcoat ambled into the shop and joined us. He asked me where I was from.

'China,' I said. Well, what would you have said? Much Itchin in the Crotch?

'China, nice country.' A glorious set of broken teeth grinned at me. 'Like China. China good.'

I ended up having lunch with them both. Well, I say lunch: I had half a dirty, cracked cup of the sweetest tea ever and a handful of what looked and tasted like greasy, underdone nans or parathas, I can never remember which is which. You would probably get them mixed up as well if you ate a curry at the time of night I usually do. Whatever they were, they were rough. But you should have seen Fatima's Refreshments up the road. They were even rougher there.

We spoke about the Taleban and Afghanistan. 'Taleban bad. We not like Taleban. That's why we leave to come here.'

About the Sharia, the Muslim law the government was beginning to introduce. 'Sharia good. Good for women. Sharia protect women from men.'

And, of course, about Pakistan. 'Pakistan good. Good people, Pakistan. But not as good as Afghan people.'

Naturally, I agreed. What else was I going to do? Start another war?

Then they offered to show me all the bores in town. Immediately I declined. One rotary club is very much like another rotary club. But it turned out they meant gun shops. Here, in the middle of nowhere, surrounded by buildings that haven't seen a lick of paint since the Stone Age and where every railing is about to come crashing down from every balcony, you can stroll into a squalid tin shack and buy everything you need to equip a modern army. Not just hand guns, but a whole string of rifles (laser-sights an optional extra), .30 pump-action pistols, shoulder-fired missiles, sten guns, even rocket-launchers, mortars, howitzers, anti-aircraft guns, shoulder-fired stingers and, judging by the huge bulge under that pile of carpets, I mean floor coverings, in the corner, nuclear bombs as well. In fact, I wouldn't be surprised if these guys didn't sell the Indians the nuclear bombs which have caused so much trouble between the two countries.

We then clambered into the toe-picker's battered old Sherman tank and headed down the road for Bassra, where all the stuff is made. I'm not saying it's one of the world's greatest armaments centres, it's just that when it comes to arms, Landi Kotal hasn't got a leg to stand on. In a town of 20,000 people, 2,000 of them are gun-makers. What is even more amazing is that everything, but everything, is counterfeit. Made by hand. By guys in tiny little shacks tucked away in a maze of narrow little alleyways.

In one is a lathe of sorts. In another a kid is sitting on the sandy floor filing away at a lump of metal. In a third a guy the size of an elephant is bashing hell out of something or other. In yet another a group of guys pedal away for days on end making sophisticated gun barrels for all kinds of weapons.

Who buys the stuff? Well now, who do you think? The Mujahidin next door in Afghanistan bought everything they could lay their hands on to fight off the Soviets when they invaded the country. The Ah-ha are supposed to have bought containerloads, and I was told there was an Irishman living at the appropriately named Green's Hotel in Peshawar until very recently. Prices? I could have bought everything I wanted for next to nothing.

I went to one shop about the size of a shoebox. All around the walls there were guns, rifles, automatics and every kind of Kalashnikov. I'm no expert on guns – I've forgotten more about them than I ever wanted to remember – but I do know one thing. The British Ministry of Defence might think the SA80 is the best gun in the world because it jams and is unreliable in cold as well as hot weather, but the odds are against them. Informed opinion is on the side of the Uzi or the Kalashnikov: the Uzi for rapid, close-up stuff, if you've got to take out a lot of guys before they take you; the Kalashnikov for practically everything else.

As far as Kalashnikovs go, there are Kalashnikovs and Kalashnikovs, especially in Bassra. A copy of a Pakistani-made Kalashnikov? For you, sir, US$40. A copy of a

Bulgarian-made Kalashnikov? No problem: US$60. A copy of
a Russian-made Kalashnikov? That's US$100. A copy of a
Chinese-made Kalashnikov capable of 600 rounds a minute?
That's the one with the metal shoulder rest. For you, sir, a
special price, US$150. The Chinese Kalashnikov is the best of
all, so the copy is obviously also more expensive. Goodness
me. Didn't you know that?

A copy of a .50-calibre semi-automatic rifle capable of
firing through a sheet of metal as thick as a manhole cover, as
used by armies, terrorists, would-be assassins, drug dealers
and even street gangs all over the world? For you, my friend,
US$250. The bargain of a lifetime. In the US, where these
rifles are advertised as 'the weapon that makes men shiver',
they cost US$6,000, maybe more, depending on the extras.
Now, where would you like me to ship the container, sir?
But the real top-of-the-market winner, I was told, was a copy
of a US-made DIVAD anti-aircraft gun, which one half of the
town said would automatically home in on the nearest sound
of helicopter blades and the other half said would merely
blow the nearest air-conditioning unit to kingdom come.
Either way, a bargain at US$10,000.

And the crazy thing is these were the prices I was quoted.
You can imagine how much lower they would be if you hag-
gled, and if you were talking about buying in bulk. Which is
scary. Because when you think about it, keeping up that level
of production at those prices over such a long period of time
can only mean that somebody somewhere is buying the stuff.

The other thing that struck me as crazy was that here, in
the middle of nowhere, in the middle of the Middle Ages, not
only could I buy any gun or rifle or rocket-launcher I wanted
(well, apart from a single bolt-action Enfield, the SA80 and
the machine-gun version, the light support weapon, which
the British government says is perfect for the British Army but
which the British Army says is unreliable, not tough enough

and jams, especially in hot and dusty conditions such as battlefields). I could also pay in any currency I wanted: pounds, dollars, French francs, punts, it didn't make any difference to them. What was more, they could give me change in any currency I wanted as well. And to think of the fuss they make when I go into my local branch of the great National Westminster Bank at 208 Piccadilly. Just to give me US$500 in cash they need three days' notice. And even then, if I'm lucky and the moon is on the right side of Saturn, I might get US$250 and the rest in whatever currencies they've got available.

So did I treat myself to a Kalashnikov with a thirty-round clip, or even a jolly old rocket-launcher? No, I didn't. But I admit I was sorely tempted. Though can you imagine the commotion when I arrived back at Heathrow? Every alarm bell would have been ringing like mad. Although, knowing Heathrow, they'd probably make less of a song and dance about it than over an extra 0.001 kilo in excess baggage. Then I thought, why not send them to different people back home with a note saying, 'As requested, sample enclosed. Await your further instructions. Osman.'

What I did buy – whisper it not to a soul – was a fountain pen. A fountain-pen gun. It's the size and shape of a fountain pen. It's got 'Made in Japan' stamped on it, even though it was made down the road in some tent. It's twenty-five-bore, whatever that means, and you load it by unscrewing the barrel like you would your ordinary fountain pen, and inserting the bullet instead of an ink cartridge. To fire it, you simply pull out the clip on the top of the pen, take aim and gently press the top of the clip. Crack. You can kill a man at 300 metres. At least, that's what I was told. All I can say is that when I saw them demonstrating it, standing on the roof of the shop and firing it into the air, it certainly looked as if it could.

How much did it cost? 150 rupees. About US$3. Did I

need an end-use certificate before I bought it? What do you think?

But the Khyber Pass is not the only dangerous place in Pakistan. The whole country from, as they say, Landi Kotal and Darra in the North-West Frontier Province to Cox's Bazaar in the south-east is virtually riddled with – or rather, machine-gunned, missiled and nuclear-bombed with – violence. And I don't just mean punch-up violence. I mean all-out war violence or, as one Pakistani philosopher type described it to me, again in particularly Pakistani terms, 'a form of casual determinism confronting moral responsibility'. He took the words right out of my mouth.

First, of course, there are the political, religious and ethnic killings. Hardly a day goes by – what am I saying? Hardly an hour goes by – without somebody being gunned down or murdered (or, as they say, 'awarded death') for some political, religious or ethnic reason. Politicians and political leaders are shot. Mosques and churches are attacked. In fact so bad have the assaults on churches become that some bishops have started organising what they call a Christian Taleban to fight back. As far as ethnic killings are concerned, whole areas of towns and cities are almost continuously under siege. Murders can easily exceed 1,000, even 1,500, in a single year. Out in the villages it's even worse. And because what happens in the villages is far away from what small semblance of law and order there is in Pakistan, nobody knows how much worse it is, or cares.

Then there are the business killings. Forget such old-fashioned concepts as fair trade, market forces and competition. The only competition businessmen seem to believe in is whether his friend's Kalashnikov is better and faster than my friend's. That's if you're actually manufacturing anything. Again and again businessmen told me stories about armed gunmen strolling into factories and lifting the monthly

payroll. Refuse to hand it over and they'll line up all the workers against the wall and shoot them. Just like that. Give them
the money and everything grinds to a halt.

Finally, there are the family killings. Husbands killing wives,
wives killing husbands. Husbands and wives having their
daughter killed because they don't like the guy she's planning
to marry. Sons being killed because husbands and wives don't
like the idea of him marrying somebody else's daughter.

Then there are all the incidentals: the car-jackings, lootings,
armed robberies, women jabbed with pins or maybe needles
labelled 'Welcome to the HIV Club'. Rockets raining down
on police stations. Even police beating up other police.
Apparently, so disorganised are they that it's not unusual for
one uniformed police force to stake out and attack another
uniformed police force. Whenever this happens it provokes a
huge public outcry because instead of just fighting each other,
normally the police kill everybody outright.

Gee whizz. I'd no sooner checked into my hotel in the capital, Karachi, got to my room and started to wonder why of all
the magazines to choose from in the world they had left me
The Defence Journal before bombs started going off outside,
injuring twenty people, smashing virtually every windscreen in
town and blowing out the windows of surrounding office
blocks. And this wasn't any middle-of-the-night attack. It
was only midday.

'My dear sir, the rule of law is purely a concept that exists
on paper,' one of the waiters told me in the hotel dining
room. 'People say there are over six thousand professional
killers in this city alone, all of them armed to the teeth. All of
them for hire.'

Another waiter assured me not to worry. The gangs were
not running riot. They were controlled by 'state functionaries'.

'How do you know?' I asked innocently.

'If there is a murder,' he whispered, 'and you ask an officer in the Border Force how long it will take to investigate it, he will say one week. If you ask military intelligence, they will say three days. If you ask an ordinary policeman, a *thanedar*, he will tell you, "Three days before it happened we knew who was going to do it, when and where. But we'll never be able to find out who did it."'

He then told me 'very good Punjabi joke. Very funny. You will laugh, sir.'

'Two archaeologists are studying ancient marble head. They are trying to work out how old it is. No problem, sirs, says typical Pakistani policeman. He takes it away. Five minutes later he comes back. 2493 BC, he says. The two archaeologists are amazed. How did you find out? they say. And to such a precise date? Easy, he says. We gave him a few strokes with a well-oiled shoe and he blurted out his date of birth.'

Even more mysteriously, another member of the hotel staff told me that most of the killings were in fact organised from a quiet back street. Hale Grove Gardens. In Mill Hill, north-west London.

'Hale Grove Gardens in London?'

'Shhh! It's more than my life is worth.'

'But why Hale—'

'Because that's where the King of Karachi lives.'

'The King of Karachi?'

'Yes, Altaf Hussain. The leader of the biggest ethnic group, the Mohajir Qami Movement. He says he represents all the downtrodden Mohajirs, or refugees, the Urdu-speaking Muslims who came here after independence. He is gradually taking over the whole place. It is like Mafia.'

'You mean . . . ?'

'No, no. I say too much already. I am going now. Goodbye.'

And he was gone.

Others say the MQM are only after their just deserts. The government hasn't had a census since 1981 so that they can deliberately ignore the newcomers and their legitimate grievances and keep all the power in their own hands. Neither have they redrawn all the constituency boundaries, which again means power is concentrated among a small bunch of powerful landowning feudals who make up 80 per cent of the national assembly while big industrial towns which thirty years ago were tiny villages are not represented at all.

'The feudals, they know nothing,' a local businessman complained to me one day. 'We have education ministers who can hardly read. We once had a health minister who thought a labour ward was for hospital workers.'

Pakistan is the only country in the world where you are likely to be arrested for riding pillion on a motorbike or sentenced to death for swearing while gunmen and crooks are allowed to go rampaging all over the place and even to form their own trade union, presumably to ensure they get a fair deal from whatever is going on. One, called the Professional Car Lifters' Union, costs 2,000 rupees, about US$45, to join. The benefits? Once you've stolen your car, you ring up the union, which then negotiates a deal with the car's owner. You get 90 per cent of the deal price. The union keeps 10 per cent. The owner gets his car back. Welcome to justice, Pakistani-style.

Not to be outdone, the rich guys have formed their own police force, the Citizens–Police Liaison Committee. If something is stolen, if people are attacked or kidnapped or even murdered, they call them rather than the official police.

'There's no police force in Karachi,' a smooth, old-school Pakistani bank manager told me. 'They are not trained. They don't have any qualifications. They don't have any equipment. And, of course, people don't trust them. Instead of working for the people, they are working for the politicians.

We started the liaison committee as a kind of Neighbourhood Watch, but we very quickly realised the problem. Now we have a fully trained force. We have phone-tapping and voice-matching equipment. We have everything a proper police force would have.'

Yet here we have some of the cleverest guys in the world. They're serious, sensible, intelligent. They're doctors, lawyers, accountants, bankers. They're running the World Bank, the International Monetary Fund and a hundred other world-wide institutions. They're even running other countries. But the crazy thing is they can't seem to run their own country.

Industry is at a standstill. The only thing anybody wants to talk about is how quickly they could move across the Arabian Sea to Dubai and what the chances are of getting a Canadian passport. Investment is non-existent. Pakistan's once world-famous textile industry is hanging by a thread. One 5,000-acre free-trade zone I as good as risked my life to visit was built in 1979 to accommodate 3,000 units. It was going to be the largest industrial site in the whole of Asia. When I went there just twenty-eight companies had moved in, and even some of them had closed down. It had no gas, no telephones, no water, no sewage system.

Banks are so wobbly people are scared to close the door, let alone slam it. Even the telephone system is riddled with what they call the Moldova virus. Somehow or other, either by accident, as a result of the glorious antics of a clever bunch of hackers, or just because it's Pakistan, you can hardly pick up a telephone anywhere in Karachi without immediately being put through to somebody you don't want to talk to in Moldova in Eastern Europe. Apart from the sheer waste of time you are then promptly billed for all the calls.

So why is the country in such a mess? Perm any eight of the following. Religion. Authoritarian rule. The military. Contempt for human rights. A rubber-stamping Parliament.

Weak politicians. A completely useless tax regime. A completely useless judicial system. A completely useless civil service. Violence. Decrepit industrial infrastructure. Decrepit transport infrastructure. Decrepit every other kind of anything. India. India. India.

Personally, I reckon it's all of them, and more. Particularly education, or edukashun, as they spell it in Pakistan, and korupshun. Fewer than 40 per cent of children go to school, compared with a world average of 80 per cent. The illiteracy rate is practically a world record, which is doubly, trebly, whatever, shocking when you can go into a shack in the middle of the Sahara and find a teacher, a blackboard and a group of kids speaking not only impeccable French but also quoting Proust, Baudelaire and all the best Bordeaux vintages since the time Britain allowed Germany to invade France.

The reason education is so bad, Pakistanis will tell you, is because parents don't want their children to be educated. They are frightened that if they are they will leave home, and then who will help them and look after them when they get old?

Then there is the corruption. I'm not saying that just because the World Bank lists Pakistan as the third most corrupt country in the world – they even fiddle the figures they give to the World Bank and the IMF – the whole place is riddled with corruption. It's just that when a motorway policeman found some money and actually returned it to its rightful owner, it made headline news throughout the country for days on end.

Take the start of all their problems, education. The government decides upon the funds for education. The local authorities allocate the funds to different areas. The areas distribute them to the school authorities. The school authorities then identify how much money each individual school will receive. The trouble is, it never gets there. It's syphoned off, stage by stage, all the way down the line until there's nothing left.

I met some guy who had just been put in charge of education for the whole of the Punjab. He told me that they had no fewer than 56,000 'ghost schools' in the province. No desks. No books. Hardly a building, either. Yet every single one of them was allocated money from state funds. I went to one school near Faisalabad, Pakistan's third-largest city. It had 450 pupils, no equipment and only two classrooms. Most classes were held in the open air. Other schools desperate for a roof over their heads used mosques, derelict buildings, any building in which there was a vague chance of a teacher being able to teach.

On the other hand, Pakistan being Pakistan, I also came across some ultra, ultra, strict Islamic schools, way out in the western Punjab, which were anything but ghost schools. They had buildings, teachers, desks, books and pupils who literally wore leg irons, welded to a chain attached to either a block of concrete or a lump of wood, to stop them running away.

'Don't be worry,' one of the teachers said. 'They eat, sleep, wash, work, learn like that. For five years, maybe ten years. After that they become teachers. They have their own school, their own pupils. They become rich men.'

As if ghost schools were not bad enough, apparently the really, really big money is to be made out of helping students pass their examinations. The trick is to get an advance copy of an examination paper, which is not too difficult when you bear in mind that the going rate for them is around ten times the examiners' annual salary. These are distributed through some vast unofficial network and sold initially to teachers around the country so that they can make certain their students know the answers to all the questions they are going to be asked. Next they sell the papers to the parents, to make certain that they make certain that their children know the answers to all the questions they are going to be asked.

In some cases, I was told, the business is now so big and the amounts of money involved so great that armed gangs will actually break into examination halls, hold the teachers or invigilators at gunpoint and then distribute the official answers to the papers to make sure that the students copy them down correctly.

'But that's impossible!' I stuttered.

'Not in Pakistan it isn't.'

An official in the Ministry of Education described to me how in the old days one of his colleagues had so much money in his house that he gave him US$2 million in cash to look after. Today, however, everything had changed. If you accuse anyone of not having a Swiss bank account you 'disrepute them', as they say.

If these are the tricks they get up to in the Ministry of Education, which I wouldn't have thought was a prime breeding ground for corruption, you can imagine what it's like in the ministries of, say, Defence, Trade and Industry and, of course, Justice. Wherever I went, whoever I met, I heard stories of earnest, dedicated civil servants and government officials plodding home wearily with their briefcases full to bursting with cash.

'A businessman wants to import something. It's going to cost him twenty million rupees. He needs a licence. He goes to somebody in government. He pays him a million rupees. But when he's got his licence, he can make much more money. You are knowing what I say is right.'

A minister appoints a friend of a friend as acting chairman of some vast, nationalised combine. Within a year he is said to have lifted over 70 billion rupees, around US$1 million. Which you have to admit is some takeaway.

I went to a meeting at a big Pakistani state holding company where everybody was wearing badges identifying them as a 'functionary'. I was introduced to a very smart, very

switched-on young guy: the new finance director, I was
told.

'*Was* the new finance director,' he corrected.

At his first board meeting, he said, he presented, among a
million other bits of paper, a list showing which directors had
company loans, how much for and the rate at which they
were repaying them, and which did not. That was it. He
wasn't even allowed to stay for Any Other Business.

Another Pakistani businessman I met, this time at the big
university in St Louis, Missouri in the US, told me that he had
once had a big flour-milling business in Karachi. The government wanted money from him. He said that he was a
businessman, he wasn't interested in what he called 'politi-
cals'. Surprise, surprise, within two weeks he was arrested and
imprisoned for three months under the Defence of Pakistan
law, which apparently gives the police the right to do whatever they want to do. When he was released, he still refused to
hand over any money, and he was jailed again. Members of his
family were sent to prison as well. Eventually he fled to Japan,
then to Dubai, then to the States. He lost everything.

'Different people. Different parties. The same thing is still
happening today,' he said. 'It's difficult to know who is more
corrupt, the politicians or the police or the army.'

So what about the small guys with sweetshops or newspaper
stands? It's the same story. Except in their case it's called
bhatta, or protection. Pay anything up to US$50 a month per
employee and you're safe. Argue about it, tell them you can't
afford it, or are on the anvil, as they say, or fall behind in your
payments and there is a Pakistani solution. Another businessman claimed that the corruption was so bad that even local
cricket matches were fixed. The good news, however, was
that, because it was all done in such an obvious way, he always
put all his money on the side he could tell was going to win.
He could then afford to pay the *bhatta* demanded of him.

What of paying taxes? First there's the question of who to pay. There are more than thirty-seven different tax-collecting authorities. Second, how much? As little as possible. Government ministers, I heard again and again, pay less tax than university professors, and you can guess how much university professors pay. In fact, of a total population of over 140 million, less than 1 per cent pays any taxes at all.

Not so long ago Karachi, the one-time capital, was the fun spot of south Asia, the City of Lights, the cleanest and most cosmopolitan city in the whole subcontinent. If, unlike me, you are keen on bars and clubs, it was the Beirut of south Asia. If you went for the restaurants and the good life, Empress Market in the city centre was another Paris. They were all there: Western, Chinese, Pakistani. Clifton Beach, with its elegant bungalows, as the Brits called them – the French, not to mention the Americans, would have called them *châteaux* – was practically Nice, give or take the odd camel.

Today, it is not even half an anna to a rupee, as we used to say in the days of the Raj. Come to think of it, it's probably not worth much more than half an anna. Far from being the City of Lights, it's more a City of Darkness. Apart from the hotels and big houses, or rather bungalows, which have their own generators, there's hardly any electricity. Come nightfall, the place is almost pitch-black. I know because the first night I was there, against the advice of everyone in the hotel, I got a cab and went in search of some booze. Well, speaking as a cow-devourer and a non-Muslim, there's a limit to how much Coca-Cola you can drink. The driver told me proudly that his car had just been given a 'fitness certificate'. I can vouch for the fact that the car was more than 100 per cent. If there was an Olympics for taxis, this taxi would have got a gold medal.

First we negotiated every obstacle you can think of: piles of rubbish which even the goats had turned their backs on; pot-holes the size of Swiss bank vaults; all kinds of animals fast asleep in the centre of what used to be roads and are now just escape routes for killers. We drove past crumbling museums and mansions and assembly buildings. We drove around the port. All the time the driver kept saying, 'I don't drink, sir. Sorry, sir. My father, he not drink, sir. But when my father dies maybe I then drink.' I was not prepared to wait that long.

Around Aurangzeb Park in the old part of the city I saw groups of drug addicts squatting by the side of the street passing syringes blithely to one another. By Sohrab Bridge I saw the poorest, hungriest and probably the most heart-breaking beggars I've ever seen. Men, women and babies, many with half their faces eaten away, many of them Afghan refugees.

At one point my non-drinking driver insisted we drove particularly slowly past a row of trees near one of the big hotels. 'Not madam, and not men, sir,' he whispered towards the shadows. 'They are waiting. They want to realise their evil intentions.'

By contrast we virtually surfed through one area, Lyari, which was awash with sewage. That made me even more eager for a couple of whiskies. Bottles, I mean. I also saw every kind of mosque, even one that seemed to be part ground floor, part cellar of a huge, crumbling block of flats. I actually spotted what looked like a real, as opposed to a ghost school, with a sign outside declaring, 'I am to learn'.

We made for Zamzam Boulevard, the swish, upmarket end of town, where boutiques and stores and bistros are to be found and where a meal for two can cost as much as the average monthly salary – if there is such a thing as an average monthly salary in Pakistan. But, typically of Pakistan, we couldn't get near it. Nearly every street we took was either being repaired or still being built.

Eventually we found what we were looking for: booze, being peddled through a hole in the wall off a side street off a side street, off a side street. Without giving anything away – you can't be too careful in present-day Pakistan – it is near a secondhand bookshop called Mr Old Books, a hairdresser called Hair Port and the back of the house of a famous woman ex-prime minister known to her friends as Big Ben. The only reason we found it was because it was the only place for miles which had a light on.

'I don't drink, sir. Sorry, sir,' the driver continued as we carried the bottles out to the cab. 'My father, he not drink, sir. But when my father dies, maybe then I drink.'

I got back to the hotel intending to lean up against the bar and chat casually about how many rickshaws there weren't in the car park, but instead I was almost hustled out of the building. Alcohol was allowed only in the rooms, not in what they called public places. Undaunted, I retreated to my room, emptied all the cans of cola in the minibar down the sink and returned to the restaurant with three refilled cans of Pepsi. Normally Pepsi doesn't have much effect on me, but this stuff was a killer, I can tell you. So much so that a number of waiters insisted on tasting it for me to check whether my health was in any danger.

The following morning things had changed dramatically. In daylight everything was a million times worse. What I could see of it, that is. Some people say Karachi has a population of 10 million, others that it is 11, 12, 13, even 15 million. To me it looked like 150 million. The place was jam-packed. The piles of rubbish I couldn't see for Afghan refugees poring over everything. Whatever they can find that's worth recycling they immediately grab, and then head for Gulshan-e-Iqbal, or the Federal B area, where they sell it for whatever they can get. Which is usually less than nothing. The potholes were hidden from sight because the roads were so solid with traffic that you could hardly tell whether there was a proper carriageway underneath or just sand and mud. Added to which, most of the policemen or *thanedars* are illiterate and can't read the traffic rules and regulations they are supposed to enforce, so they send cars and trucks up one-way streets, force oxen and camels into so-called overtaking lanes and generally make matters worse. If such a thing is possible in Pakistan.

The municipal services in Karachi are a joke. Water, as you would expect in what was once one of the major ports in the region, is as polluted as hell. Electricity is more off than on. What offices I went to were more like refugee camps, with guards on the doors, huge steel barriers, people wandering around aimlessly, children asleep in corridors, old women cooking on balconies and landings. Even the rooms where we held our meetings looked like something out of an Afghan jumble sale. On top of that, everything was covered in dust and cobwebs.

As for the essentials of life, all the bars and clubs are gone. Even the nightclub where Mrs Bhutto's strict Muslim father used to go every night of the weekend has long since closed down. The restaurants are pitiful, although the one on the corner of Preedi Street does a nice line in whatever they called it. But the Rendezvous of the Elite, as it claims to be, it is not.

And Karachi is dangerous, dangerous, dangerous. With over 2,000 people being killed here every year, it is far and away more dangerous than probably all the other dangerous cities of the world combined, so it's hardly surprising that everyone looks as though they've got at least one gun or rifle or even rocket-launcher tucked neatly into their fancy white *shalwar qamiz* or down the front of their baggy pants. It has got so bad that even Karachi's own St Francis, Dr Schweitzer and Mother Teresa all rolled into one, Abdul Saltar Edhi, couldn't take it any more. After fifty years of caring not only for the poor but also for the dead – every body he was given or he collected was washed, given the last rites at a local mosque and buried – he finally upped and left.

Goodness only knows what it will be like in five, ten or even fifteen years' time.

One evening, purely in the interests of research, I toured the illegal bars and clubs in the vast, sprawling port area. Filthy it was. Risky it was. But the only dangerous thing that happened to me was when some Filipino sailor suddenly lurched at me and, in a flash, pulled a mouth organ from his pocket. Don't ask me why, but he then proceeded to lecture me on the different notes you can get from a mouth organ: A, you blow. E, you suck. Or was it the other way round?

Lahore – the only city in the world named after the Sultan's French girlfriend – is a different matter altogether. So different, in fact, from the rest of Pakistan that it must be one of my favourite cities, if not my favourite city, in the whole of Asia. As for my world top ten, it would be up there with the best of them.

Situated on the left bank of the River Ravi in the Punjab, it has everything Karachi hasn't and is everything Karachi never will be. Yet it is still a Lahore unto itself. On the surface, it has trees and gardens and canals and parks and elegant houses. Everything the invader, or even the tourist, could possibly want. Or is it everything the tourist, or even the invader, could possibly want? I never know which one is more destructive.

Like Karachi, Lahore is packed to more than bursting point. It is teeming with traffic: original Mogul motor cars, rickshaws, every four-by-four in existence, tiny donkey caravans, beautifully groomed high-stepping horses and huge, plodding buffalos and oxen, dogs and sheep and goats.

Like Karachi, it is also violent, but it has got style. Not to mention fancy hotels, expensive restaurants, polo matches, the heaving Sootar Mandi Market, theatres, cinemas, computerised bowling alleys, charity balls. Non-stop parties, night after night after night, strictly private, of course. And last, but by no means least, it has Kulfi, the super rich cardamom-flavoured ice cream of the Punjab.

The Mall, which runs through the middle of town, is a glorious mish-mash of old colonial mansions, modern, faceless hotels and fine old neo-Mogul-Greco-Roman-Gothic-Palladian-cut-price-Pakistani shacks made up of towers and circles. At the top end, standing four-square on its own island spot in the middle of this huge, swirling mass of everything you can imagine on four feet as well as on four wheels, is Zam-Zammah, the fire-breathing dragon which is to many old colonial buffs, and to even more fans of *Kim*, the most famous gun in the world. According to the Persian inscription on the gleaming gold barrel, the Taker of the Ramparts of Heaven, at the time it was cast in Lahore in 1762 (what on earth were the Pathans doing in Bassra to let such a contract slip through their fingers?), it was the largest gun ever made. But, far more important, this is where Kim first met his lama from Tibet where 'the air and water are fresh and cool', and in what has to be one of the great adventure stories of all time set off on the Great Game.

Facing it, as all guilty and embarrassed lovers of *Kim* will know, is the Lahore Museum. Half the world will tell you that this was Kim's Wonder House, where Kipling's father, Lockwood, was curator for twenty years. To the other half, this is nonsense. The museum run by Lockwood Kipling, they claim, was originally down the road in, they say, Tollinton Market. What you see today is a modern museum built in 1894 long after Lockwood Kipling retired as director and five years after Rudyard left India for good.

As for the contents of the older/new museum, again, half the world says they are a priceless collection of rare Asian antiquities. The other half say they are all fakes; the real things disappeared years ago and copies were put in their place. After all, if some kid can build a cruise missile sitting in the dirt in the middle of the Khyber Pass, how difficult can it be to knock up any number of Fasting Buddhas, let alone various knick-knacks from the Moenjodaro, Harappa or even Achaemenian periods? Whether it's the real McCoy or not, it wasn't half as much fun as wandering around Lurgan Smith's little shop down the road from Simla Town Hall would have been, as all *Kim* addicts – oops, now I've admitted it – would agree.

Facing Zam-Zammah on the other side of the road are the law courts. But as Pakistan doesn't have any law, they can be of only academic interest. Far more fun and far more relevant to people's lives is Lahore Fort, which is actually a city within a city. Shuffle through the enormous Alamgiri Gates and you can picture what it would have been like in the days of the Moguls. Here's where the Emperor would every day appear on the balcony to greet his people. There is a private mosque for the ladies of the court. Over there is a Palace of Mirrors. Most impressive of all is the Badshahi Mosque which, with its enormous courtyard capable of holding 100,000 worshippers and huge towers on each corner, is, they say, the biggest mosque in the world. But if I were you I wouldn't say so to the mullahs in Mecca, Damascus or even Islamabad. You know how touchy people can be about this kind of thing.

Nobody mentioned to me that the fort was also the scene of one of the worst bloodbaths that occurred during Partition, when hundred of thousands of Hindus and Sikhs were trapped, their water supplies cut off, and practically roasted to death. So I didn't mention it, either.

The Minar-e-Pakistan Tower opposite the fort was built to mark the speech made in 1940 by Mohammed Ali Jinnah, the founder of Pakistan, in which he set out the case in no uncertain terms for breaking up the subcontinent. It was completed in 1968. 'Make sure you go to the top,' everybody told me. 'You'll get a fantastic view of the city.' I tried to, but the lift wasn't working.

Some people say that Pakistan never had a chance. That from day one – 14 August 1947 – the odds were stacked against it. It was never given anywhere near the industrial equipment, the military hardware and so on that was agreed in the carve-up. Even worse, it received only 200 million of the 750 million rupees it was promised. But I didn't mention that, either.

The Shalimar Gardens, hidden away behind high walls and serrated battlements, must be one of the best city-centre parks anywhere in the world. Laid out in 1641 by Emperor Shah Jehan, of Taj Mahal fame, as he laid out so many other things in his life, it covers about forty acres and features huge pools, waterfalls and hundreds of fountains. The top terrace, Farah Baksh – the Giver of Pleasure – was appropriately enough reserved for the ladies of the imperial harem. The lower section is called Faiz Baksh, which means the Givers of Quantity. You don't need me to tell you who that was reserved for. As for the middle bit, well, I never did find out who that was reserved for, but I have my own ideas.

One evening, I somehow ended up in either Modeltown or Raiwind at a private party in some luxurious mansion with an enormous garden and an unending supply of – don't tell a soul – booze. One guy there, who I took at first to be a waiter because of the number of drinks he was carrying around, turned out to be the youngest son of some rich local family. He was drinking, he told me, because they had just lost two ships worth US$30 million. The captains had been doing the clubs in Manila, got bombed out of their minds and missed the sailing date. The ships then got caught in a storm and both ran aground. The family had lost everything, and he was now, for the first time in his life, facing the prospect of having to go out and work for a living.

Next I met a gentle, elderly, intellectual type. I could tell he was a gentle, elderly intellectual because he wanted to bomb India to smithereens. He wasn't the only one. So did every other Pakistani there. They weren't just wary of India. They didn't just dislike it. They hated it, and everything it stood or did not stand for. 'The problem is not that it's just another country,' the intellectual mumbled to me. 'The problem is that it is India. If we lose at cricket to another country, we lose a cricket match. If we lose at cricket to India, we have lost everything there is to lose. That is something that is not possible. We must bomb them.'

Which is obviously why Pakistan has the bomb. If India has the bomb, they must have the bomb. If India explodes the bomb, they must explode a bomb. But do they honestly believe that India will drop their bomb on them? The amazing thing, or maybe the sad thing was, every single person at the party, and every single person I met during my trip said yes. At the end of the day, they truly thought India would be prepared to drop a bomb on Pakistan.

The only way I could make them even start to think about what they were saying was to go all intellectual on them. Or at least, to try. Did Pakistan have a duty to protect its citizens? Yes. Pakistan, therefore, had a duty to protect its citizens against a possible nuclear bomb being dropped on it by India? Yes. If India was going to drop a nuclear bomb on Pakistan, surely it was going to want to drop it where it would cause maximum damage? Yes. Which meant on a city like Karachi or Lahore? Yes. So if Pakistan had a duty to protect its citizens against a nuclear bomb attack from India, what steps had the government taken to protect people in Karachi or Lahore? Silence. So if the government had not taken any steps to protect its citizens in Karachi or wherever, it couldn't really believe that India would drop a bomb on them, could it?

Nobody said a word. They all shuffled off and I was left talking to this upmarket fashion model who, try as I might, I shall never forget for the rest of my life. Not because she said she was Pakistan's top model, but because she said that after a heavy night the only thing she could rely on for keeping her complexion fresh and healthy and smoothing out all those wrinkles was the cream her mother used to keep her haemorrhoids under control.

After that there was only one place to go. The best place in the whole of Lahore: Heera Mandi. Where the hookahs are to be found. In the old city, at the back of the Shah Jehan Mosque, go up any of the lanes and into any one of the tiny houses. There, in any of the rooms, you'll find a bunch of musicians lounging against the walls. Sitting in the middle of the floor are a million girls, either on their own or in groups, waiting to entertain you in the traditional manner. Not one of them, I promise, will mention anything about her mother's haemorrhoids.

So far I've told you what's fun in Lahore. But if you're looking for something hilarious you must, just must, go to Wagah, about an hour's drive out of town through the wheat and mustard fields by ox and cart, and three hours by taxi. This is where the death trains between the two countries came through during Partition. It was also in 1965–6 the scene of a big tank battle between India and Pakistan. But that's in the past.

Today, from the moment you get there, I promise you, you won't be able to stop laughing. First, along the whole 875-mile border between the two countries, which have a combined population of over 1 billion, this is the only crossing point. Now that, I reckon, is enough to get anyone going.

Second is the red tape involved in getting from one side to the other. To get their visas for India, Pakistanis living just this side of the chainlink fence have to go all the way to the Indian Embassy about 300 miles away in Islamabad. Indians on the other side just have to go to the moon and back to get their visas for Pakistan. That had me rolling in the aisles, not that there are any aisles in the mosques in Pakistan – they're all open-plan. On the other hand, if you're a local farmer and you're smuggling basmati rice across the border, where you can get almost double the price for it, you just make the traditional arrangements and – quick, before he turns round – you're across.

Finally, the killer: the thing that had me in a heap on the ground hysterical with laughter, the official Closing of the Border Gates ceremony. We were all huddled behind security barriers on either side of the road, which stretched right up to the big iron border gates, as if we were the biggest band of hardened criminals and terrorists the world had ever seen. If we put one foot in front of the other we were immediately hustled back into line and threatened with thirty years in jail.

It's not as if the gates themselves were particularly impressive. I've got bigger gates than that on the tradesmen's entrance at home. But the deadline for closing them was approaching. Everybody was silent. You'd have thought it was the most solemn occasion in the history of the world. I was almost afraid to breathe.

Then, suddenly, out of nowhere, a gang of Pakistani soldiers in their fancy uniforms and head plumes, all about seven feet tall and as thin as beanpoles, came marching down the middle of the street. Well, I say marching. They were actually swinging their outstretched sandalled feet as high, if not higher than their heads. Eat your heart out John Cleese. This was not just the Ministry of Silly Walks. This was the goosestepping Ministry of Silly Walks to end all goosestepping Ministries of Silly Walks. But it was for real.

They came to attention. They slapped their sandalled feet down on the ground and then did a sort of supercharged faster-than-the-speed-of-sound scurry along the road, like the

White Rabbit on heat, their arms flailing all over the place like windmills, until they skidded to a stop, slapped their sandalled feet on the ground again and resumed the swinging of their feet higher than their heads.

I looked around. Everybody was standing behind the lines. Everybody was taking it seriously, which, of course, made it even funnier But when it came to the actual closing of the border gates I don't know how I contained myself.

At Mach 3 the tallest and thinnest of all the soldiers skidded down the road to the green painted gates. With one hand he swung one of them shut. But, of course, at the speed at which he did so, it just came juddering back again. Again he swung it, and again it juddered back. What happened after that I couldn't tell you, because I just collapsed. But it taught me one thing: Pakistan doesn't need the nuclear bomb. All they have got to do if they want to take over any country in the world is to send in their troops doing their Silly Walk and the place would be theirs. Nobody could resist them.

If what you see at Wagah is hilarious, what you'll see in the rest of the Punjab – home, incidentally, to a nearly completed plutonium reactor for you know what – will, I guarantee, make you weep. It's mediaeval. It's barbaric. It's Stone Age.

One morning I headed out across the never-ending, flat, fertile Punjab plains known at one time as the granary of India – oops, I mean Pakistan – which was in itself an achievement, because in order to keep the place securely in the Stone Age, most of the feudals refuse to let the government even build roads through their territory.

The first farm I stopped at had over 12,000 acres. The feudal had no fewer than thirty families working for him. In other words, around 150 people. They had practically no food, no drink, no shelter, no medical facilities, no education. If they had the barest minimum decencies of human life they were lucky. But in spite of that, every morning they had to go to the feudal to pay their respects. They then had to go away and work their fingers to the bone for almost twelve hours solid. When they finished that, they had to go back to the feudal and thank him for granting them the privilege of destroying themselves for his benefit. If they didn't, or if they showed even the slightest flicker of disrespect, he would throw them in his own personal, private jail for as long as he liked.

On another farm I saw ten kids who could have been no older than seven, eight or nine pulling a broken, rusty, old plough. 'They are cheaper than a tractor,' said the farmer. 'Need less feed than an ox.'

At other times of the year, I was told, you can see children complete with leg irons gathering in the sugar cane. At night they are chained to wooden posts around the fields and thrown a handful of flour. Apparently most survive by eating grass. 'For the money I pay one adult, I can get three, maybe four boys who are faster and less trouble. Why not?' another feudal said to me.

In the towns and villages it's just as bad, if not worse, if such a thing is possible. I saw kids making bricks or weaving carpets up to their necks in slurry pits. In one textile mill I saw children actually chained to the floor, to each other and to the machines they were operating. If they made a mistake they were taken to a punishment room, where they were hung upside down and caned, lashed or even starved nearly to death.

Another day I tried to get to Sialkot, a small town about fifty miles from Lahore up towards the Kashmir border. There I was told that as many as 7,000 kids, aged anything from five upwards, were working eighty hours a week in virtually total darkness, making footballs by hand for the likes of Nike, Reebok and Adidas for the princely sum of US$1.25 a day. For some reason my driver couldn't find Sialkot.

Instead I spent almost all day in a rough-and-ready garage

in the middle of nowhere which, again, was more or less run
by kids. The owner, a fat jolly Punjabi in his *shalwar qamiz*,
told me he was the son of an *alim*, a religious scholar. He kept
slapping me on the back and telling me I was worrying about
nothing. It was Punjabi tradition. Children always worked and
helped their families. There was a desperate shortage of able-
bodied men. Children were the backbone of the country's
infrastructure. They were a sad but vital factor in the country's
glorious dash for industrialisation. Pakistan couldn't survive
without them. The place would collapse. What was more, the
children earned far more under the present arrangement than
they would if they worked anywhere else. They helped their
families. They raised their standard of living. In any case, it was
better than the apprenticeship-type system run by many more
unscrupulous businessmen who as good as bought children for
five years for US$150. Less, of course, their food, accommo-
dation – not that that was much – maintenance, training tools,
equipment and the cost of all the mistakes they made.

'But surely there must be laws against this kind of thing?'
I protested.

'Of course.'

There was the Tenancy Act 1950 and the Bonded Labour
Act 1992, which was supposed to outlaw all forms of bonded
labour once and for all. Not to mention a million different
health and safety regulations.

Children were not allowed to work in high-intensity, poisonous or dangerous industries such as the manufacture of
explosives, construction, transportation or carpet-weaving.
Children, that is, under the age of fourteen. Over the age of
fourteen it didn't matter.

But didn't the government check? Didn't they carry out
any inspections?

'Of course,' he grinned.

There was a whole army of International Labour

Organisation-trained inspectors. There were also lots of human rights organisations going around checking on the conditions children were kept in. Some were even buying their freedom for them.

'Isn't that a good thing?' I asked.

'Not at all,' he said.

After the children had been released and the do-gooders had disappeared, the children were rounded up, beaten and taken back into bondage again. So what was the point?

Another town I tried to visit was Rakiul Yar Khan, which is to all intents and purposes owned and run by Sheikh Zayedbin Sultan Al-Nahiyan, the holder of a wildlife conservation award bestowed upon him by Prince Philip and the ruler of the United Arab Emirates. From Rakiul Yar Khan he and his entourage go out on hunting trips for the rare houbara bustard. I especially wanted to go there because I'd seen the other end of the business in Abu Dhabi: the falcons worth US$1 million and more; the markets for falcons; the hospitals for falcons, and so on.

At Rakiul Yar Khan, I was told, there were special landing strips for 747s. There were satellites for tracking the bustards, which are protected by a string of international nature conservation treaties as well as by Pakistan's own wildlife protection laws. There were also special luxury camps in the southern Punjab fully equipped with all the necessary facilities for the bastards, I mean bustards.

Apparently, over the years, so pleased have the Arabs been with their hunting trips in the area that they've scattered Mercedes and Jeep Cherokees among the local politicians and bureaucrats and even wildlife conservation officials. One lucky bus conductor, I heard, was given such a large thank you for services rendered that he was able to quit his day job, go into politics and eventually ended up in the provincial cabinet. As for the bustards, they're now supposed to be on the brink of extinction. Why do the Pakistanis make such a fuss of them? Because, they say, if they don't, the Arabs will expel all the Pakistanis from the Gulf States, and then where would they be?

I didn't make it to Rakiul Yar Khan, either, because my driver had another mysterious geographical blackout. So instead I went to Islamabad and Rawalpindi.

Islamabad, the capital, is odd. It's a modern city – construction did not start until 1961 – but somehow it already looks old-fashioned. The only building that is remotely memorable or striking is the huge Shah Faisal Mosque which – don't tell the guys in Lahore – is supposed to be the biggest mosque in the world seating, or rather, I suppose, kneeling, up to 75,000 people at a time. Although where they would all come from Allah only knows. The whole time I was in Islamabad, I didn't see enough people to fill even the front row. All the other buildings look like a downmarket council estate.

The other odd thing about the place is that it has no places. No bus station. No market. No government buildings. No Parliament. Instead – typical Pakistani bureaucrats' approach – it has just grid references. So if you want, say, the Sitara Market, you can't ask for the Sitara Market, you have to ask for G7. Similarly, it's no good asking for the Civic Centre, you have to ask for G6. The only exceptions I discovered were the Swiss bank, which everyone seemed to refer to as 'Shhh', and the famous Juma Bazaar, the largest open-air market in the world, or more accurately the biggest open-air market in the world next to a *nullah*, a huge, foul-smelling, open-air sewer which is known as 'Phew'. If you go there, go to the open-air Afghan restaurant under the trees. I promise you, the cups of *kahwa* they serve there are truly aromatic.

Trying to fix your daily list of meetings, therefore, is like playing chess with Kasparov: F6 to G8-1, F4 to G1-3, G9 to

F7. The trouble is, at the end of it there's no way you can mate anybody. That's forbidden as well.

Rawalpindi, on the other hand, is well known the length and breadth of Pakistan. In the days of Kippers it was the biggest British Army base in the whole of Asia and in some ways, especially around Saddar, it still looks like it, although instead of being British it is now the Pakistanis' biggest army base.

Just up the road from Rawalpindi, in the hills, is Murree, which, with its neat rows of bungalows and guest houses and churches, is as much British-looking now as it was in the old days. It's even got its own whisky distillery, the only whisky distillery in the whole tea-total Muslim country. But with Murree, my driver had yet another one of his geographic blackouts.

Was it the fact it was still so British? No. Was it the fact it had a whisky distillery? No. It was because, in a country riddled with violence and corruption, and which every day is becoming more and more Muslim, and where more and more women are wearing the veil, where adultery is a crime punishable by stoning to death, Murree City had summoned up the majesty of what was left of the Pakistani judicial system and passed a full-blown law decreeing that – and I quote – 'the wearing of knickers has been prohibited on all roads of Murree City'. The only city in the whole God- I mean Allah-forsaken country where it was possible to eat, drink and be Murree, and I couldn't get there. Talk about not playing the Game, Great or otherwise.

Bandar Seri Begawan

You've got Alzheimer's. You've just had another triple bypass operation. The old prostate is still playing up. You've got Alzheimer's. You're desperate to get away not just from carrot juice but organic carrot juice, pasteurised semi-skimmed unsweetened soya milk, tofu salads and having to take handfuls of soy isoflavone extract three times a day after what are laughingly called meals. And, in case you've forgotten, you've got Alzheimer's.

Even so you want to go somewhere where you can still dream of England and all those old-fashioned, long-forgotten English things that John Betjeman used to go on about: the Church of England, eccentric incumbents, oil-lit churches, the Women's Institute, modest village inns, the Tory party, arguments about cow parsley on the altar, the noise of lawn-mowers on Saturday afternoons, local newspapers, local auctions, the poetry of Tennyson, Crabbe, Hardy and Matthew Arnold, local talent, local concerts, visits to the cinema, branch-line trains, winning the Ashes, light railways and leaning on five-bar gates and looking across fields.

Although maybe the Church of England will figure less in your dreams than the local talent.

So where do you go? Europe and the States are out. They're too close to home. The family, or at least those members of it who are still talking to you, could still drop in for the weekend. In any case, wherever you go in Europe or the States, the chances are you'll probably end up being surrounded by a load of expats waffling on about the joys of warm beer, throwing up at the mere sight of a can of lager and banging on endlessly about how much they hate the weather, the food, the drink and, of course, the Spanish, whichever country they happen to be in.

The only answer is the Far East.

Phnom Penh, Ho Chi Minh City, Yangon, Bangkok, Hong Kong, Karachi, Dhaka, Bombay, Manila, even tiny Macão, are all great fun, although I suppose not exactly ideal for someone with a heart condition, prostate problems and allergies to benzene, butadiene, nitrogen dioxide, sulphur dioxide and those tiny particles called PM 10s which block up your lungs and cause all kinds of nasty things. Including death. The same goes, I suppose, for Taipei, Kuala Lumpur, Beijing and Shanghai. Ventiane, Hanoi, Colombo and Luang Prabang are all nice and quiet, although I suppose not too many laughs. Unless, of course, you're planning to become a Buddhist monk and go around begging for money.

Which means about the only place left where you can park the old zimmer frame that is clean and warm and safe and b-o-r-i-n-g is Brunei, the tiny patch of 24-carat gold on northern Borneo squeezed between Sarawak, the land of the legendary White Rajahs, and Sabah, home to Mount Kinabalu, Borneo's highest mountain – about the same size as Mont Blanc – and the highest peak between the Himalayas and faraway New Guinea.

A few years back, long before I finally got there, which is

usually the case, Brunei was one of the fun spots of the world, a champagne-fuelled Utopia crawling with luxury yachts run by Australians of the Foster's-swilling variety. Although, come to think of it, practically every Australian I've ever met has been of the Foster's-swilling variety. Including the Sheilas.

Inland, if you could get there, that is, because the airport was invariably chock-a-block with anonymous-looking trunks with Asprey's stamped all over them full of jewels worth £10 million a shot, Brunei was inundated with polo teams from all over the world falling over themselves to get into a hotel, any hotel, and then spending the night dodging up and down the corridors making certain everybody's breakfast-order card hanging outside their room requested twenty-seven orange juices. Which explains why at one time Brunei led the world not only in champagne consumption but orange juice sales as well.

There were also strange-looking buildings that were said to contain all kinds of, er, sporting equipment, as well as all kinds of, er, sporting personnel who were more than prepared to, er, cater for your every requirement for the rest of your natural-born days. Which, I was told, was usually around three weeks. Or less, if you were lucky. Brunei was determined to conquer the world, in fun terms, if nothing else.

Now that's all changed. Sultan His Majesty Paduka Seri Baginda Haji Hassanal Bolkiah Mu'izzaddin Waddaulah, known to his friends as the Sultan His Majesty Paduka Seri Baginda Haji Hassanal Bolkiah Mu'izzaddin Waddaulah, has found religion. He is also – if you have tears, prepare to shed them now – down to his last US$30 billion. To cushion the blow he still has homes all over the world, a stack of Impressionist masterpieces, sacks of jewels, a clutch of hotels, hundreds of cars, including a mere 150 Rolls–Royces, Mercedes, Porsches and Ferraris, not to mention a clutch of McLaren F1 sports cars at £650,000 a throw. And if that's not enough to keep anyone out of mischief, he also still has his own personal aircraft hangar and more planes than the national airline, Royal Brunei. Not that Royal Brunei is some two-bit airline. It's the only one I know that has gold-plated seatbelt buckles. It's also, incidentally, the only Muslim airline I've come across that always begins its long-haul flights with prayers which are then quickly followed by the latest *Seinfeld*, which I always thought – correct me if I'm wrong – was some kind of Jewish American comedy show. But then, I never have understood the way airlines treat their passengers.

Gone, however, is the luxury yacht called *Tits*, which the Sultan shared with his brother Prince Jefri, and the speedboats *Nipple 1* and *Nipple 2*. Gone are not only all the, er, sporting personnel, who have packed what little they had to pack and left, but also all the air stewardesses on the Sultan's Royal Flight who, among other things, no doubt, used to decorate Cowdray Park or Smith's Lawn whenever the Sultan dropped in for a spot of polo. Gone, too, are Michael Jackson, Janet Jackson and Rod Stewart, who used to drop in to entertain the royal kids for the odd half-hour or so. When, of course, they were not playing with their toys. For example, the real-life Airbus the Sultan bought his daughter for her eighteenth birthday. Just the kind of present I guess any eighteen-year-old girl dreams of.

Some say the reason for the let's-get-serious move was the Asian financial crisis. Others claim it was all the fault of the Sultan's brother, Prince Jefri. Others still maintain that nothing has changed at all: the Sultan has always been a serious, sober, strict Muslim. It's just that today, as always, he's a little bit more serious, sober and strict a Muslim.

All of which, looking at it from the expat viewpoint – through the bottom of a whisky tumbler – makes Brunei the next best thing to having your own dialysis machine.

It's small. The whole country is about the size of a couple

of polo fields and the reception area at the Dorchester Hotel in London which, I forgot to mention, the Sultan also still owns, along with the Palace in New York, the Bel-Air in Los Angeles and the Plaza Athenée in Paris. The total population is around 275,000, which must be about the number of large Scotches they serve every day in the Sultan's hotels around the world.

It's pleasant. Well, with GNP per head of population at around US$20,000, one of the highest in the world, with no income tax, free social services, free schooling, free pensions, free housing if you work for the government, free trips to Mecca and all the oil and gas you could ever want, it would be surprising if the locals were not at least mildly friendly. If they're lucky they might even get a couple of juicy steaks thrown in from the Sultan's farm in Darwin, Australia, which I'm not saying is big – it's just bigger than Brunei. As most of the money comes from the Sultan's joint oil and gas operations with Brunei Shell – they reckon these make him only US$5 million to $10 million a day – the place is known locally as the Shellfare State.

Finally, it's safe, safe, safe. When I was there I heard how one of the locals had just been into a bank, his chauffeur walking behind him carrying a big suitcase. He put the suitcase on the counter. He said it contained US$10 million. In cash. One of the staff counted the money. It came to US$7.5 million. The man then turned on his chauffeur 'You're crazy!' he shouted at him. 'You brought in the wrong suitcase!'

At the same time, and to ease the old Calvinist conscience, it's not in-your-face rich like some places you come across, those, say, not a million miles from Florida. In fact, if anything, to look at it you'd say it was inhabited by Calvinists with Muslim financial advisers.

The capital, Bandar Seri Begawan, or Banders, as we old Asia hands call it, is tiny. It has a population of about 65,000.

At least, that's what they say, although I've only ever seen about seven people there, and I've been there a million times. Walk the length and breadth of the place – it's not difficult, it's about the size of half a polo field – and there's nobody around. It's like being the sole survivor of some mysterious champagne bomb that kills people but leaves the caviar standing.

The fancy, air-conditioned shopping malls are empty. You'll also notice, if you look carefully, especially in the jewellery shops, the absence of any suggestion of a cross, a crucifix, a Buddha or anything that could possibly be identified with any religion other than Islam. The Holy Prophet. Peace be upon him.

Take a stroll round the back by all the Chinese shops, again, empty. Of people. And you'll also notice, if you look carefully, especially in the shops selling hamburgers, of anything that could possibly be described as meat. Even in McDonald's, which must be the only McDonald's in the world not McSelling McChicken McNuggets, let alone any McBig Macs. Some people say it's all to do with the fact that the meat has not been prepared in accordance with strict Muslim procedures, even though this is done in next-door and equally Muslim Malaysia. One or two say it isn't so much that as that it hasn't been prepared by the right people operating the strict Muslim procedures. If you see what I mean. Most people just keep their heads down and go for the spring rolls.

As for the hundreds of tiny wooden huts on stilts out in the Brunei River, it's the same story. Empty. Incidentally, you'd expect, as befits one of the richest countries in the world, these to be, if not exactly luxury pads, at least, how shall we say, adequate. But half of them look as though they are about to collapse into the water. The wooden planks are splitting in shreds, the metal barriers are as rusty as hell. As for the wooden posts supporting them, well, I only hope they don't get any strong winds blowing up any time in the next couple of minutes.

Take a five-minute trip upriver in one of the similarly ramshackle motorboats to the 22-carat-gold-domed Istana Nurui Iman Royal Palace, a snip at US$250 million. I wasn't invited in, but those who have been tell me this is empty as well, which I suppose is hardly surprising given that, in one of the smallest countries in the world, it is the biggest royal palace ever built, bigger even than Buckingham Palace and the Vatican combined, with no fewer than 1,788 rooms. Well, I say empty. From the outside it might look like a cross between an airport car park and the Sydney Opera House, but inside it apparently has three thrones, one for himself, one for each of his two wives – one a cousin, the other a one-time air stewardess with Royal Brunei (she has the throne with the gold seatbelts and the headphones that don't work); 257 toilets, all with smoke-detectors and no paper; a banqueting hall seating 500 people; 564 chandeliers; five swimming pools; 250,000 marble and gold columns; 6,000 fountains; enough gilt furniture to fill Versailles ten times over; a stack of unopened trunks from you know who; a catering manager called Beverage, who insists on spelling it Beveridge because he is sick and tired of all the jokes, and a million waiters flown in from all over the world because the last thing any self-respecting Bruneian wants to do is wait on table for his Sultan and benefactor. The only time it gets anywhere near even a quarter-full is on the one day a year when, National Trust-style, the Sultan throws it open to the public so that they can tramp through it moaning about the curtains not matching the carpet, who on earth thought of putting that painting there and fancy having to do the dusting.

Not content with the emptiness in town, I decided to

check out the emptiness out of town. I trotted over to the polo club. It's enormous. There are a million different polo fields, each complete with luxury seating and floodlights. All of them empty. There are hundreds of huge, open-air-conditioned stable blocks. Empty. Except for a couple of horses and rumours that another 200 had been put down that morning.

Canter across to the club house, which is about the size of Buckingham Palace. All fancy blue and gold carpets, wood panelling and horse paintings everywhere. But not a soul. Gallop through the restaurant, the private dining rooms, the huge ballroom, which is about the size of half a dozen polo fields, the squash courts, the bowling alley. Not a sausage.

Take a swing through the golf club just across the way. The green is immaculate, the fountains and waterfalls spectacular. All the golf carts are lined up by the hundred ready to go. Nobody in sight.

Even Brunei's world-class hospitals are practically empty. Not because nobody ever gets ill, but because they are so luxurious and so full of all the latest technology that the last thing they want is a lot of sick people throwing up and ruining the place.

But the eeriest thing of all is the theme park, Jerudong Park, a massive, but massive, funfair, fairground or whatever you call them, 25 kilometres out of Banders. It must be about the size of a couple of Disney Worlds. But it's empty, empty, empty. And it's not because it's too expensive to get in, because it's absolutely free.

But perhaps it isn't quite another Disney World. First, sleeves. Everybody, especially women, and anyone that could be loosely described as a woman, must have sleeves. No sleeves, no rides. It's all to do with the Sultan becoming more serious, although I must say when I was there the loudspeakers kept blaring out non-stop, 'You're the one for me. You're my ecstasy', 'You've come a long way, baby', something that sounded like 'What is this thing called, luv?' and other no doubt religiously acceptable lyrics.

Second, running costs. Even though Brunei is one of the richest countries in the world, even though out of the kindness of their hearts the locals decided to build this enormous funfair to keep people happy and contented, even though they decided not to charge for anything, somebody or other decided that, to save the odd couple of dollars, they would operate the various swings and rides and roundabouts only if they had at the very least two kids on board. At any other funfair in the world it would be no problem, but here in Brunei it's a big problem. Believe me, it can take all night for another person to turn up to share some kind of roundabout, let alone a ride, with you.

As for the big rollercoasters, for some reason or other they refuse to switch on unless they have a minimum of six people. You could probably fly to the real Disney World in Florida before as many as six people show up. And back again. And you can bet your life that when there are finally six of you, somebody won't have any sleeves.

To complicate matters, everything comes to a stop five times a day for prayers. So you can imagine what a day out at Jerudong Park is like. You wait all day for five others to appear so that you can go on the big rollercoaster. They eventually turn up. You clamber on board. You get halfway round. You're hanging upside down. And then they turn the power off and go and say their prayers. It's enough to drive you to drink, except, of course – another big Muslim marketing turn-on – there's no drink.

To cheer myself up, I took a look at the world's most expensive unfinished hotel, Jerudong Hotel. It's got 600 rooms and has cost, they whisper, over US$1 billion to date. Just to break even – are you ready? – it's going to have to charge US$500 a night for a standard room and hit a minimum 90 per cent occupancy rate for fifty years. Now doesn't it cheer you up that you're not a shareholder? It did me.

The other thing that cheered me up enormously was that my visit to Jerudong Hotel extended my Malay vocabulary by one word. The Malay for fire extinguisher is, would you believe, *pe madam*.

To me Brunei has the feel of a country that hit the big time and was stung by some smart wheeler-dealers who sold them anything and everything as fast as they possibly could, got paid and then got the hell out of there before they were rumbled. Why else would they have so many huge public buildings, theme parks, hotels and shops they just don't need?

The result is that Brunei needs expats to help fill all those empty spaces. Desperately. As for being an expat in Brunei, well, it can be a million times better than being an expat in many other places I wouldn't care to mention. Providing, of course, you're looking for somewhere small, pleasant, safe and b-o-r-i-n-g.

Mornings, as long as you remember to turn your hearing aid off so you're not woken up by the local mosque for prayers at sunrise, you can sleep in until, well, until whenever you like. You can then get your Filipina nurse to wheel you downtown to look at all the empty shops. If you're adventurous, or if you need the dough, you can always give English or even French or German lessons for a couple of hours. Preferably individual, one-on-one lessons to young students. The fact you don't know any French or German need not necessarily be a problem. Most Asian accents are so bad when it comes to speaking virtually any Western language that the chances are nobody would know what they were saying anyway. If you were rumbled, you could always say it was some kind of regional dialect and nobody would know the difference.

Lunch will be some mushy rice, which shouldn't cause too

many problems for the old gums. Promise your nurse whatever she wants and she'll take you to a Chinese restaurant
where they serve – nudge, nudge, wink, wink – Special Tea.

In the afternoons, get out your malacca cane and cover
yourself up with tartan blankets and you'll be spoiled for
choice. You can go to the local Churchill Memorial
Exhibition, where generations of young Brunei schoolchild-
ren sit for hours on end entranced by tape-recordings of
Hitler's rantings and ravings. What they make of them I have
no idea. On the way back you could take in the royal palace.
Invariably, whenever I go there, there is a bunch of guys from
Asprey's clambering all over the roof taking measurements for
yet another solid-gold model of the place for someone or
other to give to the Sultan as a surprise birthday present. Or,
if you prefer to look forward rather than back, the Malay
Technology Museum is always worth a visit. Don't forget
that for Brunei technology means fishing, boat-building and
tool-making, which, fortunately, is much easier to understand
than all this hi-tech electronic, ball-grid array and microchip
stuff. If, on the other hand, you suddenly feel weepy and
want to recall the happy days you spent with your loyal band
of friends at work, you can always hunt out the local snake
temple for a quick reminisce. If it's the love and affection of
your family you miss, there's bound to be an alligator farm
somewhere.

Evenings are for locking yourself behind closed doors with
a bunch of other old buffers called Jeremy or Tristan or Felix
and chuckling about the fact the Sultan's tailor, who flies out
from London a million times a year to run the imperial measure up the imperial inside leg, is called Slacks.

You can hear them now.

'Prince Mohamed, the elder brother. Not as tough as they
say. Even though he once kept me in his office for six hours
arguing about five hundred pounds on a million-pound bill.'

'The Sultan's ceremonial sword. You know it's got two inches missing at the top? Caught it on some spiral staircase in the Dorchester just before going off to some fancy do at Aldershot.'

'Well I never. I haven't heard that before.'

'Still very military. Very tough. Keeps up his connections with the Irish guards.'

'That's what Montague-Fitzherbert told me.'

'Before he got religion, never worked Fridays. Now he's serious, often get called in on Fridays – and Friday is supposed to be their holy day.'

'Not unusual to see the Crown Prince wandering around a government office meeting people. Nice chap.'

'Yes, but does he have the breeding?'

'Gun? Of course he carries a gun. Trouble is trying to spot which side it's on.'

Failing that there are always meetings of the local branch of the World Red Swastika Party where, for hours on end, you can debate why the Americans say it's wrong for Asian governments to bail out their banks but perfectly OK for them, the great champions of free enterprise, unfettered markets and rip-roaring capitalism, to bail out their own.

If you have any trouble getting to sleep at night, all you have to do is either flick through the latest Eric Newby or switch on any one of a million cassette tapes of sermons which, wherever I go in Brunei, I find being hawked around town by some minister of the Church of Scotland. Two seconds, I promise you, and you'll be off. If it's the sermons you go for, it'll take at least ten seconds.

Not everything in Brunei is sweetness and light. There are rules that you break at your peril. You must not, for example, wear anything yellow. Yellow is the official colour of the Sultan. Wear it, especially in his presence, and you're likely to find yourself barred from the New York Palace, the Bel-Air in

Los Angeles, the Plaza Athenée in Paris, the Dorchester in London or any other B&B that he owns. It is also considered mildly treasonable to point with your thumb, cross your legs or to sneeze. Do all three at the same time and you'll be left dangling between *Nipple 1* and *Nipple 2* until there is no life left in your body. But even worse that that, is trying to estimate Brunei's international currency reserves, if such a thing is possible. Do that and you can end up in jail for three years.

Not that Brunei is not a democracy. It is. It's just that democracy has been outlawed since 1962. Mention it, even think about it, and in the old days you risked being thrown into prison. Today, however, they'd probably make you listen to the Church of Scotland guy for a couple of hours instead. Not even the Bruneians are cruel enough to make you finish the Eric Newby.

The most important thing of all, far more important than such trivia as democracy, elections, freedom of speech and all that, is the booze. Thou shalt not drink it. Or rather – subtle, these Muslims (the Holy Prophet, peace be upon him) – thou shalt not drink it in public and get found out. If you drink it behind closed doors you can get bombed out of your mind from the moment you arrive until the moment your body is carried, pickled, to the local DHL office to be shipped back to Blighty for scientific research. The result is that every expat in Banders is perpetually bombed out of his mind. Swimming pools are not used as swimming pools. They're used as ice buckets. Although one glorious couple of expats I stumbled across swore that they had filled their swimming pool with vodka on the basis that it was much safer than water.

'The theeper thou thinks the thigher thou thets,' they maintained.

The trouble with this is that once a week, or maybe even every other day, you must, must, must find time to write to whichever members of your family haven't yet walked out on you in disgust, the odd friend still talking to you and as many strangers as you can think of, inviting them to come and stay with you if they're ever on a swing through the area and decide to swap planes at Banders in order to take advantage of the cheap flights offered by Royal Brunei.

Not that you are the slightest bit interested in them or in what they have to say. After all, you've heard everything there is to know about Sir Oswald a million times. It's just the easiest, quickest, and safest way of getting hold of more booze. It's not that Brunei is strict about the demon drink – they run so many 'save water' campaigns that in many ways you're performing a public service if you save the odd bucketful by sticking to the real thing – it's just that you are only allowed to bring in two bottles or twelve cans of beer per person, which can be pretty restrictive, especially if you've had your fill of travel and all you want to do is see out the rest of your days slumped under the nearest oil rig. The other problem is that whenever you bring in your two bottles you have to fill in some long, boring government form declaring it. The first time I filled in the form I got all confused. Where it said *Namal*/Name I thought it meant the name of the drink, so I put down Pierre Smirnoff. Under *Alamat di negara Brunei*/Address, I put St Petersburg. *Tarikh lahir*/Date of birth: 1842. *Kerakyatan*/Citizenship: Russian.

It didn't make any difference. The customs guy just stamped the form, scribbled all over it and gave it back to me.

'Do I have to keep it?' I asked him in a weak Russian accent. 'And hand it back in again when I leave?'

'No,' he said. 'You can throw it away now if you like.'

Which seemed to me to be the ultimate bureaucrat's dream: creating bits of paper and all kinds of inconvenience for absolutely no reason whatsoever. But you try to smuggle in 140 cases at a time, as some big shot from the local yacht club did, and you're likely to be fined, to have your house and car seized and to be thrown out the country. So I suppose there's a lesson there somewhere. Don't get caught.

As for the locals, they're fantastic. The beauty of retiring to the Far East is that everyone is polite, civilised and courteous, or at least, they pretend to be. Unlike in Europe or the States. They even say unusual things like yes, please and no, thank you. Instead of boring you to death about their beer-mat collection, they listen to you when you're talking to them. They even appear to be interested in what you're saying. It makes a change from those people who won't let you finish whatever it is you're saying because, they say, they know what you're going to say before you even say it, and who talk about you in front of your face as if for all the world you're already in the final stages of Alzheimer's. What was I saying? Oh yes, I remember. Then, of course, when you want peace and quiet, they wander off happily and, instead of blasting the hell out of you with their videos or their Walkmen, they are content, good Buddhists that they are, to spend hours mumbling away before their family shrine until you're ready once again to regale them with stories of how you singlehandedly fought off the Norman hordes and with a solitary musket personally won the Battle of Bosworth or wherever.

And when you hit the final curtain, there's no squabbling over insurance policies or complaining because the mortgage still has to be paid off or because you didn't leave anything to that pain in the neck who criticised everything you ever said or did during your short, innocent, blameless life. All they do is pour you into a jar and stick you at the back of a shelf in a local Buddhist temple or shove a few handfuls of you into your favourite pewter tankard and bung you behind the bar of the polo club until some temporary barmaid decides to have a clear-out and throws you in the bin with the rest of the rub-bish.

You might think that as your last-but-one resting place it's a hard regime, but I've come across a million expats all over the world, and the only pair I've ever had the pleasure of actually staggering into were in good old Brunei. They really had it organised. Up in the morning. Wash. Shave. Downstairs on the dot of seven, large glass of Scotch in one hand. Fantastic. Into the old four-by-four, what. Quick drive into Banders. One hand on the wheel. The other sloshing back the booze. The other holding a mobile phone. What could be better? Especially when doing a U-turn or reversing at 120 kilometres an hour across a motorway intersection by a sign that says, 'DANGER, slow men at work'. Somehow or other it sobers you up wonderfully. Straight into the office. Burn up the paperwork. Couple of meetings. More paper-work.

Lunchtime. Back home. A quick dip in the ice bucket. Try to avoid banging into all those bottles. Then a long, cool plunge into half-a-dozen huge vodkas. Light lunch. More vodka. Quick siesta from two till three.

Then back to the office. Telephone calls. Faxes. E-mails. More meetings. A quick visit to the palace. Yet another group are clambering all over the roof taking measurements for a you-know-what surprise for you know who. A couple of dis-creet meetings with men in suits with Central European accents. Out of the door by seven.

Dinner at eight. Time for a quick half-dozen before the guests arrive. Sit down to eat. Then another. And another one. And another. Crash.

The end of another busy day in-hic-dialysis-paradise.

In the old days at La Florida in Havana, Hemingway thought he was doing well if he shifted sixteen Papa-sized frozen daiquiris in a night and then went home and slumped into an alcohol sponge bath. Let me tell you, he was a babe in arms compared to some of the expats I've come across in Brunei.

If you don't think the old liver can quite stand the pace, there's one or two other nice, clean, safe, wrinkly paradises scattered over the Far East where you can park the old empty tumbler; where the G and Ts go down as fast as the returns you are getting on your portfolio managed by those so-called whizzkid investment managers recommended by your dozy son-in-law who was too stupid to even be an estate agent; and where they don't pollute the environment, don't throw up on the pavements and don't go on and on about tofu salads.

Tokyo, for example, is great fun now you can see the sky again. Not only that, but it's blue as well. The sky, I mean, not Tokyo. Not so long ago it was like the bottom of a cup of organic coffee. Decaffeinated, of course. There was so much smog you could hardly tell whether it was day or time to hit the nightspots, start knocking back the whisky and go in for a spot of *nanpa*. Factories were belching out so much smoke, cars were pumping out so much exhaust, that you were forced to change not just your white salary man's shirt but also your face mask three times a day. If there was an earthquake I doubt whether one in a million would have found their way to the shelters.

Now the smog, the sludge, the smoke, the fumes, the face masks have all gone. Though not the white shirts, at least for those who are still lucky enough to have a job. The threat of earthquakes, of course, remains.

Some people give the government the credit. They've gone all environmentally friendly. They've introduced more and more controls on cars and the traffic flows. Civil servants have to leave their cars behind on Wednesdays in winter and use public transport instead. Recycled paper is the watch-word for documents and business cards. Ministries pool their deliveries. And wherever they can plant a tree, they plant a tree, if not two or three. Others say it's nothing to do with the government. It's direct action. Local people suddenly got tired of choking for a living and started campaigning for a cleaner environment. Where, for example, the government takes air samples at eighty odd sites throughout the city, they take samples at more like 18,000. Where the government is encouraging motor manufacturers to build cleaner cars, they are actually suing motor manufacturers for failing to protect them from the fumes. And wherever they can plant a tree, they plant two or three hundred.

Whoever is responsible, today Tokyo is super-clean. You can eat your sushi off the pavement. It's also, another big plus you can't steal from it, super-safe. Nobody locks their front doors when they go out. Not that it is likely to make any difference when you live in a house with paper walls.

It has also smartened itself up. It used to be drab and dull. Today, especially since unveiling its new Narita Airport, it seems to have opened up. Not quite like Los Angeles or Barcelona, but heading in that direction. The four upside-down pyramids which make up the Big Sight Exhibition Centre, the Telecom Centre, with its huge satellite dish and the slab of meccano with a globe on top have all appeared on an artificial island in Tokyo Bay. Then there's the Tokyo International Forum between the Imperial Moat Tokyo station and the Ginza, which is a fantastic conference, exhibition and cultural centre.

But let's drink to my favourite building of all: the new head office of Asahi Breweries. The jazzy old-and-new style of Murphy's Brewery headquarters in Cork is small beer compared to Asahi's, which looks just like a giant frothing glass of beer. Not their awful, tasteless Beer Water, but the real thing. Cheers.

There are also a million things to do, even for a wrinkly. You think London, Paris or New York are busy? You should see the local Tokyo *What's On* guide. It's about the size of your typical downtown Yellow Pages. The trouble is, the necessities of life are not only very expensive, but half of them are not fit to drink.

Osaka, which is squeezed between traditional Old Kyoto and modern, swinging Kobe of beef fame, is similar. I'm not saying it was seriously polluted, but in the old days the fish had so much mercury in them they could take their own temperature. Locals said it was because they were downwind of a steel mill, a power plant and about a million factories. Today Osaka seems to suffer from a different kind of pollution. Wherever you look, it seems to have developed a love affair with the English garden. The Hankyu department store, I seem to remember, is not content to have just one typical English garden planted on its roof, it's got eight of them, and three what they call garden consultants on hand to tell you how to create one yourself. They even sell big, fat, fluffy ginger toms. Not to ruin your English garden, but for company. Except that the cats are not real, they're electronic. Every time you pick them up and pat them, not only do their eyes roll but a million little computers inside them whirr and whizz around, transmitting everything you're saying and doing, not to mention your heartbeat and the contents of your bladder, to the local old people's welfare centre. Anything out of synch and a robot ambulance and a couple of robot doctors will be round at your place in no time to sort you out. On the plus side, the damn cats won't get fleas, scratch the furniture, pee in the middle of the carpet or scratch the hell out of you at three in the morning.

But that's not why I go to Osaka. I go there for the restaurants. It is not called the kitchen of Japan for nothing. The trouble is, whatever restaurant you go to, Japanese, Chinese or Western, they somehow can't seem to get out of the habit of serving food Japanese- or Chinese-style. In other words, as soon as the food is ready, they bring it. Not that I'm criticising them for a moment. There's a lot to be said for starting dinner with cheese, going on to a sticky chocolate pudding and light fish dish combined and ending up with an enormous meat thing. With the odd glass of red and white wine thrown in along the way. And the whole thing is over in exactly sixteen minutes, including working out how many yen you have left in your pocket and paying the bill.

But as far as expats of mature years are concerned, the best Fukuoka place to go in Japan is Fukuoka, away up on Kyushu, their largest and most westerly island. For centuries it was the major port of entry for China and Korea. With the bay on one side, mountains on the other, it has a pleasant, semi-tropical climate. It's not too big, not too small. You can easily stagger from one side to the other in the time it takes some people to decide to open a bottle of *saki*.

It's also green, but without getting up your nose, if you see what I mean. Although one day their green policies almost cost me my life. Coming out of my Nishitetsu hotel and walking down the road looking for a Nishitetsu bus to take me to Nishitetsu Industries, I was forced to jump out of the way to avoid a cyclist careering along the pavement and was practically mown down by one of those tiny, sit-up-straight electric cars. As if that wasn't bad enough, the driver, who looked as though he had just had a rubber tube pushed up what expats call his Gary Glitter, then had the cheek to call me a *sangokujin*, a term which, I can assure you, does not mean 'Welcome to our country, honoured stranger'.

For entertainment, Fukuoka has got everything: a football team, a baseball team, an annual sumo competition and a real grown-ups' Juradong Park on an island in the Naku River with wall-to-wall bars, clubs and everything else you'll need, especially if you're planning to spend all your hard-earned money on yourself and not leave it to an ungrateful wife so that her toyboy can shove it up his nose. In fact, it's so good that guys in Tokyo think nothing of making the seven-hour journey out to Fukuoka by bullet train for a night out and then back again the following morning, or rather, afternoon.

It's also easy to get away from. From Fukuoka I've covered Japan, China, and Hong Kong. The only problem is that whenever I'm there or passing through, I've never yet had a secretary who has been prepared to courier stuff out to me because it has meant telling DHL the zip code for the hotel I was staying in was ANAFUK. And as for the luggage tags they put on your bags at the airport, they're collectors' items.

My one regret is that I've yet to go to their local Kinki University. I just feel somehow I might have learned something there that I didn't learn studying Latin and ancient Greek for all those years. Never mind. Maybe next time.

Just down the road, or at least, it seems just down the road when you take the bullet train, is Hiroshima, which may not exactly be everyone's first choice as a retirement home, although for some reason it does seem to boast more old people than anywhere else in Japan. Last time I was there the country's oldest inhabitant, Asa Takii, had just died at the age of 114. She had been sixty-one when the bomb went off, killing her entire family. Somehow she survived not only the blast but the radiation as well. Whether it had anything to do with her living to a grand old age nobody could tell me.

After Japan, I suppose the next cleanest, safest and best-organised place has to be Singapore. Personally, I hate the place, not just because it's so goody-goody-two-shoes but because it's also so nannified. You can't do this. You mustn't do that. And don't forget to wash your hands afterwards. Try to do anything on your computer, for example, and it will immediately flash up, 'You have performed an illegal operation. It is also bad for the environment. PS Don't forget to pull the chain.' Singapore is so squeaky clean that if you go to a disco – and discos are few and far between – you're likely to end up, especially if you're in Sentosa, in an ankle-high bath covered from head to toe in soapsuds. Join the local Taoists, however, and you would end up sitting in a giant wok covered in boiling oil with a bunch of monks throwing sesame oil, rice wine, ginger, soy sauce and herbs at you. Just don't look at your watch if you're driving or operating heavy machinery.

But in spite of all this – see how objective I am – it's got to be up there with the angels. Singapore really is your ultimate green city. So green, in fact, that the whole place looks like some upmarket golf course. The infrastructure is superb. Traffic is kept strictly in its place. Public transport is unbelievable. Unbelievably good as opposed to unbelievably bad. Not a blob of sulphur dioxide, let alone nitrogen dioxide, is allowed to escape into the air. The locals are almost too afraid to touch it, let alone stroll around and gambol in it. Come on, you haven't forgotten your gambolling days! Their idea of a day out is being enveloped in air-conditioned luxury at Changi Airport looking at the planes trying not to break the sound-emission levels.

It's not cheap, but then, it does have a solid economy; modern, beautifully cared for infrastructure; huge reserves; no debt. And if you call an ambulance, you know it will get there. It won't get stuck in the traffic. What's more, they've livened up Orchard Road, not to mention Boat Quay and Clarke Quay, so maybe it's worth it.

If you were brought up on all things Asian and modern, make for Georgetown way up in the top north-east corner of Penang Island in Malaysia. It's not so clean or so safe or so organised, but it's a million times more fun. An old colonial trading post – it was claimed by the British in 1786 – Georgetown is what South-East Asia used to be like. Literally. It's British. It's Indian. It's Chinese. It's Thai. It's Tamil. It's Sindhi. It's Gujarati. It's Hakka. It's Burmese. It's Muslim. It's Armenian. It's even a touch Malay. It also has more scruffy, dirty, narrow, bustling alleyways and prewar buildings than any other major city in the whole of South-East Asia, so any expat is guaranteed to get lost there, no problem.

If you're hooked on Straits architecture, or even if you just want to look at some broken old relics to remind you of home, there is nowhere like it. I don't know anywhere else east of wherever which has so many of your original tiled Chinese shop houses, Thai parlours, white stucco colonial bungalows, ornate clan houses guarded by stone dragons, and even your super-rich, expensive mansions such as Cheong House, the home of Asia's Rockefeller. This has twenty-eight rooms, five courtyards, seven staircases and 220 windows. The amazing thing is that most of the buildings are still in their original condition. Many of them even have the original inhabitants still living in them.

Georgetown also has more than its fair share of temples, mosques and churches. The Chor Soo Kong, the Snake Temple, I always think is great fun. First of all because there are hardly any snakes there. Second, because of the sign outside saying, 'Mediums are forbidden to fall into a trance in the Snake Temple or its precinct to avoid causing inconvenience to worshippers or visitors.' Goodness me, whatever next? It's amazing how inconvenient some people can be. It makes you wonder what Lourdes or Fatima or some of these Southern Belt hot gospel churches you see on American television would be like if they were being run by these guys.

My favourite, though, is the Kek Lok Si Temple. Perched on top of a hill overlooking the whole town, it's not just one of the biggest in South-East Asia, it also boasts over a thousand Buddahs, all Chinese-, Thai- and Burmese-style. But the reason I enjoy going there, just as I enjoy going to so many Anglican churches – well, apart, maybe, from Liverpool Cathedral, which seems to me to be a Gothic cathedral designed by Lutherans – is to see what the gift shop is like. At the Kek Lok Si Temple, it's unbelievable. First, it's enormous, about half the size of Liverpool Cathedral. Second, it's full of masses of highly reverential items like ice cream, Tower of London pencil-sharpeners, African masks, a complete range of 'fartoholic awards' and a selection of signs saying very Buddhist things like 'Shirt and Shoes Required', 'Bra and Panties Optional' and 'Avoid Hangovers – Stay Drunk'. There was even a ridiculous one which read: 'All profits proceed to the temple building fund'.

Mornings you could spend checking out the place. Up Armenia Street. Down Burma Road. Along Ceylon Lane. Back through Yahudi Road. Then there are all the temples and mosques and churches. Failing that there is always Fort Cornwallis. It's not worth going inside, but there are a couple of stalls outside selling soft drinks where I once spent a happy couple of weeks sheltering from a tropical rainstorm.

For lunch, you can take your pick. Georgetown has all the food and restaurants anyone could possibly want: Malay, Chinese, Indian, French, Italian, American, you name it. You can slurp noodles in any language in the world. They are also pretty hot when it comes to serving food the traditional way: local prices for locals, bigger prices for non-locals. So make certain you grow your hair into a pigtail, or, better still, shave off the lot.

In the afternoons it could be back to the buildings. Try to spot the governor's residence which has never been used because it gave off all the wrong *feng shui* vibes. Alternatively, you could pop into the Wat Chaiya Temple, with its huge, reclining Buddha – 'Beware of shoe thieves', says a sign outside – and have yet another go at learning all thirty-six different things to look for in a statue of Buddha: the ears, the rings of flesh around the neck, the hair on top of his head, the curls, and so on. Or what about the opera? But don't forget that it's Chinese opera, and takes place on rickety old platforms outside the various pagodas. And there's never ever anybody else there, or at least, there hasn't been whenever I've gone to see one. But they are free. Better still, catch one of the famous Hindu ceremonies in which they go around smashing their nuts in the middle of the street in some kind of homage to the god Lord Murugu. If you feel that would bring tears to your eyes, you could always have a bit of a siesta to prepare yourself for the evening, because Georgetown, let me tell you, is no Singapore, especially if you can get into some of those old Chinese mansions.

I forgot to mention that Georgetown is also the disk-drive capital of the world. It is responsible for over 40 per cent of total world production. It is also full to overflowing with electronics companies. Not only is it the hi-tech centre of Malaysia, it also boasts one of the largest concentrations of hi-tech companies in the whole of Asia. But believe me, you'd never guess it wandering around the back streets and temples. Anyone want this near-life-sized paper model of a Lexus to burn on their funeral pyre?

Another town I like in the Far East which I reckon would be suitable for expats is Suzhou in Zhejiang Province, about two or three hours south of Shanghai. Beijing, Shanghai, Xian are all great, but, oh, if you knew Suzhou like I know Suzhou. Oh, oh, oh, what a town. Sorry about that, it's the way it affects me. Even the Chinese refer to Suzhou as heaven on earth. It has a beautiful climate, not hot and sticky and humid like Hong Kong. It's full of canals – the Venice of China, they call it. It also has its fair share of classical Chinese rock gardens. Not so long ago it was little more than a tiny village; today it is one of the fastest-growing parts of China and has developed enormously over the last few years. There are great four- and five-lane highways swinging backwards and forwards through the middle of town, massive hotels all over the place, and just outside there's a vast factory estate full of hi-tech companies. But it's still China.

If you want to play mah-jong all day, you can. If you want to bet which fly is going to lay its eggs in the centre of whose milk pudding first, you can. And if you feel like a bit of action, you can always hit Shanghai up the road.

Cebu in the Philippines is also nice. Nowhere near as exciting and fast-moving as Manila, of course, but OK for expats, especially as they've built that big new hotel in town, installed a twenty-four-hour casino and opened up a whole string of fancy golf courses where for some reason or other I cannot imagine they always seem to be offering huge boxes of Viagra to whoever can hole-in-one.

But at the end of the day, for an expat looking for somewhere that is clean, warm, safe and b-o-r-i-n-g, Brunei still takes the Golden Zimmer Frame Award. Especially when seen through the bottom of that whisky glass, or rather, tumbler. Give it a try, get the supplies organised, and I promise you, you'll have no aggro, no risks. You'll live to be 100 per cent proof, if not more. Because if you do it properly you'll be completely pickled morning, noon and night. If by any chance you do sober up, or if those so-called friends stop coming and you have to go and get your own booze, there are one or two other boring places nearby worth a quick visit. And I do mean quick, because, as far as I can tell, the rest of Borneo is nothing but inconvenience, discomfort, rainforests, wild orchids and warrior ants – which, I warn you, figure high on the local menu because they're supposed to be high in protein and low in cholesterol, whatever that is. And whatever you do, wherever you go, you have to make blood offerings to everything under the sun.

If you go for a drive, you have to make an offering to the gods of the engine. Time for a meal? You have to make an offering to the gods of the table. Start building a house, and you have to pour your lifeblood into the foundations, whereas we just give it all to the bank or building society. Every building site has to have not only its own god but its own bunch of priests as well, a bit like the Canons of Westminster Abbey, I suppose, although these priests don't seem to argue among themselves so much.

Take Sarawak, the land of the White Rajahs, to the south. I'm probably wrong, but I reckon the local Sultan only gave the place to young, handsome, debonair James Brooke because he wasn't interested in keeping it himself. All those savage head-hunting Dyaks. It meant too many problems, too much aggravation. Sensible man. Brooke took it because it was the lesser of two evils: it was either that or get married.

The capital, Kuching, is a rambling old affair on the twisting and turning Sarawak River. When Brooke first saw it he described it as 'a very small town of brown huts and long houses made of wood sitting in brown squalor on the edge of the mudflats'. Well, all I can say is that the brown huts are even browner than they were then. I cannot imagine why people call it the Seville of the East. There's nothing Seville about the place.

As for the tropical rainforests, I don't fancy them at all. If I want to have my blood sucked dry by a mass of leeches, I can assure you I don't have to go all the way to Sarawak. As for walking around all day in a swarm of mosquitos, wearing a pair of socks soaked in Dettol or some local jungle juice with some guy with a penis gourd and a feather headdress waving a razor-sharp parang all over the place, no thank you. Neither am I keen on the idea of crawling into some underground cavern the size of five St Paul's Cathedrals feet-deep in bat droppings.

Sabah, to the north, is better value. Especially on the Sabbath. The capital, Kota Kinabalu, or KK, as we locals call it, is quite fun. Parts are a bit seedy and run-down; parts look a touch Joseph Conrad, especially the traditional buildings on stilts which, for some reason, are blocked off from view by enormous screens. Funny that. But the new town they're building across the tiny bay is way out. It's all jazzy buildings – the chief minister's office looks like the bottom half of a spaceship – and vast, sweeping lawns. The new State Mosque looks like it's surrounded by a row of giant chessmen. Best of all, on a good day, is the early-morning view of Mount Kinabalu. But Sabah is now desperately doing everything it can to bring in the tourists, so you'll have to cross it off your list.

The alternative – and I hate myself for saying this – is Labuan, about fifteen minutes across the bay from Brunei by plane or about an hour by boat. Forget all the nonsense about it becoming a big Malaysian international offshore financial centre. Forget the big, swish hotel out on the beach where one evening I waited over an hour for them to find a bottle of champagne. Forget the Hotel Tiara out near the airport unless, of course, you can get Room 419 because, shhh, don't tell a soul, the key also opens not only the door to the bar, but all the drinks cabinets as well. Don't ask me how I know. All I can say is I've had the hangovers to prove it. Labuan is the perfect place to retire. Providing, of course, you haven't got Alzheimer's, you haven't had another triple bypass operation, the old prostate is not playing up and you haven't got Alzheimer's. It's small. It's so small there's not enough room for an eighteen-hole golf course – it only has a nine-holer – let alone a full bottle of whisky. All the bottles I saw were no more than half full, if not almost empty. There is a great mish-mash of people: Malays, Indians, Chinese, Kadazans, Dusuns, Bajaus, Muruts, Rungus, Lotuds, Orang Sungeis, Kadayans and everything else you can think of. There are even the odd one or two expats. There are hundreds of tiny bars and cafés full of old men playing *jenga* which, I've noticed since the big financial crisis hit Asia, they've stopped referring to as dominos. There are hundreds of authentic local restaurants – so authentic they think nothing of beating the hell out of a fish on the floor in front of you, killing it with a swift twenty-seven strokes, cooking it and then bringing it straight to your table. There is also the Yacht Club restaurant, which isn't really a yacht club restaurant. It's a huge, open-air wooden shack on the beach, the ideal place for riotous assemblies. Whatever you slop on the floor, they just sweep it all up and get you another bottle, no problem. The Beach Club is a bit more prim and proper, but ask for Daisy, and she'll look after you.

As for getting to Labuan, ask any expat and he'll tell you straight away. The flight and boat times will be engraved on his swollen, throbbing liver.

The reason I like Labuan is because, living there in a house on the beach, is my dream expat retirement couple. They've no worries, all the sunshine they want and as far as I'm concerned, they're the world's greatest experts on all forms of liquid pleasure. Of which, I hasten to add, swimming is the least. But if you're thinking of heading out there with the old zimmer frame and doing the same thing, don't. You'll have the time of your life. Stick to Brunei. You'll live longer. Because, by comparison, it's as b-o-r-i-n-g a-s h-e-l-l.

Ulan Bator

It might be the birthplace of Genghis Khan – pronounced T-chin-giss by the Mongolians – be the size of Europe, have a population of just 2.5 million people compared to 30 million animals, stink to high heaven of rancid mutton and be gummed up with *airag*, yaks' milk, but Mongolia is not a country. At least, not a real country with houses and streets and fences and pavements and policemen creating enormous traffic jams. It's more of a giant assault course designed and created for nothing but Jeep thrills. The world's biggest, muddiest, slushiest, smash-'em-to-pieces testing ground for four-by-fours by far.

If you like your countries to have horizons lined with busy highways, this is definitely not your kind of place. There are hardly any roads in the towns. What am I saying? There are hardly any towns. In fact, with less than 1,500 kilometres of roads in the entire country, more or less every square inch of the place is geared to those who want to do nothing more than point their bonnet in whichever direction they fancy, give it a bit of welly and skid for it for all their life is worth.

From, appropriately enough, Moron and Lake Hovsgol, which contains 2 per cent of the world's fresh water, way up in the north, almost touching the border with Russia, down to the petrified forests and the Gobi Desert and the border with China in the south.

Speaking as an old Land Rover man myself, or, as we off-roaders call ourselves, among other things, Landyman – although I must admit that my Land Rover was like my mother-in-law: it drank like a fish, smoked like a trooper and did nothing but cause me trouble – Mongolia is everything your souped-up Series 11A Stationwagon, with 650×16 Dunlop eight-ply triple-traction tyres, a cracked exhaust manifold and a driver as thick as his two rear tyres, could wish for. Soil. Grass. Gravel. Pebbles. Rocks. Sand. Sandstone. Gullies. Dried-up riverbeds. Great, sweeping plains awash with colour – the colour of thick, grey, icky mud. Golden valleys under flawless blue skies. Huge mountain ranges. A million yaks gawping at you wherever you go and whatever you do. Horsemen galloping around all day long, standing in their stirrups and waving at you like mad. Eagles perched on every telegraph pole in sight. Winds from Siberia which cut through you like a knife through six-month-old rancid yaks' butter. Temperatures as low as –40 degrees centigrade.

In other words, not to put too fine a point on it, for the dedicated Landy, Mongolia is a 101 Forward Control without the NATO green paint, offering as many do-it-yourself elk tests and 60-mile-an-hour slaloms as you like. Here talk of going topless and My God, she's a capable beast takes on a whole new meaning. It's where men are men, roads are for cissies and breakfast, lunch, dinner and supper is boiled mutton. As they say in my local off-roaders' club, grinning from gear to gear, he who tyres of Mongolia tyres of whatever they say it is. And they auto know. To the more elderly married men – those over twenty-nine-and-a-half – it is, they say, the only place in the world where they can put up with yak, yak, yak, morning, noon and night because it's also got those other three essentials of life: horses, vodka and an almost total lack of vegetables.

I say horses. They're more like ponies. They have short, stocky bodies, little legs, long ears and the stamina of an ox. Called *takhi*, or Przewalski wild horses – Przewalski was the name of the Russian soldier who first discovered them – it is said that they can be traced back to the Ice Age. Personally, my only experience was tracing one back to a wild, moth-eaten Bactrian camel to which he seemed to take a fancy when he slipped his moorings one morning while I was being plied with yet more curdled sheep's stomach scrapings and another gallon of yaks' milk. No sooner had the ponies, oops, I mean horses, been discovered than they were almost wiped out again by Europeans who wanted to take them home as pets. And no wonder. They go like a bomb. In fact, I reckon T-chin-giss, which means Universal King Who Lives Off Nothing But Mutton and Vodka, never really intended to hit Vienna. It's just that once the ponies' little legs got going there was no stopping them. Bless them.

The problem is the tack. It's not really tack at all. It's everything you find at the bottom of the drawer in the cabinet at the back of the garage. The bit that goes in the horse's mouth is not your proper, highly crafted, precision-engineered bit you get from Mandy in that essence of Edwardian England Swaine Adeney Briggs. It's an ordinary, everyday strip of copper or whatever other metal they can find. Ditto the bridle. Forget your beautifully polished, top-of-the range Dobert double bridle lined with gold or silver from Germany. It's a mass of different bits of string. As for the saddle, well, that brought tears to my eyes. It's no Jefferies lightweight flyover saddle, or anything even remotely like a saddle you'd find in your Pony Club handbook. It's bits of stick thrown over the horse's back with strong, upright wooden supports fore and aft. The upright wooden support at the back is fine for leaning back and pulling the thing to a halt. As for the strong upright wooden support at the front, there's no way I could see it doing anything other than damaging your enthusiasm. Just think about it. You're bombing across the open steppes when a snow leopard suddenly leaps out at you from the middle of nowhere. The thing slams on its brakes. You shoot forward in the saddle and slam straight into the wooden support at the front, and bang go your chances of singing tenor, never mind baritone, in Handel's *Messiah* in the village hall at Christmas. I know because I tried it. Riding across the steppes, I mean, jammed tight within a tiny Mongolian saddle on a tiny Mongolian pony. Not singing in Handel's *Messiah*. I'm usually dragging myself round the village singing more traditional carols like 'We Three Queens of Orient Are' and 'I Saw Daddy Kissing Santa Claus'.

Anyway, they are not a saddle for anyone interested in developing and maintaining a stable relationship. They're obviously OK for the Mongolians, but for us big boys they can present all kinds of problems. As soon as I clambered on board and grabbed hold of Granddad's old pyjama cord I knew it wasn't made for me. Vroom. We were off across the wide, open plains like a Mitsubishi Shogun 2.5 turbo diesel on heat.

Whoosh. Wasn't that the railway station just outside Alma Aty?

Whoosh. Was that Buda? Or was that Pest?

Whoosh. 'I'll have a *schwartzwaldekirsch torte bitte. Mit sahne. Danke.*'

As if getting the hang of the saddle was not bad enough, the *uurga*, the Mongolian lasso, had me all tied up in knots.

But the amazing thing was, apart from the noise of the old

ticker belting away like mad, the silence. The total, all-enveloping silence which – I know this sounds stupid – seemed to wrap itself round you like the peace and contentment you feel cruising at way over 150 kilometres an hour at night along a German *autobahn* in a Toyota Landcruiser. It was unbelievable. There was nothing there. No animals, no birds, nothing. If the old pony hadn't been puffing and panting as well, I reckon you could have heard the grass growing.

Nothing made me stop when it came to the vodka, either. Partly because it was not just chilly, it was Sir-Ranulph-Fiennes-has-just-lost-another-finger-Antarctic chilly. It was like those mornings after you've been forced, because it's the only way you know how to earn a living, to go to another boring business dinner and, through no fault of your own, you haven't got back home till four in the morning. Know what I mean? The first vodka the next day was always a bit rough. Maybe it was something to do with drinking it before breakfast, I don't know. The second glass, however, always seemed to be better than the first, the third than the second, and so on until you get to didn't I leave the Land Rover parked around here somewhere?

The other advantage I found to Mongolian vodka is that, if it's not exactly a fuel substitute, it certainly gets those little Russian four-by-fours moving. Once I got stuck halfway up a sand dune somewhere in the Ukhaa Tolgod foothills leading up to the Gilvent Mountains. We were heading for Xanadu, a gap between two low hills littered with 80-million-year-old dinosaur eggs. The driver immediately grabbed a vodka bottle, jumped out and poured the lot into the tank. The whole thing practically exploded. But we were moving again. Why eighteen out of the nineteen vodka distilleries in the country failed their Hygienic and Virulent Audit Service I have no idea. As far as I'm concerned they should all be rated four-star. Premium.

As for the almost total lack of vegetables, if, like me, when you're at home you're being forced to overdose on cold organic beetroot and chickpea purée, it's fantastic. Or, as Jeremy Clarkson would probably say, it's a 1991 five-door complete with window-tinting. Apart from a bit of rice and, I suppose, the vodka, which, come to think of it, is really a vegetable in liquid form, there are hardly any vegetables the length and breadth of the country. The trouble is, what little other food there is, apart from mutton, takes some getting used to: camels' curd the size of doorsteps; fermented mares' milk; salty tea with a dash of rancid butter; a dollop of axle grease and all kinds of stuff out of strange-shaped bottles. But given the choice between yet another natural fennel quiche and a lump of rotting camels' curd, I'd take the rotting camels' curd any day. And, of course, a dash of traditional unhygienic, virulent Mongolian vodka. I'd even take that three times a day.

Horses, vodka and the almost total lack of vegetables apart, Mongolia is for grown-ups. Unlike at all those silly kid-sized testing grounds and cross-country drives you see all over the rest of the world with all their don't do this, don't do that nanny signs all over the place, in Mongolia you can do what-ever you like. In whatever gear you like. If you want to do it, you just do it. Nobody's going to come at you wearing an anorak, blowing a whistle and waving a clipboard about, or get into a panic about whether you've got permission or not and give you a long, boring lecture about the damage you're doing to the environment, not to mention the two springs and selector fork over your dog-clutch selector shaft. You just press the old yellow knob, slip into the usual wrong gear and within minutes you can be scaring the life out of whole flocks of eagles and falcons, reversing into the secret hideaways of rare snow leopards or really busting the dust and crashing through whole piles of dinosaur bones. You get an extra ten points if you hit a dinosaur embryo, especially down in Omnogobi, which is just across the border from China, where they will fetch enough to buy a 110 LWB five-door Stationwagon.

But be warned. If your wing mirrors are not too clogged up with mud and sand and in between the odd glug of vodka you spot a gazelle in the overtaking lane, take care. Not only can they do 60 miles an hour, but they love nothing better than a game of chicken, dodging from left to right in front of your bonnet like a bunch of dolphins playing in front of a ship. If, however, you are overtaken by a gazelle being chased by a wolf doing 60 miles an hour, you either need to take more water with it or you're way overdue for a new coil-sprung 80-inch 3.5 EFI five-speed Santana box with PAS, full-cage spaceframe construction with twin shock mounts.

If you like you can even destroy your Landy, and yourself as well, come to that, and nobody will say a word. In fact it is doubtful that anybody will even realise, unless you're eaten by a snow leopard and turn up in years to come in an autopsy carried out by a student attached to some Chinese–American–Russian research expedition trying to find the foundations of the Statue of Liberty.

If all that is still too tame for you and you feel you'll have nothing to tell the folks at your local Land Rover club when you get home, a word in the right ear and the Mongolians will gladly make matters a million times worse for you. Forget the lumps of frozen carbon dioxide and drops of silver iodide that the Americans, Russians and even the Australians keep on about. The Mongolian military are only too happy to fire scores of shells into the overhanging clouds to deliberately create your own personal snowstorm. Usually they do it to try to stop forest fires, but I'm told that for a pair of Land Rover spotlamps, STC 8481, with or without the tool kit, they'll oblige. After all, now that the Russians have left them in peace, they're wheeling and dealing as much as any Toyota agent trying to break into Land Rover territory.

Ulan Bator, the capital of Mongolia, is the greatest capital city in the world. Not because in the seventeenth century it was home to the high priest of Tibetan Buddhism, the religion of the Mongols. Not because it was at one time a major cross-roads for caravans running between China and Russia. Not because in 1911, when China's Qing Dynasty fell and Mongolia finally became independent, it was known by the startlingly original name of Niislel Khureheh, the capital of Mongolia, which, as a name style for capital cities, somehow didn't quite catch on. And not even because, when the Communists took over in 1924, it became Ulan Bator, the Red Hero, which somehow didn't catch on either.

Ulan Bator is the greatest capital city in the world because – Paris, Rome, New York, eat your hearts out – like the rest of the country, it has also been conceived, designed and created solely for the use of four-by-fours. For about eleven months of the year, it's buried in snow and ice – it is the coldest city in the world – so whatever the handbooks say, it's the perfect place for testing the new heating system you know you should never have had put in cheap by the garage down the road. For a couple of weeks, it's covered in slush, so you can try out those super, maximum, world's-best slush-protectors you know you should never have bought from the guy in the Landy Club with the collection of badges. Then, when it finally thaws out for about three days, you can pull back the yellow lever and cruise around like any other Sunday-afternoon dawdler.

Whatever the conditions, switch on the old V8, put your foot down and it's a dream come true. Half the roads that should exist, maybe more, don't. They're either hard, sandy track or deeply rutted rock. And wherever there does happen to be a decent bit of road, it's full of potholes, some the size of genuine Freelander rigid loadliners, others big enough to take a fully loaded 101 built on a box-section basis. The little bit of space not taken up by potholes is full of . . . what do they call it? Oh, yes, tarmac.

As if that's not enough excitement, there are piles of earth and sand and rubble all over the place. They even use the stuff to block off a road. Instead of putting plastic barriers and red tape and cones and things across it they simply pile up a ton of earth, which is yet another example of their determination to do everything they can to provide as much fun as possible for off-roaders.

There are few buildings, either, to get in the way of a really good burn-up. Most of the 250,000 population seems to live in *gers*, funny-shaped wigwams you see on the outskirts of town. When you look at the state of the typical apartment block, you can hardly blame them. At least in a *ger* you know you can trust the wooden poles and white canvas covering, which is more than can be said of the cement and mortar used in most buildings in Ulan Bator. You also know that if you've had it up to here with the in-laws or you've fallen out with the neighbours – beautiful though it is, even Mongolians can have too much of *hoomi*, the traditional throat-singing – you can always pull down your *ger*, ship it out on the backs of a couple of yaks, put it together again somewhere else and be inside again in twenty minutes, all warm and cosy, brewing up another couple of gallons of *kumiss*, fermented mares' milk, even in the teeth of a 140-mile-an-hour gale.

The poor two-by-two creatures that shuffle along the sides of the so-called streets, drenched from head to toe in the mud you're kicking up, are also doing their best to make you feel at home. Half of them are wearing trilbies and what they call a *del*, a long coat buttoned to the neck with a bright sash around the waist, which is obviously the original design for a car coat. The other half, the ones with the gnarled weather-beaten faces and wispy beards, are wearing exactly the same long coats buttoned to the neck, but they're twice as big and three times as heavy. They're the women. In fact the reason why, even today, Mongolian wrestlers wear those silly Y-fronts with a long-sleeved jacket open at the front is to make it easier for the judges to spot a woman illegally entering the competition, thrashing all the men to death and walking off with all the prizes.

The young people, though, were not as I expected. In a country which is supposed to be more Tibetan Buddhist than Tibet – at one time, before Stalin got to work, over a third of the population were lamas – most of those I met were Christians. Not just Sunday school Christians, but active, Bible-thumping, hymn-singing, slightly over-the-top Christians. This surprised me, until a passing yak whispered in my ear, 'The reason they're Christian is because most of the churches in Mongolia are American evangelical churches, and most young people think that if they become Christians, they can get to America on some training or preaching scholarship, get the Green Card and stay there. That's why they're all Christians.'

But young or old, Buddhist or would-be Green Card-seeking Christian, everybody is as superstitious as hell. Forget walking under ladders, throwing salt over your shoulder or touching a piece of metal if you walk past a nun, as the Italians do. That's kids' stuff. These guys are in a class of their own.

It starts the moment they wake up. Some days are good days. Others are days when you're forced to drive a Chrysler Voyager. How you tell the difference nobody could explain, but apparently, if a Mongolian opens his eyes in the morning and decides it's a Chrysler Voyager day, nothing will shift him. He'll stay huddled under his pile of sheepskins all day.

Those who do step out of the door of their *ger* will never tread on the doorstep. It's bad luck. When they have a quick drink of whatever, they'll flick some of it into the air with their third finger as an offering to the blue sky and then, again with the third finger, put a drop on their forehead for good luck.

If they walk down the street or ride across the steppes and see a wild ass, that's good luck. If they see the dust kicked up by a five-year-old horse they'll practically do cartwheels in it. It doesn't just mean good luck, it means good luck for the whole year.

Spot an *oboos*, a pile of stones with a stick stuck in the middle and a piece of silk at the top of it, and you've hit the jackpot. Walk around it three times, put three more stones on the top and one day your four-by-four will be as clean as the day it was bought. It's as good as done.

One day shortly after I arrived I was at a loose end. I had seen everything there was to see and done everything there was to do. I think it was my first evening in Ulan Bator. I decided to drive across town from my hotel to a restaurant called, unbelievably, Churchill's which, I was told, came complete with mock-Tudor façade, a sign showing the Old Bulldog demonstrating in the traditional manner his appreciation of Mongolian culture, and inside, as much fish and chips as you cared to eat.

Outside the Bayangol Hotel, down towards the River Tuul, in a bracing 25 degrees below zero, I spotted a Honda CRV heading towards Sukhbaatar Square, named after Dam Diny, or rather Damdiny Sukhbaater, the man who caused all the problems for Mongolia in 1921 by making it only the second country in the world to go Communist.

In front of the Parliament building we nearly ran into the back of a Toyota RAV4 with its permanent four-wheel drive unitary construction and independent suspension all round. It was parked outside a shop. Which is about all it's good for.

Outside the Khan Brau pub near the post office, where the band seems to play nothing but old Beatles hits and everybody drinks nothing but beer, I hit the off-roaders' jackpot. I saw a luxury Mercedes M-class, complete with four-wheel electronic traction system, not to mention its own electronic stability programme. But this was obviously up the chute. It had crashed into the back of some Russian truck the size of a multi-storey car park.

Exactly what it was I spotted loitering carelessly outside the bar, which is installed in a plane parked near the back of the railway station, I forget now. All I know is that, even though it was smoking profusely, the bodywork was in great shape. Later I was told by an expert on the subject that it was the Naked, the unbelievably named new four-by-four just launched by Daihatsu, the Welsh car manufacturer.

The old V8 was cruising comfortably when I finally got to Churchill's. But it didn't last long. I flipped a couple of gears and went into overdrive when I was told I couldn't get in because the place was packed to the rafters with what looked like a visiting German trade delegation.

Another evening, probably because people know how I am obsessed with curves and bumps and gradients and sudden inclines – the things I do for my country – I was invited to an enormous Stalinist monster of a hotel for the launch of what I thought was going to be yet another evening of traditional Mongolian steppe dancing. Instead it turned out to be what was billed as an important event in the country's history: Mongolia's first erotic revue, which I thought was going to have everyone firing on all their V8-powered cylinders.

Erotic? It was about as erotic as a Landy bring-and-buy sale. We all sat in a room about the size of a holding bay full of unsold Chrysler Voyagers, munching our fried chicken and rice. Somewhere in the distance something moved. There was a roll of drums. A flash of lights. A group of what could have been girls suddenly appeared wearing fancy headdresses and I couldn't tell you what else or what not else. And that was it.

All the same, it was another great evening in Ulan Bator.

On the way back to the hotel, parked outside the Boar's Tusk between the university and the Cuban Embassy, I spotted a Land Rover trailer, and later, along Little Ring Road, what looked like a very well-preserved 1982 Series III Country Stationwagon. Just outside the bar installed in the plane parked near the back of the railway station, I was somewhat distracted and just missed this huge Alvis Stalwart which was driving in a straight line, completely demolishing everything in its way. Its driver was obviously as distracted as me.

By far the best thing in Ulan Bator, apart from the Genghis Khan Hotel, which, even though it's the most expensive hotel in town, with platefuls of caviar costing as much as US$1.90 and a whole bottle of vodka US$2, still looks like an old-style Chinese workers' hostel – there were even cattle grazing outside on the grass – is the monument to Soviet power and might. If it's buried deep in snow, it's worth waiting for it to thaw, because it shows a huge Russian tank heading up a steep incline before facing a massive drop on the other side. I only hope the designer is released from jail while he's still got the strength to hold a pencil in his hand so that he can come up with another glorious tribute to the Russians' prowess as a colonial force.

As for the rest of the country, talk about Montana, East Dakota or even the West End of Newcastle being empty: Mongolia makes them seem positively New York. The old capital city, Khara Korum, for thirty-two years the centre of the massive Mongol empire and for 140 years the capital of Mongolia, is about 350 miles from Ulan Bator. In any other country in the world you could do it in, say, three or four hours max. Not in Mongolia. It takes about three weeks. Depending, of course, on whether you've still got that Chrysler Voyager or you've built your own Mud Bogger complete with 3.9-litre engine. In which case it would probably take three months, because it would be so much fun getting there, swerving and skidding and kicking up mud in all directions. But, however long it takes, I promise you it's worth it.

Once you head out of Ulan Bator, past the railway station and past that bar installed inside the plane, you're off road practically the whole bumping, jerking, bone-shattering way.

By the time you catch sight of the sacred mountains of Songino Kharkhaan Uul, which apparently means the Onion Mountain, you're weeping, not with joy at the sight of such natural beauty, but with frustration because, out of loyalty to the Germans, you stuck with the faithful British and didn't switch to the much more comfortable Japanese Toyota Landcruiser. By Lun Soum, the old back's beginning to ache like hell. You can feel the teeth loosening. And you're beginning to regret not tying a blue ribbon to the outside aerial. The sweeping, green Khustain Nuruu gives you an excuse to stop to try to spot some Przewalski horses, although you and I both know it's really to rest the joints, try to get the blood circulating again and to calculate roughly how much it's going to cost you to pay that fake physiotherapist to twist you back into shape if you ever get back home. Then it's back on board, across the River Tuul and a comparatively gentle swing close to the Saijrakh Uul Mountains, where there are heaps of dinosaur remains just waiting to be smashed to pieces.

Devsen Bulagiin Rashaan is a famous Mongolian spring. In fact, it's probably the nearest you'll ever get to a Mongolian spring in your life. But as it is only a deadly mix of bicarbonate, calcium and magnesium it's not worth wearing out the brake linings to stop and have a look.

The Batkhaan Uul Mountains are much more interesting,

as long as your back hasn't been shattered completely and you haven't been strapped to the roof as an instant offering to the bearded vultures hovering overhead.

Finally, there's the Khugnu Khan Uul and the ruins of two seventeenth-century Buddhist monasteries, which, as far as I can gather, are the most unvisited places in the country. Either because by now people have lost the ability to walk ever again, or because they're so desperate to get to Khara Khorum that they just slam the throttle flat to the floor and bomb straight past.

When you finally get to Khara Korum itself, you can't fail to notice that it is the world's very first purpose-designed and -built four-by-four city. When they eventually got round to building it in 1220, they carefully paced it out so that it measured exactly 4 kilometres long by 4 kilometres wide. So it has remained, although the condition it's in today, and the state of its non-roads, makes it, you'll be pleased to hear, more a four-by-four city than a four-by-four city, if you see what I mean.

It was from here Genghis – 'I am the punishment of God' – Khan ruled most of the land between the Adriatic Sea and Beijing and from southern Russia down to India, the biggest land empire in history. It might now be the middle of nowhere, but at one time roads and tracks spread out from it in all directions. Every 50 kilometres along each road across the Gobi Desert, to Beijing, to Ulan Bator, to Vienna, there were relay stations with up to twenty horses ready to gallop their hearts out. Riders could, therefore, carry messages backwards and forwards anywhere across the empire at the rate of 400 kilometres a day, which is probably a darn sight faster than many courier services could manage today with all their motorbikes and earrings and mobile telephones.

But in spite of such efficiency, the great T-chin-giss was no good at organising his own personal affairs. Nobody knows where he was born. Nobody knows where he died. It was only in 1999, after 800 years of intensive research, that a group of Mongolia's top historians and scientists from the International Centre of Chingis Khan Studies and the Chingis Khan Memorial Complex Fund even made a stab at it. They plumped for 31 May 1162 as his date of birth and 1227 as the year of his death, although where it happened is anyone's guess, because the Mongols did everything they could to prevent his grave from ever being discovered. The old Mongolian history books even talk about thousands of horses being driven backwards and forwards over it to make certain it was never found. The experts' guess is that he was buried on Burkham Khaldun Mountain. But the last time I checked there were nine different mountains called Burkham Khaldun. My money is on the one near Gurvan Nur, the three lakes where there was once a huge Tibetan monastery, with over 1,000 lamas, which was destroyed by the Communists in the drive against Buddhism in the 1930s. I'd say there has to be a reason why there was a huge monastery there in the first place, and there's not much else on any of the other Burkham Khalduns.

Today, however, the man who destroyed cities, used prisoners as human shields, slaughtered whole populations and is rated one of the most brutal murderers the world has ever known – during Communist times, the mere mention of his name could land you in jail – is revered like a god. Streets, hotels, vodka, they are all named after him. Look at almost any of the tiny Buddhist shrines to be found all over the country, and I'll bet you any money you like, in front of them, carefully wrapped in some fancy cloth, will be a prayer to T-chin-giss. Even the local television – the final confirmation, if any were needed – runs one blockbuster after another about him.

The experts have also recently rediscovered the Great

Destroyer's personal black flag, which has been remade using the hair of 1,000 horses and adopted by the Mongolian Army as their banner. To mark the event the president, N. Bagabandi, and the defence minister, R. Odonbaatar, turned out for a special parade on Oguumur Mountain to watch the army kneel before it and offer fire, vodka, incense, *hadakh* and food to the mighty military spirit to ensure that it brings them good luck. But, between you and me, they don't have a hope in hell. Because in the crowd watching the ceremony was a single woman and, as all good Mongolians know, a single woman means many things, but rarely good luck. Afterwards, to mark the event, both the president and the defence minister engaged in a spot of target practice. The president hit the target eight times, the minister of defence twelve. Both, however, failed to even wing the unlucky single woman.

Don't breathe a word to the Mongolians, but T-chin-giss is also pretty big in next-door Kazakhstan. So big, in fact, they even claim him as a Kazakh. The only reason, they say, the Mongolians make out he is one of theirs is because in the days of the old Soviet Union of unhappy memory the Russians didn't want the Kazakhs to know he was a Kazakh in case it gave them ideas above their station. But now, with the Russians out of the way, they can reclaim their national heritage. So far, however, they've yet to hoist their black flag of 1,000 horsehairs, let alone shoot a woman spectator, so I can't see them keeping T-chin-giss to themselves for long.

A word of advice, though. Don't, whatever you do, when talking about T-chin-giss in Mongolia, mention, hint or even think about T-chin-giss being Chinese. It will, I promise, guarantee at least 1,000 horses being herded backwards and forwards over your grave – and you won't be dead at the time. The Chinese claim that not only was he buried in Ordos in northern China, but they have his tomb as well, much in

the same way as they claim Tibet is part of China. Not that
T-chin-giss himself is to blame for that. It's all the fault of his
grandson, Kubla Khan, he of the pleasure dome and founder
of the Chinese Yuan Dynasty. At one time, say the Chinese,
he ruled both what is now Mongolia and what is now Tibet.
When he then conquered China and moved his capital from
Mongolia to Beijing, he in effect transferred authority for
Tibet from Mongolia to China. Hence, they say, Tibet is still
legitimately part of China.

Today, however, T-chin-giss's capital city is gone; all the
ornate official buildings, the hundred temples, the huge
Palace of Worldly Peace and the fancy fountain Marco Polo
went on about when he came calling with his bag of brushes.
It's nothing but a sad, pathetic, collapsing collection of prehistoric Soviet factories, apartment blocks, a couple of shacks,
and about 200 yards of roadway.

Not that this has stopped some Mongolian members of
Parliament demanding that it once again becomes the country's capital. It is, they say, not only the centre of Mongolia,
but also the geographic crossroads between the Gobi Desert,
the Hangai Nuruu and the northern steppes. It has enormous underground water reserves. It would also take the
pressure off Ulan Bator, which is attracting around 10,000
people every year who, for one reason or another, are quitting
the countryside for the town. They've even, with the genius
of members of Parliament the world over, set up a special
committee to examine the proposal. If the British system of
special committees is anything to go by, that should kill off
the idea altogether.

Within skidding distance of the old capital, however, are
the remains of Erdene Zuu Monastery, the world's first four-
by-four Buddhist monastery. Built in 1586, its square not
only measures 400 metres long by 400 metres wide, but it
also has four gates, one on each side. Inside the crumbling

brick wall around the square, on ground that would be ideal for any Land Rover cross-country weekend, are various temples, more the size of double garages than your real thing. You don't even have to take your shoes off to go inside them, which I always think is half the fun. Something to do, they say, with the weather and padding around in your bare feet in temperatures of –40 degrees centigrade. Soft, these Mongolians. It would never have happened in the days of T-chin-giss. He must be turning in his grave. Wherever it is.

Shoes or no shoes, the Jansresek Temple is a must. In the chapel on the left, if you look closely, you can see a collection of musical instruments. Made from the bones of an eighteen-year-old girl. I asked one of the lamas or monks what kind of music you can make on the bones of an eighteen-year-old girl, but I don't think he understood the question. He did, however, show me a skull which was kept in a silver container on the right of the altar. It was completely empty inside.

'Woman,' he grinned.

Maybe he had understood my question after all.

The Eastern Temple is also fun. I don't know about you, but I swear the Janraisag Buddha, with that gentle, enigmatic smile, is a dead ringer for Sir John Gielgud. Either that or the good Sir John is a reincarnation of the Janraisag Buddha.

Of all the different temples, my real favourite is the Temple of Zuu. The idea of a guardian king protected by all those wicked, evil, designer goddesses is almost enough to make you want to turn Buddhist.

Out of Khara Khorum, point the bonnet south and the wide, wide, open, never-ending steppes begin to turn to wide, wide, open, never-ending dust, which then begins to turn to wide, wide, open, sandy desert: the Gobi, the second-largest and the most unusual of all the deserts in the world. In my time I've bombed, swerved and skidded my way across some of the most hostile and inhospitable parts of the world – the

Sahara two and a half times, the Rub al-Khali, the Kalahari, the Negev, the Namib and the centre of Newcastle-upon-Tyne after dark on a Friday and Saturday night – but the Gobi, which is about the size of France and arguably a touch more sophisticated, was a first. To start with it's dust and gravel – 'Gobi' means stony desert – that goes on and on for miles and miles and miles. Then it's grass. Not just odd tufts of grass, but vast areas of the stuff. Then it's sand. Tiny little patches as well as huge mountains like you get in the Sahara, the Kalahari, and I can't remember all the others. Finally, most amazing of all for a desert, it's glaciers. Massive glaciers containing enough ice to supply a couple of Landy Christmas parties. Then there are the storms. Suddenly they seem to roll up across the desert towards you, they batter you to kingdom come, and then they roll on again.

Such is my luck in life, I got the lot: sand, wind, rain. Even hailstones.

The sand was the worst, because it went everywhere. The wind just rocked you backwards and forwards. Face the wrong way at the wrong time, or hit a ridge at the wrong angle, and the force of the wind could turn over any four-by-four. Even a Morris Marina with a Toyota chassis and a Ford V6 engine. As for the rain and the hailstones, as long as the old wind-screen wipers were OK, there were no problems. The cold was also rough. The Sahara I remember being cold, but that was more the drop in temperature at night. The Gobi was cold, cold, cold. The worst we got was around –20 degrees. Sometimes, especially in the depths of winter, it can drop to as low as –40 degrees. Everybody keeps telling you not to worry, because once you're inside your *ger*, or even your gear, it's warm and cosy. Don't you believe it. The benefits of sleeping in a *ger* in the Gobi Desert in the middle of winter I can count on the fingers of a big, frozen, leather mitten.

We all know the theory. A wooden frame covered with

white canvas or, better still, animal skins, which can be trans-
ported by two yaks or camels, can be reassembled in a
howling storm in thirty minutes, complete with a colourful
wooden doorway facing south. In the Bogd Palace Museum
in Ulan Bator they have a *ger* made out of 150 leopardskins.
Inside, to the east of the doorway, is always your traditional
Mongolian riding gear: a pile of string, a bundle of sticks and
bits of wood, a couple of old blankets and that lethal wooden
clamp of a saddle. In the middle is the combination cook-
ing/heating stove. To the west is the living area: 100 gallons
of fermented camel milk, 100 gallons of fermented mares'
milk and about 2,500 tons of rancid mutton. Gazing down
with pity on everything is a small Buddhist altar and a picture
of Jeremy Clarkson in yet another pair of designer-faded blue
jeans.

In practice, however – at least in the cheap, fraying, moth-
eaten *ger* I was in – it was more like the winter of my discount
tent. There was no riding gear. The furniture looked like the
stuff I made at woodwork class. The living area was dominated
by a huge can of *airag* which tasted like cold sick. In desperation I added more vodka to it to see if it would make a
difference. It did. It made a dramatic difference. After that it
tasted like a cup of warm cold sick. In the centre was a wood-
burning stove that had obviously been used by T-chin-giss
after his second visit to Vienna. Above the stove was a gaping
hole which not only showed Mars in conjunction with the
moon but all the onlookers as well. Or it would have done if
you could have seen them for the thick clouds of black smoke
belching through it.

Now we come to the clever bit. Leave the door open, they
say, and the fire will be stocked up with wood by some mysterious Mongolian wood fairy throughout the night. The
trouble is, with the door open you freeze to death. Close the
door, and don't put any wood on the fire, and it goes out in

two hours. I tried both and the result was always the same. I'd wake up every morning frozen solid with birds all over my bed. Which, I can tell you, is not always the best way to start the day.

By Mandalgov, your original two-track town, in the Middle Gobi, everything was green and fertile. Then we hit dry sand and gravel and literally hundreds of ancient graves. They tell you they're the graves of famous warriors. Don't you believe it. They're the graves of ancient visitors who couldn't get the hang of the traditional Mongolian central-heating system.

By Dalandzadgad, which is practically the centre of the desert, I'd lost it altogether. I decided that if I was going to suffer there was only one way to really suffer. I hired myself a Russian-made four-by-four, a Uas, complete with a Mongolian driver who had a smattering of English and a non-stop supply of typical Mongolian jokes. As far as I could gather, every Mongolian joke has to do with fleas. In comparison, glugging back bowls of warm sick and then freezing to death every night suddenly had its attractions.

With the Uas coughing and choking for its life, the first thing I thought I'd better do was explore Dalandzadgad before it expired. As it turned out it was difficult to tell whether it had already expired or not. Dalandzadgad, I mean. Not the Uas. The town consists of little more than a single street, a muddy square, some appalling Stalinist blocks of flats and a couple of hundred *gers*. Two minutes later we were heading out across the desert, which I must say left me Gobi-smacked. This time it had everything. Rich, luscious grass. Sand. Soft red sandstone. Thousands of miles of gravel and pebbles. Huge areas of absolute nothingness. Not even a tree, let alone a telegraph pole. Then, suddenly, you're between rocks and even harder places like boulders the size of Jeremy Clarkson's ego.

We drove, or rather we juddered and screeched and jarred

our way along dried-up riverbeds, across muddy lakes, halfway up sand dunes – the poor old Russian four-by-four could never make it to the top – and again over mile upon mile upon mile of nothing. We saw craggy, jagged peaks. We saw massive curtains of rocks. We saw moonscapes more real than the real thing.

One morning we chugged our way to the Flaming Cliffs, or Bayan Zag, the most famous dinosaurs' graveyard in the world. Famous, that is, as far as dinosaur freaks are concerned and far more fun than all the dinosaur sites in Montana in the US. First discovered in 1922, it's virtually a huge, gaping gash in the sandstone. We skidded to a halt on top of what was no doubt the last dinosaur egg in existence – Russian four-by-fours don't believe in flash incidentals like brakes – and clambered down into the graveyard proper which is, I suppose, about the size of your average international four-by-four and military show. It was just like being in the office. There were old fossils all over the place. If I was a dinosaur freak, or rather a dinosaur Sherlock Bones, I could quite happily have stayed there for the rest of my life and catalogued every bit of dirt and dust and broken bone.

I've seen dinosaur eggs and bits and pieces before in dirty, battered old showcases in empty museums on rainy Wednesday afternoons in different parts of the world. But to be actually where they lived was something else. Climbing back up the cliffs to the Russian four-by-four also made me very hungry and very thirsty so we celebrated the way the Mongolians have been celebrating since the days of the dinosaur: we had a hunk of rancid mutton and a large slug of vodka. And a large slug of vodka. And a large slug of vodka. And a . . . what did you say this was called?

Another day – or was it another week? – we chugged our way to Gurvan Sayhan, in other words the Three Beauties, which, I must warn you, in Mongolian terms means Big,

Huge and Help, I Give In. See what I mean about Mongolian women being built like wrestlers? Here they didn't have the usual pile of dinosaur bones scattered around. Instead there was a mass of crazy rock formations which looked as though they'd been put together by some sand-dune freak high on fermented yaks' milk.

I even, by chance, became the world's greatest living expert on some filthy, thick, matted, greasy, mangy animal covering. Cashmere. Take a herd of skinny, long-eared, pot-bellied goats and what do you get? Fleas. That's what I used to think. Not so, said my teacher, who I at first took for a merchant banker because he milked everything in sight. Every spring you comb out the grease and the dirt, and underneath you'll find an undercoat of soft down which, per goat, produces just three or four ounces of cashmere. Three goats and you have enough to make a cheap US$1,000 sweater. Blend it with merino wool, camel or yak hair, horse's mane or even *shah-toosh* from Tibetan antelopes and, of course, the price comes crashing down to a much more realistic US$995 per sweater. Well, you know what retail mark-ups are like.

For the poor farmer, however, the three or four ounces of pure cashmere means television sets, video-recorders, motor-bikes, even, if he's unlucky, a Russian Uas. Ten years ago there were only three big cashmere manufacturers in Mongolia. Now there are dozens. Unfortunately, because there are so many, and because your pure cashmere is no longer as fashionable as it used to be, the price has crashed. In the old days it used to take 5 kilos to get a television set, 10 for a video-recorder and 50 for a motorbike. Now it takes 10 kilos for the television, 20 for the video-recorder and 75 for the motorbike. As for the Uas, the price remains what it always was. Nothing. They can't give them away.

The most unbelievable place in the whole of the Gobi was Yolyn Am, the Mouth of the Vulture. It's like a lost valley in the middle of the desert. One minute you're driving across a million miles of grey dust and shingle, and the next you're passing through a tiny gap in the mountainside into a beautiful, wide, open, green, fertile valley that time forgot. It's the kind of trick you imagine Steven Spielberg would have pulled if he'd been asked to design the Gobi Desert. Inside everything seems extra vivid. The air is like cut glass. It is also very, very cold. As you go further into the valley, you come across a small lake with ice a metre, maybe two metres thick which never melts, even though outside in the desert proper, temperatures can soar as high as 40 degrees in the height of summer. Overhead, nesting in the top of the mountains surrounding the tiny valley, are dozens and dozens of eagles. Some people rave about the giant condors in the Colca Canyon deep in the Andes. A few are even awestruck by the sparrowhawks you can see hovering over the Millennium Dome at North Greenwich. This, with apologies to Peter Mandelson, is a million times better.

After that everything else was a bit of an anticlimax, like driving a 1999 Land Rover Discovery after a 1983 Lightweight. Wherever you turned there were black-tailed gazelles, wild camels which look like tame camels without humps and – yawn – the rare ibex. Then there were – yawn – falcons. I'm not saying the place is overrun with falcons, but wherever you turn they seem to be there. Sitting by the side of the road. Hovering over the poor Russian four-by-four whenever we parked. Swooping across the windscreen whenever we hit our top speed of 27 miles per hour. Most of them, especially around Omnogobi, seemed to be your ordinary, everyday falcons as opposed to the fantastic white falcons you see in, say, Uzbekistan and Kazakhstan which, if they're the right size, shape and colour, can fetch anything up to US$1 million among the falcon-hunting sheikhs of the Middle East.

But I'm not complaining. I wasn't even disappointed not

to see a *madzaali*, the dark brown Gobi bear, which is so rare it's only actually been seen once, by two Russian scientists after a heavy lunch one day in 1943, let alone the almost as rare snow leopard. But I did meet one old friend of T-chingiss who told me that, as a boy, he thought nothing of going out and killing a couple of wolves, half a dozen foxes and a snow leopard before breakfast, or rather, before the first helping of rancid mutton and vodka of the day.

So, a word of advice, as the chairman always says in our local Landy club newsletter. Much as the wife might like doing the school run or popping down the road to Sainsbury's in the old V8 Range Rover with its Israeli-made Alliance tyres, that's not what it's made for. It's made for wide, open spaces. It's made for skidding across deserts, racing across swollen riverbeds and hurtling up and down mountain passes. Before it's too late, and you have to sell the V8 for a Chrysler Voyager because all the other school mums have got one, point the bonnet in the direction of Mongolia. It won't cost you a four-by-fortune. It'll be an experience you'll never four-by-forget. Believe me, if you don't, you'll never four-by-forgive yourself. Ever.

Astana

'Coke adds life.'

This was translated into Chinese as 'Coke brings your ancestors back from the dead.'

'Tasty crisps in attractive packaging.'

This was translated into Greek as 'Tasty crisps delivered in coffins.'

'He had a firm in Africa but it didn't last very long because of the way it was handled by so many different government officials.'

This was translated into Polish as 'He had a hard in Africa but it didn't etc.'

You think these are bad? You should go to Kazakhstan. It's a translator's nightmare. First of all, you don't know whether it's Kazakhstan, Kazakstan or even Sazakhstan. Or even where it is, come to that. Some say it's in Russia – including President Yeltsin, which sent a shiver down everyone's Swiss credit cards in Kazakhstan, Kazakstan or whatever you want to call it. Others say it's in China. Especially the Chinese, who refer to it in passing as Xi Yu, their north-west province.

The Uighars, the guys with the long beards, high cheekbones and fancy embroidered skullcaps, in and around Xinjiang swear that it's all part of Uighurstan and argue till they're blue in the face that the Chinese have no more reason to be there than they have in Tibet. But that's another story.

I've even seen American books which claim that it is not in Russia or China or so-called Uighurstan. It's nowhere. It doesn't exist. Which isn't bad, when you consider that Kazakhstan is in fact slap bang in the centre of Asia, covers a million square miles, stretches all the way across from the Caspian Sea to China, and from Siberia in the north down to the fantastic Tian Shan range of Heavenly Mountains in the south, was the second-largest of the old Soviet republics and is now, after Russia, China, the USA, Australia and India, the sixth-largest country in the world. Then there are all the incidentals. It's the size of Western Europe with the population of London. It looks like it was designed by the Dutch. It's flat, covered in grass, with virtually nowhere to spend anybody else's money. It wins more medals at the Olympics than we do.

Way back in the 1930s, after a decade of Russian terror which wiped out all traces of Kazak culture, not to mention anything between a third and half of the population – some say as many as 3 million lives– it became a huge dumping ground for people unwanted by Stalin. There were labour camps all over the place. Solzhenitsyn himself was one of its more famous old boys.

As if they hadn't done enough for the country already, the Russians then decided, out of the kindness of their hearts, to make it the main testing and launching site not only for their space programme but for their nuclear missiles as well. As a result, Kazakhstan is today also the fourth-largest nuclear power in the world, and has a huge nuclear complex at Semipalatinsk which the Americans, who spend more on military matters than every other country in the world combined, and whose weapons are at least one generation ahead of their nearest rival, have probably also never heard of.

As for the people of Kazakhstan or Kazakstan or Sazakhstan, some call them Kazakhs or Kazaks or Sazakhs, or just plain Saks or Sachs. Others call them just plain unlucky. Another American book I saw, for some reason best known to the CIA, referred to them as Kyrgyz, which is a bit like calling the Americans Spaniards. I don't know about you, but as far as I'm concerned Kazakhs are Kazakhs or Kazaks or even Sazakhs, the direct descendants of the Golden Ordu or Horde or Tribe or Army – see what I mean about the place being a translator's nightmare? – in other words, the wild, unruly we-khan-do-anything mob which under good old Genghis ran all over Eastern Europe in the thirteenth century, while Kyrgyz are Kyrgyz, and live next door in Kyrgyzstan. But maybe the Americans know something we don't know, like where to find the Chinese Embassy in Kazakhstan.

Whether you call them Kazakhs, Kazaks, Sazakhs, Saks or Sachs, or even Kyrgyz, the one thing they can't stop you calling them is a minority. They make up less than 40 per cent of the population of their own country which, I suppose, shows there are some disadvantages to neglecting your domestic duties and running wild all over Eastern Europe. By the time they got back they were too exhausted to do anything but slump down in front of the television and fall asleep.

Yet even though there are so few of them, they still think of themselves in terms of *ordus* or hordes or tribes, or even armies, depending on which Kazakh–, Kazak– or Sazakh–English dictionary you get hold of.

The Big Ordu live in the south, down near the border with China.

The Little Ordu live out towards the west and the Caspian Sea.

The Middle Ordu live in the middle, and up towards the north-east and the border with Russia.

The trick, of course, for all the *ordus*, big, little or medium, is to make certain that no other *ordu* or horde or tribe is a bigger *ordu* or horde or tribe or has more influence than any other *ordu* or horde or what the hell. The president, therefore, being not just a big guy but a Big Ordu, or Big Horde guy, has a Middle Ord, or Middle Horde, prime minister, who, he insists, is the best guy for the job. Which I'm sure is true. The fact that most of the country's enormous mineral resources lie in Middle Horde territory is, of course, just a big coincidence. Similarly, the oil and gas minister is a Little Ordu, or Little Horde, guy and is, I've no doubt, the best Little Ordu, or Little Horde, guy for the job. The fact that most of the oil and gas in the country is in Little Ordu, or Little Horde, territory just proves what a dirty, twisted, cynical mind you've got.

Way back in December 1986, when President Gorbachev fired Dinmukhamed Kunaev, as first secretary of the Communist Party in Kazakhstan because he was as corrupt as hell, the Kazakhs, Kazaks or Sazakhs, Big, Little and Medium *ordus*, hordes or whatever went bananas. There were riots all over the show. Not because they didn't think Kunaev deserved it, but because his replacement wasn't one of the you-know-whats. He was a Russian. In the end Gorbachev relented and appointed a one-time shepherd boy, Nursultan Nazarbaev, a Big Ordu, or Big Horde, guy, who is still Big President, I mean president, today. Which, I suppose, proves what a big you-know-what he really is.

Most Kazakhs, once safely tucked up in their traditional yurts or tents or large circular felt structures, depending on which guidebook you've stolen, sipping a glass of *koumiss* or fermented mares' milk or yuk, will tell you that the Big Ordu, or Big Horde, think they run the place, the Middle Ordu, or

Middle Horde, actually run the place, while the Little Ordu, or Little Horde, do all the work.

After that it's lights out and a very quick *gosh-sau bolyngdar*, *jaksh kalyngydzar* or even a quick *khal zhaghdayngyz galay*-your-father because, spurred on by television commercials sponsored by the president's wife, Sara, they are now all more determined than ever to do their bit to ensure they don't remain a Big, Medium or Little Ordu, or Horde, minority for much longer. In fact, in true let's-overrun-the-world, Genghis Khan fashion, the government gave a year's salary free to the parents of the first 2,000 babies born in the year 2000.

To many people, however, the whole thing was a shocking, demeaning, disgusting publicity stunt. They believed they should be offered ten times the money to have a baby, if not more. Well, have you seen what most Kazakh women, or Kazak old bats, or even Sazakh old bags look like? According to Kazakh tradition, and also to the gentle and humane teachings of Genghis Khan, if a Kazakh fancies a woman he is supposed to be able to ride up behind her, grab her, drag her on to the back of his horse and disappear for ever into the sunset in order to show her the steppes. That's the theory, anyway. In practice, they reckon that today, what with all that *koumiss* and *laghman* and dumplings, they'd need a forklift truck and a horse the size of an elephant to try to make off with anyone.

Should they ever fancy a Kazakh woman in the first place, of course, because sweet, innocent and subservient they are not. Many people reckon that the reason Genghis Khan and his merry men went careering all over Eastern Europe was because they couldn't stand being at home, even with somebody else's wife.

A few even claim that Kazakh women are your original Amazons. In Pokrovka, up in the north towards the Russian border, they insist on showing you great big, hairy ancient skeletons of women practically the size of mammoths. They are bedecked not only with all the usual beads and bits of coloured glass all self-respecting Amazons get from Body Shop, but also with iron daggers, enormous quivers holding anything up to forty arrows, and around their necks pouches containing bronze arrowheads. A number of them even have their left breast missing, which one poor, pathetic, shrivelled-up little male expert whispered quietly to me was a clear indication that they were prepared to go to any lengths to make certain that once they got a man within their sights, nothing would obstruct them in their resolve to severely damage him or destroy his life altogether. Not, I suppose, that much has changed over the years.

Because today it's not much better; at least, that's what I was told behind closed doors, or rather tent flaps, in the dead of night in the middle of the steppes. Most Kazakh women were brought up on the steppes. Unlike their sisters in other parts of Central Asia, they've never had to wear the veil. They've never been Muslims or come under Muslim influence. They've never had to keep their eyes to the ground, shuffle along three paces behind their lord and master or be totally responsive to his every whim. None of those glories of Islam which are so much admired around the world. Well, around half the world. As a result, not only are they the stroppiest and most independent women in Central Asia, but many of them are also fighters and wrestlers. Lots of them also do it for a living.

As for the rest of the much faster-growing non-Kazakh, non-Kazak or non-Sazak population, it's all one great mish-mash of over a hundred, some say, different ethnic groups. Chief among them, apart from the Russians, being the Uzbekis, Tatars, Ukrainians, Georgians, Belorussians, Azerbaijanis, Poles, Turks, Chechnyans, Bashkirs, Greeks, Dungans, Moldovians, Tajiks, Kurds, Armenians, Ingushians,

Churashians, Kyrghyz and, of course, our friends the Uigurs. There are even Koreans dumped there from the Soviet Far East during the Second World War. There also used to be, especially up in the north, lots of Germans whose families emigrated to Russia in the days of the Czars and were then packed into sealed lorries and trains and shipped out to Kazakhstan by Stalin immediately Hitler declared war on Russia in 1941. But as soon as the Berlin Wall came down and the German government gave them the all-clear to come home, they were off. Without so much as an auf Wiedersehen, pet, I'm leaving.

There used to be lots more Russians than there are now, too. Almost half a million more. Among them were many Cossacks, descendants of the fierce legendary brotherhood of Russian soldier-peasants the Czar sent in to take over the country in the first place. Most of them have left not northern Kazakhstan, Kazakstan or Sazakhstan, but what they called Southern Siberia, and gone back home.

Then there's the language they speak. Apart from the occasional stray donkey left behind by Genghis Khan when he was riding roughshod all over the place, the Kazakhs or Kazaks or Sazakhs started speaking Kazak, or should it be Kazakh, or even Sazakh, only when the Soviet Union split every which way. So nowadays you can't tell whether they're speaking Russian Russian, Russian Kazakh, Kazakh Kazakh, Sazakh Sazakh or Chagatai, an exotic mixture of Kazakh, Mongol and Turkish written in Arabic script and pretty well invented by the younger son of Genghis, who was obviously not given to riding roughshod all over the place like his father.

Now far be it for me to complain about anyone's foreign-language skills, although there was a time, if I say so myself, when I was a dab hand at Evé and could pass as a native in virtually any village east of the Akosombo. Well, all right, then, the end of the week was easier than the beginning. But in Kazakhstan not even the president speaks Kazakh, Kazakh Kazakh or even Sazakh Sazakh. True, it's not unusual for people not to understand a word their leaders are saying, but still.

As far as Chagatai is concerned, there is an excuse. As far as anyone knows, and that includes UNESCO, only one person in the world still speaks the court language of the Mongols which was at one time to Central Asia what Latin was to Europe. He is a Kazakh linguist, Maksud Shafigi, who maintains he should be declared an historic Kazakh, or perhaps that should be Chagatai, monument. What does he have to say about the language issue? I have no idea. I told you he's the only person who understands Chagatai. How the hell am I supposed to know what he's talking about?

Inevitably, with such a great mish-mash of people and languages they also have a great mish-mash of religions. Islam. Russian Orthodoxy. Catholicism. Judaism. Lutheranism. Protestantism. Buddhism. Especially among the Koreans. After seventy years of religious repression, they've now got the lot, although, Allah help me, the Muslims are way out ahead. Which is not bad going when you consider that, for a nomadic people, they started off with virtually no Muslim tradition at all, unlike, for example, the Uzbeks next door with their Samarkand and Bukhara, the Kyrgyzs, the Tajiks, the Turkmenis and everybody else west of the Big Goose Pagoda in Xian. That, plus the fact that even though under the constitution everyone is entitled without fear or favour to practise the religion of their choice, the Muslims are the only ones to have only five programmes on radio every week, not to mention an hour-long television programme every Friday. Yet across the country they are managing to open an average of four new mosques every month and to attract to their Friday prayers mere thousands of worshippers as opposed to the usual two or three spinsters of the parish, the churchwarden and the vicar's wife who turn up nowadays for your typical Church of England morning service. Unless, of course, the vicar's wife feels she's got better things to do, like visiting the vicar in the next parish. If she does, even she won't bother to turn up.

But whether they're Muslim, Russian Orthodox, Catholic, Jewish, Lutheran, Protestant or Buddhist, the Kazakhs' biggest religion of all is wheeling and dealing. And I mean wheeling and dealing. The country might be one of the least densely populated places on earth – about one left leg, two horses and a handful of wheat to the acre – but in terms of the amount of business they do, it's downtown Lagos.

In any street or alleyway anywhere in the country, from Qaraghandy or Karaganda or the capital of the Gulags in the north of the country to Zhambyl or Sambole or even Shamble in the south, you can hardly move for boxes, benches, tables and enormous stalls piled high with every-thing under the sun, from horse-intestine sausages and smoked horsemeat – which, incidentally, goes down well with cold noodles – to all your usual hi-fi, television and video gear, smuggled in, they say, with the help of the Uighurs of wherever, although I suspect that the French have a hand in it as well. Especially when it comes to the horse-intestine sausages and the smoked horsemeat.

As for vast, untapped natural resources, they've got the lot: oil, gas, coal, iron, copper, zinc, lead, titanium, gold and silver. Their problem is that they also have huge natural resources nobody else has got. Like anthrax and enough strontium 90 to light up the night-time sky. What am I saying? There's enough strontium 90 to light up the daytime sky from St Petersburg to Vladivostock because, whichever way you translate it, apart from all the nuclear bombs and space research, poor Kazakhstan was treated by the Russians from the beginning as one huge, empty wasteland ready to be used for the worst of everything.

First the Czarist Russians moved in. Of a total population of 4 million, 1 million Kazakhs were promptly killed, or died of starvation, in what the Russians called a 'civilising mission'. Then came the Communist Russians, who did exactly the same thing. They took a nomadic people who, for thousands of years, had roamed the steppes of Central Asia, slaughtered their cattle, burned their grain and forced them into huge, state collective farms. Rather than agree to such a thing, many Kazakhs killed themselves, their families and their herds. Others fled to China. Those who stayed either died or were sent to labour camps at Kengir and Samarka. Not just your ordinary, everyday, inhumane Russian labour camps. These camps were so much worse than any camps anywhere else in the old Soviet Union that the prisoners actually turned on their guards. But to no avail. They were overrun and literally crushed to death by Soviet tanks. This whole, sorry process cost the once-proud, fiercely independent Kazakhs another 2 million lives – 40 per cent of the population.

As if that wasn't more than enough for the poor Kazakhs to put up with, the Russians then decided they were going to industrialise the country. They shipped in hundreds of thousands of Russians, Ukrainians, Poles, Belorussians, Georgians, Azerbaijanis, Kurds, Chechnyans and whoever they could lay their hands on. They dug huge coal mines. They built giant steelworks, lead smelters, phosphate plants, cement works, copper foundries and chemical plants. They even started drilling for oil.

Within a matter of years, industrial output soared by a staggering 4,000 per cent. Or at least, that's what the Russian statistics said.

Then came the big one: the Russians decided that all that wide, open space in Kazakhstan, where in any case they outgunned and outnumbered the poor Kazakhs by two, maybe three to one, was the ideal place to test not only all their space rockets, but their nuclear bombs as well. The upshot is that today, practically anywhere in the country, you are guaranteed to experience the warmth of a genuine, old-fashioned, Russian welcome. And there's no need to rush. The radioactivity in the atmosphere, never mind the lumps of strontium 90 all over the place, will last for thousands of years to come.

You are also guaranteed to see more people than you would ever want to see suffering from cancer, leukaemia, a range of skin diseases, not to mention a mass of serious congenital disorders, irreversible damage to the central nervous system, blindness and goodness knows how many other birth defects. Because the Russians, in their infinite wisdom, made Kazakhstan home not only to their massive Khrunichev Space Complex at Baikonur, close to Leninsk or Leninogorsh or even Leninskoe, way out towards the Caspian Sea, but also to their even more massive nuclear testing site named after Igor Kurchatov, the father of the Soviet atomic bomb, at Semipalatinsk – or is it Semeypalatinsk, or Semey, or just plain heartbreaking? – up in the north-east.

Apart from all the jokes about space exploration being a big steppe for the Russians, let alone the Kazakhs, and the risk of bits of our favourite rusty old Mir space station falling into their backyards, or rather, the space in front of their *yurts*, the space complex did not create, given everything else they've had to cope with, too much of a problem for the Kazakhs. Even so, there must have been some reason why the Russians decided to base mission control a million miles away in Star City, just outside Moscow.

At least, the space complex didn't create any problems to start with. In the first four years the Russians only managed to launch the first space satellite, the first dog in a space satellite, the first rocket to the moon and the first man in space, Yuri

Gagarin, from Baikonur. Now, however, they've gone commercial. And because of their location tucked away in the middle of the desert, they don't, unlike Cape Canaveral, have to contend with storms, let alone hurricanes, and with their far superior liquid fuel technology, they are sending up rockets practically every week, which, I'm told, is driving the Kazakhs, not to mention their camels, out of their minds.

Most of the satellites behind the whole worldwide mobile telephone and digital television multimedia revolution are being launched by the Russians, would you believe, in Kazakhstan. Plus the odd short-range interceptor rocket for their own A135 antiballistic missile system. Which, of course, nobody talks about.

In other parts of the world where rockets are being let off on an almost daily basis they at least collect as much of the debris as they find, recycle what they can and destroy the rest. Your environmentally friendly Russians, on the other hand, just leave all the rubbish and space debris where it falls and get on with the next job. So if you happen to be in the area, you happen to meet one of the locals, and he invites you back for a quick cup of *koumiss* and a *laghman* before the wife lumbers home from another wrestling match, beware. The beautiful, traditional Kazakh tent you are about to stumble into could be the nose cone of a Soyuz-Proton rocket. And that 40-foot long shack where he keeps the cows that provide the *koumiss*? It might well be the burned-out shell of either the first, second or third stage of one of the booster rockets that fell away and crashed back to earth. Contaminated as hell.

The nuclear testing site at Semipalatinsk is, however, a different story. A real horror story. At seven o'clock on 29 August 1949, the Russians exploded their first atomic bomb there, 37 metres above ground. For the next forty years, usually, for some reason or other, on a Saturday morning, they merrily carried out another 470 nuclear tests: 150 above or at ground level, the rest below ground. At least, that's what they say.

Not only did they explode such a huge number of nuclear bombs – on average just over one a month – but they didn't take even minimal precautions. I'm no expert on anything, but even I know, from my occasional visits to Lop Nor deep inside Western China and the Mururoa Atoll in the Pacific, that if you're going to explode a nuclear bomb underground you have to build a shaft 800 metres deep and between three and four metres wide, stick the thing at the bottom and seal the top so that when it goes off, the basalt rock immediately around it vaporises and the rock further away vitrifies or, to be technical, goes like molten glass, which then, with a bit of luck, seals in the radiation.

Not the Russians. Sometimes the holes for the bombs they let off were half the depth they should have been. Sometimes the wind was blowing in the wrong direction. Sometimes local people were told to disappear. Other times they were told to watch the tests. Just like that. Completely unguarded and unprotected.

Everybody and everything in the area has now been so totally exposed to radiation that you can hardly see the vast, open plains surrounding the site where the bombs were exploded for tiny particles of plutonium, caesium and strontium blowing in the wind. And radiation levels in the area are an unbelievable twenty times the norm.

Once on a trip to Portland, Oregon in the States I met a young girl from Semipalatinsk working in the airport bookshop. She told me that in addition to everything else there was also what the locals called an atomic lake, created by an enormous underground nuclear explosion, that was so dangerous that just to look at it made your hair drop out, let alone anything else you might have under wraps. As for fishing in it, forget it. You were more likely to go fission in it than anything else.

In a nearby village, Akzhav, with a population of around 1,000, there is someone in every family, I was told, who is either mentally or physically handicapped or riddled with cancer. Children are suffering from congenital heart disease. Many are born with Down's syndrome. Many are cruelly deformed. Some have no bones on the top of their head. One boy is reputed to have been born with only one eye. In the middle of his forehead.

In Dolon, the once-secret Soviet long-range bomber base an hour away by car, as well as in other villages, such as Sarzhal or Zhamenka, 80 per cent of the population have anaemia. Blood disease and cardiovascular defects are 30 per cent higher than the national average. Mental illnesses are twice as high.

To make matters even worse, if such a thing were possible, when the Russians finally upped and left, they did it the Russian way. Not for them the orderly handover. Not for them the planned retreat. They just pulled on their boots and disappeared, burning down, as a final gesture, the Palace of Culture in Semipalatinsk, and inside it all the documents on which nuclear bombs they had let off, where and how and, more important still, the extent, exact location and current levels of radioactive waste throughout the entire region. Which must set back any hope the Kazakhs have of controlling, let alone solving, the mass of horrifying and inhumane problems left behind by the Russians by thirty years at the very least.

Yet incredibly, it was only in 1989, after 500 bombs had been exploded, that anyone even tried to do anything to stop the testing. After two nuclear tests one Saturday afternoon, a radioactive cloud actually drifted slowly over northern Kazakhstan. Within a few days, protesters in the area had collected over a million signatures calling for an end to all nuclear testing. Not just by the Soviets, but by the USA as well. See how political they can be when they want to be? A few more days and there were demonstrations, the first mass protests in the whole of the old Soviet Union. A few days after that the Communist Party of Kazakhstan was also calling for a ban. What did the Russians do? Nothing. But there weren't any further tests.

One woman who lived in Beskaragai even wrote to President Gorbachev. Whenever there was a test, she said, 'we were herded into a deep ravine and told to lie on the ground, face down, with our mouths wide open, which was supposed to protect our eardrums from bursting.' Overhead would come the aircraft carrying the bomb. It would drop it. The bomb would explode. Then came the vast mushroom cloud.

'Sometimes it would blow towards the Abolsk region. At other times towards us. There was also the soundwave. It would come more or less immediately, knocking people off their feet. During one of the exercises the top storey of our school was sliced off, as if with a knife. Many houses collapsed. There were never any medical check-ups in spite of the radiation we were exposed to. People in our village began to die of leukaemia, but for some reason it had to be kept quiet.'

Was Gorbachev interested? Did he reply? What do you think?

However, to be fair, which is something I'm not used to being, when a local Kazakh politician raised much the same kind of question, the Kazakh government were so grateful to him for drawing their attention to the matter and arguing his case so forcibly that they promptly promoted him to the prestigious position of ambassador and packed him off, oops, I mean appointed him, to their Embassy in Rome.

I don't know about you, but whenever I'm unlucky enough

to be in the United States I often find there is nothing better to do on a lazy Sunday afternoon than to wander up and down Interstate 90 in South Dakota taking a look at their old nuclear missile sites. Some of them, in typically American style, they've even turned into Minuteman Missile National Historic Parks. I thought I'd try the same thing in Kazakhstan.

At Semipalatinsk the nuclear reactors, the nuclear research facilities and the uranium plants were all still there. At the Kazakh Institute of Radiation nearby, I was told, you could also, if the spirit moved you, examine thousands of deformed, stillborn or aborted foetuses. Could I go and have a look at them? The answer was yes and no. Yes, they had no objection to me going to see either the nuclear reactors or the Institute of Radiation. But no, I couldn't go by myself. I would need a guide. Unfortunately, there were no guides available at present. The next time a guide would be available was in three months. It would also cost me US$1,000 just to get there. Travel, transport, hotels, guide, glowing, red-hot meals were all extra. In other words, the whole thing was going to cost me a bomb.

So I tactfully declined. Instead, I said, I'd go and see their ambassador in Rome. It would probably be more informative and certainly a darn sight cheaper.

Having poisoned the atmosphere with radioactivity for generations to come, you'd have thought the Russians would have been content. But no. They opted to destroy the environment as well. The vast northern steppes, they decided, they would turn into the breadbasket of Central Asia. In poured still more Russians, more Ukrainians, more Poles, more Belorussians, more everybody they could lay their hands on. They ploughed up no less than 30 million hectares, an area about the size of 30 million polo fields.

They had two good harvests and then – nothing. There was no way the semi-arid steppes could support wheat and barley. Which was why – surprise, surprise – for thousands of

years the Kazakhs had been nomads, drifting from one place
to another trying to survive on a patch of grass here, a patch
of grass there. But of course, the Russians weren't interested
in practical details like that.

Then it was cotton. Down in the south, the Aral Sea straddles the border with Uzbekistan. To the Kazakhs – or at least
to the Kazakhs who have never been anywhere near the
place – it's the location of one of the greatest Russian land
and water rehabilitation schemes ever undertaken in the history of the world. It's also home to one of the greatest
contributions ever made to world peace. To the local
Kazakhs, as well as to anybody else who has been down there,
the greatest Russian land and water rehabilitation scheme
ever undertaken can be translated into plain and simple
English: a Complete and Utter Disaster. To make the Soviet
Union self-sufficient in cotton, the Soviets dug huge net-
works of canals not only throughout Kazakhstan but across
neighbouring Uzbekistan and Turkmenistan as well. Then
they diverted water from both the Syr Darya, one of the great
rivers of Central Asia, and the Amu Darya River, which flows
into the Aral Sea, even though half the water they diverted
promptly evaporated or drained into the sand. Now the Aral
Sea is fast disappearing. The surface area has shrunk by half,
and in terms of volume of water, it is down by three quarters.

Temperatures in the area now soar to an unbelievable 50
degrees centigrade in summer and then plunge to minus 40 in
winter. And because water in the Aral Sea, and what's left of
the Syr Darya, which is supposed to flow into it, has all but
disappeared, the concentration of chemicals in the water is
now at danger level, so much so that the United Nations
have declared the whole region an 'ecological disaster area'
comparable with Chernobyl. 'There is hardly another region
on the planet where a powerful environmental crisis has
affected such a large area,' says their report.

Worse still, the massive increase in the summer temperature has strengthened the local winds to the extent that all the sea salt exposed by the disappearing waters is being turned into huge, toxic duststorms which are in turn polluting the surrounding 'ecological disaster area' even further.

As for those vast fields of cotton, what do you think happened to them?

Much the same applies to one of the Russians' greatest contributions to world peace. This, it might come as a shock to you to know, translates as Aralsk 7, once the Soviets' top-secret biological research station. Based on Vozrozhdeniye Island in the shrinking Aral Sea, it was at one time home to over 1,000 people, all merrily working away on one deadly biological killer after another: anthrax, brucellosis, Q fever, tuberculosis, viral hepatitis, throat cancer, tularaemia and something called Venezuelan encephalitis.

The trouble is, with water levels rapidly falling, the island is not going to be an island for much longer and the tons of deadly anthrax, bacteria and other goodies the Russians, with their usual regard for safety procedures and the health of the local population, happily buried in the sand when they finally quit will not stay buried much longer.

Already, I heard, there have been reports not only of rats but of rabbits as well finding their way to the island, and presumably back again to the mainland with goodness knows what under their fingernails.

One old boy also told me that once some herds of antelopes, grazing casually on the banks, as they do, suddenly all dropped dead in under an hour.

'How many?' I wondered. 'Ten? Fifteen? A hundred?'

'Half a million,' he said.

You can guess what could happen when the water disappears altogether, the island becomes part of the mainland, all that deadly anthrax and what have you starts leaking straight into the surrounding area and those three-eyed, 200-pound, red-hot rats with teeth the size of Janet Street Porter's start spreading it around. Especially as the Russians, God bless them, made everything deliberately resistant to antibiotics. I only hope the Kazakhs have got enough embassies left in which to put all the people who are going to go bananas about it.

Conversely, the Caspian Sea, which Kazakhstan shares with Russia, Azerbaijan, Iran and Turkmenistan, is rising still and rising. In the last ten years, they say, it has risen almost practically twenty feet. If it continues at that rate, over 500,000 hectares of land will be under water, whole towns and cities will be flooded and more than 265,000 people will have to be evacuated and rehoused.

I'm not saying that either of these events was one of the reasons why the Kazakhs, Kazaks or Sazakhs moved their beautiful, relaxed, sunny capital city from downwind of any fall-out, never mind a plague of anthrax-carrying rats, to the middle of a flat and open plain a million miles from anywhere. But, let's face it, it could have been.

When I first thought about going to Almati, Almaty, or even Alma Aty, the home of one of the most important deeply spiritual shrines in the world, the Elvis Presley Memorial Kitchen, as well as to the gloriously named fast-food operation Shaggie's and all the wild cannabis you can pick, they immediately translated, if that's the right word, the capital to Aqmola, or rather Akmola, some obscure industrial hideaway in the north of the country which in summer is bitterly cold, –40 degrees centigrade, and wolf-infested, and in winter a mosquito-ridden swamp. Or maybe it's the other way round.

Well, I say new capital city. Maybe in Kazakh, Kazakh Kazakh or even Chagatai it can be described as a new capital city, but I must tell you, Brasilia it is not. It's not even Milton Keynes.

Talk to any Kazakh speaker, if you can find one, and he will tell you that Aqmola is, appropriately enough, Kazakh for white graveyard, although Kazakhstan's non-Kazakh-speaking president disputes this. To him it means 'big city in nowhere middle of from both Russia and China safer is we hope'. But that's not the end of the translation problem.

Before it was called Aqmola, when it was run by the Russians, it was called Tselinograd, and then Aqmolinsk, when it was run by another bunch of Russians, if that's not too confusing. According to one translation I saw, Tselinograd means 'city of the land of the virgins' and Aqmolinsk means 'the only virgins you're likely to find around here are in their graves'.

When I finally got around to going there, as if it hadn't had enough name changes, and chopped down enough trees to put up more and more signposts, which obviously accounts for the fact that it is surrounded by 1,000 kilometres of nothing, they immediately translated it again. This time to Astana.

OK, I thought. They're trying to tell me something. But why should I take the hint? Nobody, not even the descendants of Genghis Khan, get off that lightly. So, undaunted, I adopted the only strategy I know that is guaranteed to work in such circumstances. I pretended I didn't want to go anywhere near the place. Instead, in order to fool them, I made out I wanted to go next door to Kyrgystan. I fixed the flight to the capital, plain, simple, unchanging Bishkek. I booked myself into the Dostuk, the fancy Turkish-owned hotel on the edge of town. I even booked a car to meet me at the airport. That done, at the last minute, talking all the time in a loud voice about the delights of Kyrgystan, I switched all my bookings and instead made for Akmola, I mean Aqmola, or rather Akmola.

But as soon as I landed at the airport – I say airport: the runway was some kind of dirt strip and as for the terminal building, I've seen better warehouses – I was sure they'd rumbled me. There was nothing there. Well, next to nothing. The clever Kazakhs, I thought. Somehow or other they had heard about my change of plan and moved the whole city somewhere else to stop me from seeing it.

But I very quickly realised that this wasn't the case. Of all the cities in the world, they didn't have to worry about living up to my expectations or anybody else's. There wasn't a city there in the first place. Well, nothing you could call a city. It was more one big yawneroo, a collection of piles of sand and cement and a lot of guys hanging around obviously talking about football. The only people I saw doing any work were the beggars. And, believe me, they were going for it. Clearly they had all bought huge tracts of land on the wrong side of town. When the government started building the city where they did, they must have lost everything.

The main street, or at least the street with the biggest piles of sand and cement in it, was lined with giant posters promoting the delights of Kazakhstan: Pepsi Cola, Coca-Cola, Reebok, Nike, Toshiba and a host of yet-to-be-built, half-built and fully built but still empty office blocks.

All the buses appeared to have been a generous gift from the refuse department of some bankrupt borough council somewhere. Most of them seemed to be plastered with ads for Tic-Tacs. I couldn't read the blurb but I assume it said something like: 'Tic-Tac – the box will last you the whole journey.' With a bit of luck. Not because Tic-Tacs disappear quickly, but because the buses looked as though they'd take ages to get anywhere.

The cars and trucks were in even worse shape. The car I got from the airport broke down, or rather ran out of coal, on the ramshackle old bridge over the River Ishim – named after an old Kazakh phrase used a lot when the Russians were around meaning, 'It's not me. It's him over there.' I got out and walked the rest of the way.

The side streets were full of guys unloading crates of Heineken off the back of big German lorries and stacking them in a long line of Ladas. No, I tell a lie. They were full of guys unloading crates of Heineken and huge cartons of Camels off the backs of big German lorries and stacking them in a long line of Ladas.

The first hotel I went to was full of cement-mixers and fork-lift trucks. At first I thought I'd missed reception and strayed into the kitchens by mistake. But it turned out the place was still being built. Instead I ended up in another hotel which looked as though it had been built in the 1930s but was still not finished. There was no plumbing, no heating and practically no food. Well, no food worth eating, anyway. Even worse, smelled as if it had been used for testing Turkish cigarettes. So it was back to the vodka diet again. Cheers. As for the rooms, they were so small, I spent the whole week curled up underneath an air-conditioner that didn't work and which was called Arcelik. What the translation of that is I dread to think.

The rest of Astana was much the same. The main square was apparently being built with all the loving care and attention to detail that produced the Mir space station. On one side of this great mass of bits of paving stones was a dead ringer for a 1930s Soviet department store, all empty shelves and officious-looking women not charging exorbitant prices for tiny lumps of bread and even tinier lumps of fat. Because the bread had not been delivered neither had the tinier lumps of fat. On the other side was the President's Office, a giant red, domed, loudspeaker of a building, again all empty shelves and officious-looking women. Or maybe it was the other way round.

Then came a mass of government buildings: huge imposing pillars, enormous wide, open stairways, miles of iron railings, acres of marble, thousands of statues and plaques, radio masts that almost grazed the sky and a thousand fountains that didn't work. In front of all of them were guys carefully painting walls that even I could see were bound to be knocked down by tractors before the paint was dry, or neatly planting trees and shrubs that were going to be flattened by the next lorry that careered into them, or putting the finishing touches to beautifully tiled pavements and roadways that would be dug up for gas mains before the week was out.

Further down there were more traditional Kazakh or whatever you call them buildings: a Casa Italia, a Hanover restaurant, a Kodak shop, an Adidas store, which, for some reason which escapes me just now, all seemed to be built, completed and open for business.

I went into one huge office block: I think it was the Ministry of Strategic Planning, but nobody could tell me for certain one way or another. From the outside it was all intricate loopholes, which seemed appropriate enough. Inside it appeared that they had tied themselves into knots. Part of it looked like your typical 1920s Soviet extravaganza: wooden floors covered in a mismatched assortment of worn-out rugs and carpets and no lightbulbs. As for the rest, it was all smoked glass, stainless steel and flashy telephones that didn't work.

From here they are trying to run not just the Tengiz oilfields out near the Caspian Sea, once the largest in the old Soviet Union, and even bigger than the oilfields in Alaska, but also the Karachaganak gas fields in the west, which are three times the size of the gas fields in the North Sea. Overall, they reckon they have the world's sixth-largest reserves of oil and natural gas, as much as the Saudis have, if not more. And as if that's not more than enough for anyone to cope with, they also have huge deposits of iron ore, manganese, chrome, nickel, cobalt, copper, molybdenum, lead, zinc, bauxite, gold and uranium.

I say 'trying to run' because, for all their bragging about privatisation – of all the old Soviet republics, Kazakhstan was the first to begin privatising farmland –and free enterprise, they are still very Russian. I once, between vodkas, casually asked, as one does, one of the officials at their Ministry of Strategic Planning what the daily milling rates were at Dzherzkazgan, their enormous copper operation. You'd have thought I was asking for the private telephone number of the president's wife so I could volunteer my services to her great campaign. It was a state secret, he blubbered. How dare I ask for such sensitive information? The private telephone number of the president's wife, he would probably have given me straightaway, no questions asked.

On the other hand, when the need arises the Kazakhs think nothing of breaking practically every international agreement in the book, such as when, for example, they sold no fewer than forty old MiG fighter planes to North Korea in order to make a couple of dollars. Well, US$8 million, to be precise.

Before staggering back to the hotel and ordering myself a nice, juicy vodka dinner, I took a turn down Republic Prospekt, which the locals had already labelled Potemkin Prospekt. Behind all the fancy aluminium cladding were the same old crumbling, faceless, Russian-style concrete blocks.

The following day was a fête worse than death: brass bands, mounted Mongol warriors – I say warriors, but Genghis Khan would have turned in his grave if he'd seen them – sword-wielding folk dancers, fireworks, prancing horses, twenty heads of state, twenty boring speeches and a desperate shortage of telephones, not to mention silly little things like gas, electricity, water, bars, restaurants and foreign embassies. It was the official opening ceremony of the new capital city, Aqmola, I mean Akmola, I mean Astana.

'This is our new capital city,' declared the non-Kazakh-speaking Kazakh president, Mr Nursultan Nazarbaev. 'This is serious and for ever. This is the new face of the Kazakh state.'

He then promptly about-turned, raced to the airport and caught a plane back to Alma Aty. Not that anyone thought of blaming him in the slightest. They all did the same thing. You think I'm joking? Even the chief architect of the project, Bayir Betov, admits that he didn't know what he was doing when he built the place. Or rather, half-built the place. 'We didn't really have any style in mind when we designed the city,' he confesses. You can say that again, Bayir.

Still, it's probably not surprising given that Astana is built on the very spot where, in the eighteenth century, the Kazakhs were so severely thrashed by their enemies, the Jungars, that they did the one thing nobody should ever do, even with a knife at their throat: they asked the Russians for help and protection. Which immediately changed everything. The knife was immediately removed from their throat and plunged into their back. And twisted. And twisted. And – cough, cough, excuse me, the anthrax is getting to me – twisted again.

The official opening ceremony over, I'm back in my excuse for an hotel. Who do I get a telephone call from? Well, apart from the usual, it's the guy at the Ministry of Strategic Planning who bounced me all over their so-called town because I had the temerity to ask him about the daily milling rates at Dzherzkazgan. He wants me to help him with some translations. Could I meet him and his colleagues at his office? In Aqmola or Akmola or Astana? Of course not. He couldn't stand the place. It would be in Almati, Almaty or even Alma Aty.

What could I say? Well, on the basis that I've always believed, whatever the country, that foreign-investment trans-actions speak louder than words, I mumbled something like *la qansha*. Why I agreed I have no idea. Translations are about the second-biggest headache in the world after won-dering what on earth to buy your wife for Christmas after she has already said she can't stand the sight of any of the 2 million presents you've already given her. Everybody's an expert. Everybody speaks better English than you. Everybody grammar English knowing better is than also you too. Especially the French.

Years ago I used to be responsible for turning a string of beautifully designed, written and produced French annual reports into bland, boring, meaningless City blah-blah-blah so that they could be understood by all the big bankers, brokers and institutional investors in London. All hithertofore, the aforementioned and up with which I will not put.

There was no problem until *un jour* along comes this *nouveau* finance director at L'Oréal, the big French perfume house, all Yves St Laurent suit and '*nous sommes les greatest*', who looked as though he couldn't tell one end of an interpreter from another.

We ploughed our way through his Report of the Financial Director, which was about as exciting as a back number of *Le Monde Diplomatique*. I changed *appuyer sur le champignon* (to press the mushrooms) to 'to increase the rate of'. I changed *copains comme cochons* (friends like pigs) to 'our colleagues, the auditors'. I changed *soulever un lièvre* (to stir up a hornet's nest) to 'take due consideration of the views of the shareholders'. He agreed. Then we came to the section on new board appointments. I wrote down the usual waffle, 'During the year under review, there were many changes in the boardroom', etc. He went *loco*. He swore. He cursed. He damned. He blinded me. Wrong! Wrong! Wrong! he screamed. 'Changes' was the wrong word. According to his bible, *Le Petit Larousse*, it should have been 'mutations'. I quickly agreed. Life, I found out too long ago, is too short to argue with the French. So their annual report went out announcing: 'During the year under review, there were many mutations in the boardroom.' The laugh was that nobody noticed, which must say something about the British view of French companies, although I'm not quite sure what.

Another time I was turning a Spanish annual report into blah-blah-blah so that the City could understand what was going on. Again everything was going fine until the arrival on the scene of a *nuevo* finance director. This one brought with him one of those tiny translation computers. You know the kind of thing. You type in a word and out it comes in half a dozen different languages. Except in this case something always seemed to be not quite right. About two seconds into checking the chairman's report he hit '*necessario*'. He typed the word into his computer. Out came 'Swiss bank account'. Then came business. He typed in 'business'. Out came '*corrupción*'. And so it went on. Until we came to the sign-off. In he typed 'el presidente'. Out came 'torturer'. Following the president's example, and that of the rest of the government, I headed south.

The only good thing about the two-hour flight in the Soviet-built Antonov propeller plane, complete with net curtains, was that it wasn't a twenty-two-hour train ride north across the baking, unrelenting heat of the steppes to Aqmola, Akmola or even Astana. But it was worth it. The Elvis Presley Memorial Kitchen apart, Almati, Almaty or even Alma Aty is a find. I could also understand why nobody wants to leave there, apart from the fact that Astan is closer to all that nice warm radiation.

Originally called the City of Apples, the Father of the Apple Tree or the City Apple of the Tree Father, according to which translation you're trying to stagger through, Alma Aty is 2,600 feet above sea-level, in the foothills of the so-called heavenly Tien Shan Mountains, and about 200 miles from the Chinese border.

Once a tiny, insignificant trading post on one of many different highways and byways that make up the now legendary

Silk Route, but which at the time was nothing but many different highways and byways stretching all the way from Vladivostok in the east to Harrods fashion department in the west. Then, around 200 years ago, the Russians moved in. They immediately started building a fort which, they claim, is scheduled for completion any day now. By 1867 there were enough unfinished buildings around for it to become a town. They called it Vierney, an old Kazakh word for 'we're still waiting for the cement'.

Twenty years later, in 1887, whatever buildings there were were destroyed by an earthquake. The Russians instantly did what they're best at. They issued a whole raft of predated invoices to the poor Kazakhs for cement that was never delivered for buildings that were never built. Smart guys, the Russians. The Kazakhs, of course, have been paying for it ever since.

Today, even though in many respects Alma Aty is your typical Soviet city, it doesn't feel like it. It feels quite pleasant. The streets are lined with trees. There are huge parks and patches of green. Some shops and stores are pure Russian – empty shelves, empty counters, long queues of people still waiting to pay for what they bought when the shelves and counters were full – but there are more and more modern, swinging, fashionable places opening up all the time. There are plenty of bars and restaurants and hotels. Wherever you go you can get whatever you want, as long as it's Greek brandy. As for food, make sure you go to the snack bar in the Kazakhstan Hotel. There's no other snack bar like it in the world. It closes for lunch.

Old Central Asia hands claim that the place has changed more radically and faster since *perestroika* than any other city in the region. Maybe it's the location. Perhaps being in the earthquake centre of Central Asia – for years they couldn't put up anything higher than a two-storey building – gives them a carefree, relaxed, slightly indifferent view of the world. Maybe it's being just 200 miles from the Chinese border. They're open to Chinese influence, style and fashion as well as to practically every other influence, style and fashion under the sun.

Maybe it's all the cannabis growing naturally up in the mountains. Many's the time I've been up there, checking the crop, examining the leaves, working out the best time to pick and wondering why on earth they're called the Heavenly Mountains. A small plot, don't forget, can produce around 5 kilos, which is plenty to keep anyone smiling through life's adversities – such as snack bars that close for lunch – for a couple of months. It might even be enough to see me through a visit to the Elvis Presley Memorial Kitchen. Failing that, a quick word in the ear of any passing Chinese Uighir trader and I'm sure he'd be more than happy to take the lot off your hands for, say, US$10,000, which is more than enough, in a country where the average wage is US$100 a month, to put a smile on anyone's face.

On the other hand, it could just be the booze. Even the elephants in the local circus get a litre of vodka a day. It used to be up to 5 litres, I was told, but they had to reduce the rations because of lack of funds. For the same reason they cut out their daily dose of brandy and French Cahors wine.

Then, of course, there are all the sights. Brezhnev's old house in Fumanov Koshesi, not far from the US Embassy. The world's highest ice rink just outside town. The second-tallest wooden building in the world, a cathedral built with no nails, which they seemed to think is remarkable, although as far as I could tell the whole country looks as though it was built with no nails. Either that or the amount of radioactivity in the atmosphere melts them all as soon as they are hammered in.

'So what holds the timbers together, then?' I asked two old

soldiers who were playing chess on a rickety table outside the cathedral.

'Wooden pegs,' they said.

'But aren't those nails?'

'No,' they insisted. 'They're wooden pegs. They're not nails.'

Translation subtleties of argue with who am I to.

Much the same applies to the Elvis Presley Memorial Kitchen. Apparently the whole thing, stainless-steel counters, refrigerators, cookers, even the old-fashioned Coke machine, was bought by Elvis Presley as a present for the regiment in which he was serving as a GI in West Germany.

In 1994 it was packed up and, for some reason known only to the US Foreign Service, shipped out to the US Embassy in Alma Aty, where it was soon dubbed 'The Hound Dog Hole'. Precisely how that translates into Kazakh or Kazak or even Sazakh, I was frightened to ask, but it might account for the fact that so few locals seem to want to be seen in it.

No nails or no no nails, Elvis Presley Memorial Kitchen or no Elvis Presley Memorial Kitchen, much against my better judgement, come Monday morning, bang on the dot of nine o'clock, I find myself in a grubby conference room in a derelict shack, also apparently thrown together without a single nail, wooden or otherwise, round the back of a building site. Nobody else is there.

At around 9.45, in comes this worry-wart. He is the Ministry of Strategic Planning's official English translator. He is accompanied by his secretary.

He tells me his name and his secretary's name. They are both, he goes on, 'ordinary pipple' from a 'pissful village' way out in the middle of nowhere.

'I am dirty,' he adds. 'My secretary, she is dirty also.' Or at least, that's what it sounded like. Which is a great start to any meeting.

Famous Translations
'You are invited to take advantage of the chambermaid.'
Sign in a Japanese hotel.

Then in comes a very smooth-looking guy. He is from the Ministry of Strategic Planning. In no uncertain terms he tells me he knows very well English. Why present I am not necessary. Eton was school he went to. Then he was off on some rigmarole about divs and beaks and something that sounded like F-tits. Did I know what he was talking about? No, I admitted. 'Eton slang!' he shrieked and collapsed into a chair at the head of the table.

No sooner had he hit the chair than, as if on cue, in trooped a gang of guys carrying prehistoric bundles of files and papers and mediaeval cardboard briefcases. They all looked as though they kept budgerigars, collected stamps and dreamed of being inspector-generals. For about the next three hours I shook every sweaty palm in the room. Finally we all sat down round the big table.

One guy, who appeared to be wearing very cheap prosthetic make-up, probably as a result of all those bombs going off in Semipalatinsk, tapped his pen on the table. We were in business.

One of the eager young men who had barged through the door carrying bundles of files began to speak in what sounded like a long, slow American drawl. Either that, or he was on 40 grammes of valium and a bottle of cheap vodka a day.

He was a Kazakh, he mumbled. From Phlumwahski. He'd studied at the Shchardovka as well as in Moscow. But he'd been to America. He understood Americans. He spoke their language but not their dialects. He knew how American business operated. The *Harvard Business Review* he knew very well. He'd once made the cover. Now, however, he only had time to 'page' through it.

Famous Translations
'Drop your trousers for best results.'
                              Sign in Bangkok dry-cleaner's.

'OK,' I began. 'But the purpose of the meeting, as I understand it—'

'We want them to butt out,' he said. 'I'm businessed out.'

'Butt out,' I repeated slowly. 'Businessed out.'

His English was obviously KGB English. Everything was 'rapaciously exploited'. They had experienced 'petit-bourgeois capitalist deviancy'. It was necessary in the light of circumstances to take 'the sternest measures'. He was so old-school he could have made 'yes' sound like a negative.

He turned to the interpreter. 'Please, you repeat,' he grunted.

The interpreter, who, I suddenly realised, was suffering from an acute form of irritable vowel syndrome – or should that be irritable consonant syndrome? – so he was not so much dirty as thirty, was then on about 'phonological characteristics' and 'reduplicative compounds' and the principle of what he called 'normative assimilation' and somebody or other suffering from 'rectal cranial inversion' since 'three years this following September coming up'.

By now, I was losing it. If they'd told me W.C. Fields meant toilet pastures I would have agreed. I was in some run-down government office. I'd been asked by some guy I met in the lobby of the Ministry of Strategic Planning way up north in Aqmolo, Aqmolinsk or even Astana to help him 'reintermediate' some English translation they were working on because, he said, he was information-stressed. I agreed. I'd done my duty. Instead of spending a trying day sampling the local vodkas, I'd turned up for their meeting. Now what the hell were they on about? What on earth was I doing there? What, if anything, did they want me to do?

'You've got to tell it like it is. Wax on, baby. Wax on.'

We all looked at each other.

'Butt out,' he repeated. 'They've got to learn to hang with us.'

The guy from Eton stopped flicking through the pages of his big, black leather diary, which he'd been doing since he sat down.

The guy with the make-up dropped his pen on the table.

The interpreter and his secretary suddenly looked as though they were having thirty thoughts about each other, although goodness knows why: he couldn't have got her on his horse if it was a brewer's dray.

Famous Translations

'It is forbidden to enter a woman even a foreigner if dressed as a man.'

Sign in Chinese temple.

The American expert threw an armful of files all round the room. 'OK! Let's rock and ride!' he yelled.

Then he was off, talking like a bad hand of Scrabble. Decomplexify the results. Diaggregate the business. Zingering a strategy. A new, calculative trust. The llama factor. Neptuning an option. Developing a flexible, self-generating, dejobbing market.

This was not the kind of meeting I am used to. I much prefer it when we all go into a room and just headbutt each other.

Finally, he stopped.

Again, we all looked at each other.

'OK,' I began again. 'What you're saying is—'

'Yup,' he grunted. 'We're going to buy the dip. It's on the radar screen.'

'Well why didn't you say that before?' I slapped the table. Then, lapsing into the jargon, I added, 'OK. I'll throw my best pitch at it.'

For what seemed like three weeks we were caught up in a real gabathon. We worked on some text all about calculating certainty . . . equivalent rate of returns . . . mutant quadratic equations . . . outside the box . . . paradigms . . . implicit pluralinguistic ratios . . . inherent matrix parameters . . . passive aggressive multiple concurrences . . . by-products of predispositions . . . escape avoidance. Then it was dysfunctional coping mechanisms of micromanagement, and something that sounded like bedroom pioneer, low-cost provider, horizontally accessible and vocally appreciative, although I wouldn't swear to it.

As the sun started to disappear for about the fifth time we broke for what the American expert called 'a heartwise snack with a double-decaff low-fat light-froth latte', although it looked to me like the usual black sludge and biscuits I used to get in the evenings from the snack bar that closed for lunch.

Halfway through his heartwise snack, I thought for a moment that our American expert was going to ask if someone could doggy-bag it for him as they do in the States. But the guy in the make-up grabbed it off his plate when he wasn't looking.

Then it was back to the text, which, even then, was a few drafts short of *War and Peace*.

Famous Translations
'Special cocktails for ladies with nuts.'

Sign in a Hong Kong bar.

Finally, after a few more months, it was finished.

'OK,' said the guy from Eton, closing his black leather diary. 'Is that clear?'

We all nodded in agreement, although, to be honest, I only understood the first two words of our beautiful English translation, which were 'Dear Gentlepersons'. The rest was about as meaningful as a Tony Blair speech.

Turning down the offer of another 'heartwise snack with a double-decaff low-fat light-froth latte,' I made for the nearest bar.

What had I spent my life helping them to translate? It was only later that I discovered it was a demand that the Kazakh Government renegotiate some deal about leasing an oil refinery to foreign investors by playing games with their single controlling so-called golden share.

Did it do the trick? On my way back to the airport I bumped into the guy from the Ministry of Strategic Planning who got me involved in the first place. I asked him what he thought of the document.

'Horse waste,' he said.

Which translates as: 'Never get involved with guys from the Ministry of Strategic Planning in Aqmola, Akmola or Astana in Kazakhstan, Kazakstan or even Sazakhstan. Especially if it involves translations. Worth it not it is.'

Bishkek

A ship?

A ship made out of bricks and mortar?

A ship made out of bricks and mortar, the same size and shape as the battleship *Aurora*, which, as every capitalist schoolboy knows, fired just one shot in the whole of its existence – and that was a blank – yet somehow managed to bring about the collapse of Czarist Russia, the rise of the Bolsheviks, the birth of Communism and the founding of the Soviet Union?

A ship made out of bricks and mortar, the same size and shape of the *Aurora*, here in the middle of Kyrgyzstan in the Tien Shan, the Heavenly Mountains, which start next door in Kazakhstan and then stretch for over 1,500 kilometres deep into China?

Behind it, as flat as a sheet of glass, is Lake Issyk-Kul, the world's second-largest lake after Lake Titicaca, and, I must say, about the bluest stretch of water I've ever seen. Not that I'm an expert on anything to do with water.

On either side are more spectacular, snowclad mountain

ranges, some over 4,000 metres high, which is not surprising when you bear in mind Kyrgyzstan – or, to give it its new name, the Kyrgyz Republic, which ruins all those old jokes about Central Asia being full of nothing but -stans – is 95 per cent mountain, three quarters of which are covered in snow and ice the whole year round. For mountain freaks, this includes the highest spot in the country, and the second-highest in the old Soviet Union, Pik Pobnedy, which is Kyrgyz for 'it's so cold up here I can't get my bloody pick in the side of this Godforsaken mountain'. It was like being in the middle of the most fabulous Alpine scenery, except it was far more Alpine and far more fabulous than, well, the Alps, now that they are full of skis strapped on top of roofracks, sailboards, mountain bikes, bungee-jumping, canyoning over waterfalls, hydrospeeding along anything that's wet and getting piste out of your mind in Les Deux Alpes.

This was the Alps of happy memory. Meadows full of poppies, primroses, gentians and a whole mass of other wild flowers whose names I can never remember. Fields of hay. Pine trees. Herds of horses. Mountain streams. Goodness me, for a moment, I expected Julie Andrews to come leaping into sight and ruining everything.

Kyrgyz is a famous mountain paradise, the happy hunting grounds of the Moguls, the Turks, the Chinese and the place where Tamerlane, or, rather, Timur-the-Lame, used to come for his summer holidays. Even today it is still a land of bears and snow leopards, where crusty old nomads with straggly beards, tribes of flat, red-faced daughters and white felt hats called *ak-kalpaks*, with usually black or sometimes even red trimming and little tassels, think nothing of sending up flocks of trained falcons to hunt down gazelles by pecking their eyes out while their sons play polo with headless goats all day or chase girls on horseback – which, incidentally, contradicts the claim that most Kyrgyz women are not chased at some time or other in their lives. But if a bloke doesn't succeed, then all the other blokes turn and chase him instead which, I suppose, if you spend all your life in the mountains surrounded by nothing but sheep and cattle, is one way of passing the time. Even Kyrgyz guys with proper jobs in the towns can't wait to head for the hills in summer to live in their own *yurts*, those domed, circular tents made out of wooden poles and masses of carpets, and indulge themselves in a spot of *udarysh*, or horseback-wrestling.

In fact this is still a land of honour and trust and integrity where they rate their horses above everything else. Even their wives. What do you think is the greatest honour they can bestow upon a guest: to lend him their wife for the night, or to give him their horse for the day? You've got it. What the horses think about it is another matter. Not much, I would have thought. One, because they must wonder what the point is of being ridden around all day if they don't see a single fox, and two, grateful as they must be for being sponged down at the end of every day, they must pray that eventually the Kyrgyz will stop wiping first their backsides and then their nostrils.

So you can imagine how I felt in this land of horses to be suddenly faced with this dirty great brick-built boat in the middle of nowhere. And I hadn't been drinking, either, which only made it worse. It wasn't as if I set out to find it. I was supposed to be checking out some of the sites along the old Silk Route which runs from Balasagun through the Chu and Issyk-Kul valleys, which are a bit like the Highlands of Scotland without the bagpipes. I also wanted to investigate the way to the Torugart Pass, which everybody told me was the best way into China because the first hotel you hit once you're past the border is the gloriously named Hotel Semen.

I'd finished all my calls in Bishkek, the capital; I'd even

taken in Tokmok, the centre, I was told, of the Kyrgyz electronics industry. All I can say is that if this was the centre of
their electronics industry, there's a lot to be said for gas. It
was more Silicon Carne than Silicon Valley. Outside one factory I was met in typical Kyrgyz fashion by wild eyes,
distended nostrils and heaving flanks. That was the director.
His horse, by comparison, was immaculately groomed, beautifully behaved and impeccably mannered. As for the factory,
I'm not saying it was old-fashioned, but I actually saw the
director's secretary, a fat old *babushka* with a white lace collar
who looked as though she was going through her second
menopausal meltdown, sitting by the fax machine taking
down in shorthand the various messages as they came in.

Just south of Tokmok, in the middle of the Sham Shin
Valley, I hit the Burana Tower, which, according to the books,
is one of the most important historical monuments on the
entire Silk Route. It was a veritable lighthouse, they said, to
the merchants and travellers who flowed backwards and forwards along the route year after year after year. Nonsense. It
wasn't a tower at all. It was all that was left of some enormous
eleventh-century mosque which had at one time been the
centre of a town full to overflowing with scientists, philoso-
phers and poets, not to mention more mundane facilities such
as a constant supply of cold water from the nearby canyon; a
bath house, a sewage system and, as the local historical book
puts it, 'a flourishing of crafts, trades and religions'. But it's all
gone.

All that is left is the tower itself and, surrounding it, masses
of odd, Humpty-Dumpty-like stone faces stuck in the
ground, Easter Island fashion, grinning up at the odd visitor
who happens to come by for a quick look-see. Which, I suppose, is only to be expected, given that it's in the middle of
nowhere, it's falling to bits and you can't even go inside
because it's in danger of collapsing.

Outside the tower, however, were a couple of horses tied to a pole Wild West-style and the official Burana Tower state archaeological and architectural museum, established in 1976 by the Republic's Council of Ministers 'taking into account the scientific, the historical-cognitive and the cultural value of the excavated monuments'. In other words, a two-roomed wooden shack run by a woman who, as soon as she realised I was English, although how on earth she knew that I cannot imagine, kept following me around wailing, 'I want to go to Canada. I want to go to Canada.'

What I thought was going to be the works, offering hours of fascinating insights into life on the old Silk Route, turned out to be a bit of a flop, apart from my discovery, no thanks to the wailings of the would-be Canadian museum guide, that Balasagun, the town that disappeared, was also home to Khas Hadjib Usuf Balasagun, the Muslims' answer to Machiavelli. Like *The Prince*, his catchily titled Kutadgu *Bilik*, better known in Kyrgyz circles as 'How to run the country and get away with murder, not to mention fraud, smuggling, money-laundering and everything else under the sun, and let the World Bank pick up the tab', has perhaps not surprisingly been widely translated into Russian, Ukrainian, Belorussian, Kazakh and all languages east of Venice.

So, for ever the adventurer – Thesiger's got nothing on me – I decided to head for Lake Issyk-Kul, which, even though it is so high up in the mountains, around 1,600 metres above sea-level, never freezes. Why nobody seems to know. My guess is that it's because of the mysterious Lake Issyk-Kul monster, which is so secret that nobody has yet discovered it. Why else would the Russians have kept this place off-limits until the late 1980s?

Just the other side of Balachy, a scruffy town of cement works and empty factories, I'd survived a raid by about thirty policemen all eager to collect what they called an 'ecology tax'. I told them that the longer they held me up, the more carbon dioxide and other horrible, noxious fumes my beaten-up old Trabant would pump into the environment, so the quicker they let me go the better. In any case, I didn't have any money, at least, not enough for thirty of them. So they let me go. But not before they made me write down the registration number of the car in some book the size of two Family Bibles, along with my name, address and job title. Which I was happy to do: Vladimir Ilych Ulyanov Lenin, Finland Station, St Petersburg. Housewife. Nobody said a word.

We then chugged our way through Cholpon Ata, which, compared to Balachy, was quite swish. Well, at least the line of unbuilt hotels along the banks of the lake looked as though they might eventually be quite swish in a Russian kind of way. They all had four walls and a ceiling and what seemed to be arrangements for water pipes.

I stopped at one of the banks in town to change some money. They didn't have any. Roubles? Dollars? Swiss francs? Nothing at all, they said. They'd completely run out of the stuff. Thinking that either this must be a faraway branch of the NatWest, where I always have much the same kind of problem, or just a traditional way of welcoming strangers, and thus one of the explanations for the collapse of the Silk Route, I later sent my driver in with some dollars to exchange. But it was the same story, and he returned empty-handed. It really was a bank with no money. A genuine branch of NatWest in the Kyrgyz Republic.

Now, all of a sudden, a few miles the other side of Cholpon Ata, here I was staring at a real-life, rock-solid Soviet battle-ship which turned out to be the one-time top-secret hideaway clinic or health farm for all the big Soviet big shots. Brezhnev had been here. Khrushchev had been here. Andropov had been here. Chernenko had been here. Gorbachev had been here. Obviously this was one reason why the whole country was off-limits to foreigners up until the late 1980s. None of these guys wanted even to be seen, let alone photographed by the world's press, plodding down to take the waters in their no doubt enormous black-and-white-striped, one-piece Soviet-designed Victorian swimming costumes.

Seeing as they were clearly used to dealing with senile, drunken old has-beens, I did the least I felt I could do in the circumstances. I checked in. All for the price of US$10. Not for a week. Not for a month. But for a whole year. Which included treatment for my throbbing liver as well.

Baden-Baden it was not. Neither was it Bath-Bath or Marienbad-Marienbad. Neither was it one of those New Age Native American fitness centres you find all over the States, which go on about measuring your *vata* and your *pitta*, not to mention your three *doshas*, and then insist on locking you up in some body tent poised precariously over a boiling cauldron of hot water and administering things called ylang-ylang, bergamot and patchouli before, heaven help you, opening up your third eye in the middle of your forehead.

No, it was a million times better than any of them. For this was not just your genuine Russian health farm, this was a real, 100-per-cent Russian soap-opera health farm. Sure, there were mineral water fountains everywhere. Sure, the place smelled of chlorine. Sure, there were plenty of old party officials sitting around marinating gently all day long in dirty, sweaty, lumpy armchairs. And what came out of the mineral water fountains looked more like what comes out than what goes in, if you see what I mean; the chlorine brought tears to your eyes and the old party officials were a mixture of decrepit ex-army officers who thought that cellulite was some kind of portable unit you carried around in your back pocket along with your favourite pair of tiny electric tweezers, former KGB officials with malignant tumours caused by having some Soviet-made mini-microphone the size of a cartwheel jammed up their lymphatic glands for most of their lives, and a collection of old women who spent their days sitting behind tiny desks on huge hotel landings and were now jealously nursing between their breasts things that far younger and far less experienced women are still unable to nurse. Like their wellingtons.

Did I feel a touch uncomfortable among them? No way. In fact, I was thrilled to bits. With friends like these, I thought, who needed enemas? After all, everything was as regular as clockwork: it was all run strictly on Soviet, as opposed to Russian, lines. In fact, there was nothing Russian about the place whatsoever.

The corridors were as long and dark and narrow as, I suppose, the many long, dark and narrow corridors people have taken in the history of the Soviet Union. In this case the only danger spots were the corners, where even the concrete beneath the padding beneath the carpet beneath the mat had worn so smooth you risked breaking a leg like people do when they're receiving the greatest care and attention while in all kinds of custody or, shall we say, supervised restraint.

As for the rooms, I have no complaints – well, apart from the fact that maybe they could have been hosed down now and then, and had a little bit more fresh straw thrown in perhaps a little more often.

We all queued up at nine o'clock sharp for breakfast. We each had a dollop of something slopped on our plates. Whatever it was, I'm sure it came from Siberia. Well, my lumps did. They were always freezing cold.

Lunch, which was served from two to three, was again typically Russian. We formed another queue and, from the second person in line onwards, we all hoped like hell there would be nothing left for us by the time it was our turn. But it was not to be. There was always enough left for me. What it was I couldn't tell you, although every day it looked as if it had been in a worse and worse car accident. Throughout lunch they insisted on playing, or rather blasting, through their somewhat fragile loudspeakers what they called their 'international tape', which consisted of the latest pop songs in French, Russian, Uzbekistani, German, Kyrgyz and English, although the English ones could have been Mediaeval Mongolian for all the sense they made to me.

The afternoons we all spent in the gardens by the lake, trying to get away from the microphones in the trees and bushes. Well, old habits die hard, especially when you've been the guys hiding them all over the place for the whole of your life. I always strolled down to the boat tied up at the end of the pier. I wondered who it belonged to. We were never offered any trips on it. The other thing that puzzled me was why, since nobody seemed to use it, the crew were always busy loading and unloading stacks of booze whenever I went down there. But I never found the answer to that. Maybe one day the body of a dead frogman will be discovered underneath it.

Dinner was from seven to eight o'clock. But the less I bring that up, the better. If you see what I mean.

On the other hand – think positive, think positive – it was the only health farm I've ever come across which provided not only hot and cold running tea but hot and cold running vodka as well. Not just during opening hours, but twenty-four hours a day. Just inside the entrance. In the corner. You couldn't miss it. A bar serving everything you wanted. As much of everything as you wanted. For practically nothing at all. It was unbelievable. You could also have all the meat you could eat, although I will admit that some of the stuff they served up looked as though it had been eaten before. As for cigarettes, the air was so thick and foggy I could hardly see who it was who was whining on about something or other not working, or coughing up blood all over the place or, of course, telling jokes, Russian jokes. Like the one about the old KGB lady who kept asking to see a psychiatrist.

'What do you want to see a psychiatrist for?' said one of the old KGB officials. 'Are you thinking of opening a bank account?'

The only trouble was, the more vodka we had to drink, the funnier we thought they were.

There was one joke we kept telling each other, though, that always made everybody laugh. It was: what's the difference between capitalism and Communism? Capitalism is the exploitation of man by man. Communism is the other way round. We didn't need any vodka to laugh at that because the poor, innocent Kyrgyz had been the victims of some of the biggest frauds ever carried out in the history of the old Soviet Union. Bigger than the wine frauds in Georgia. Bigger than the caviar frauds in Azerbaijan. Bigger even than the fishing frauds in the Baltics. In fact, at one time the entire country was just one giant fraud.

In Bishkek, the capital – I say capital, it's more like a small town covered in trees – you can see the signs of it everywhere. Slap-bang in the centre is the usual massive statue of Lenin, complete with regulation waistcoat, his arm outstretched pointing to the Alatau Mountains way in the distance as if to say, 'These are our targets, comrades. This is what we must achieve for the glory of the party.' In front of him is the big main government street, Chui Prospekt, so called because this was where all the party bosses used to gather together to chew over their prospects for meeting the higher and higher targets they kept being set by the central planners in Moscow, and to wonder how the hell they were going to get anywhere near them.

Around the edge of the square are the usual elaborate buildings, or rather, façades of elaborate buildings. Behind them is all your typical falling-apart, genuine two-parts-water, one-part-blood, one-part-cement Soviet architecture.

Behind the statue of the great man, or more appropriately, behind his back pocket, is what they call the White House, the presidential and government offices. Goodness knows why, because the last thing it is is white, let alone whiter than white. Behind that is a park and some kind of kids' funfair. The White House is where all the party officials' problems were solved because it was here that Leonid Ilych Brezhnev, later to be first secretary of the party, arrived one day. He was the miracle-worker. In other words, the hammer and fickle. He could take any disaster and turn it into a glorious success. His solution to their problems? Forget the targets. We'll make it up as we go along. Quotas, targets, total production figures, deliveries, the lot. All the planners want are statistics. So we'll give them statistics. Lots of them.

In Moldova, which to me was the Italy of the old Soviet Union, Brezhnev had done it with apples. In Kazakhstan, he did it with grain. Khrushchev was desperate for somebody to turn around his huge virgin lands scheme to finally make the Soviet Union self-sufficient in grain production. Brezhnev did it for him. By making it all up.

In Uzbekistan, he did it with cotton. He boosted production figures to such a high level that the Soviet planners couldn't believe their eyes. Neither could the Soviet space scientists when the Russian spy satellites started sending pictures back to earth showing one derelict field of Uzbeki cotton after another after another after another.

Brezhnev, of course, was safe. The big guys always make certain they're safe. In any case, who could think, let alone say, anything about a guy as big as Brezhnev? What's more, this guy was an expert. He once, no doubt over buckets of caviar and champagne, told a bunch of cronies, 'No one lives on wages alone. I remember in my youth we earned money by unloading railroad freight cars. So what did we do? Three crates or bags unloaded, and one for ourselves. That is how everybody lives.'

But out went the boss of the party in Uzbekistan, Sharaf Rashidov. Out went the chairman of the Uzbeki Council of Ministers. Out went over 50,000 government officials. Out, too, went Uzbekistan's deputy interior minister, a certain Yuri Chubanov, who just happened to be the son-in-law of you-know-who. For his trouble, he was later sentenced to twelve years in jail, although one of the first things Boris Yeltsin did on seizing power after the coup in August 1993 was to pardon him. Now, I wonder what made him do that. And so soon after taking power. Makes you think, doesn't it?

Brezhnev is addressing the Central Committee of the Communist Party.

'Comrades, at the end of the next Five Year Plan we will be able to prove the superiority of Communism over capitalism. We will then conquer Europe and the Third World.'

'But why not the United States as well?' shouts out one delegate.

'Don't be stupid,' says Brezhnev. 'Where are we going to get our wheat from?'

While Khrushchev was going around saying, 'If people in our country would stop stealing for a single day, Communism would have been built long ago,' Brezhnev was to do the same thing again in the Kyrgyz Republic. This time, with meat.

'How many tons shall we deliver this year?' he would ask the party functionaries who were obviously sharing the gristle, if not some of the fat. 'Shall we say ten, fifteen maybe even twenty million?'

'Whatever you say, Leonid Ilych. You are the party leader,' they would no doubt grin back at him. 'Would you like one record harvest or two?'

With another target met, they would then break open the vodka and celebrate for the other 364 days of the year. It sounds unbelievable, I know, but not for nothing was the Kyrgyz Republic known as the *altyn beshik*, or the golden cradle.

How much did he lift? Whichever way you do the sums, an awful lot of money. Some people say that as much as one sixth of all government funds just disappeared into thin air. Or rather, into the thin air of another Alpine-like country.

Brezhnev is on a visit to the United States.

'Your economy must be in bad shape,' he tells an American diplomat.

'How come?' he says.

'Because,' says Brezhnev, 'people here are too poor to buy anything. If anything here in the US was on sale in Russia, there would be queues a mile long. In the United States I haven't seen one queue.'

One official in today's slightly whiter White House – they've taken down Brezhnev's door plaque, the one that reads: 'Thou shalt not pass through here unless thou be prepared to pay at least 40 per cent' – told me that wagonloads of gifts were continually sent from Bishkek to Brezhnev, even when he was first secretary of the whole party and running the whole of the Soviet Union. An old man I met in the bar told me that was nothing. Next door, in Kazakhstan, where

he was finally caught, the first secretary of the party had managed to stash away in his own name 247 hotels, 414
apartments, 84 cottages, 22 hunting lodges and 350 hospital
beds.

'If a first secretary can do that, how much could a man like
Brezhnev take?' he said.

There's a top vacancy in the Ministry of Economic
Affairs. Three people apply: a Ph.D. from Moscow
University; a specialist in international law and a former
diplomat who speaks seven languages and used to work
with the World Bank. Who got the job?
  Brezhnev's cousin.

My own guess is that he probably took everything. You
only need to look at the number of trees and parks there are
in Bishkek. The Second Biddlecombe Law of Corruption is
that the more trees and parks there are, the more opportunities there are for people to get away from the microphones
and do deals. Certainly not for nothing was Bishkek known as
the leafiest capital in the whole of the old Soviet Union. Sure
Chisinau, the capital of Moldova, has plenty of trees. So does
Alma Aty. Tashkent has some, not many. But none of them
come anywhere near Bishkek.

Then there are all the blokes you see playing chess all
hours of the day and night. They're the fixers. They have to
make all the detailed arrangements for the deliveries to take
place.

'OK, I'll ship my stuff from here to here.'

'You move yours from there to there.'

'Agreed. This means I can now move my other assign-
ment from—'

'*Niet. Niet*. Do that and you'll be caught.'

'Yes, yes, comrade – I mean, my friend. Instead I'll move from here to here and . . .'

'That's the church taken care of.'

'And the prawns?'

'What about the old Queen?'

'Don't worry about her. She's neutralised.'

'I'll take care of the prawns, then.'

'Which means, mate, we've finally come together. The arrangements are in place.'

The First Biddlecombe Law of Corruption? That'll cost you a brown envelope, I'm afraid.

Brezhnev is on his way back by train from Bulgaria with his wife. She keeps asking him where they are.

Brezhnev puts his hand out of the window. Somebody kisses it.

He says, 'We're in Bulgaria.'

Next time he puts his hand out of the window somebody spits on it.

'We're in Romania,' he says.

The next time he puts his hand out of the window he says, 'We're in Russia.'

'How do you know?' asks his wife.

'Because someone has just stolen my watch,' he says.

And the amazing thing is that it's still going on. The Russian Ministry of Finance lends US$150 million to the Moscow Aviation Production Combine to help it build MiG 29s for sale to India. An audit by the Chamber of Accounts discovers that not a single rouble has reached the combine.

What's more, when the loan was made, the MiGs had already been built and were awaiting shipment.

The total bill for the first Chechen War was US$3 billion. How much money actually reached Chechnya? US$150 million.

The World Bank loaned Russia US$90 million to help compensate victims of bank frauds and various kinds of pyramid-selling schemes. How much of it reached the victims? You've got it. Nothing.

That's the big stuff. Or, rather, a tiny, tiny portion of the big stuff. Apart from the electronics factory where the boss's secretary took down faxes in shorthand, I visited another tiny electronics company in Tokmok. There, in spite of all the rules, the regulations, the promises made hand on heart to the World Bank that this time we promise we really, really, really will put our financial house in order, they were carrying on in the same old way. International accounting standards, the even stricter US generally accepted accounting principles, they'd never heard of them. They'd never even heard of Russia's Chart of Accounts which, I must admit, I mentioned more out of academic interest than anything else.

The finance department, as far as I could see, consisted of another fat old *babushka*, wearing another frilly, crocheted collar over a severe black dress, a big, fat accounts book and a mountain of used carbon paper. How could she control, all by herself, all the accounting of a company she said employed over 1,000 people? Easy, she smiled. She was a professional accountant.

But how could she do it without computers, without records, let alone a single calculator?

She smiled again. She got in early in the morning, she said. 'Was the company making a profit?'

She stopped smiling. 'That,' she said, 'is a commercial secret.'

Who says Brezhnev wasn't a great leader? Look at the enormous influence he had and the number of people all over the old Soviet Union who, even today, over twenty years after his death, are scrambling to follow in his footsteps. And to think I feel guilty if now and then I tear a cheque slightly so that it has to go through the system by hand which, of course, gives me a week's extra use of the money.

Brezhnev is in his official car. His chauffeur is driving him through the countryside. They come to a little village. Suddenly, a pig runs out across the road. The chauffeur brakes but hits the pig and kills it.

'You'd better go and apologise to the family who own the pig,' says Brezhnev.

Off goes the chauffeur to the nearest house.

One hour goes by. Two hours. Three hours later, the chauffeur comes back to the car, bottles of champagne in his pockets, jars of caviar in a bag in his hand, balloons and ribbons around his neck, a girl on each arm.

'What's going on?' says Brezhnev. 'You've been three hours.'

'I don't know,' says the chauffeur. 'I did as you told me. I went to the nearest house. I told them the president was outside in the back of the car and I killed the pig.'

The original Russians who arrived in Kyrgyz did not, of course, have the same standing and moral integrity as Brezhnev. They just wanted to go around killing people. The Czar was feeling nervous. The further and further south he could push his borders, and the more people he could eliminate in the process, the safer he felt. The Russians, of course, didn't put it like that. They said they were there to help one tribal chief against another. The first thing they did, therefore, was to destroy a fort called Pishpek which lay on the caravan trail from Tashkent to Kashgar. Well, the Russians called it a fort. The Kyrgyz say it was more of a collection of huts.

The Kyrgyz wanted nothing to do with the Russians. For some reason or other they didn't fancy the idea of settling down. Instead they preferred to be continually on the move, living in their *yurt* tents, looking after their sheep, breeding horses and generally enjoying life. Something to do, I guess, with being nomads.

Come the Russian Revolution, Pishpek became Frunze, named after a Russian Bolshevik general who was born there, sent to Tashkent to prevent a counterrevolution and ended up a Soviet hero. Then came the Soviets with their belief in the dictatorship of the proletariat and the rule of the common man. Again they tried to force the poor Kyrgyz to stop moving around as they wanted to do. This time, however, the Soviets insisted, in most cases at gunpoint, that not only did the Kyrgyz do the last thing any bunch of self-respecting nomads ever wants to do, but also that they worked together. In other words, they collectivised them. The lucky ones grabbed their horses, their camels and their women, in that order, and made for China. As for the unlucky ones, well, nobody really knows what happened to them, but you can guess.

In order to show their appreciation that the Kyrgyz had none too voluntarily given up thousands of years of tradition, their way of life and even their country, the Soviets then promptly banned their language and started shipping in hundreds of thousands of Russians, Ukrainians, Uzbeks and other Slavs to take their place. By 1936, with the arrival of still more Russian settlers lured by some pretty hefty land grants, which, of course, were not in the gift of the Russians to grant, the place became a fully fledged Soviet Socialist republic. The Kyrgyz, or at any rate the few who had managed to survive, were now a minority in their own land.

When the end of the Soviet Union came, it came swiftly like, I suppose, a meat chopper through the jugular. The Kyrgyz president, Askar Akayev, was in Moscow at the time of the coup. A mirror image of Yeltsin, apart from the standing-on-a-tank bit, he immediately opposed it. When the local KGB chief arrived at the presidential palace to arrest him, he was arrested by the president's own guards. Akayev then ordered the troops, still loyal to him, to surround the headquarters of the Communist Party. He ordered television and radio, also still loyal to him, to broadcast Yeltsin's call for resistance against the coup. This they did.

On the collapse of the coup, Akayev, like Yeltsin, quickly resigned from the Communist Party. This ensured that not only did he remain in charge, but he could also lead the move against the party of which he had been the glorious leader and call for its suspension and the confiscation of all its property. The top party guys promptly fled to Moscow. The members of Parliament became independents. The guys in the middle, the bureaucrats, the managers of all the big state enterprises and collective farms, became rich. The ordinary blokes, as ever, became confused. As for the Russian population, they became increasingly nervous. Out of nearly a million of them, around 75,000 left in six months.

So successful was Akayev at managing the switch that he was soon invited to Moscow and offered the job of vice-president of the old Soviet Union. He turned it down. Instead, he said, he wanted to stay at home and establish democracy in Kyrgyzstan. Which he has more or less done.

The capital, Frunze, they've finally renamed Bishkek. Pishpek, they say, sounded more Kazakh rather than Kyrgyz, although I have my own theories. You try pronouncing

Pishpek after hitting the vodka. There is still a Frunze Museum, however, which contains the original house our Russian hero lived in during his days in Kyrgyzstan, although I notice they've taken his name off his statue opposite the railway station.

Kyrgyz is now the official language. Not Russian.

Whether or not it is down to all the independence celebrations, the population is now not only over the 4.5 million mark – although there are still three times as many cattle – but the Kyrgyz are at last a majority in their own land once again. A majority of just 52 per cent, according to the latest census returns. The Russians, who've obviously had other things on their minds, are down to 21 per cent. The rest of the population is everything else: Ukrainian, Uzbeki, Tatar, Chinese, Muslim, Korean, ethnic German, and, of course, Turkish. As far as I could see, the Turks are big players in Kyrgyzstan and determined to be even bigger. Turkey has been a big foreign investor in the country, and the Turkish are for ever stressing their linguistic and cultural links with Kyrgyzstan, even though they don't speak the same kind of Turkish there as they do in Turkey. Not that that has stopped the Turks from beaming all kinds of Turkish-speaking television programmes at them.

The Kyrgyz Republic is also a Muslim state, but not an official Muslim state. Well, being nomads, it was difficult to get them to the mosque regularly every Friday. There was also no way women were going to wear the veil. State and religion, as a result, are separate. Political parties are not allowed to be based purely on religion, which came as one hell of a relief to the Russian minority.

Down in the south, however, in Osh, which runs along the border with Uzbekistan and would to all intents and purposes be part of Uzbekistan today if it hadn't been for some whim of Stalin's in the 1930s, some people, mostly Uzbekis, had other ideas. There were even rumours that they were going to break away and return to where they thought they belonged. Things came to a head in June 1990 when a local Kyrgyz tried to take over an Uzbeki-run collective farm. Kyrgyz security forces poured in to back up the Kyrgyz. Uzbekistan rushed to the aid of the Uzbekis, though only morally and financially. I was told that the clashes left over 100 people dead and 500 injured. Others said there were 300 dead and nearly 1,000 injured, most of them Uzbekis.

Because of the discrepancy in the figures, violence flared up again in Bishkek towards the end of the year. This time over 1,000 Kyrgyz demanding the true figures went on hunger strike. The situation was resolved only when Askar Akayev flew in from Moscow, stood for election as executive president, and won.

Since then, the Kyrgyz Republic has been virtually trouble-free. Well, I say trouble-free: every now and then the Kyrgyz seem to stop and seize trains trundling through town on their way from Iran to anti-Taleban forces in Afghanistan; trains loaded with up to 700 tons of military ammunition marked, 'Humanitarian Aid'. There is also, I notice, the odd guy hanging around the back door of the White House, obviously still waiting for his brown envelope.

My treatment aboard *Aurora* was finally over. But I couldn't leave because my car was blocked in. Some Kyrgyz big shot was arriving, presumably for another decoke, surrounded by a host of hangers-on.

So I sat in the health bar, taking the usual cure with some of my fellow KGB spies and experts on the peaceful uses of such goodies as anthrax, smallpox, plague, brucellosis and tularemia. One old boy who, up until this point, had only ever asked me, 'Are you a trade union member? Which trade union do you belong to? Have you seen all our important art galleries and exhibitions?' suddenly announced that he wanted to tell us his favourite Brezhnev joke.

Stalin, Khrushchev and Brezhnev are travelling by train. It breaks down in the middle of nowhere. 'Fix it,' Stalin barks. They fix it, but still it doesn't work. 'OK, shoot everybody,' barks Stalin again. Then he dies.

Khrushchev now takes over. 'OK, rehabilitate everybody,' he says. They rehabilitate everybody, but still the train doesn't move. Khrushchev dies.

Brezhnev now takes over. 'OK,' he says. 'Close the curtains. Let's pretend we're moving.'

Laugh? I thought they were all going to die there and then.

'Do you know that the Communist Party announced a competition for the best political joke about Brezhnev?'
'No. What's the prize?'
'Fifteen years.'

One of the old KGB women, who looked far older than I thought anyone had the right to look, shuffled up to us. I told her that, rather than face Manas Airport at Bishkek, I was going to drive all the way back across the border into next-door Kazakhstan and across the steppes to Alma Aty. She cackled away like mad, which I took as her subtle KGB way of asking for another bottle. Once she started glugging it back she talked to me about 'Manas', the famous Kyrgyz epic poem, which is twenty times longer than 'The Odyssey', and you remember how long that was. It tells the story of the Kyrgyz people and a certain Khan Manas, and how he practically singlehandedly fought off the foreign devils with the aid of the occasional magic horse, and slew the odd dragon, watched by his wife, Kanykey who, of course, kept telling him he was doing it all wrong.

It was nothing, she said, but another glorious Russian fraud.

During the 1930s she'd worked in the National Museum. At the same time as the Russians were busy slaughtering anything that moved, they were also busy trying to create separate identities for all their Central Asian republics. One of them had the idea of suddenly discovering an epic poem telling the story of the Kyrgyz people from more or less the year dot. They then strung together all the old Kyrgyz stories and poems they could find to make up a single, long epic which they then proclaimed, as a result of their diligent research, dedication to the Kyrgyz people and their culture, economic use of government funds, blah, blah, blah – you can almost hear the speeches rolling off those bureaucratic party members' tongues – they had discovered in some long-forgotten pile of empties and completely restored to its original mint condition to take its place in history alongside blah, blah, blah.

Who was going to contradict them? Not the Russians. As for the Kyrgyz, well, we all know what condition they were in at the time. And the rest, as they say, is homework for today's poor Kyrgyz schoolkids.

Did my treatment work? Was it worth it? They had completely removed the vodka lines from under my eyes. Now they were all over my face. As far as my liver is concerned, it is not only still throbbing merrily away, it now throbs to the chorus of 'The Red Flag'. My chronic – yawn – fatigue – yawn – syndrome is still there. My ability logically to think to sensibly constructively and write are unimpaired.

But I don't care. All I know is that before the treatment I thought I'd seen the cruiser *Aurora* built of solid brick 1,600 metres up in the Heavenly Mountains. After the treatment, it not only looked like the *Aurora*, it was rocking backwards and forwards as well. As for the cannon that fired that single shot, it was now going off non-stop like a machine-gun. Deep inside my head.

Why, I wondered, would all the Soviet bigwigs come here

for a health cure that left you feeling so much worse than when you went in? Call me bitter and twisted and cynical if you must, but one morning ambling around the gardens trying to work off the effects of my breakfast bottle of vodka, I discovered, reading between the pines, that at the far eastern end of the lake which, don't forget, is so cool it never freezes, was a red-hot property: the old Soviet Navy's big, top-secret military research establishment. So important was it to the Russians that even after the collapse of the Soviet Union they still wanted to keep it on. The Kyrgyz said *niet*. So today it has been shut down and just left to rot. Which is a pity. They should have tested one of the Soviet hit-precision torpedos on it.

Now, you're not thinking what I'm thinking, are you? That all this business about the boat and the health spa was an elaborate cover? That in the old days – don't forget, this place was only opened up to the outside world in the late 1980s – if the big guys were ever discovered here, they could say they were simply enjoying a spot of R and R when all the time they were actually planning one hell of a health cure for an awful lot of people all over the world.

After all, when you think about it, it's a good cover story. US presidents always go off to Martha's Vineyard. The Chinese noodles make for the seaside at Beidaihe. Our Tone heads for Chiantishire. Why on earth shouldn't the Russian leaders keep coming here for the pure, sparkling water, the gorgeous, thin mountain air and the hot and cold running vodka?

So you think I'm suffering from a touch of the Le Carrés? In that case, how come, since they shut down the big secret weapons research establishment, none of the big Russian guys have bothered to come here any more? Huh?

Manila

As they come into the floodlit ring, a hush descends on the vast stadium. The two contenders eye each other warily. The one in the left-hand corner turns and looks at the crowd. The other struts up and down, eager for the fight to begin. Both are in tip-top condition. Lean. Sleek. Alert. The pick of the bunch. And trained killers.

For this is a cockfight. In a basketball stadium. In Manila, the centre of world cockfighting.

Apart from being the Filipinos' second-favourite pastime – they say that whenever two or three Filipinos gather together, they love nothing better than to get their cocks out and have a fight, and then afterwards sit up all night buffing their trophies – cockfighting is big, big business. Which, honestly, is not just some cocktail-part story I'm telling you. Practically every town, village or couple of shacks has its own cockpit. Over 1,500 of them are registered. Probably another 1,500 are not. Registered or not, each cockpit could employ, directly or indirectly, 200 to 250 people, or cockers, as they call themselves, as opposed to, I suppose, roosters. On top of that the government takes anything from US$2 to US$10 in tax on every ticket sold for every cockfight anywhere in the country.

There is a huge supporting industry: a million breeders, trainers, handlers and feed merchants selling everything from vitamins and conditioners and high-protein super-strength pellets to slugs of testosterone and great lumps of digitalis to make the birds' hearts beat faster, not to mention various things to stem the flow of blood if the worst comes to the worst.

Inevitably, like every other industry under the sun, it also has its own string of trade magazines and, judging by the articles and stories I've read, its own technical terms. How big is your cock? Has it got a beautiful sheen? How often do you caress and massage it? What conditioner do you use on it? What do you use to stop it bleeding? To which, of course, the only possible reply is, 'Sure it's in peak condition, thank you very much. How's yours?'

There are also – not that size is important – big breeding enterprises; huge liveries where you can have your cocks lovingly looked after morning, noon and night and, of course, whopping great worldwide buying-and-selling operations. Cocks from Manila, for example, end up in all kinds of obvious places like Haiti, Cuba or the Dominican Republic, as well as in many not so obvious places like Ireland or Italy or Malta. But so far, I was told, not one has yet ended up in St Lucia, let alone St Vincent. A lot end up in chicken chow mein, but that's a different story.

I don't want to ruffle any feathers, but like most popular, everyday sports – dog-baiting around Wilmington, Delaware, goat-throwing in Manganeses de la Polvorosa in Spain and the first twenty-seven minutes of any football match in which Gazza is taking part before he is sent off crying his eyes out – it's also a great leveller. Rich or poor, *maginoo* or *sabungero*, it doesn't make any difference. Once you're hollering your guts out around a cockpit, everybody's the same, whatever their place in the official pecking order. Even the women who are, I suppose, called chicks. Perhaps not surprisingly, once they come out of their shell they seem to be able to holler louder and longer than the men. But that might well have something to do with all the practice they get at home.

As for politicians, I don't want to cry foul, but forget garden fêtes and jumble sales. Cockfights are the only place to go to get votes. 'If you don't go cockfighting, you don't get elected. It's as simple as that,' one congressman I met at the cockfight in the basketball stadium told me.

'But isn't it, you know, cruel?' I hesitated.

He was astounded that anyone could even think of asking such a damn fool question. 'No way,' he spluttered. 'People like to see me coming and enjoying myself with them at cockfights.'

'But what about the cocks?'

'They enjoy it as well,' he said. 'They're natural-born killers. They love it.'

'Even with their guts hanging out?'

'Sure. Why not?'

Apart from your run-of-the-mill cockfights – run of the mill to the spectators, that is: the cocks usually end up dead – there are local, regional, national and even international contests or derbies like the International Slasher World Cup, the biggest cockfighting event in the world, which attracts entries from Korea, China, Mexico, Thailand (where, when it was classified as a gambling activity, it was banned, but, now reclassified as a traditional sport, it is alive and well and spitting blood) and even parts of the US where cockfighting has not been banned, or where nobody has heard about it. Like Maurice, Louisiana, the Smoky Mountains in Tennessee or virtually anywhere in Mississippi, Arizona, New Mexico or Oklahoma. In Missouri it had been banned for over a hundred years until a bunch of cockers got together in 1985 and had the legislation thrown out as being too vague.

Not that we didn't go in for a spot of cockfighting in the UK as well. Come Shrove Tuesday in mediaeval times, boys would take their prize birds to school. They would then arrange fight after fight until they found the prize cock. All the dead birds would then go to the local Ye Olde Kentuckie Friede Chickene. The head teacher would then, as is the norm, claim the best cock in the school for himself. Today, like everything in this world, the cockfights are still there if you look hard enough for them. The nearest one to where I live takes place regularly in a shed at the back of a caravan park in Belvedere, Kent. But don't tell anyone I told you, otherwise I could be in trouble.

Talk to the Filipinos, however, and you won't be surprised to learn that they don't rate anybody else's cocks but their own. Not even the so-called big all-American cocks. At first, they say, the Americans bred better birds. They also trained them to be tougher fighters. They taught them, for example, to roll and skip out of the way of danger. They strengthened their legs for the killer blow. They also made them either fliers or grounders, a critical distinction, apparently, in the world of cockers. But no longer. Over the last twenty years, the Filipinos say, they have fought back and regained their traditional world dominance. Partly because they have poured enormous amounts of money and resources into it. Partly because, let's face it, there are now so many Filipinos living in the States that they virtually dominate the sport there as well. As a result today, they say, the Americans have to be drugged up to their eyeballs before they can even think of doing anything. Then they invariably get it all wrong.

As for the fights themselves, some are four-, six- or even eight-stag events, which means an owner brings four, six or eight birds along with him. Whoever gets the most victories wins the competition. Some fights are between equals. The organisers match the cocks for size, weight and skill. Others, such as the derbies, are between cocks selected at random.

There's also a mass of rules and regulations about what you can and cannot attach to your cock to increase its effectiveness. Some cocks, I was assured, are made for such things as gaffs, long, rounded needles. Others for short knives ranging from one to two inches long. Others, inevitably the strongest of all, need no additional assistance whatsoever.

To the owners of the winning cocks, most prizes are nominal, although some, like those for the big Slasher World Cup, can be up in the millions. People do it for the love of the game. The cocks, of course, may have another opinion. The real money, however, is made breeding and selling. Establish a reputation for having a killer cock and your services will not only be in demand all over the world but you'll also be able to name your own price. Some cocks have fetched as much as 50,000 pesos, or US$775, for a single appearance. With or without any guarantees that it will do the job expected of it. Then, of course, there's the money to be made from the betting that inevitably surrounds the performance of any outstanding cock in peak condition. Few owners, however, seem to go in for sponsorship, which surprised me. I'd have thought it would be ideal for somebody like British Airways, which nowadays seems to be dedicated to one cock-up after another.

If only the cockers could run the country itself, because whenever I go to the Philippines, I never know whether to laugh or cry.

I know this is going to offend the half of the world that has cheap Filipina nannies and childminders, not to mention a couple of Filipina dancers and bargirls hidden away somewhere, but to me the whole place is like some giant funfair or even freak show.

First, of course, there were the shoes. In all seriousness, how could any woman need so many shoes? I know plenty of women do crazy things. But I ask you, 1,200 pairs, including the ones with the flashing heels for secret late-night visits to the best discos in town. Second, it's a crazy country: 7,107 islands. And that's at low tide. Nobody has worked out how many there are at high tide. Probably 8,107, knowing the Philippines. I mean, how can you possibly govern that lot? Not that everybody agrees that the Philippines should govern them all. Some, including the appropriately named Mischief Reef and the Spratly Islands, are claimed by China, others by Vietnam, Taiwan, Malaysia and even tiny little Brunei. Third, the actual state of the place.

Agricultural production is down. In rice production they lag way behind Indonesia. Irrigation systems are fouling up. Most of their forests have been destroyed. Similarly industrial production. Costs are high, efficiency desperately low.

Unemployment is climbing. People are so desperate for jobs that when they advertised for someone to be the country's new official executioner they were inundated with applicants, many from doctors, dentists and even clergymen. Girls, however, seem to be the exception. From birth they are brought up to believe that, in spite of all the odds against them, they have a long list of career opportunities ranging from escort to call girl.

Services are appalling. Take the banks, for example. They're almost as good as my branch of the NatWest. They think nothing of keeping you waiting for forty-five days to clear a travellers' cheque, let alone an ordinary cheque. As for foreign-exchange transactions, it's all *mañana, mañana.*

Violence is endemic. Forget the fact that the police pay US$5 for every 1,000 dead flies anybody hands in. They even get prisoners to count them to make certain they are not being swindled. Forget the fact that the police run Christmas raffles offering as first and second prizes a 9mm Daewo pistol and a .45-calibre automatic. Forget the fact that the traffic police gun down other policemen when they are caught red-handed taking bribes from motorists.

I ask you, would you appoint a convicted torturer and a man accused of being an accessory to the summary execution of suspected kidnappers as the head of the national police force? They did in the Philippines.

Finally, regardless of the money they make out of cock-fighting, the tax take is minimal. What government revenue there is is no longer, thank goodness, devoted to supporting the worldwide shoe industry. Instead it goes on running costs and paying off the country's debts. The little left over goes on roads, schools and various long-overdue infrastructure projects. Except, thanks to the startling efficiency of the Philippine civil service, it is very rare for anything at all to get to any roads, schools or various long-overdue infrastructure projects.

The only thing that seems to keep the place afloat are all those little brown envelopes all those Filipina nurses, nannies and childminders keep sending home, not to mention the huge money transfers made by all the chastitute dancers and bargirls, who, I'm told, are to be found in bars and nightclubs all over the world. With the Philippines already the world's largest exporter of labour – the world's ports are awash with Filipino seamen – they reckon those little brown envelopes are worth anything from US$5 to US$10 billion every year. Which is one hell of a lot of babysitting, bar tips and horizontal tangos.

Not that the government is not grateful. Whenever they return home on holiday, overseas workers or *balikbayans* are given their own fast track to clear customs. The bigger their suitcases or cardboard boxes, the faster the track. Neither do they have to pay any airport fees or travel taxes. Officially, that is. Unofficially, like the rest of us, they still have to pay the immigration officials.

So concerned is the government that those little brown envelopes should continue to find their way home that the Labour Department has set up special training courses and skills tests for Filipinos going abroad as domestics and baby-sitters, presumably to avoid headlines like 'HOSPITAL FLIES IN FILIPINO NURSES'. Whether they are going to set up similar training courses and skills tests for Filipinas going abroad to work in the biggest business of all, I couldn't find out. If I do, I'll let you know.

But given all their undoubted skills and unique ability to make money, there has to be a reason why the Philippines is not a big, fluffy, pink Asian Tiger and instead has to rely on all those envelopes.

In the quiet corners of an upmarket Manila coffee shop, some Filipinos will admit that they're all mixed up because, they say, they've spent 400 years in a convent and forty in Hollywood. Others maintain it's because they have none of the so-called Asian values of their neighbours. Instead, they tell you, they have the *mañana* of Spain, the machismo of Latin America, the messy political system of the United States and one hell of a lot of unsold shoes.

In the more downmarket Manila coffee shops, which are much more fun, they simply confess, in between shots, that they're baffled because the country is called Philippines, the people are Filipinos, the women are Filipinas, everything is Philippine, while Manila is the world capital of brown envelopes.

But to me it's simpler than that. They're in a mess because less than 4 per cent of the population are Chinese, and wherever you go in the world, if you get only a handful of Chinese, you get low economic growth. QED.

All praise, however, to President Ramos. When he was in power the government announced that he and his Cabinet had agreed to adopt 'a longer-range vision for the Philippines

from Philippines 2000 to Philippines 3000 to propel the
country into the ranks of the industrialised nations'.

Wowee. Nobody can accuse them of underestimating the
seriousness of their situation and their determination to come
up with the solution as quickly as possible. But while we're all
waiting for the year 3000, when they plan to take their rightful place in the ranks of the industrialised nations let's take a
look at the capital, Manila. It's simply unbelievable. It's
Bangkok, Jakarta, Kuala Lumpur and the road from
Rotterdam to the Hague all put together. About the only
good thing about the city is that they've no longer got the
Marcoses.

Just walking down the street is impossible. It's hot. It's
steaming. The pavements are jammed solid. There are old
men and young boys repairing bikes and motorcycles in the
middle of the crowds. There are chickens tied upside-down,
hanging from what used to be parking meters when Imelda
bought her first pair of shoes. On every street corner small
groups of people are huddled together over a cardboard box
playing *jueteng*, a home-grown numbers game.

And everywhere there are shanties. Beneath road bridges,
along railway tracks and riverbanks. Tucked under odd corners of office blocks. Even backing on to other shanties.
Unless, of course, there's a big important international con-
vention in town, like a Miss Universe competition or an
Asia–Pacific summit meeting. Then they are all, regardless of
what the poor inhabitants think, bulldozed and swept away in
the name of what Mrs Marcos used to call beautification.

As if all that's not bad enough, there's the noise. I don't
mean from the traffic. I mean from the bands. They're all over
the place. In the middle of the pavement. Outside offices.
Inside the Coconut Planters' Bank. In the shopping malls. In
the hotels. In the lift going up to your room. Inside the minibar. The traffic creates other problems. Manila is the perfect

place to take a driving test because the traffic never moves. At first I thought it was because they were still trying to shift all those shoes, but it's just the way it is. Any journey anywhere, I promise you, takes at least two to three hours. On second thoughts, it takes that long to pull away from the kerb to get into the stream of traffic. Then it takes another two to three hours to get to wherever you want to go.

Because the congestion is so bad, it's not unusual for people to walk 5 or 10 kilometres to get to work. During my last trip, for example, there was a huge jam all the way along EDSA from Balintawak to Makati, caused by flooding at the underpass between EDSA and Shaw Boulevard. Rather than wait for the jam to clear, people just accepted it and started to walk the whole way instead.

Some people do get annoyed. Well, I say annoyed. One guy, before he got off a bus on which he had been held up for hours on end, shot the driver with a .45-calibre pistol. Then he disappeared into the crowds. Because the traffic is so bad, the last I heard was that they were still waiting for the police to arrive at the scene.

The only good thing about the roads are the Jeepneys, the flashy, multicoloured, all-singing, all-dancing minibuses or maxi-taxis, depending on how long you're stuck in them and with how many people. I can honestly say they're among the best hotels I've stayed in anywhere in the world. Originally built from bits and pieces of US army Jeeps left behind after the Second World War, like the African Mammy Wagons, they're invariably decorated with slogans such as 'God is With Us', 'Jesus Saves' and 'Jesus is my Co-Pilot'. The trouble is, the way they drive when they get the chance, I often feel as though I'm going to be meeting the Co-Pilot before the journey is over.

One morning, in despair at the mere thought of yet again battling through the traffic, I thought I'd try the local train.

I went to the nearest railway station. There's not a hope in hell of getting on a train. So what have the Filipinos done about it? They've built their own self-propelled carts which, in between the trains, they push backwards and forwards themselves along the rails from station to station.

Another day I tried to go to the airport, but I couldn't get anywhere near the place. Not that I was particularly worried. Grand International, a big domestic airline, had just announced that one of their office workers had flown a Boeing 737 200, with passengers on board, all the way from Manila to Cebu and back. Afterwards passengers said they could tell he wasn't a fully qualified airline pilot because the plane left on time, arrived on time, and pulled up at the gate on time. There was no turbulence, no silly remarks on the intercom, no weak smiles as you got off the plane.

Pick up the local newspaper, the *Philippine Star*. It's full of reports about three Filipinos going in for a world-record-breaking chilli-eating competition just to get into *The Guinness Book of Records*. Geronimo Millesa tucked into 150, Grison Nación 167 and the wonderfully named Bert Gonzales polished off a stomach-blowing 300. They all had to be rushed to hospital afterwards and only later discovered there was no category in *The Guinness Book of Records* for eating chillies.

Rabies is a big problem throughout the country. Not only is it one of the most infected areas in the world – it ranks number four after Pakistan, India and Bangladesh – but the problem is getting worse every year. What are they doing about it? They are planning to immunise every one of the 7 million infected dogs in the country. How many doses of vaccine do they have? Forty-two thousand. In the meantime, in San Lazaro Hospital in Manila, which has the only rabies ward in the country, they simply strap the victims to the beds and wait for them to die. Out in the villages, I was told, they do much the same thing, although some herbalists are making a fortune selling rabies stones. If you're bitten by a rabid dog, you put the stones on the wound. It'll heal up a treat. Well, that's what they say. In the meantime, whatever you do don't give that nice little doggie a bone. It might be the last thing you ever do.

Fancy a meal out? Take my advice. Forget the hot dogs. In spite of all the fuss about rabies, the government has only just got round to banning dog meat. Not because of any health risks, but because the killing of anything other than cattle, pigs, goats, sheep, poultry, rabbits, horses, deer and crocodiles is cruel. Except, of course, when it is done for religious purposes. As for chargrilled cats, choose your open-air barbecue with care.

Eggs are not recommended, either, unless you like the idea of a local delicacy such as *bahut*: hard-boiled, fertilised duck eggs, sometimes served within hours of the duckling actually hatching and pushing its way through the shell on its own.

Fish can also be a bit dodgy. Best to check the weather forecast first. A red-tide alert in the South China Sea means that it has been hit by some killer algae and all the shellfish are in danger of being infected. If this happens, stick to the *kare-kare*, oxtail or knuckles, cooked in a spicy peanut sauce and served in some kind of salty pink gunge which I'm told is the local shrimp paste. And lashings of Scotch.

But if you want to be 100 per cent safe, stick to rats. Especially the big 10-inch-long ones. The Filipinos kill them, marinate them overnight in salt, sugar, soy sauce, vinegar and lemon juice, fry them then sell them the following day as a high-protein, low-cholesterol poor man's aphrodisiac called star meat. Which, of course, is 'rats' spelled backwards. Which gives a whole new meaning to one-star, two-star or even five-star restaurants. They even organise rat-catching competitions and have a whole plague of Miss Rat beauty competitions. OK. You can throw up now.

To avoid the slightest possible risk of being invited to lunch at a restaurant with no matter how many stars, I decided to head for Cebu in the centre of the country on the rugged, mountainous Visayas Islands. Two down, 7,105 to go. It meant I had to pass on the famous rice terraces of Banaue in northern Luzon, not to mention the finals of the famous thread-eating competition in Paranaque, where everybody competes to swallow a whole reel of sewing thread for the grand prize of US$1.90. But you know me. Dedicated to the end.

The oldest city in the country, Cebu is where Magellan, the Portuguese explorer, the Chris the Colon of the East, first set foot in the Philippines in 1521. It's also the site of the famous monument to Lapu-Lapu, the local chief who killed him not very long afterwards.

To many people, it's one of the nicest, if not the nicest, city in the country, because it was the centre of opposition to Marcos. Marcos countered by starving it of government funds and assistance, which was the biggest favour he could have done it, for it forced Cebu's citizens to look after themselves. Today, as a result, it is booming. 'We say it is Cee-booming,' one local businessman, who had obviously had more than his fair share of star meat, told me.

There's a big industrial zone near the airport which is home to over 120 companies, many of them household names. It is also home to no fewer than seven of the biggest Filipino Chinese tycoons. What did I tell you about Chinese hard work and prosperity? Confucius, he say, give me Chinese and I will give you big boom. Foreign investment is pouring in. Unemployment is way down. There is no gridlocked traffic. No Jeepneys mounting the pavements looking for a short cut. None of that frantic hustle and bustle. No noise. Apart from the nineteenth-hole cackle of golfers flying in direct from Hong Kong, Tokyo and Taiwan for the city's three golf courses, which are, apparently, flight and hotel included, far cheaper for them than staying at home and playing a single round on one golf course. It's also, I was told, about half the price of playing in Manila. It seems it is so popular among the high-flying Far East golfing community that many visiting golfers go home with a bigger handicap than they had when they arrived: a Filipina bride, which they can buy with all the necessary guarantees for anything from 200,000 to 400,000 pesos, between US$3,000 and US$6,000. A Chinese woman, by comparison, costs only 50,000 pesos. But then, she doesn't have all the, how do you say, attractions of the Filipina model.

On a hillside is a huge Taoist Temple which is more like a Taoist theme park, with big, colourful dragons all over the place and its own model of the Great Wall of China. But for kids, it is not. A sign outside stresses, 'Please observe solemn and silence. Keep this temple clean. No smoking inside. No immoral acts allowed.' There's also, on another hilltop, the huge twenty-two-storey Cebu Plaza Hotel, where I'm sure everything is allowed.

Cebu has its share of problems, of course. Slums. Starving kids. Beggars. Open sewers. Side streets teeming with people. But here it all seems much more controllable, more solvable. Even the mayor is so relaxed that every day he slopes off around lunchtime for a round of golf at the Cebu Country Club. Not many mayors can do that. Usually they take the whole day off.

But I wasn't there for the golf. Neither was I in the marriage market, although I had something equally dangerous to do. I was there to visit the gun factories. For between you and me and the guys in half a dozen pubs in and around west London where, with a stack of readies, you can pick up virtually any kind of gun in thirty minutes, behind all the long, sandy beaches and golf courses and casinos and luxury hotels, Cebu is also one of the gun-making centres of the world.

Within ten minutes of landing, I was being driven up rough old country tracks, far from the Taoist Temple and the twenty-two-storey hotel, to shady barns in the middle of sugar-cane plantations and being offered enough guns to line the walls of a couple of hundred silage pits not a million miles from Stormont Castle. Why are they based in shady barns in the middle of sugar-cane plantations? Because whenever everyone hears a car coming they drop what they're doing and disappear into the sugar plantation, of course.

Unlike, say, Austria's Glock GmbH; Italy's Beretta SpA, manufacturers of the sleek 9mm pistol which replaced the US Army's .45-calibre Colt pistol back in 1985; Germany's Heckler and Koch GmbH, which is, whisper it not, a subsidiary of British Aerospace plc, or even Arsenal, the once near-legendary Bulgarian manufacturers of Kalashnikovs tucked away in Kazanluk in the foothills of the Balkan Mountains, the gun-makers of Cebu are not major players. But for all that they know their business. They also know the rules. They told me they were allowed to sell guns only to people who'd got a licence. But that was no problem. They could get me a licence in three weeks. Maybe less. Depending.

'Depending on whether the licence is in your name or the name of your Filipina wife,' the manager of one of the gun companies told me.

'But I haven't got a Filipina wife,' I said.

'Well we can get you one of them as well, if you like,' he grinned. 'All included. No extras.'

If I wanted to try any of them out before I made up my mind – the guns, I'm sure he meant, not the Filipina wives – there was a special shooting range past the huge San Miguel brewery alongside the equally huge Coca-Cola plant close to the airport. He'd be happy to make the necessary arrangements.

That, for what it's worth, is the official side of the business. For the unofficial side, you have to go down the road to Danão, once a rebel stronghold where, not so long ago, the first thing everybody had to do every morning was to clear away all the dead bodies left by the night's activities. Here all the real illegal firearms operators are based. Here, just like in Bassra, way up in the Khyber Pass, you can buy a fake anything: a fake Beretta; a fake Colt; a fake any kind of Smith and Wesson, from the tiny, small-frame 60LS up to the large-frame, long-barrelled 629 Classic DX revolver. With the right introductions you can also buy a fake Uzi sub-machine-gun and/or a fake MP5, every terrorist's favourite toy. I was even offered a Lapu-Lapu revolver, named after the local chief who took care of Magellan way back in 1521. But I politely declined. I'd been told there was something even more powerful than a Lapu-Lapu: sprinkled kneecaps.

There are gangs going round the country digging up dead bodies to steal their kneecaps so that they can grind them into a powder for people to sprinkle around their homes. This, Filipinos believe, will protect them from people carrying guns. Even Lapu-Lapus.

Back in Manila, I decided, powdered kneecaps or not, I'd had enough of guns. It was time to tackle the important things of life: bars. Because, let me tell you, there are bars and there are Filipino bars, like the one I stumbled into full of salt-rimmed margaritas late one Friday night, or was it early Saturday morning.

I'd been doing the usual. Too much work. Too much hustle. Too much everything else. I'd spent most of my time in Makati, the business and financial end of town, which, after seven o'clock in the evening, is about as many laughs as the City of London. They'll assure you it's a second Hong Kong, bursting with about-to-be-done deals. Don't listen to them. It looks swish. All those neon lights. All that chrome.

All those new hotels, especially the twenty-eight-storey Shangri-La. All those typical Filipino restaurants like the Hard Rock Café, Studebaker's, TGI Friday's, Tony Roma's. But a market trader in Hong Kong, and I mean a street-market trader, does more deals in a day than these guys do in a week.

I didn't fancy the usual drag: drinks at the Giraffe, some fancy French meal at Le Soufflé, which, however good it is, seems crazy in the Philippines, and more drinks at the appropriately named Zor. I wanted to get away from Makati, and especially from any risk of being dragged off to the expat hang-out, the Prince of Wales.

So I headed for Malate, on the other side of town, down near Manila Bay, where I was told there were one or two bars, one or two clubs and a joint is a joint is a joint. In order to make certain I was there by six, I was outside the Peninsula, where I was staying, and in a cab by 2.30. You can never be too careful with Manila traffic and I definitely wasn't going to hitch a ride on one of those railway carts, however cheap it was.

I was lucky. The jams weren't too bad, and at just gone five o'clock I was in the famous Manila Hotel – famous because everyone says it's famous, like Hemingway, who remarked, 'It's a good story if it's like the Manila Hotel.' Famous because everybody raves about the views of the bay at sunset, though they are probably looking at it still waiting for room service to deliver their breakfast. Famous because, no sooner have you staggered through the door than everybody is telling you that that great old American war hero and liberator, General – duty, honour, country – Douglas MacArthur spent five years there in a penthouse apartment when he was commander of US Army Forces in the Far East before the last war.

However, I can't see that he was a great old American war hero and liberator. Mother's boy, yes. When he went to West Point Military Academy, she took a hotel room overlooking his so that she could make certain he did all his homework. Drama queen, yes. He was arrogant, overweening, obsessed with his own self-importance. He would have dropped a nuclear bomb on China just to get on the cover of *Time* magazine if Truman hadn't got rid of him. I know that sometimes it takes ages for messages to get through at the Manila Hotel, but that can't possibly explain why on earth MacArthur, the moment he heard about Pearl Harbor, refused to disperse his own aircraft stationed across town at Clark Air Base. Instead he left them on the ground for the Japanese to virtually wipe out in a single strike. Neither can it explain why it took him another unbelievable nine hours to launch a counterattack by bombing Japanese positions on Formosa, now of course, Taiwan.

And if that's not enough to discredit him for ever, look at what happened on Luzon Island. The Japanese under General Masaharu Homma began landing their troops on 22 December. MacArthur always said he would fight them on the beaches, or words to that effect. Instead he immediately turned and ran. He ordered around 70,000 American and Filipino troops, as well as 26,000 civilians, to retreat to the Bataan Peninsula, where they were very quickly hit by lack of food, lack of medical attention and lack of practically everything and started dying from scurvy, beriberi, malaria and dysentery. In the meantime, having got his trusted aide, Colonel Sidney Huff, to do his Christmas shopping for him, our great war hero and liberator celebrated Christmas with his wife, Jean, and three-year-old son Arthur in Manila, and then, just as the Japanese were moving in, scarpered with the Filipino president, Manuel Quezon, and the few remaining members of his government across the water to the comfort of the island fortress of Corregidor.

For that he was awarded the Congressional Medal of Honor.

But the plight of the American and Filipino troops and the civilians was far from over. On 9 April they surrendered to the Japanese and were forced to make the sixty-five-mile Bataan Death March to special prisoner of war camps at the base of the peninsula. Over 500 Americans and as many as 10,000 Filipinos never made it. They died along the way.

In the general's great comeback, the battle for Manila, more people died than were killed by the atomic bomb in Hiroshima. The devastation was worse than the devastation at Warsaw. Yet nobody seems to talk about that. Maybe it's because the fighting hadn't even started when MacArthur declared the capital officially captured. 'PRIZE OF THE PACIFIC WAR. MANILA FELL TO MACARTHUR LIKE RIPENED PLUM,' proclaimed *Newsweek*, before even a shot was fired. Nobody said a word. Everybody went along with our great war hero and liberator.

Was the US grateful to the Filipinos? What do you think? On 22 June 1944, the US Congress voted in the GI Bill of Rights, which gave full benefits to everyone from no fewer than sixty-six different countries who had served in the US forces, regardless of their race, religion, colour or nationality – except for the Filipinos. They even went on to revoke the decision they had taken two years earlier to give all Filipino veterans the right to become naturalised US citizens. And so matters still stand today.

Not surprisingly, whenever I go to the Manila Hotel I am always desperate for a drink. I headed straight for the Tap Room. But while I was waiting to be served – maybe it wasn't MacArthur's fault after all. Maybe the messages really didn't get through – I picked up a newspaper and saw a big advert for some property company, which was promoting its flats. 'Family will pamper you more! Wife will care for you more! Girlfriend will love you more!' For some reason it made me think of Remedios Circle.

Now, you might find this difficult to believe, but I've been in one or two bars in my time. The filthy, downmarket ones in Moscow. The Russian bar in Lan Kwai Fong in Hong Kong called the Yelts Inn. There was no kitchen, no food, practically no staff, but, boy, was there enough to drink. Once I even spent a whole evening in the Vatican, a bar in Kildare, Ireland. And, of course, on the odd occasion, much against my will, I've been forced to go to those kind of bars where there are girls walking around stark naked for all the world as if they'd been born like it. In Malate, let me tell you, they've got the lot. And some more.

I started in the Penguin Café on Remedios Circle itself. Everybody told me that this was the place to be. Place to be or not, the Café de Paris on the Via Veneto, or even the World Famous Smith's bar at Island Harbour in Anguilla, it wasn't. After that it was Patio Guernicas, Eva's Garden, some faded old air-deco hang-out, the building round the corner with the tiled balconies, a hole in the wall that gloriously proclaimed itself 'an outrageous rip-off on food and drinks all night long', where they were running low on what they called voddies and instead were serving their own killer combination of beer and tomato juice. Then it was on to a place with a girl band called Better When Wet, which seemed to be full of preppy American MBAs (Married But Available). I asked one of them, a guy with this Thriller from Manila who looked as though she could suck a football through 50 feet of heavy-duty garden hose, what it was like. He said, 'Touch and go. Touch the glass, or anything else, come to that, and immediately go for a medical.'

Just as there was an acute risk of blood entering my alcohol stream, I stumbled into the strangest place. It was practically pitch black. It was packed. It was noisy as hell. Suddenly, I got this feeling there were lots of things flitting backwards and forwards around me which were not your usual eye candy. It was a bar, would you believe, run by midgets. I did what anyone would do in my position, never before having spent an evening with anything small and wrinkled. I pushed and shoved my way to the bar and asked them if they had any shorts.

Midgets you see all over Asia, usually sitting begging by the side of the road. In parts of India they're in great demand at weddings, where they make a great show of standing on tables by the entrance to welcome all and sundry. In more civilised parts of the world, it's supposed to be great sport to throw them off the tops of buildings. But this was the first bar I'd seen actually run by midgets. At first I thought that it was all a clever Filipino marketing dodge to make the drinks look bigger, but this wasn't the case.

Drink in hand, I retired to the edge of the scrum while some American was asking one of the guys for a drink off the top shelf. After the barman had fetched the ladder, clambered all the way up it and finally got the bottle, the wise guy American, of course, said he was only kidding, he'd take beer instead. Another bunch of Americans – the United States gave them their independence in 1946, but you'd never think it – was asking the guy behind the bar where they advertised for staff. When he said 'In the small ads,' you'd have thought one of their nuclear bombs had gone off.

All the same, it was great fun. Especially the retelling of all the old midget jokes, like the one about the wife who made her husband promise to stop chasing girls. The following week she found him in bed with a midget. 'Hey, you promised to stop chasing girls!' she yelled at him. 'Well,' he said. 'I'm cutting down, aren't I?' In fact it is now – sorry, Smithy – one of my favourite bars in the world. And when I finally left, no, I didn't ask for a miniature as a souvenir. Because I didn't have any small change.

If you feel a bar run by dwarves would be too much for you don't, whatever you do, get yourself invited for a Sunday after-

noon out with a typical Filipino family. A typical Sunday afternoon out for a typical Filipino family invariably means a visit to
the local freak show. Kids with twisted legs are billed as mermaids. Kids with an arm or a leg missing are lame ducks. Kids
with all kinds of strange skin diseases are half human, half rep-
tile. Kids with an extra limb are spider children.

Much the same goes for grown-ups. At Boom Na Boom
funfair in central Manila, I was told, Thalidomide victims are
kept naked and chained up inside cages while their so-called
keepers throw them raw meat to eat. As if that's not appalling
enough, many of them are also made to take part in various
circus acts, like knife-throwing. They're invariably on the
receiving end, of course.

If you think the organisers of such horrifying spectacles
should be thrown in jail, think again. One businessman I
met, who looked as though he had all the right connections
in all the wrong places, told me that in the Philippines life
behind bars was considerably safer, cheaper and more comfortable than life in front of them. Selected prisoners were
allowed their own colour television sets and video-recorders,
and in some cases even their own air-conditioners as well,
while the select of the select were also permitted to build not
only their own tennis courts but their own private homes
within the prison complex.

To avoid being invited to a Sunday out with a typical
Filipino family, I would normally suggest going to church
instead. But in the Philippines going to church can mean
watching any number of people walking miles on end on
their knees until they bleed, crowning themselves with thorns
and hammering nails through their hands and feet. See what
I mean about the whole place being some giant funfair or
freak show?

Have a nice weekend.

*

Suddenly, the whole stadium erupts. Everybody is on their feet, waving their hands all over the place and shouting and yelling and screaming at the tops of their voices. One man near me is hollering like a wounded rhinoceros and dangling all ten fingers in the air. Two rows down another guy is jabbing two fingers at the ring. Across the way a woman, all wrinkles and no teeth, is waving three fingers. This, believe it or not, is betting, Filipino-style. Somehow or other, from all over the stadium they are placing their bets with the *kristors*, bookies or bet-takers, as they call them, who are all packed together in a pit by the side of the ring. No money changes hands. No confirmation is given. No receipts are issued. Somehow everybody remembers everything. Everybody trusts everybody. This being the Philippines, there are also supposed to be middlemen all over the stadium checking who places bets and with whom, placing bets on behalf of people who, for one reason or another, do not want to put them on themselves and – perish the thought – making certain that losers don't disappear out of the door without paying.

How much do people bet? That depends where you're sitting. In the best seats, the first two rows around the ring, the minimum bet is 1,000 pesos, around US$15. In the next block it's 500 pesos minimum, then 400 and so on, down to 100 pesos in the gods. The guy in front of me, all Elvis Presley haircut, denim jacket, denim shorts and about the size of a tank, seemed to be betting millions with every bet-taker in sight. On the other side of the ring, I was told, was a group of local politicians and congressmen. I couldn't see them yelling and shouting and waving their hands in the air. Presumably they were using middlemen. But then, that seems to be the custom for politicians and congressmen in the Philippines.

With the betting in full flood, now comes the warm-up.

The owners gently pick up their prize birds, by the legs or around the wings. Obviously cocks repay careful handling. They then jab them again and again in front of another cock to get their juices going. Some birds are raring to go after just a couple of jabs, pecking at everything in sight. The feathers around their necks are all flared out, their feet are going nineteen to the dozen. Others take longer to get started, as if they're bored with the whole process and, cool killers that they are, just want to get the job over and done with. Once the birds are quivering, wild-eyed and spitting blood, the owners put them on the floor, with one end of a bit of string tied firmly around one of the cock's legs and the other end clamped under their own shoes. The cocks begin to eye each other. But because of the string, they're unable to do the business. Into the ring now comes the *sentenciador*, the referee, a scruffy guy in a white Pizza Hut T-shirt and jeans. The owners pick up their birds.

As the yelling and shouting and screaming gets even louder, they begin to unwind the twine that has been protecting the super-razor-sharp, three-inch spur attached to each of the cocks' legs. Wild cocks fight with their own bony back spurs. Fighting cocks, however, have them cut off and the super-razor-sharp spurs attached in their place.

As more and more of the twine is unwound, the two spurs begin to glint and flash in the spotlights.

It might look like a simple fight to the death, but there are rules, just as there are in any other sport. Like bullfighting in Oman, camel-fighting in south-west Turkey or horse-fighting on Mindaou Island, also in the Philippines.

Interfering with your opponent's cock is forbidden. Quite right, too. Apparently, some owners go to pat their opponent's cock on the head and in so doing accidentally on purpose break one of the tiny bones in its back. Others go and give it something to eat. Something poisonous, of course.

Interfering with your own cock is also forbidden. These are some of the favourite tricks.

Packing a whole load of foul-smelling gunge under its wings. Foul-smelling, that is, to other fighting cocks. Once the other birds get a whiff of the stuff, they are finished.

Gluing a tough piece of goatskin on its chest and covering it with feathers to provide added protection in any really close-in fighting.

Dabbing pesticide on its hackles. Not only does that stop the other cock from pecking, it also means that if it does, it's a goner.

In fact, so cautious are most owners that not only do they keep their cocks hidden away until the last possible moment, but they even arrange for them to be looked after by security guards.

The spur is the spur is the spur. No deadly poisons are allowed to be smeared all over it. If you see the referee wipe the spur with cotton wool and then trickle the liquid down into the cock's beak, you know he suspects something. As for the fighting, it's no holds barred – unless one of the birds, for some unexplained reason, suddenly stops fighting. The referee then counts to twenty. If the cock is still not fighting, it's back to its corner for another count of twenty for a session with its seconds. If it still hasn't got the fighting spirit, it has lost. Or unless the cock hits the canvas and, after three counts of ten and one of twenty, as opposed to five counts of ten, it's out. Or unless it simply turns and runs.

The fight begins.

The bird in the left-hand corner, under the sign saying 'Meron', the favourite, is the first to move. It struts up and down, looking out of the ring at the crowd. The other, under the sign saying 'Wala' – also-ran, underdog, loser – begins to peck at the floor. The huge stadium grows quieter and quieter. The two birds now eye each other as if they're wondering what to do. The one on the left goes back to strutting up and down and looking at the crowd. The other takes a step nearer to it. And another. And another. The strutter turns, and in a flash it is on top of the other bird. They are both rolling round and round in the ring. Squawking like mad. Feathers all over the place. The stadium erupts. Everybody is on their feet, yelling and screaming.

Now the birds separate. Both stand there staring at each other. The pecker goes to move. The strutter jumps over him. The pecker tries to move again. Again the strutter jumps over him. Then they're in a bundle, somersaulting about the ring, feathers spurting up into the air. The noise is intense. Then, suddenly, the two birds stop rolling around. The referee bends down to pick them up, one in each hand. He holds them head to head, or rather, beak to beak. They go to attack each other and he drops them back on the floor again.

The screaming gets worse. A pair of wings begins to flap. Is it the strutter or the pecker? The flapping becomes slower and slower. The strutter has made another kill. The guy with the Elvis Presley haircut looks like he's won a security vanload of money. Tiny bundles of notes are suddenly flying all over the stadium. Less the 5 to 10 per cent commissions.

The strutter could now be worth anything up to US$25,000. The pecker? He's now just Kentucky Fried Chicken. Unless, of course, somebody slipped him some fancy dewormer, in which case he's probably eaten away with cancer by now and not worth a handful of feathers.

Such is death in Manila. But not in the afternoon. This was midway through the evening. And there was another six hours of it to go.

Macão

Broken Tooth. That's what they call him. Even though he's probably got the best set of molars east of Harley Street. It was a name he got when he was a daisy, probably from some big-hearted fakeloo on secondment from what used to be the National Health Service. You know what they're like.

So there he is in this cosy little courtroom about the size of a bartop radio. Broken Tooth, the mighty Triad, boss of 14K, with over 10,000 slippery noodles under his left boot, every single one of them ready to take the long walk, just for him. And because they don't want their granny hit by a 40-ton truck while she's at home, in bed, fast asleep. Anyway, there he is, all dressed in black. Black jacket. Black trousers. Black shirt. He's so black you can't see where he ends and his shadow begins. Which is how it should be with all good bodyguards.

It's billed as the trial of the century. Flouting the gambling laws. Making a mockery of the system. Holding the judiciary up to ridicule. And just to put the judge in a good mood, old Broken Tooth has just financed a film of his own life. A rags-to-riches, kung-fu, one-man-against-the-system thriller, glorifying everything you shouldn't glorify, like carving up the place with rival Triad bosses over a couple of tarts. Egg tarts and tea. Driving boilers over the legs of innocent people. Throwing lead outside the local cop house. Blocking Macão's main bridge to film a procession of 200 cars, when filming, the film itself and everything to do with it had been banned by the authorities well before shooting began. Not to mention before filming began.

In comes the judge. He's all fire and brimstone. He's just itching to give Broken Tooth the long goodbye. But within ten minutes it's all over. Seven key witnesses – get that, seven key witnesses – suddenly developed coughs and colds. They all sent in doctors' notes with big, yellow streaks down the back of them. The look on the judge's face felt like it stuck inches out of your back.

Collapse of case.

The big razzoo, real name Wan Kuok-Koi, the most feared underworld chief in practically the whole of South-East Asia, is out of the Big House. The guy who's got more foot soldiers and more firepower under his control than any police force in the region is free as a bird. Then, it's farewell my lovely. Off in his Lambo, hitting on all eight. Away into the sunset. He has escaped once again from the jaws of justice, or rather, from the soft, flabby, pink gums of justice, to shake down a few more fairies.

The boobs who sent sicknotes, and those who didn't, were obviously relieved that after so long under the eye of Broken Tooth they could now scram out and get their soiled laundry taken care of. Not that you can blame them. I once got myself ordained, got all my ordination certificates and became a church minister just to avoid sitting on a jury. All for the price of US$10.

As for the judge, there's no way he's sending flowers and get well soon cards to the seven missing jurors. He is busy flicking through the Lisbon Yellow Pages. He's just ground what few teeth he has left to dust. He's desperate for a whole new set, this time of reinforced steel. Just as soon as he stops shaking with rage.

The moral of the story: don't play a French defence against a Steinitz. In other words, if you don't want to end up cleaning your teeth through your backside, don't mess with the Triads. Ever.

Welcome to Macāo, the one-time tiny Portuguese enclave of 450,000 people, covering just over twenty square miles at the tip of the Pearl River estuary, a quick one-hour, 65-kilometre jetfoil flip across from Hong Kong. It's where the sophistication of southern Europe meets the gentleness of Asia. Well, that's what they say. To W.H. Auden, the nance with the craggy face, it was a 'weed from Catholic Europe'. Not being another W.H. Auden – I don't have so many lines on my face, at least, not yet – all I would say is that it's the kind of place where, Catholic weed or not, you should never feel a stranger. In other words it's the most rip-roaring, free-and-easy, devil-may-care crooks' paradise on earth. Paradise, that is, for the big boys who know all the tricks. For the rest of us, it's more like hell on earth.

The oldest and the last remaining European colony in Asia – at least it was, the last time I strolled by – Macāo might look like Hong Kong's sweet-and-sour little sister, all cobblestones, pretty, pretty gardens, baroque churches, mini skyscrapers, pastel-coloured houses, cracked washbasins, mosquitos, tiled street signs, shops selling everything from unmentionable vegetables that look like dog vomit to unmentionable lumps of meat that look like dog vomit, sick jurymen and old men kicking the gong around, numb with heroin, playing mah-jong all day long. But believe me, it isn't. To put my cards on the table, which is something you should never do in Macão, the whole place runs, hops, skips and jumps on rats and mice. In other words, gambling. People gambling that they'll win a fortune at the tables. People gambling that the gold on the wedding ring will last at least until the weekend is over. People gambling that they won't catch anything celebrating afterwards.

That's as far as the punters are concerned. For the guys holding the cards, this is no down-at-heel brains emporium. They might look as though a slice of *spumoni* wouldn't melt in their mouths, but for them it's no gamble at all. They're holding a deck with all the aces, not to mention what's stashed away under the table. In fact some clever hunks with slide rules they bought with other people's winnings reckon gambling brings in between US$500 million and US$750 million a year. Which makes it bigger than Vegas, bigger than Monte Carlo, even bigger than the bingo club down the church hall on Friday nights. Sorry about that, Father Corleone.

Macão is also one huge, sweetheart safety valve for Hong Kong where, thanks to the British, all forms of gambling are banned, apart, of course, from horse racing, a few licensed mah-jong parlours, the local lottery and, of course, the biggest gamble of them all, marriage. Officially, that is. Call it a hunch, but you can bet your wife's life that everyone there is trying to grab a buck by gambling on everything, like the possibility of people betting on the fact that everyone is gambling on everything.

But, as at your bingo club down the church hall, there's nothing clean about gambling in Macão. Here cut-throat competition is just that: cut-throat. Pick up a throwaway US$100 chip. Underneath it, it's the Alamo, Chicago in the 1930s and Las Vegas all rolled into one. This is not just Triad territory, this is Triad versus Triad versus Triad versus the police versus whatever moves, shoot first, ask questions later, in any case half the jury won't bother to turn up anyway territory.

First – backs to the wall, eyes on the door – there's the home team. Broken Tooth, who many people say virtually runs Macão and, more likely than not, the whole of southern China, with the assistance, helpful and otherwise, of the bosses of other rival Sunday school classes like Seui Fong, Gasosa, Big Circle and Bli Nkayu Adedman.

Then there are his Hong Kong buddies from across the water, such as Sun Yee On, Wo Shing So and Soi Fung, who are all behind the eight ball with problems brought on by Chris Patten's weepy holiday in the area and are looking for richer pastures.

Next come the Taiwanese Triads, who, having been shown the door· by increasingly tough police operations, are also looking for a new place to call home.

Finally, there's all the bindle punk from mainland China, from Guangdon Province, desperate for a place in the big, wide, outside world. They are said to be under the notorious leadership of someone called Shu Ting Yu, although I may have been misinformed. I shared a bottle of Igloo Industrial Drinking Water with some pikers, all designer jackets and bulges under their shoulders, one evening in an upmarket opium den near the ferry full of society-page has-beens – well, what would you have done? Gone for the PP Drop Quality Water? They were bumping their gums and banging on about even the Chinese Ministry of State Security itching to ice the champagne and give the *foie gras* a hammering. What's more, they said, the ministry already owned one hotel-casino. How did they know?. The day it opened, they said, the Chinese received a welcome-to-Macão-present bomb in the lobby. Not that that would be likely to make them turn yellow. And what is more often than not found lying alongside the body of the latest murder, or chopping, as they call them? A traditional Chinese magnetic health pillow? No way. A Chinese People's Liberation Army pistol, that's what. Not that I'm saying a word, mind you. I'm not carrying the ball for anyone.

As a result, with something like 10,000 to 12,000 Triad members around town, compared to, say, 4,000 to 5,000 cops, bent or otherwise, there's no such thing as a quiet game of mah-jong, a quick flick of the cards or a discreet stroll down to the nearest police station to contribute to their widows' and orphans' fund. The day of the traditional chopper, or butcher's knife, is over. Instead, progress being progress the world over, and this being the Portuguese storm before the Chinese lull, they cop the full libretto. Cars set on fire. Cars set on fire outside the police headquarters. Firebombs. Beatings. Beatings with iron bars. Motorcycle shootings. Machine-gun attacks. People's arms chopped off. Dismembered bodies in dustbins. Everything from live snakes delivered by post with their tails sliced in two, the traditional Triad *arrivederci*, to the worst, most agonising death of all, a glass of Mateus Rosé. And if that's not enough to make you throw up, they're quite prepared to go the final mile and throw in half a glass of *aguardente* brandy as well. In short, wherever you go, it's the end of the pier and a wooden kimono for somebody.

Pop into the Caravela Coffee Bar near the promenade for a quick pancake 'stuffed with mouse chocolate', as I did one morning, and some gun punk is likely to put his head round the door, or through the high window, and have one of your fellow customers frothing at the mouth. But not with the *cappuccino*.

Stagger through town after lunch of giggle juice, trying to forget you've actually eaten pickled pig's-lip soup, complete with pickled pig's lips – Macão is also famous for its East-meets-West cuisine – and you're likely to see one of the police chiefs, or maybe even one of the top officials in the Gambling

Inspection and Co-ordinating Directorate, being blown away by a dropper in a black mask by the side of the road.

Drop your nickel by the governor's mansion while trying to digest your lump of beef with a fried egg on top, and the chances are you'll see three Triad chiefs being pumped full of daylight in a car parked outside.

One evening, try the shark-fin soup in Mou Wei's restaurant, where they don't dare to serve oysters unless there's a pearl in them. Before you can even think of crying, 'Waiter! There's some shrapnel in my soup!', as likely as not a chopper squad will burst in, put the din into your dinner and juice you in the wrong part of town so you'll never have to worry about asking for Tabasco ever again.

Go for a stroll on Bamboo Bay. Ignore the looker in the lake and, just past the seafront villas, pause for a moment too long by the tennis court, and it's all England to a china orange you'll be overrun by squads of armed ginks in black balaclava helmets who look as though they might be on the way to sing 'Mother Macree' at a local old people's home. Not so. They'll probably be throwing lead not only at a top-secret Triad command centre controlling smuggling operations throughout the whole of the South China Sea, but also at a huge warehouse hidden away underneath it which contains millions upon millions of contraband cigarettes, not to mention thousands upon thousands of chick flicks.

For at stake is not just the gambling which makes up more than 40 per cent of all government revenues, but all the extra doodly-squat as well, such as prostitution, smuggling, loan-sharking and extortion, not to mention the pawn shops which opened in 1860 along with the first casino and haven't closed since. The environment, which is definitely not lead-free, is so bad that they say it takes twenty-nine people to change a lightbulb. In Hong Kong this is one to guard it and twenty-eight to fly to Beijing to ask permission to change it. In

Macão, one man just does it. He knows exactly what to do, and gets on with it. It takes the other twenty-eight people to check with all the Triad gangs.

One of the seven hills surrounding the city boasts, as a tribute to the power and influence and prestige of the Triads, one of the finest Christian churches in the whole of Asia, the cathedral dedicated to St Paul who, you will recall, perhaps because he always saw everything through a glass darkly, preferred drinking out of the same bottle with the likes of the Triads rather than chinning it with us poor, honest, upstanding members of the community. In this case there's not even a wall to let him down. It all burned down in 1835. Some say it's because they didn't pay the, how do you say, boomshakalaka. And, no matter how good your contacts, I Corinthians 13 notwithstanding, if you don't pay your, er, boomshakalaka, you get hit like the rest of them, whoever you are. Which seems a bit unfair because from the moment the Portuguese, at the time the world's number one colonial power, landed in 1557, a full 200 years before the Brits made it to Hong Kong, they've worked hard to play woolly bear with the guys running the show. They also worked with the Chinese. As a result they know far more about China, which is just 300 yards away across a tiny strip of water, and the way they play solitaire than the Brits ever learned in Hong Kong hanging around the Captain's Bar in the Mandarin Oriental, tipping it at Grassini's in the Hyatt, not to mention the pool at the Shangri-La, which must be the biggest family-run hotel in the world because, as I recall, when I stayed there once, all the girls were wearing badges with the same name, Trai Nee, on them.

Come the end of the Second World War, however, and the Portuguese really began to capitalise on all their old contacts and the specialist skills they had developed over the years. The trouble was, their old contacts were shacked up in the jungle in various parts of South America and their specialist skills were melting down gold bars with or without Nazi Reichsbank stamps all over them. But before long, heavy wooden boxes were being delivered to Gate 16 in Macão's outer harbour, all heavily secured with dental floss and reeking of suntan oil. After that it was duck soup.

The boxes would regularly be trundled across the main drag by a bunch of goons who were obviously not in the carriage trade to a dirty, rundown building with a steel grille in front of it the size of the letterbox at St Quentin. The steel grille would be lifted and the boxes would disappear inside, never to be seen again.

The West very quickly caught on to what was going on, and after about ten years sent somebody from Naval Intelligence to wash the windows; somebody with an even greater literary reputation than St Paul. He was the creator of probably the cruellest, cunning, most sadistic sleuth of all time, Miss Marple. Or, at least, I think it was Miss Marple. Anyway, he was some smoothy boozehound with a bow tie like a sick chicken called Ian Fleming. He arrives on the scene, no doubt fresh from Firefly Hill in Jamaica, where he had been spending another love-in with 'dear Noël and the girls', ready to give them the third.

For all his abilities, he didn't solve the mystery. At least, not the mystery of the gold bars. Maybe somebody put a lean on him. It didn't take him long, however, to discover the secrets of the nine-storey Central Hotel round the corner on the Street of Eternal Happiness. Or so I was told. The higher up you went, the better the bars, the gambling and the, er, raw meat, until you reached the ninth-floor nirvana, where all you had to do was knock twice, ask for, would you believe, Garbo, and tell her the captain sent you. After that the last thing on your mind was how the hell Chairman Mao managed to survive the US-led Cold War trade embargo, let alone finance his Cultural Revolution.

~ But fair's fair. Our great jingle-brain from Naval Intelligence didn't fall asleep on the job. Somehow or other he came up with the bright idea of somebody cornering the gold market and painting what's-her-name all over in yellow paint. The rest, as they say, is histrionics.

In 1962 this guy Stanley Ho Hung-Sun, a non-gambler, breezes into town. He goes around, shakes a few hands, hey, bos everyone in sight, hands out a few cigars, and before you know it, it's eggs in the coffee. He's persuaded the government to give him the gambling monopoly for the entire island until the year 2001. The price? A big kiss and a smile. After which he changed his name to Stanley Ho-Ho-Ho.

Today he's turning over think of a number and double it. He's the biggest honcho in Macāo, with well over 10,000 staff. He runs practically every casino there, plus a string of hotels and goodness knows how many offices, shops and other properties. So much so, he's now called Stanley Ho-Ho-Ho-Ho-Ho.

The Portuguese, however, even then, had had it up to here. They wanted to take a powder, cash in their chips, pack their bags and blow. They kept trying to hand the place back to the Chinese, but for some reason the Chinese didn't want it. One guy I met outside Wanco Shops – he was a genuine Macanese: half Portuguese, half Chinese and half everything else under the sun – told me that even the Red Guards wouldn't take it back.

Portugal at the time had the shakes. It was going through its own revolution-cum-civil war-cum-let's ditch Salazar and get at the drinks. They sent a bunch of high-ups to put the bite on Macāo. They got a trip for biscuits. The teenage Red Guards didn't know the difference between a *Little Red Book* and a cow's caboose. They couldn't believe there was a place called Portugal, that they ran another place called Macāo, or that they wanted to dust out and be shot of the whole damn thing.

Talk to the 100 per cent Chinese, however, and they will say that the Red Guards were not just doing their *qiqong*. They knew exactly what was what. Even they were aware that Macão was a useful back door for all kinds of tricks. Yet again Occidentals try cause trouble between Orientals. Once more and I kill you.

Either way, there was always much more of a buddy-buddy, *guanxi*, pitching woo relationship between Macão and China than there ever was between Hong Kong and China, especially during the days of Chris Patten, or Fat Pang, who went out of his way to make certain the Chinese recognised the fact that Hong Kong was British and would remain British until the stroke of midnight on whatever day it was that Jonathan Dimbleby was scheduled to publish his objective hagiography. Only then would the Union Jack be lowered, hankies raised and the place handed back to China. The Portuguese, on the other hand, were more than happy for China to look upon Macão as chicken chow mein under Portuguese administration. For them, for example, it was no big deal to allow the Chinese living in Zhuhai, the sprawling, faceless boom town just over the border, to wander across every day to work in their textile factories as well as to roll the dice, deal the cards, pay off the police and provide any other services they cared to provide. They were also happy to ban books, plays or whatever if they thought for a moment they might upset their masters in the slightest. And, of course, unlike the Brits, who always kept their gundogs in Hong Kong, there were no Portuguese troops in Macão rushing to repaint their barracks to leave everything spick and span as the Prince of Wales's own did when they left Hong Kong.

As for democracy, it was better than a kick in the kidneys. They had no hang-ups about it one way or the other, probably because they had only recently developed a taste for it themselves.

In fact, so casual were the Portuguese about Macão that the last time I was there it was already the big sleep. If you didn't know it you'd never guess it hadn't already been handed back, largely because, I admit, the population had never been more than 3 per cent Portuguese. And most of what Portuguese there had been had already fled to the old country, where they knew they'd be loved, honoured and appreciated. Like Guinea Bassau. Or Cape Verde. Or São Tomé. Or even Brazil, which for generations kept Macão supplied with the only tender meat it ever received. Come to think of it, I swear that each time I went there there were more Chinese around getting washed and fed than ever before.

They were with the law boys, jamming the roscoe in their button and busy redrafting standing orders – 'In future in all official announcements, comments and otherwise the Chinese mainland will be referred to as the Chinese mainland and not mainland China' – and checking to see how the new school history books would objectively handle such sensitive issues as the Opium Wars, not to mention Mao Zedong, the 1949 revolution, the flight of Chiang Kai-shek and the founding of Taiwan.

Would-be ministers were no doubt beginning to grapple with the harsh realities of power, discovering that a quick buck is not always something you eat and instituting ways of putting their hands in the till without being dropped, unlike one previous Portuguese administration, which was forced to resign for taking backhanders on the construction contract for the new airport. Because it was discovered they were not taking enough.

As for the town itself, in the old days the Largo do Senado, the main square, with its black and white mosaics flowing in waves like they do on the Tagus embankment in Lisbon, its big, imposing government offices and all its pastel-coloured buildings, always had a distinctly Mediterranean feel about it. Like a plate of *pasteis de bacalhau*, a traditional Portuguese mish-mash of salt cod. Now it had a slight whiff of the South China Seas.

Gone were the traditional Portuguese singers who had always been there in their Sunday-best black suits, big black hats and cheaters. Instead there seemed to be nothing but Chinese flatties. Even in the grand old church of São Domingos at the far end they were always lounging in the back pews, chatting away to each other. And instead of your usual church music, military music was coming over the loud-speakers. Which may or may not have been significant.

It was the same wherever I went. From a building company called, with refreshing honesty, Iam Wong, to a firm of solic-itors, Kokit Tup, whose secretary, as innocent as an English muffin, was, I swear, named Dysentery, the Chinese seemed to be all over the place.

I wandered up to St Augustine's, which has already burned down and been rebuilt three times – I'm not saying a word. I reckon it should really be called St Sebastian's. It's the only church in which I can remember seeing such a louche statue of the saintly limp-wrist, impeccably groomed, leaning oh so casually against the stump of a tree, the odd arrow sticking out of him, obviously causing him the most exquisite pain. Standing staring at him was a tall, thin, Chinese hop-head with a long, thin pair of scissors, oh so carefully snipping the hairs deep inside his nose.

As for the Chinese temples in town, they obviously knew better than to stop their payments. They were positively blooming.

At the old fortress built by the Jesuits – to keep out not the Chinese, but their fellow Europeans, especially the Dutch, which they did with a single hit on their ammunition dump on 24 June 1622, a day still celebrated in Macão today –

there were even more Chinese. In baggy pants. In Oxfam rejects. In razor-sharp suits. All with cameras. All bowing and smiling to each other. All typical tourists, not understanding for a moment what they were looking at.

Even at Gate 16 at the harbour was a group of Chinese chuckling, I swear, over the way they had completely out-foxed the great spy expert. Across the road, the building where the gold was taken and melted down for shipping across the 300 yards of water to China, is now a bank, modern, faceless, all plate glass and chrome and full of old ladies who looked as though they were living off the money they earned all those years ago on the ninth floor of the Central Hotel.

The back streets and alleyways, crowded with tiny shops with such delightful names as Steals Direct Computer Superstores, CXC Software Engineering Company and Tack Kee Plastic Watch Co., were as chock-a-block with Chinese as ever, if not more so. My favourite shop of all time has to be the gloriously named leather goods shop Gofuku. With a name like that, I can only assume their advertising agents must have been Saa Tchi and Saa Tchi. I also spotted Hydro The rapist, which may or may not have been a kuok-up. Like the sign I saw driving around Hong Kong one night years ago. I went down this mean street and came across a flop-house called the Vermin Beach Hotel. In daylight, of course, or with all its lights working, it was really the Silvermine Beach Hotel.

The Chinese influx could be seen in the restaurants too. The Macanese used to go on about their cooking being 'the most refined, the most voluptuous and succulent cuisine in the world, thanks to the spices from the Orient, the tangy bits from Brazil and the art of using sugar from the sweet-toothed countries Turkey, India and the Moors of North Africa'. Not any longer. With the Chinese moving in, I found the most popular traditional dish wherever I went was 'choice of bugger with cheese'. Although one evening I did splash out. I spent two hours sipping a glass of La Vile Puripied Drinking Water from Vietnam, chewing what I was told were codfish balls and wrestling with something called African chicken, although mine looked more like African canary. Judging by the price, however, it must have been African golden eagle.

At the Hyatt Regency, seeing as they were coming over a bit heavy – a notice in my hotel room read, 'Please note that letting fireworks off in hotel guest rooms is strictly prohibited' – I thought I'd forgo the Big Boy nuts and Pokey biscuits and go straight for the tarts instead. First the Chinese ones, then the Portuguese. The Chinese ones, I was told, were plain and simple. And, of course, cheap. You could pick them up on any corner at more or less any time of the day or night. If it's the uppercrust ones you're after, they are only to be found in the oddly named Lord Stow's Bakery, a tiny family-run hideaway off the main drag on Colôane Island. The Portuguese ones, however, are the class act. Bigger, sweeter, creamier. More nobbly. And, of course, they cost more bucks. You can pick them up in most hotel lobbies. Being a man of somewhat discriminating tastes I didn't fancy either, flaky egg tarts not being my particular hammer.

I decided instead that if I was going to gamble I might as well gamble. The problem was there were too many things on offer. Kite-flying? Horse racing? Dog racing? Macão has one of the biggest dog tracks in the world. It's also the only place in Asia, well, the only legitimate place, where you can go bullfighting Portuguese-style. They don't kill the bull as they do in Spain. They just stick darts in its back. The Chinese, however, don't like it. It's not violent enough.

I opted for the casino. Now, I'm not saying that the Lisboa, the number one hotel in town, is big, but by the time you've checked in and negotiated the lobby – which, no matter what time of day or night it is, always seems to be full of twists with charming names such as Pubic Ha, Chi Kee, Chuan Kee and Scru Ying Yu, wearing a smile and very little else – you already owe them for a week's rent.

As I was handing over my life's savings this Jasper comes up to me. He looks like he's eager to horizontalise anything in sight, including his little sister. He says they call him Woo Ping. 'You want virgin? I get you virgin.'

'How do you know they're virgins?' I wonder.

'I know,' he snarls, in his best man-of-affairs drawl, 'I've tried them all myself.'

Downstairs the casino is full of crap tables. It's got some pretty lousy chairs as well. It's about the size of an aircraft hangar and crammed with every slot machine ever created. Everything is on offer. European phooey like baccarat, blackjack, roulette. Chinese things such as fan-tan, some ancient Chinese game, which involves spilling buttons out of a silver cup, whose rules are known only to the winner; dai-siu, some ancient Chinese game, which involves spilling dice out of a silver cup, whose rules are known only to the loser, and the biggest gamble of all: being selected to serve on a jury charged with deciding whether some big Triad guy is innocent or very innocent.

But this was no Bel-Air high-roller territory. This was lower-middle-class cheapy coffee-and-doughnut territory. Small-time Chinese jocks, bored Hong Kong housewives clutching a nickel's worth of nothing. Package tourists from Taiwan wearing T-shirts celebrating 'Winnie the Poon'. Even the women croupiers were all doing their thing in thick, woolly cardigans. At least, I think they were. The blue fug was so dense it looked as if they were burning a stack of old car tyres by the pool of blood by the blackjack table. It was enough to make anyone want to get out their han kee and weep.

Upstairs in the special VIP rooms – minimum bet around US$125 – it was different. It was like being in a room in which someone had just died. Everybody was working out how much money they had coming to them. Everything was on tap. The punters were more upmarket, although they weren't displaying any of the obvious signs of wealth you'd see in, say, a McDonald's in Glasgow or even Manchester. These were your medium- and big-time honchos, I mean government palookas, from all over: Hong Kong, China, Taiwan and, of course, Macão itself. Apart from a couple of tuxedos knocking back the vintage Cognac and Coke, whose testosterone patches seemed to be on overcharge, none of them looked like they would be smothering their wives with diamonds. They'd find a cheaper way of doing it instead.

One guy, however, a Chinese chemist called, would you believe, Au Choo, who was busy chewing on a stray blonde just about still in her best threads, kept telling me he was 'red, raw nappy'. Whether he'd found the way to do it, he wouldn't tell me.

The only real red, raw nappy emotion I saw was some fink in a sweater, dirty jeans and a long, greasy pigtail who was marching up and down, a plastic bag in one hand, hitting himself red raw on the forehead with the other. From what I could gather, he had every reason to be worried. Not only had he screwed up big time and lost a packet, he'd also lost the money some friendly guys in Chicago overcoats had generously loaned him at some astronomical interest rate that was soaring higher and higher by the second. Which, if you know Macão like I know Macão, meant it wouldn't be long before someone put the finger on him and he was getting not a baby chick, but a snake with its tail sliced in two, and being told to bring his own relish.

The only place, however, I didn't see any Chinese was in a one-time private mansion, language school, secondary school and refugee camp on the slopes of Penha Hill. The beautiful white and ochre Hotel Bella Vista, with its views of Praia Grande Bay and the Macão –Taiya Bridge and a fireplace in every room, is to Macão what Raffles is to Singapore. All pigskin suitcases, oyster-white raincoats and 'Get me my broker. I just want to check my internet stocks again before I blow my brains out.'

Some creepy French philosopher who obviously talked a good game, Bernard Henri-Lévy, once called the Bella Vista 'a magical place, a mythological place'. But I am sure that was because of the speed with which they made your money disappear once you set foot inside it. In any case, those days are long gone. Now it's being converted into the new Portuguese Embassy for Macão. At least, that's what they say, but I don't believe it. There's no way they need anywhere that size, that lush, that lavish. Just filling it up with second-rate civil servants would indicate that the Portuguese were going to involve themselves far more in Macão affairs after they've left than they ever did when they were running the place. For my money, it's one big cover. Once they've finished it, I reckon they'll sell it to the government of Macão. In other words, to Broken Tooth. Just so that they'll get something back for all the time and money they spent on it.

But whatever you do, don't tell him I said so, otherwise I shall be in for the big one.

Kiev

Psst. Fancy a bit of harmful fun? A spot of S and M? Or, perhaps to whip up your enthusiasm, you'd prefer more of the M to the S? If so, forget all your ropes and rods and belts with nails inside them, all the leather gear, not to mention that weekend you were promising yourself with the in-laws. I won't go into any more detail in case you're of a nervous disposition, but just make for the Ukraine, the biggest country in Europe. I promise you, not only will you have a spanking good time, but you'll also be able to wear your welts with pride. It's also a damn sight cheaper than the rates you are probably currently paying, judging by the small ads I occasionally stumble across in what I am told is the S and M fraternity's own weekly journal, *The Times Literary Supplement*. In fact, I don't know anywhere else in the world which seems to glory so much not just in discomfort but in degradation and personal suffering as well. They seem to positively relish every single second of it.

I'm not exactly an expert on all aspects of aversion therapy – as far as I'm concerned, the only thing that beats a healthy dose of self-flagellation, is, for example, somebody else doing it for you – so this is going to hurt me more than it hurts you, I'm pleased to say, but the whole place is like one huge masochists' theme park. Crucifixions a speciality.

Go there as an ordinary, boring, well-adjusted, middle-aged businessman, and I can guarantee that you'll come back knowing more about bonds and bonding than you ever imagined, even if you're an accountant. If you don't, you can beat me black and blue all over. Twice. Slowly.

If you want to completely surrender your will, to be insulted, injured, treated with contempt, trodden into the dirt, mercilessly abused, beaten, lashed into submission and walked all over or, as Freud, perhaps more professionally, put it, 'bound, painfully beaten, whipped, in some way maltreated, forced into unconditional obedience, dirtied and debased', believe me, there is nothing better on earth than getting out the uniform, whip, handcuffs, thumbscrews and leg irons, and, of course, the high heels, and spending a few days holed up in a Ukrainian hotel with a bunch of other victims going for the burn. With or without the sticky toffee pavlova. Any Ukrainian hotel. In fact they are not hotels. They are domination centres. Instead of stars they should be rated using whips, or maybe rubber boots. For pain. For humiliation. For submission. For domination. For absolute unwavering obedience. And that's before you even check in.

A typical Ukrainian hotel looks more like a rest centre for the homeless. There are beggars scouring around outside. There is a mass of young and not-so-young ladies from the service sector blocking the doors. The windows are smeared in grease. At least, I think it's grease. There's no hot water, no heating, practically no food. The warders, sorry, I mean staff, all look like camp guards just back from the gulags who, like all good masochists, are now having the time of their lives. Most of them are about 10 feet tall and 30 stone, appear to have been halfway through a series of sex-change operations when they ran out of money, and are built like Ukrainian diesel-driven T80 UD battle tanks. And that's just the women.

And service? There's definitely no service. The cost? Two hundred and fifty US dollars a night. In cash, no credit cards. Bring your own sleeping bag, insect repellent and US$10 to get your passport back from reception, US$20 if you don't want it all covered in greasy fingermarks and . . . my God, I hope that's not what I think it is. And don't forget, ask for a receipt for your passport as well as for the US$10 or $20. You'll marvel at how long it takes for the bruises to heal.

I've lost count of the number of hotels I've stayed in which are hailed in the leaflets and brochures, and pictured in photographs, as glorious examples of Ukrainian architecture and wonderful, unparalleled havens of peace and quiet with huge baths, huge beds and furniture covered in expensive fur. Ukrainian architecture? They're more like glorious examples of Ukrainian architorture.

When you check in – now this may hurt a little: if it does, good – you find they're not only unbelievably expensive, even compared to the likes of Le Crillon in Paris, they're also jaw-droppingly awful. There's no bath. The washbasin has two taps: blue for cold, red for very cold. The bed is practically on the floor. And the fur is not only on the furniture, it's on the walls, the ceiling, the pipes, the door handles and everything else. Which is great for the wildlife, I suppose. There's no soap-on-a-rope, or even just a rope. Instead there's a cat-o'-nine-tails. No, no. I'm joking. There's a red-hot razor-sharp cat-o'-eighteen-tails.

Underneath the bars of the window will be a rough wooden box which passes for a table. On it will be the final humiliation: a set of vouchers to eat in the hotel restaurant which, I always reckon, is pushing it a bit. After all, you don't mind being a masochist as long as you don't have to suffer for it. As for the telephone, it's so expensive you can't afford to look at it, let alone call for help.

What do you do? In desperation you grope your way down the long, dank, dark corridor. Lights? In a Ukrainian hotel? Are you kidding? You complain to the retired KGB torturer-in-chief stationed on the landing outside the lift, which doesn't work, no doubt because she's got all her microphones and tickertape still connected up to Moscow and is siphoning off what little electric supply there is.

A word of advice. Whatever you do, don't mention anything about spiders under the bed. Unless, of course, you really want to turn professional as a masochist. All she will do is either sell you a bottle of vodka that's already been opened and half drunk, or offer to call her friend. Don't ask me why, but I always go for the vodka. Many's the time, however, that she won't even have any vodka. Then there's no alternative but the hotel bar, which, I must tell you, is not the usual hotel bar. If you go in there and order a drink you could still be waiting for it when hell freezes over. Instead, if you want to make it hard on yourself, do what I do. Try the unofficial hotel bar, which is invariably a bedroom turned into a bar by a group of very service-oriented, Freud-fixated young ladies, obviously embarrassed by the lack of facilities provided by the hotel. I've always found them, whichever hotel I'm staying in, to be very nice, very pleasant and very accommodating. The range they have on offer might not be very extensive, but you never have to ask twice for anything. And they never, ever rub you up the wrong way.

If any country's hotels deserve the Lubianka Award for Excellence Beyond and Below the Call of Duty, the Ukraine's do. The capital, Kiev, for example, doesn't have one home-grown five-, let alone four-star, I mean four-whip, hotel, never mind a Hilton, a Sheraton or an Inter-Continental. Which must be some kind of record. The hotels they do have are clearly geared to making their guests, or rather victims, as happy as a Slav. Either they appear to have been built with the bricks left over from throwing up a gents' toilet or they look like a super-modern airport designed by an Afghan tank commander. With one eye.

Take the Hotel Moskva – please. It's in an ideal position, on the hillside looking down on Khreshchatyk Boulevard, the main street running through the centre of town. On the other side is Independence Square. Outside it is like a budget version of a Stalinist monstrosity, with all kinds of big, imposing fiddly bits. Inside, well it's no San Fran soda parlour, I can tell you, although it does boast a better class of cockroach than any other hotel in town. And every one of them, I'm pleased to say, is an omnisexual sadist.

The Hotel Khreshchatyk is no better. It's dark. It's miserable. And I hate to think what's behind all those curtains. The restaurant, however, is unique. You can't tell where the table ends and the food begins. Talk about pain being pleasurable.

The Hotel Dnipro is even worse. Not only do the telephones never work, but the bar doesn't work, either. Or not the way it should. Every time I go there the blowsy old woman behind the bar always gives me a far, far bigger measure than I ordered. But she has this fetish. She then grabs the glass and promptly pours half of it back into the bottle again. If she's doing it, you can bet your life – excuse me while I throw up – that every other barmaid in the country is doing it as well. It's no wonder they have outbreaks of cholera all over the place. Stick to the Belorussian tractor diesel. It's safest.

The Hotel Lebid on Victory Square is where the swingers are supposed to go to celebrate the victory of capitalism over Communism. All I can say is, if they think the Hotel Lebid is living it up, there must be a secret floor in there somewhere.

Otherwise it's more bondage-a-go-go than anything else. The bars, especially the one on the ground floor, always smell of disinfectant. All they ever have to eat is cake, which, not surprisingly, always tastes of disinfectant. The other thing is the lifts. They do work: it's just that the buttons don't. Whichever button you press, you always seem to end up on a different floor from the one indicated by the number on the button. Maybe it's all the endorphins in the atmosphere. Or maybe its because of that secret floor.

The National Hotel, for all its so-called reputation in the old days as a home from home for top-ranking Communist Party officials, is just another three-star Intourist hotel. The food shop on the ground floor, however, is not bad. I always go straight there after a meal in the hotel restaurant. It's not that the food there is that bad. It's just that it looks as though it was used for something else before it was slopped on to the plate.

The Salyut Hotel is literally out of this world. It's shaped like the Sputnik, and like the Sputnik, it is forty years out of date. Inside, however, it boasts all the smooth efficiency of a Mir spacecraft. In the restaurant it's touch and go whether it's quicker to order a meal or wait for the American rescue mission to arrive.

As for the Hotel Myr, don't be misled by the dilapidated-looking interior, the men in raincoats or by all the dumpy women hanging around. Just look at all the Porsches outside. For this, believe it or not, is where the real action is. There are also plenty of other sporty models in the Flamingo Club next door, who always seem to be slipping out to the car park for something or the other. My guess is it's for the other. But if you do decide to go there, don't make any Godfather jokes, let alone mention the Sointsevskyas or Podolskayas in Moscow. If you do, you could find that instead of choking on your own vomit you'll choke to death on somebody else's. You have been warned.

Are the Ukrainians worried about the state of their hotels and the fact that cities like Tirana, the capital of Albania, has a brand-new, sparkling hotel and they don't? No more than any dominatrix worries about any of her clients' capacity for suffering. When the mayor of Kiev was asked if he thought the state of the hotels would stop people coming to the Ukraine, he shrugged his shoulders. 'We may not have hotels, but when they see our women they'll come,' he grunted. The fact that the City Council owns practically all the hotels, and somebody, somewhere is no doubt taking a hefty slice of the action is, of course, quite incidental.

It's the same with the restaurants. Any restaurant. Wherever you go will be paradise. For the cockroaches. They all have the same awful food, the same service with a snarl, the same loud music to drown the howls of pain as people trying desperately to eat with their eyes closed keep missing the plate and jamming their fork into the hands of the people sitting opposite them.

Like all true masochists, the Ukrainians have mastered the art of doing disgusting things with food. There's so much of it to make you suffer I don't know where to begin, and I don't just mean the whipped cream. With the *salad delikatsy*, which is more katsy than salad? With the gherkins that buckle the fork as you chase them round the cracks in the plate and are so crunchy you can't hear the shrieks of some poor slave screaming out to his dominatrix, 'Kalinka! Kalinka!' for the fiftieth time? With their very best Kabernet, guaranteed to take the enamel off your teeth? With the eggs, which are practically white, including the yolks? With the sour cream, which can be virtually anything you like: thick or thin, white or yellow, tasteless or quick, call the fire brigade?

Wait a minute. I know where to begin. With the *salo*. The French have champagne and *foie gras*. The Russians have caviar. The Americans have eggplant mousse with tapenade croutons and cabbage rolls stuffed with lobster and garnished with fried zucchini flowers. Very simple people, the Americans. The very pinnacle of Ukrainian cuisine is *salo*. Pig fat. Yes, pig fat. Great, thick, greasy, fatty globs of creamy-white pig fat. They go into raptures over it. They're so much in love with the damned stuff that they even write poems about it. Whether it's best all wobbly or as hard as a brick. Whether it should taste of nothing but fat, or whether it should be salty. Whether it's tastiest on its own or with onions and cucumbers and a lump of thick, black bread or with bits of garlic or bacon mixed in with it. I even met a bunch of miners from Donetsk, the heart of the huge, sprawling, grime-encrusted Donbas industrial region, who reckoned it was best after it had been wrapped up in a newspaper all day. Which newspaper they wouldn't tell me, although my guess is it would have been *Pravda*. Because there's not much else in *Pravda* to get your teeth into.

So convinced are the Ukrainians of the nutritional value of these solid lumps of cholesterol that they don't just shovel them down their own throats as often as they can, they even went around handing out great mountains of the stuff to the victims of the Chernobyl disaster, to help reduce the effects of radiation.

I once went into one restaurant where they not only had *salo* on the menu but chewing gum as well. When I asked for it, however – Well, I had to, didn't I? – this great, fat, greasy waiter with a ring the size of Piccadilly Circus through his nose and a funny blond wig told me in no uncertain terms that all I could have was cold appetiser. 'Cold appetiser. You have cold appetiser. Yes?'

'Yes,' I obeyed instantly.

Some Ukrainians who came in after me were then given the works: soup, chicken, some kind of dessert, coffee. But did I complain? Did I ask to be lashed and thrown into a bowl of boiling *salo*? I didn't say a word. Because every time the waiter bent over to serve them, the blond dye from his wig splashed on to the food. The Ukrainians didn't complain, either. They just lapped it up. It probably added some flavour to their food. But then, who can blame them? In the old days the restaurant wouldn't even have been open. They all closed at lunchtime and dinnertime, so that the staff could get something to eat.

The other thing that amazes me about Ukrainian restaurants is that whenever they slop a plate of hot, or more often than not cold, what-the-hell-is-that? in front of you, not only does it have a broken leg, but its wings are tied behind its back as well. Obviously a case of old habits dying hard.

The only time I have ever seen any decent food in the Ukraine was one evening when I arrived back at my hotel exhausted after a long day waiting for a piece of paper to be stamped. I staggered up to the restaurant, which was about to close. There, inside, was a table with a whipping great pile of the most fantastic selection of meats and fish and cheese you could imagine. All with their legs broken, including the cheese. Sitting around it were all the restaurant staff. 'Yesterday's food,' snapped the manager and, in true Ukrainian tradition, slammed the door in my face.

As for service, I've tried all the usual tricks to try to get served, such as telling them, when they ask you where you want to sit, 'By the waiter.' But none of them have worked. All hotel and restaurant staff are either skilled at giving the impression that the last thing they want is to be considered a pleasant, friendly, everyday human being or else they genuinely don't want to be considered a pleasant, friendly, everyday human being. I once waited so long for my lump of pig fat in the Hotel Ukraina while the one and only grease-cake of a waitress concentrated on cutting up a pile of paper napkins into eight tiny pieces that to pass the time I went out to the world's biggest off-licence, installed outside in reception, bought a bottle of vodka, brought it back to the table and had drunk practically half before my *salo* finally arrived. As for the slimy meat, greasy cheese and funny-looking blackcurrant thing I ordered to follow, I'm still waiting for them.

As well as being undoubtedly the first nation in the world to put the glob into global food, the Ukrainians have brought a whole new meaning to the phrase 'meals available around the clock'. In the Ukraine this means that if you order a lump of pig fat at any time of the day or night, you can expect to get it sometime within the next twelve hours. Complete with broken leg. The laugh is that these were the very same guys who invented fast food by storming into all the cafés in Paris in whatever war it was and shouting, 'Bistro! Bistro!' – Fast! Fast! – at all the poor *garçons*.

Even the secretary-general of the European Bank of Reconstruction and Development, Antonio Maria Costa, the man who handed over no less than US$600 million in loans to the Ukraine, was once bounced out of a big hotel in Kiev, not just because he was talking business over breakfast – 'If you want to talk business, you must go to the business centre,' snapped the waitress – but because he wanted to pay the bill, US$48, with his credit card. 'We don't take credit cards,' Miss Ukraine Service 1502 snarled at him. 'Don't you have cash?'

A fellow poor, overworked, underpaid businessman told me that he had once called the National Hotel from the States. The guy he wanted wasn't in his room. He was probably out desperately searching for something decent to eat and drink. So the businessman asked if he could leave a message in English. The switchboard operator, he said, hissed at him, 'If you want to leave a message in English, call a hotel in England,' and put the phone down on him. It took him three days to get through again. By which time, of course, the guy he was after had either starved to death or moved on.

In the end, I'm ashamed to say, the pain was too much for me. I just gave up and stuck to the breakfasts, which were always far more reliable. Cold slices of cardboard. Cold slices of chipboard. Cracked cups of some cold, black, oily sludge. Even better, I could serve myself rather than wait two days for nothing to turn up. And there were no broken legs to worry about.

Now to more serious matters. However you put it down on your expenses, whether you're a regular at the oh so exclusive Monolith Club in Moscow, with its Piano Bar and never-ending range of Scotch whiskies, its lavish dining room and never-ending supplies of fish soup, baked sturgeon and New York strip and the guy from San Diego with his never-ending impersonations of Frank Sinatra; or at the glitzy Manhattan, with its Happy Herb Pizza laced with marijuana in downtown Phnom Penh, or even at the Blankety Blank on the beach in St Tropez, the nightclubs in Kiev will come as a shock to the system. They might all look as though they were expressly designed for the punk and disorderly, but they are plastered with signs offering 'Ladies free before midnight', 'Ladies free for special events', or even simply 'Ladies free'. Which, you must admit, makes a pleasant change from other clubs in other parts of the world.

But they're all a big gamble. You never know, if you go in them, what you're going to come out with. Like cholera. It started in the south and spread to fifteen other cities, killing twenty people on its way. Like mushroom poisoning. Eat the wrong type and you can be dead in four hours. All the big, fresh, juicy ones, don't forget, come from Chernobyl, which is less than a hundred miles away. Didn't they mention that on the menu? Or like Natasha, whose enthusiasm grows more infectious every day, especially if you enter into the spirit of the Ukraine and suggest a whip-round. Or so I'm told.

For complete, guaranteed, 100 per cent protection from whatever they throw at you, there are only two things you can do. You can stand in the middle of the club and sing three choruses of 'Lydia, the Tattooed Lady', which will clear the place immediately so that you no longer need any protection. Or you can go back to your hotel room, switch on the television, watch something called *Name that Tune*, which as far as I can discover involves playing the same Russian folk song over and over again giving it a different name each time. It doesn't matter what time it is, or what day of the week, it always seems to be on.

There's no protection, of course, from shops, shop managers, shop assistants or any dominatrix even remotely concerned with any organisation whose sole aim in life is to cause maximum grief. They are all bad; bad; quick, just once more with the whip.

The customer is always right? The customer rules the roost? The customer is king? Forget it. A Ukrainian shop assistant would no more pay the slightest attention to a customer than a Ukrainian dentist would think of sending you a birthday card and a polite reminder to pop in and see him while you still have at least one tooth left in your head. As far as they're concerned, Communism and capitalism are the same thing. Communism meant being rude to customers; capitalism means being equally rude to them. Except that under Communism you were forced to be rude to customers, whereas under capitalism you can at least choose when and where you want to be rude to them.

So whether you're groping your way round Milk Store No. 47; queuing up for the third time in Gastronom – the first time to check the price of what you're buying, the second to pay, the third to get the receipt for what you've bought – or standing in line at a traditional Kiev sausage bistro to be told there's no sausage, no bread and nowhere to sit down and not eat it, either, you're on your own. As if that's not enough, when the winds start howling and the snow begins to settle, the ultimate consumer nightmare happens. The lights go out.

It's not just in the hotels, bars, restaurants and shops that people suffer, obviously. It's everywhere. Houses are falling to pieces. Schools are shut. Hospitals are surviving on nothing. One hospital down in the south, for example, was so strapped for cash that in order to save money they decided they had no alternative but to suspend their ambulance service: a horse and cart which they had bought as a part of their previous cost-cutting exercise.

As for doing business, or, rather, trying to do business, it's a whole new experience in self-flagellation. The companies that have survived so far will do anything to get two pennies to rub together – or, to be more accurate, two hryvna, their new, unpronounceable currency. Yushmash, the world's largest rocket factory, based in Dnepropetrovsk, is building toy guns and trolleybuses to keep going. In the odd one or two other firms still operating you come across businessmen, especially foreign businessmen, who are not only suffering but paying out millions, if not billions, of dollars for the privilege. Who said this was not a masochist's paradise?

First of all, they are tied up with red tape. To start a business, any kind of business, in the Ukraine you need no fewer than eighty-seven different licences, secured by providing eighty-eight different little brown envelopes. Eighty-eight? Of course. Don't tell me you've forgotten the guy who also wants airline tickets for his wife. To get an export licence you need permission from twenty-five different people in return for twenty-four different little brown envelopes. It's only twenty-four because this time the customs officer wants a new Mercedes.

You then have to keep five different sets of books for different inspections and pay more than twenty different types of tax, not to mention those special taxes levied by the inspectors themselves. And how often does a government inspector come calling to make certain you haven't strayed from the straight and narrow? Every four days.

The entire country is being strangled by red tape and slowly being ground even further into the dust. After the death of Patriarch Volodymyr, the leader of the Ukrainian Orthodox Church, his congregation naturally wanted to bury him in his beloved St Sofia's Cathedral, which has the most miserable-looking painting of Our Lady I think I've ever seen. When they turned up with the body, officials said they hadn't got the necessary bits of papers. They couldn't take him home, so they buried the poor man outside. Under the pavement.

Again and again I came across companies, domestic as well as foreign, eager to establish what I think Freud called a contractual scenario, and what others who know the Ukraine refer to in equally technical terms as doing a St Sebastian. In other words – promise you won't laugh – they want to invest in the country. They've got the rope. They've got the box. They've got these two . . . Oops. I got carried away. What I mean is they've completed all the forms, have attended no end of meetings with subofficials, officials and even ministers, and still they are left dangling from the ceiling. To meet just one of the twenty-five different people you need to see to get permission to risk your money in their country, you can hang around in your overcoat, in unheated offices with no lighting and no telephones for one, two or even three weeks, not knowing whether the meeting will take place in five minutes, five hours or five months. I tell you, you'll need more than two oranges to keep you going for that length of time.

Then they keep turning the screws. Eighty-seven licences? Sorry, we should have said ninety-three. Twenty-five people to get that export licence? We should have said fifty-three.

And did we say no fee was necessary for a mobile phone licence? Sorry. We should have said there was a small fee: US$65 million a year. Yes, a year.

Agree and they'll hit you with a job for the son, two months' holiday in Florida for the wife, a big, fat cheque in the bank in Cyprus and 'Come and see me tomorrow. There's somebody I'd like you to meet.' Disagree, even if it means you won't break even for 327 years at the earliest, and they'll think nothing of driving a six-lane highway through your backyard. You think I'm kidding? They've done it before, even though it meant tearing up a stack of diplomatic protocols and picking a fight with practically every ambassador in town.

So difficult is it for foreign investors to do business in the Ukraine that the last time I was there the only evidence of foreign investment I could find was a restaurant staffed by Marilyn Monroe lookalikes, which, for the Ukraine, was more than appropriate. I waited seven years to get served, and then all I got was a cup of coffee.

One Dutch businessman I saw there told me that there was only one way to survive in the Ukraine: hire a local fixer with good contacts with the local mayor or minister, and let him get on with it. 'It's wrong. But it works,' he said as we waited and waited for a Marilyn Monroe lookalike who really did look as though she had had an itch for seven years to bring us another coffee. 'If you want to do business here, it's the only way,' he advised as we gave up and left.

It's the same story out in the rural areas, where roads very quickly give way to lanes, lanes to tracks and tracks to mud. Stop at one of the mysterious-looking shacks by the side of virtually any country lane anywhere in the country and you'll hear farmers complaining about how wrestling with the latest technology – nineteenth-century technology – goes against the grain. Not that there's much grain now in the Ukraine.

Once the bread basket of Europe – the steppes have some of the richest soils in the world – today the place is more of a basket case. In the old days, with no fewer than 42 million hectares under cultivation, the Ukraine produced over 25 per cent of all foodstuffs for the entire Soviet Union, including 25 per cent of the grain, 30 per cent of the potatoes, nearly 60 per cent of the sugar . . . I won't go on in case you think this is turning into a cereal.

Not only has production fallen by 80 per cent over the last ten years, dairy herds by 50 per cent and poultry by 70 per cent, but the Ukrainians are now completely incapable of feeding even themselves.

Driving through the country, across it or into it is like sticking safety pins in your nose. There's no transport, no lighting, no power. What equipment there is has broken down. I mean what horses there are have broken down. All the tractors died years ago. Goosing is unheard of. There are hardly any geese left to throw down chimneys to clean them. What am I saying? There are hardly any chimneys left to be cleaned.

Yields are so slow that when I was last there there was talk of shipping in food from Europe and the States to help the Ukraine to survive, except, of course, for the patch up in the north-east near the border with Belorussia. There they have potatoes the size of footballs, carrots as long as your arm and leeks like nothing on earth. But the only counter they can get them onto is a geiger counter. They come from Chernobyl. Some less conventional farmers in the area have diversified. What with the cheap land, the complete absence of any controls and the huge growing potential of the soil, they have come up with what they claim is the ultimate cash crop: opium. The heroin produced from this doesn't just blow your mind, it riddles you with radioactive poisoning and slowly destroys you from within. On the other hand, maybe that's a big marketing plus for the masochistic. If the radiation doesn't get you, the heroin will.

The Ukrainians call this successful way of managing an economy *shakhmatka*. To me it's more chicken Kiev, which must have been designed by a Ukrainian. Who else would get such pleasure from causing people the maximum discomfort and degradation? Think about it. Plunge in your knife, or innocently prick the skin ever so gently to try to find out what's inside, and for your trouble you are immediately sprayed and scalded by hot, spicy, garlicky butter. A true masochist's delight. Especially when you have your best suit on. In a crowded restaurant. And when you're treating the secretary to a little light supper after her hard day slaving over her nails. Perhaps it would have been better for all of us if S and M stood for Sausage and Mash.

Yet it is not all doom and gloom. While other countries that also broke free from the Soviet Union cut back the role of the state, privatised like mad, boosted their economies and began to really motor, the Ukraine has not only halved the size of its economy, pushed itself to the brink of bankruptcy and notched up the worst economic record of all the fifteen former republics, it has managed to lift over US$100 billion out of the country. The Ukrainians have set up a vast network of locking and interlocking overseas companies, banks and trusts, as complicated as the mass of chains and locks you'll find in any bondage parlour, which controls, experts say, way over 60 per cent of the whole economy. When, for example, they privatised their largest aluminium works, three local companies put in bids. Only later did some clever researcher discover that not only were all three companies owned by the same organisation, but that organisation was Russian.

They have also done everything they can to boost the profits of the most expensive banks in the most expensive parts of the world, not to mention real-estate prices in Marin County, northern California: when the Ukraine finally split from the Soviet Union, anyone who was anyone grabbed everything they could and ran. Including the prime minister, who has since admitted he was pocketing between 8 and 11 per cent of the total turnover – turnover, not profits – of all Ukraine's state-run industries. If they were to bring even half the money back, they could stop recycling their currency by turning it into toilet paper, double their foreign reserves and start moving again. But will they? Have you ever met a reformed masochist? Unlike the proletariat, the last thing they want to lose are their chains.

So who's to blame? Some take masochistic delight in saying it's nobody, that it's in their genes. While we go all dreamy about King Arthur and the Knights of the Round Table, the oldest surviving Ukrainian book, *The Chronicle of Bygone Years*, goes into lavish detail about the national pastime of drenching yourself with cold water and then lashing and torturing yourself to within an inch of your life. Others who understand the masochist psyche far more than I do say that it's because they've yet to get over the fact that for most of the last 1,000 years they've been dominated, whipped, thrashed or been under the thumb of somebody else. First it was the Mongols, then Russia and Poland. Then Russia, Poland, Romania and the Czech Republic. Next Germany – Hitler even wanted to ship out the rich, black soil from the steppes to boost German agricultural production. And, of course, finally Russia which, under Stalin, just wanted to ship all the Ukrainians out and leave the soil behind.

Admittedly, for the last 350 years, give or take the odd attempt by the Cossacks, they've also botched, blown and generally ruined any chance they had to break their bonds and gain freedom. That sounds to me to be a classic case of masochism.

The nearest they got to actually pulling it off was in 1919, when, suddenly, like the flick of a whip, the eastern and western parts of the country united to form virtually the first independent Ukrainian government in history. But it was not to last. Within two years it had been crushed by the Bolsheviks. A few years later, a group of Ukrainian Communists seized power in the east. But again they were defeated. Stalin then moved in with a vengeance. He centralised everything. He collectivised everything. He Russified everything. Between 1932 and 1933, in what most people believe was deliberate genocide, he was responsible for the deaths of between 5 million and 7 million Ukrainians in the Great Famine. Although from what one can gather from reading the history books, it was not what he intended. He actually wanted every single Ukrainian out of the way.

But, masochists to the end, even when the Soviet Union fell apart, many people were still desperate to remain part of Russia. What finally decided them against it was an old sadist: Mrs Thatcher. She suddenly turned up in Kiev and lectured everybody in sight, telling them all in no uncertain terms that the Ukraine had no more right to be independent of Russia than California did of the United States, and then disappeared again. Which, as you can imagine, had a galvanising effect on everybody. They all decided to do the opposite, to finally break away from Moscow and stand on their own two feet. Keeping the leg irons on, of course.

Some people are still firmly in favour of the place being hung, drawn and quartered. In other words divided into four, because they reckon it's really four countries rather than one.

The north, they say, is nothing but poor soil, pine forests, log cabins and black bread. And when it rains a thin film of white powder settles on everything, which some people maintain has something to do with what's-the-name-of-that-power-station? and the government insists is only salty water from the Black Sea.

The east is Russian-speaking and Orthodox. Three hundred years ago it was part of the Russian empire. Today you've only got to wander around, say, the unpronounceable Dnepropetrovsk, and its huge steel mills, where the atmosphere is so thick with pollution that you can't see whether the giant statues of Lenin still dominate the main square or not, to realise that it has lost none of its Russian atmosphere.

The south, by comparison, is all sunshine, pretty little cottages, big, imposing castles and palaces, white bread, huge forests literally being eaten alive by silkworms and soil so rich that this time the Russians are trying to ship it all back home. The south, of course, is also the Crimea, which not only believes that it should be a country in its own right, it also knows, deep down, that, but for a quirk of history, it *would* be a country in its own right.

The west is everything the east is not: Polish as opposed to Russian, Catholic as opposed to Orthodox and agricultural as opposed to industrial, apart from the odd town like Krivoy Rog, which is known for its iron-ore mills and where it takes three hours to drive down the main street. Not because the traffic is so bad, but because the street is 160 kilometres long. The people of the west also seem to have a completely different outlook compared with those in the east. Take Symon Petliura. In the west he is hailed as a hero because of his campaign against the Bolsheviks in 1917. In the east, however, he is reviled as a traitor and mass-murderer. So be careful who you hail as a great Ukrainian, and where.

Then there is the language problem. Apparently, Ukrainian Russian is not only different from Russian Russian, it varies from region to region as well. Take the world *druzhyna*, for example. In western Ukraine it means wife. In the east, however, it means troops or warriors. So what happened when the mayor of Lviv in the west invited the mayor of Mariupol in the east to drop by for a couple of days with his *druzhyna*?

You've got it. He immediately chartered a jet, filled it full of officials and took off.

The government has now decided that this situation cannot continue. They want to unify the nation and make certain everybody understands exactly where they are and what they've got to do. They've decreed, therefore, that Ukrainians must speak Ukrainian unto Ukrainians, even though, being an old language dating back to the days of the first Ukrainians – the Russians call it *Selianskoe mora*, the peasants' language – it doesn't have any modern words or phrases, like brown envelope, commission, offshore trust, apartment in New York, 'Well I don't care what you think, she is my secretary'. But the government has spoken – in Russian, of course, because had the announcement been made in Ukrainian, nobody would have understood it, would they?

For everybody, from the president up, this has meant going back to school. The result is either speak-it or don't-speak-it people; varying degrees of proficiency with it speak; *surzhik*, call what they a mixture of Ukrainian and Russian, speak people; own version individual words with their own and mistakes speak their.

To encourage people to learn their own language, the government has also said that in future all top Ukrainian jobs will go to Ukrainian speakers, which sounds fine in theory. What is happening in practice, though, is that the poets and folk singers who have kept the language alive all these years are replacing all the Russian-speaking civil servants, top administrators, even university professors and lecturers, and are becoming the new leaders, which makes everything even more complicated.

Maybe the place is in such a mess today because nobody understands what anybody is saying any more, so they all just have to get on and do their own thing in their own way. Like the man in Zburyevka who bit off his wife's nose during a row – and then swallowed it so that the police wouldn't find any evidence. Or Kiev. For the life of me, I can't understand what they're doing there. Over 1,500 years ago it was the capital city of the old Kievan-Rus empire, the booming crossover point for a mass of trade routes running between the Mediterranean and the Baltics. Under the Soviets, it was their third-largest city after Moscow and Leningrad/St Petersburg. 'If Moscow is Russia's heart, and St Petersburg its head, Kiev is its mother,' they used to say. Not any more.

Today Kiev is the place for serious sadists and melancholy masochists. It straddles the Dnipno River. It's built on hills and slopes, whereas other cities are built between hills and slopes. It's a mish-mash of every kind of building you can think of: neo-classical, neo-classical with Soviet statues, byzantine, byzantine with Soviet plaques, baroque, baroque with Soviet carvings, renaissance, renaissance with Soviet friezes.

The main street, Khreshchatyk Street, is the best street I've ever heard anywhere in the world. There must be more loudspeakers there blaring out military music than there are in the whole of China. One morning . . . I said, one morning, when I was . . . ONE MORNING WHEN I WAS STROLLING ALONG IT I thought I bought a *pirozki*, a kind of local dumpling, from an old *babushka* outside the main post office. I'm not saying it was heavy, but after I crossed the road to Independence Square, I had to sit down to try to get my strength back. When I unwrapped my *pirozki*, I realised that the music must have been so loud the old dear must have thought I'd asked for an old Second World War Russian hand grenade. Frightened to leave it lying around in case it caused a bomb scare, I slipped it under the second-largest advertising hoarding in Kiev, hiding where the second-largest statue of Lenin in the Soviet Union used to stand until, come independence, they started lobbing *pirozkis* at it. Then I wandered over to the far corner where, engraved in the pavement around a statue of the Archangel Michael, Kiev's patron saint, are the names of all the capital cities of the world, which I must say I felt was a very courageous thing to do. Because there, in black and white, is proof, if any were needed, of how far behind every other country you can possibly think of the Ukraine is. Well, apart from Zambia and Zimbabwe, but that's nothing to be proud of.

As for the locals, the blokes all look as though they live at home with their mothers. If you ask them a question, they are uncertain whether to reply. If they do decide to reply, they don't seem to know what to say. The women all take after their mothers, especially the ones in the big, central Bessarabski Market, whose idea of giving you a sample of their honey is to smear it on the backs of their thick, leathery hands and expect you to lick it off. And the girls. They might have the longest legs in the whole of the old Soviet Union, as the Mayor of Kiev maintains, but they've got the longest faces as well.

It came as no surprise to me, therefore, to discover that over the centuries many blokes have just given up, thrown in the *pirozki* and, for the want of some peace and quiet, gone off to become monks, mostly at the famous Lavra Caves Monastery on the other side of town on the slopes above the River Dnipro, and stayed there happily, underground, for the rest of their lives.

When I dashed in there one afternoon between meetings I almost decided to join them, except that I could hardly get in the place for beggars. Not that I've got anything against beggars. I'm probably going to end up one myself, considering all the money I spend on, er, travelling. But these guys were not just hustling, they practically knocked me off my feet. The reason, I learned later, was that they, in turn, were at the mercy of the local Mafia, which charged them, can you believe it, US$20 a day for the privilege of begging from the visitors. No US$20 and they were out. Which tells you a lot about the

Ukraine, the Mafia and how much these guys must make to be able to pay that amount of protection money every day.

Then, before I even ventured underground, in the monastery museum, which actually contains more gold than the Hermitage in St Petersburg, I got shouted and screamed at by all the old women who act as guides because I decided to go my own way rather than follow their signs. 'It's the regulation!' they kept bawling at me. Another *babushka* who'll never live long enough to be as old as she looked then went potty because I couldn't believe it when she said that during the war the Russians had blown up the tower of one of the cathedrals inside the monastery in order to slow the advance of the German army.

Deep underground, however, all was peaceful. The tunnels linking the various chambers together were so tiny I could only just stand up in them. Squeezing past people coming in the opposite direction could, I could imagine, give rise to the odd unmonkish thoughts Especially if they weren't Ukrainians. The piles of bones, the skeletons, the mummies, the glass coffins, the candles everywhere . . . far from being intimidating and claustrophobic, the catacombs were surprisingly refreshing and calming. This was where the monks lived, wrote, read, chanted, mourned, kept silence, prayed and no doubt lashed themselves for their entire lives. Some of them, I was told, even went in for what they called *stolpnichestvo*: standing there without moving a muscle for years on end. One guy, apparently, stood stock-still for thirty years.

Not that this is unusual today. Many's the hotel clerk and waiter I've come across, not only in the Ukraine but all over the world, who stands stock-still without so much as batting an eyelid, flinching a muscle or even attempting to speak, however much you try to attract his attention.

Afterwards, full of peace and contentment, I guessed it was time to take in the big Russian-designed monument to its national heroes. Not because I'm collecting war memorials – normally I only take them in if I happen to spot them – but because one of the monks recommended that I look through the crook of the arm of Volodomiev the Great. It was the best view in town, he said. But I never got there. The battered old Lada I was in broke down. So instead I decided to take a look at Victory Square. I was just beginning to wonder what type of victory it was meant to commemorate when suddenly my whole faith and confidence in Ukrainian human nature was miraculously restored.

There, by the edge of the pavement, by the big stone was this big, black wallet. Being a good citizen, I bent down to pick it up so that I could hand it in at the nearest police station when – whoosh – a young guy in a black leather jacket grabbed it ahead of me. Hey, I thought. He turned to me and, honest man that he was, suggested we went through the wallet together to look for the name of the owner. As there were so many notes in there, literally wads of hundred-dollar bills and hundred-deutschmark notes, he gave me the wedge of dollars to hold while he clutched the stack of deutschmarks.

He must have spotted something in the wallet that gave him a clue to the owner's identity, because suddenly he took off at top speed for the local police station, the thick wad of deutschmarks in one hand, the wallet in the other, obviously forgetting that he had left me behind, standing in the middle of Victory Square holding a roll of notes that did not belong to me.

Realising that this could perhaps be difficult to explain, given that the Ukrainians were not yet quite up to it in Ukrainian, I ran after him. For some reason this seemed to make him run even faster. But, fit and healthy specimen that I am, I intercepted him just outside the Hotel Lybid on the corner. I thrust the dollars in his hand. 'Here,' I gasped. 'You take these to the police as well. I can't be bothered with all the complications.'

Clearly recognising me as a fellow good citizen, and still eager to get to the police station as quickly as possible, he grabbed the dollars, turned and disappeared around the corner. I only hope he got his just reward.

But for people chasing people you can't beat, if that's the right word, Odessa, the most elegant, most exciting, most dynamic, liveliest and most cosmopolitan Ukrainian city ever created. By a Frenchman. Imperial Russia's most booming and successful warm-water port, the so-called Pearl of the Black Sea, its first governor, appointed by Catherine the Great herself, in the odd moment when she wasn't playing around with all those young stallions, was the smooth, suave, handsome Armand-Emmanuel, Duc de Richelieu, who fought under Potemkin against the Turks, as I think anybody would have done, and not just because he was the size of a battleship. He was also, of course, the grand-nephew of Le Grand Cardinal himself, who, incidentally is one of my heroes because he was the first to come up with the line, 'If God meant wine to be bad for you, why did he make it so good?' Though you have to remember that he was speaking before the days of Beaujolais Nouveau, Wine-in-a-Box and what the hell did you call this, Chardonnay? I suppose, strictly speaking, to coin a masochistic phrase, I should say that Odessa is one of the most elegant, most glorious blah-blah Turkish–Russian–Italian–Moldovan–Dutch–English and, of course, Jewish cities ever created by a Frenchman.

Turkish because both the original port and fort were built and run by the Turks from around the 1520s.

Russian because Prince Potemkin grabbed it off them in 1794, even though Catherine the Great inevitably claimed all the credit as, no doubt, she also did whenever her stallions turned in a stunning performance.

Italian because de Ribas grabbed it and turned it into a *porto franco*, attracting Italian wheeler-dealers whose activities were so graphically described by Pushkin as the 'tongues of golden Italy which ring out along the laughing street', not to mention the Italian architects who were responsible for its elaborate buildings.

Moldovan because the poor Moldovans more or less built the place. As a result, the local accent remains what they call Moldavanka rather than the common or garden slurred Russian accent.

Dutch because you've only got to look at the straight lines and right angles all over the place to realise that the street plan was laid down by a Dutchman, Franz de Voland.

English because – Attention, present arms! – English shipowners were the first to see the commercial potential of the city. They built up the shipping business and obviously enjoyed themselves so much that they were the first to put in sewers, most of which are still there, leaking away to their hearts' content.

And finally, of course, Jewish. Known today as home to Oistrakh, Richter, Milstein, Heifetz and other men of note, or, I suppose, notes, before the revolution a third of the population was Jewish. You only have to read Isaac Babel's brutal short stories on turn-of-the-century Odessa to get the hang of the place. Buckets of buckwheat porridge, lumps of sugar in the borscht, vodka downed by the cupful. Old people living in a home one day, being taken by the Department of Social Security for a treat to the theatre with its gilt tiers, velvet partitions, brilliant chandeliers but no liver sausage sandwiches, and the next being thrown out on to the streets. Which surprised me. When I went to the theatre in Odessa, all the dancers looked as though they had been living on liver sausage sandwiches since the turn of the century. Especially the ballerinas. Then there were Babel's stories about gangsters like

Benya 'the King' Krik, who thought nothing of smashing people to smithereens and then stealing or destroying whatever he wanted. He even slaughtered a poor old man's cattle and then had the nerve to ask permission to marry his daughter. A modern-day Isaac Babel, though maybe not quite as short-sighted or quite as laconic, told me that much the same thing still goes on today, except that the Benya 'the King' Kriks of the new millennium live in Tel Aviv and, would you believe, in Hampstead, north London.

Odessa was also, of course, home to lesser literary lights, such as Gogol who, as an escape from his dreary life, is reputed to have written stories about the Ukraine, which only makes you feel even sorrier for him. Or Pushkin, who, they say, had an apartment opposite the Hotel Krasnaya. To me it looked like one small half of one small room, but seeing as he was having an affair with the governor's wife, the Polish Countess Vorontsova, almost the whole time he was there, it probably didn't make much difference to him, especially as he had the right half of the room. And Mickiewicz, who was Polish, lived in Lithuania and was deported to Russia, which was in effect the Ukraine, if that makes sense.

Today, for all its French influence – after sorting out Odessa, Le Grand Duc went back to France where, during the Restoration, he twice served as prime minister – the place has lost that certain *je ne sais quoi*. Even so, it's still one of my favourite cities, with its wide boulevards, lush, overhanging vegetation, beautiful nineteenth-century buildings, dilapidated Czarist mansions, crumbling art-deco decoration, leafy courtyards, broken cobblestones and potholes. And, most important of all, the secret KGB number plates which, as everybody knows, start with 04. Who says I don't give you all the lowdown?

As for the Odessites, as opposed to the Odessans, you'd have thought, with such a cosmopolitan past, they would have been a wild, devil-may-care bunch. Especially when almost everybody you meet east of Berlin tells you, 'If Odessa is the mother of crime, then Rostov is the father.' But according to my Odessa file, somehow or other they just don't seem to have managed to get it together. They are more worried and introverted than you would ever imagine. Along the Parisian-style boulevards, in the open-air bars and cafés and restaurants along Deribasovskaya Street, named after De Ribas, where everyone is tucking into sturgeon, *shashlik* and bucketfuls of wine from the Crimea and Moldova, you'd expect to find people laughing and joking and enjoying themselves. They're not. They're sitting staring silently at each other. Now, I know this is par for the course for the middle-aged and married, but I'm talking about young people. People like you and me. In their thirties. Well, mid-thirties. It's the same with the kids. Not that I know much about kids, but it is odd to see them not knowing how to play with balloons or jumping up and down in bouncy castles in total silence.

One evening, purely in the interests of research, you understand, I dragged myself away from all my files and papers and half-written reports and took a walk along the tree-lined promenade. A Russian band was playing what sounded like 'Yesterday', but I could have been wrong. On a bench somebody had scrawled, 'No matter how long you live you'll be dead,' which really cheered me up. Almost opposite I noticed a plaque identifying the Sanitary Epidemiological Inspectorate of the Black Sea Basin, which made me feel even better. Next door was the Londonskaya Hotel, whose long, echoing corridors, fussy chandeliers, enormous staircases and huge rooms always make it look and feel to me more like a vast ministry of foreign affairs than somewhere to put your head down for the night and dream of Luang Prabang. Or whatever. Although I suppose a ministry of foreign affairs is where you put your head down for the day. Even the lift is the size of a minister's private office. Every time I got in it about 350 girls managed to get in there as well.

Further along from the ministry, I mean hotel, is the toga-clad statue of Richelieu, the governor. However, with too many vodkas inside you, you could mistake him for the old Cardinal himself. At the foot of the statue are the most famous steps in the old Communist world, the steps used by Eisenstein in that famous scene of the storming of the Winter Palace in *The Battleship Potemkin*. Why he shot it here and not in St Petersburg, where all the action took place in real life, and why he made up the bit about the steps I have no idea. Unless, of course, he thought he was making another factual documentary for Channel 4 in which the truth didn't count.

At the bottom of the steps, still littered with bodies which must have been left over from the shooting, of the film, that is, although maybe not – you never know what film directors, even Russian ones, will do for a spot of realism nowadays – is the passenger terminal, which has just had a US$10 million facelift. Beyond that are the docks, home to the US$1 billion, 25,000-employee Black Sea Shipping Company, the second-biggest shipping company in the world.

Just south of the docks is what they call Arcadia, which, to prove that in spite of everything they're still a bunch of masochists, is not some Greek paradise with half-clad goddesses leaping around all over the place but a scruffy, oil-stained beach with collapsing piers and crumbling balustrades, so crowded that there's not a German in sight. Not because they're not welcome, but because there's literally nowhere for them to put a handkerchief, let alone a towel. Even Arcadia is not as bad as Nikolayev, out to the west, which boasts something even more unique for a Black Sea resort: *vibrio cholerae*. Yes, the real thing. So severe is it that whole stretches of the beach have been closed because of contamination.

Again purely in the interests of research, I dragged myself

around Odessa from bar to bar, slot-machine shop to slot-machine shop, or automat, as they call them here, from bar to bar again and from casino to casino. Everywhere there was silence. No giggling, no laughing, and definitely no hysterical out-of-control shrieking. Even in the Irish pub, in spite of no end of Guinnesses and Kilkenny's and Paddy chasers, there wasn't the slightest hint of the crack. It was more like a wake.

In the automat round the corner I saw one guy win a stack of coins. Total silence. In the casino there wasn't a murmur. Not a flicker. Not a raised eyebrow.

And this is the city even the Russians, let alone the Ukrainians, tell me very seriously is not just the font of all humour, but the ever-popular host to the Comedy Festival of Eastern Europe. There, I knew that would get a laugh.

'So what kind of jokes do you tell at the festival?' I asked one miserable-looking guy in the local town hall one morning.

'OK,' he said. 'Are you ready? I tell you best jokes of festival.'

'OK,' I said. 'Shoot – I mean, try me.'

'Man gets bird mark on his jacket. Just as well cows don't fly, yes?'

'Yes.'

'What is a bus terminal? A place where people were told there will be no bus.'

'Yes.'

'A Communist, a Fascist and a Ukrainian Jew on a plane. God tells them the plane is going to crash. But before it crashes they can have one wish. The Communist says he would like all the Fascists to be killed. The Fascist says he would like all the Communists to be killed. The Jew says, 'Well if you're going to grant their wishes, I'll just have a cup of coffee.'

After I picked myself up off the floor I wandered back to my hotel.

I'll say one thing for Odessa, though. The streets are safe at night. It's the buildings that are dangerous. Because so much limestone was dug out of the ground to build them, many of them are held up only by the pressure of the buildings either side of them and are likely to collapse at any minute. Maybe that's why people don't burst out laughing all the time. Perhaps they are frightened that the vibrations might bring the whole city tumbling down. Already three palaces have gone, and many other buildings are likely to follow suit. To save the theatre, an exact replica of the Vienna Opera House, they pumped tons of molten glass into the empty caverns below it. Whether it will work or not I don't know. Most people seem to doubt it, judging by the absence of the standing ovations and foot-stamping that seem to be the usual thing in all the other Russian opera houses I've been to. Having said that, the theatre has managed to withstand all those rugby-playing ballerinas up until now.

Not that some people don't know how to enjoy themselves although I doubt whether it involves much stamping of the feet.

Going about my business in Odessa, I pitched up for a meeting in an office in a scruffy hotel overlooking the main square. What I was told was a company specialising in encouraging foreigners, especially Americans, to invest in Ukraine's finest assets turned out to be a rip-roaring, no-holds-barred, dating agency/marriage bureau/do whatever the hell you want operation for a bunch of sad-faced masochists. And they were making millions.

They persuaded first girls from the Ukraine, then girls from all over Eastern Europe, to send in their photographs and a bit of blurb about how they looked after their mothers, cared for the environment and wanted to become brain surgeons. These they printed free of charge in an enormous meat catalogue, which they sell at an inflated price to a load of sad, hormonally challenged matrimoniacs in the States, all of whom no doubt have strong right hands and an interest in life's more solitary pleasures. They then charter flight after flight after flight to bring these sad-faced mothers' boys from all over the US to Odessa to meet up with the girls, who, of course, as we all know, are only interested in one thing: getting the Green Card so that they can quit the Ukraine for good for the land of Mickey Mouse, McDonald's and guys who drop bombs on innocent people and spend the rest of their lives saying, 'Now you have yourself a great one.'

In Odessa they give the guys a quick tour of the town – these are buildings, these are streets, that's the sea – then it's off to the port for a quick round-the-lighthouse tour of the harbour where, if they've never done it before, they can experience the joys of being tossed on an ocean wave before finally hitting the first getting-to-know-you sessions in the main office building of the port which, I was told, in spite of conditions of strict security, inevitably ends up awash with seamen.

'How can you do such a thing?' I asked the guy running the foreign-investment company.

'Do you know anybody in Israel?' he said. 'I want to set up a similar operation there. They have lots of guys looking for girls. We have lots of girls looking for guys. It is good business.'

'But it's . . . it's . . .'

'Profitable. We make big profits,' he grinned.

'I know, but—'

'And the girls, they are happy. The men, they find what they want.'

'Yes, but—'

'Some keep coming again and again.'

Well, there was no answer to that, was there?

In the Crimea, however, they kept going and going. At

least, the Light Brigade did. Straight into the Russian guns. Not that it's the only charge that's ever been made in the region described by Potemkin as 'the wart on Russia's nose'. Today it's where the red sail with the fun set. Or, at least, try to.

Surrounded on all sides by the Black Sea and connected to mainland Ukraine by a strip of land just big enough for a drunken politician to overshoot it and drown his secretary, it is Nice or Marbella or Biarritz run by masochists. Or rather, Intourist.

The Crimea has everything. Beautiful scenery. Subtropical temperatures almost the whole year round. Lush vegetation. Vineyards. Orchards. Pine and juniper trees. Cypresses. Fantastic palaces and houses. Spectacular gardens. More sunshine than they get in the south of France. No wonder one of Lenin's first decrees was on 'the use of the Crimea for Rest and Treatment of Workers'. It was where, he said, the heaving, sweaty masses should go on holiday. Well, wherever you are, Comrade Lenin, I can assure you I saw nothing but heaving, sweating masses when I went there.

But somehow or other, again, they don't seem to have got it together. It's full of Russians. Around 70 per cent of the 2.5 million population of the Crimea are Russians. Which is not exactly a recipe for fun, fun, fun. Unless you are in Moscow on a Friday night in the Hungry Duck on Ulitsa Pushechnaya – where the girls don't just have a generous nature, they're more than prepared to show you how generous nature has been to them as well – you're bombed out of your mind trying to drink your body weight in vodka, and you're about to be engulfed by a rising tide of DNA.

Maybe it's because most of the Russians you meet don't want to admit why they are in the Crimea: that, for example, they came voluntarily, in the Russian sense, that is, to virtually colonise the place. Or, if you like, make it Russian. That they came, again voluntarily, of course, to replace not only those who died in the famines of the 1930s but also the Tatars, who Stalin virtually packed up in freight trains one day in 1944 and shipped out to Central Asia. In fact, the Crimea was only given to the Ukraine on the spur of the moment, by Khrushchev in 1954. Which, of course, the Russians have regretted ever since.

Perhaps that's why the Crimea is virtually impossible to get to. Well, from the West, it is. From Kursk or from Momsk, or even from Omsk, it's probably as easy as anything. But from this side, appropriately enough, it's nothing but pain. You fly to Simferopol, the capital, in the middle of the island. Anywhere else this would be a big tourist centre. Not here it isn't, unless you're hooked on statues of Lenin, Stalinist architecture and talk about the undercover help the local Tatars are giving to the Chechens. Even the local Hotel Moskova the locals say is *karpoot*. It's so bad that, like the poor monks in Kiev, the locals long ago decided to forget the whole thing and go and live in the caves.

In the limestone hills surrounding Bakhchysaray, a tiny town just outside Simferopol, you can see where they carved a whole city out of the caves. In the hills of Chufut-Kale, there is an even bigger cave city. At Manhup-Kale there are even more. And I don't just mean holes in the ground, I mean the real thing. Real houses. Real rooms. Real corridors. Real stairways. Real stroppy neighbours.

Now comes the exciting bit. You must decide whether you're going to suspend all sense of judgement, take your life into your hands and get the local bus, or whether you're going to beg, borrow or, more usually, bribe a taxi with three dodgy wheels and no insurance to drive you over the arid Ai-Petri Mountains of central Crimea and then, brakes squealing like a bondage session gone wrong, swoop down to Yalta and the Black Sea. Either way, when you finally open your eyes, you won't be disappointed. Yalta is on the most perfect bay you can imagine. Apart from all the other most perfect bays, of course.

From as far back as the first millennium BC it's been a sunspot. As at Pompeii, archaeologists have excavated bars and restaurants and hotels way over 3,000 years old. Except here they found people still sitting there waiting to be served. In 1860 the Russians finally got round to endorsing its benefits, which proves they can work fast if they have to. Two doctors, S. Botkin and V. Dmitriyev, declared, 'Pure air and the sun are the most powerful, unsurpassed curing forces. It would be hard to find a match for Yalta as a resort basking in the sunlight with a mild, warm climate, subtropical vegetation and tender sea. Yalta offers a healing combination of the sea, mountains and the air of the wood.'

Well, of course, that did it. As happened with the south of France, all the big guys fell for it: Tolstoy, Rachmaninov, Tchaikovsky, Chaliapin, Stanislavsky, Gorky, Chekhov and, of course, Pushkin, who went into raptures about the place. 'How beautiful are the shores of the Crimea, in the light of the morning star,' he trilled. Even the Czar, once he got tired of freezing to death in Finland which, for some reason he previously chose for his summer holidays, built what he called his peasants' country cottage to take advantage of the climate.

But it was the Communists, inspired by Lenin's rallying cry, who really opened up Yalta. Having perfected their skills in shifting huge populations from one end of Europe to the other in the 1930s and 1940s, in the 1950s and 1960s they had no problem shipping back into the Crimea anything up to 10 million visitors a year, although I gather it took them a long time to get used to the idea of return tickets.

In came, in groups of 5,000 at a time, the brightest and best and most promising of Soviet youth, all ruddy-cheeked Young Friends of Policemen, Young Friends of Border

Guards and, of course, the Young Pioneers, with their red kerchiefs and Socialist ideals, eager to spend weeks on end at the Artek Youth Camp on the outskirts of town having the time of their lives learning how to sweep paths, harvest fruit, put flowers on Lenin's statue and rat on their parents.

Into all the sanatoria came all the workers who had devoted their lives, not to mention their health, to achieve impossible production targets, to be cured of all their incurable diseases and then, after three days, to be sent back where they came from.

Into the hotels came all the *apparatchiks* and managers, the real backbone of the Soviet economy, who could, at the sight of a bottle of vodka, let alone a brown envelope, fiddle production quotas, meet output targets and make all the non-existent deliveries you wanted.

Then, finally, into all the big villas around town came the really, really big guys from the KGB, who, no doubt, had their own particular form of R and R activities, and, of course, all the old buffers on the Politburo itself.

Now that everything and everybody has to be paid for, however, they barely get enough people to fill a park bench. Kids still come to the Artek Youth Camp, but today it costs them US$1,000 a week. In advance. And instead of studying sensible, practical things like Marxist-Leninism, the dialectic of the proletariat or how to stick a microphone up the kitchen sink when your parents are not looking, they concentrate on more boring, totally unrealistic things like management, marketing and why a Calvin Klein T-shirt is worth more than a fuddy-duddy, boring old Marks & Spencer's one.

The few remaining workers who have not died of asbestosis, radioactivity or just breathing the air they live and work in are still entitled to stay at their favourite sanatorium. Except now, once they hear the price, they'll probably have a heart attack and that will be the end of them.

The same goes for the *apparatchiks* and managers who have dedicated their lives to the success of Communism. Either they're no more because there's no more business for them to mismanage, or they've hit lucky in their new-found enthusiasm for capitalism and are whooping it up in Cyprus, in Marbella, in huge suites in the Negresco in Nice or in Courcheval, a ski resort way up in the Alps where, I'm told, the temperature especially in Les Caves, the local *boîte de nuit*, is hotter than anywhere on the coast. So hot, in fact, it's best to get the chocolate body-paint job over and done with as quickly as possible.

The KGB is no more. Most of the old buffers have all gone. Those who are left prefer Sochi instead. It's almost as hot, it's on the Black Sea and it's still in Russia. Well, the last thing you want to do is to stretch out on a foreign beach next to some young, ambitious Spanish judge. You never know what might happen to you.

The only people who seem to come to Yalta nowadays are those who can't afford to go anywhere else: the young with no money, the middle-aged with no money and the old, or rather, those who in spite of all the odds have survived, and have no money.

For most this means staying not in a hotel or sanatorium but in a traditional Russian, or rather Ukrainian, *domik*, a wooden garden shed. And some gardens are nothing but back-to-back *domiks* with people sharing everything. But so eager are they to get away from the grinding agony and cold and desperate conditions they have to put up with in Moscow or St Petersburg, or even Kiev, that they are prepared to pay good money to live in a shed in the sunshine for two days, two weeks or however long they can afford to shake it in the hay.

If you don't fancy what has to be the ultimate masochistic accommodation – well, apart, maybe, from hanging by your wrists in some underground dungeon – your problem then is finding a hotel. Oh, there are plenty of them around, most of them empty, but – the Ukraine being the Ukraine – the difficulty is finding one that is not too awful.

Don't go to the Yalta, up on the top of the cliffs. It's so big – it has over 2 million rooms – that it is unwieldy, and slow even by Ukrainian standards. The Orienda is not bad bad, if you see what I mean. It's in the centre of the main promenade and overlooks the sea. Everyone is quite pleasant, although it was here, I must tell you, in the downstairs semi-circular coffee-type shop, that I discovered the Ukrainian interpretation of fast food. It means they keep you waiting as long as they possibly can but, gee whizz, as soon as you get it, are they determined to have you finish it and out of the place in double-quick time. I'd read the first half of *War and Peace* waiting to be served, agonised over the menu and ordered the only thing they had left in the kitchen: lumps of cheese and some kind of thing with a broken leg with chips. I'd finished the second half of *War and Peace* waiting for the food. After that, though, it was clearing the table, trying to whip the tablecloth from under my plate and bringing me the bill before I'd even swum through the grease on the plate to try and tackle the thing, which looked as though it was riveted to the middle of the plate through its broken leg.

If you really want to be adventurous, try a sanatorium. There are around 160 in town, and they are much cheaper than hotels. If you can convince them you're the other genuine, dedicated Russian worker, they won't charge you a kopek. You'll also be much better looked after. But I warn you that the treatment you're likely to get might not be what you're used to. Their techniques and procedures were all developed specially at the I Sechenor Institute of Physical Methods of Treatment and Medical Climatology of Yalta. Although once you've got over their somewhat unique approach to colonic irrigation and can sit down again, I'm told you can quite happily settle into the routine of things. If, however, you get found out, there's no point getting a heart attack about it. Individual medical sessions will cost you around 200 to 250 kopeks a throw. All of 10 cents.

As for the town itself – once your eyes have stopped running for long enough to take it in – it's a bit like a downmarket central planners' Costa Brava. The setting is spectacular, and some of the streets are quite stunning, such as the slightly more upmarket, tree-lined Vulitsa Pushkinskaya, which runs alongside the tiny Vodopadna River. There are lots of old, wooden houses as opposed to garden sheds.

But everywhere you look people are struggling to survive. Along by the railway station old women in thick, heavy overcoats hunker down to take your blood pressure with what looks like a wooden hammer and a couple of bits of rusty Meccano. Outside the post office, a couple of ancient men who probably rode with Tolstoy are rummaging through a pile of rubbish. Dustbins are a luxury, even in Yalta. By the cathedral an old sailor has a peacock chained to a table. Give him a few coins, and he'll take a photograph of you with the peacock. Providing, of course, you've got a camera. On every corner there are small kids, big kids, thin kids, fat kids, clean kids, filthy kids playing accordions, *babushkas* selling what looks like cherry juice from the back of lorries or trailers. Or it could be paraffin. Tucked away behind the bus station there's a rip-roaring traditional market selling everything to delight the holidaymaker: sacks of potatoes, rusty old nails, battered oil cans, old shoes, piles of clothes, half a dozen onions.

What on earth inspired the likes of Chekhov, the thinking man's Somerset Maugham, to come and live here I have no idea. Apart from the seagulls, the cherry orchards, a cantankerous old uncle, a bunch of sisters and lots of ladies with broad-brimmed hats walking up and down the quayside all day long with their snappy little, white Pomeranian dogs, there's really nothing here to get excited let alone frustrated about. The books say he came to Yalta for the sunshine and the warmth because he was dying of TB. But I don't believe it. I went out to his house, which is exactly as it was when he died in 1904, even down to the bakelite telephone upstairs in his study which brought him news of the first nights of his plays in Moscow and no doubt how he had been damned by the critics but hailed by the public. If anything, I reckon it was the house that killed him rather than the champagne he was sipping when he died, because whenever you want to go up or down the stairs, the fat old *babushka* sends you out into the open and up and down an outside staircase which, however good the climate, cannot be good for someone suffering from a touch of the critics, which is enough to make anyone spit blood, as well as with TB. I'd have thought any medical student, let alone a fully qualified doctor, would have known that.

As I'm allergic to water, naturally I try to stay as far away from it as possible. But in Yalta I did actually see the sea, largely because my driver kept on asking me: 'Do you want to spend a day on the bitch?' Not wishing to disappoint him, and not wanting to risk the journey back by bus, I finally agreed, as one does. Imagine my surprise. It was the same as all the other bitches, I mean beaches, I've managed to avoid. Great mountains of lard or, I suppose, *salo*, lying around all over the place. Wives fiddling with their ice cream and moaning because Natasha next door has got a tin bath, Sophia across the road can afford to eat bread twice a week and that her mother says he is a no-good, lazy layabout she should never have married. Poor, henpecked husbands trying to make their one beer last a lifetime. Then, of course, the inevitable Russian touches. Dumped here and there on the beach are rusty old Jeeps with rocket-launchers strapped on their backs. Bill Haley and the 747s, or whatever they were called, blaring out of all the loudspeakers. About the only good thing about it was the absence of Kiss Me Quick hats, candy floss, kids shouting and screaming and running around all over the place and the fact that the fat *babushkas* kept their clothes on. Well, most of them did. Otherwise I don't think I could have coped.

Further along the coast, I kept being told, things really hotted up. Here, not only were there golden beaches, nude bathing, partying till dawn and all the drugs you could wish for, but all the action took place in the shell of what had once been a Chernobyl-style nuclear reactor. As soon as the Russians turned their backs on the place everything was stripped bare, including the nuclear reactor. Some smart guys then moved in and turned it into a non-stop Reaktor Party, which brought a whole new meaning to the phrase spit-roast shuffle, and where top-end drop-outs have nothing to do with being sent down from Eton. The order of the day, or rather night, is to down a pint of deep-fried marijuana in one go and live to tell the tale. Well, live for at least three days to tell the tale.

Speaking of which, it was Yalta, of course, that delivered a severe shock to Europe's system from which it took practically fifty years to recover. For Czar Nicholas II's 'peasants' country cottage' was where the Yalta Conference took place in February 1945. Although why Stalin proposed holding the conference there when he was continually joking, 'If only there weren't forty million Ukrainians I'd deport the lot them,' I have no idea. Probably because he didn't fancy any of the hotels in Kiev.

Today you would never guess that this is where we put our trust in Uncle Joe, who then promptly threw it back in our faces by carving up Europe, keeping a huge slab of Poland,

promising he would hold free elections – which, of course, he
never did – grabbing the rest of Eastern Europe, not to mention the Balkans, and in the process condemning millions of
people to starvation, untold misery, and death. He did, however, keep one promise: to declare war on Japan. But only
after the Americans had bombed Hiroshima, which meant
there wasn't much left to fight about anyway. I have no particular axis to grind – it just strikes me that, for all Churchill's
Treat-Uncle-Joe-as-a-member-of-the-club-and-one-day-he'll-
behave-like-one-of-us approach, the Allies obviously thought
that the quickest way of ending the war and the killing of
innocent people was to hand Eastern Europe over to the
Russians, look the other way and pretend nothing had happened.

Politics aside, what would amaze you is how much they've
learned from the National Trust about opening up grand
country houses to the general public. First of all, they make
them impossible to reach by public transport. When you
arrive by car, they make it impossible for you to park anywhere within five miles of the place. You then have to queue
for about two hours to get in, partly because, I will admit, the
old lady at the ticket desk has gone off, again National Trust-
style, for a large vodka and a little chat with the rest of the
staff. Once through the door, they make you put on these
fancy canvas slippers over your shoes. As well as wanting to
make you feel at home, presumably they aren't keen on
Russian jack or any other kind of boots stamping all over
their property.

Finally, you're inside what the books describe as a sumptu-
ous Italian Renaissance marble-and-stucco-style summer
palace. Whether it is or not I couldn't for the life of me tell
you, because it was packed with Russians chattering away
among themselves and taking photographs and videos of each
other with their Nikons and Canons and Sony camcorders,

standing in front of a fireplace, by a desk, beneath a mirror or below the two sleeping stone lions with enormous Prince Charles ears over the front door. They didn't even stop when we trudged through the Grand Reception Room, which was turned into F.D.R.'s own private apartment during the conference, or in the vast ballroom where, at the large, round table, the deed was done.

The only time everybody stopped gossiping was when, upstairs in the Czar's private quarters, we all assembled for a group picture under a huge tapestry of the Romanovs, who are, of course, revered as saints not by the Romanov Catholic Church but by the Orthodox Church. Funny, that.

After that it was the storming of the Winter Palace again as everyone made a mad rush for the souvenir shop which, even though it would have done the National Trust proud, frankly I found a bit disappointing. There were no maps showing Europe pre-Yalta, no maps showing the Europe that was agreed at Yalta and no maps showing Europe post-Yalta. There were also no T-shirts saying, 'I went to Yalta and all I brought home was Eastern Europe and the Balkans'. But for all that, I notched up a minor triumph. Seeing my masochistic, hangdog expression, the old lady at the cash desk thought I was Ukrainian and charged me only 2 whatevers. Russians she was charging 4 whatevers, and any Americans and English people she was hammering for 8 whatevers. Now, where can I get a T-shirt that says, 'I came to Yalta and saved 6 whatevers'?

Having visited one Ukrainian National Trust or, I suppose, National Distrust property, there was only one thing to do: visit some more. First I took in Koreiz, the one-time KGB fun palace. This is where Stalin stayed during the conference. It is also where he hosted the big dinner with Churchill and F.D.R. Locals say it was because it was the least lavish of all the palaces used by the different delegations. Others maintain that, because, being the KGB's

Crimean fun palace, it was practically the only place in the country with no microphones hidden behind the panelling. Today, or rather tonight, if you fancy a turn in Uncle Joe's bed, it can be arranged. Some guys told me it would cost US$200. Others said US$400. A particularly mysterious *babushka* cackled away at me like mad and said US$500.

Either way, it's cheap at the price. To sleep in Lincoln's bed in the White House, I seem to remember, set some poor Asian guy back US$1 million. And I'm sure that didn't include room service, either. Not to mention a reduction for all the noise coming from the Oval Office.

After Koreiz I went next to the ideal venue for diplomatic conferences, the Alupka Palace, where Churchill stayed. Ideal because it has two faces. One side, overlooking the sea, is like a Moorish fun palace, all towering turrets, intricate patterns and inscriptions attributed to Mohammed, the Holy Prophet, peace be upon him, taken from the Alhambra Palace in Granada, Spain. The other side is a rock-solid, austere, Calvinist Scottish castle, complete with battlements, which is said to be a copy of Sir Walter Scott's pad at Abbotsford. Running down to the sea is an impressive stairway, guarded by three different marble lions. Seeing the sleeping one at the bottom on the right-hand side, Churchill is reputed to have remarked to Stalin that all it needed was a cigar, and it would look just like him. He then asked if he could take it home with him. Stalin said no, it wasn't his property to give away. Which I always think was a bit rich coming from a guy who was about to grab Eastern Europe as well as the Baltics.

Set in around 100 acres of rolling lawns, miniature, mysterious grottos, mighty cedars, waterfalls and sweeping parkland, it was built by a British architect, Edward Blau – obviously a two-faced British architect – for the incredibly rich Count Mikhail Vorontsov, whose father was at one time Russian ambassador in London and a big buddy of Sir

William Pitt. There is a bust of him peeping through the curtains in the conservatory windows. Vorontsov himself, who was governor of Odessa after Richelieu, was a big fan of the UK. He went to Cambridge, had an English butler, an English secretary, spoke English whenever he could, and wherever he was lived to all intents and purposes like an English milord. Which is probably why Odessa is so miserable today.

In fact the castle he built is so authentic that on the day I went there they threw in some traditional Scottish weather as well. Because of the National Distrust rule about not being allowed to park anywhere closer than ten miles from the property, by the time I had run, slipped and slid through the pouring rain, splashed through puddles the size of the Black Sea and finally reached the main door, they decided to close for the day. One old *babushka* said it was to protect the floor and furnishings. But, knowing the traditional Ukrainian standards of hospitality and service to the customer, my bet is that because of the rain they just wanted to get home early.

However, having got into the National Distrust way of doing things, there was no stopping me. The following morning I set off to visit the big, once top-secret Russian naval base at Sebastopol.

We headed out of Yalta past a genuine picture-postcard Bavarian castle built in 1912 by a certain Baron Steingel, a German businessman who made millions out of oil in Baku in Azerbaijan, for his gypsy mistress, who then promptly thanked him the way women do by jumping out of the window and killing herself on the rocks below. Today it's a swish Italian restaurant owned and run by an Italian mamma who imports everything from Italy. Otherwise I suppose she would have thrown herself out of the window years ago as well.

On past a huddle of red roofs on the cliffs facing the sea.

This was once Gorbachev's famous *dacha*, complete with escalators going down to the beach where he was seized and taken prisoner on that fateful Sunday, 18 August 1991. Although, according to the locals, it was a pretty low-key affair. One guy, who looked like an old KGB operator gone to flab, told me that as soon as he heard the news on the television and saw Yeltsin clambering onto tanks and doing his bit in Moscow, and Rostropovich packing his cello to go home, he got his car out and drove all the way to the *dacha* without seeing any police or military. He couldn't get down to the villa, he said, because of the usual security guards. Three days later, when Gorbachev flew back to Moscow, the coup began to collapse and the Ukrainian government finally threw in their whip in favour of the winners, it was still no big deal, he said. Just a couple of cars outside the *dacha*, and that was it. But apparently, the *dacha* didn't belong to Gorbachev. It belonged to the Ukrainian government. He, along with a string of other VIPs, merely had the use of it. The Ukrainian government are now trying to privatise it. So if you fancy it, give them a call. Don't forget the brown envelope, though. It always helps. And the whip.

A bit further along I threw an anchor out of the window to stop the Lada. We shuddered to a halt by a rough old farm track which appeared to be heading in the right direction. Along the track we went until we came out in the open on to what was known as Cathcart Hill, after Sir George Cathcart, commander of the British 4th Division, Rifles, a name famous in Northern Ireland and at what's left of the BBC External Services. There, on one side, was the tiny, and I mean tiny – it was less than the size of a tennis court, and scruffy, weedy and overgrown – main English cemetery, visited briefly by Churchill after the Yalta Conference. A few yards to one side was a pile of rocks and a plaque proclaiming that a new memorial had been commissioned by the three British regiments which took part in the Crimean War. Over 150 years later, the new memorial has still to be built. Which must be some kind of record for honouring those who gave their lives for their country. But then, for over thirty years there wasn't even a plaque at Babi Yar, the deep ravine outside Kiev where around 100,000 people, most of them Jews, were stripped, tied up with barbed wire, machine-gunned and buried by the Nazis, so maybe it's par for the course.

A little further still along the road – it's hardly worth trying to put your Lada into second gear, if you can find it, that is – is a tall, thin, white limestone post in the middle of a vineyard: the site of the Charge of the Light Brigade.

> *Half a league, half a league*
> *Half a league onward*
> *All in the valley of Death*
> *Rode the six hundred.*

And all that.

On the post an inscription reads simply: 'In memory of those who fell in the Battle of Balaclava, 25 October 1854.'

Having stopped and tramped across the Valley of Death, my first reaction, I have to admit, was not what made them do it, but what the hell, with all those Turkish, Russian, French and British bones buried in the soil, does the wine taste like? And don't say it's bound to have a lot of body.

OK, I'm no old soldier – not that I haven't been in a few battles over the years – but standing there in the middle of the vines, you can actually get an idea of what happened. So now, as the old colonels say, if you look at the mess table in front of you, I'll explain what I would call the real crime here, I mean Crimea.

Russia wanted Turkey. Britain and France wanted chicken.

No. I mean Britain and France were against it. So, of course, was Turkey. In 1854, when Russia moved in on some Turkish provinces north of the Danube, the Turks decided enough was enough. They opted to invade the Crimea and put an end to Russian ambitions. But it was tougher than they thought.

OK, so it's 25 October 1854. Here in the centre of the table, where the waiter has left the Cheval Blanc '47, are the Russians. The place is heavily fortified. There are batteries and dugouts all over the place. Here, by the cork, is the main parapet. This, by that glass, is the officers' headquarters. This is where they also store some of their ammunition. All around are the French and the British.

Over there at the edge of the table by what's left of the caviar, you can see Sebastopol. The place is in flames. Across the entrance to the harbour are two rows of ships which the Russians have sunk to prevent the British and French from getting in. But, of course, it also means the Russians can't get out. Clever guys, the Russians.

At the top of the hill here, where the Petrus '45 is, are the Russian reserves, waiting, ready to move in. Further along here, where the corks are, are soldiers from the Chernigov Regiment.

Now way out by the napkins, near the edge of the table, you can see the French being repelled. Which is not surprising: I've always said they were a farce to be reckoned with. Rather good that, what. By that spoon is the Nikiforov Battery. They're pushing back the French, but they're being hammered into the ground.

Here, by that awful bottle of water, is Dasha Sevastopolskaya, the Russian Florence Nightingale. She is bringing water to the soldiers.

By the pepper and salt are Pyotr Koshka and Feodor Zaika coming back from a night sortie checking out the French positions. Koshka, you don't need me to tell you, is one of the great Russian heroes. He is a kind of one-man SAS. He carried out sortie after sortie after sortie. A real pain in the neck for our chaps.

Up there by the decanter of port – what vintage is it? 1963? Taylor's? Jolly good show – is the famous Admiral Nakhimov, hailed as one of the great defenders of Sebastopol. His picture and statues are all over the place. His is the number one monument outside the harbour gates. The present statue has its back to the sea and is facing inland, but the previous one was facing the other way round.

Along here by the – who left that on the table? Disgusting – is a defence tower. The parapet is on fire. There are wounded everywhere. Just in front of it – will somebody get that thing off the table? Anybody would think this was a private house – a sailor is pouring water over a bomb. A sailor? Yes, of course. While the blockade kept the French and British fleets out of Sebastopol, it also kept the Russians trapped inside. As a result all the sailors were drafted in as reinforcements to help fight the land battle.

OK, so here, by the Stilton, the guys are pushing back the French. Looking on, on the slope, is General Juferov. Behind him his batman is gulping down some water from a barrel.

Is all that clear? Good. I'll continue.

Where the butter dish is is the critical point of the whole battle. The French have broken through. They have overrun the Gervais Battery and are now hoisting the tricolour.

In the centre by the biscuits – I wonder, could I have some bread, please? – is General Khrulev, on his white horse, surrounded by Russian soldiers trying to fight them off. Over there, by the celery, Khrulev's adjutant is galloping furiously to bring in reinforcements. The French, by a stroke of luck more than anything else, have done it. They're in. The Russians are now turning and running for their lives. But they can't escape because they've blockaded the harbour. Instead, overnight they build a bridge of boats across the harbour and . . . No, wait a minute. That's not the Charge of the Light Brigade. A week in the Crimea, and I get confused with all these battles. That was the defence of Malakhov Hill. Sorry about that.

OK, so back to the Charge of the Light Brigade. Tell you what, this time, instead of being a bunch of old colonels having dinner in the mess, imagine you're having dinner at home. You remember home? The place where you used to keep the spare suitcase.

Here, by all the empty bottles of mouthwash, sorry, I mean mineral water, is what's left of Balaclava, the British base the Russians have been trying to seize. But they have been fought off by a bunch of gallant Highlanders and the Heavy Brigade. The Heavy Brigade of Cavalry, that is.

Over here, at the other end of the table by the tofu salad, are the Russians. They're about to drag away a whole load of these organic rainforest toothpicks, sorry, I mean 12-pounder naval guns, which they've captured from the Turks. Not that I can see why on earth anyone would want to keep them.

On top of this mountain of sludge, I mean wonderful spinach roulade, is Lord Raglan, the British commander-in-chief. He sees what's going on. He scribbles an order in pencil to Lord Lucan, telling him to charge and stop the Russians from getting away with the toothpicks, I mean guns.

He gives the order to this lump of cold cabbage, which is, appropriately enough, his aide-de-camp, Captain Nolan, to deliver to Lucan way down at the bottom of the hill, where he couldn't even see the Russians, let alone the 12-pounders they were dragging away. Nolan delivers the order. Naturally Lucan asks where the guns Raglan wants him to get back from the Russians are.

'There, my lord,' says Nolan, waving his hands all over the place. 'There, my lord, is your enemy.'

What does poor old Lucan do? The only guns he can see

are not the guns the Russians have grabbed from the Turks, but this string of glasses of organic carrot juice – ugh – I mean Russian 6-pounders at the end of the valley, where the cat is now spreadeagled across the table licking that awful white, er, stuff, completely protected by cavalry and infantry.

So he says to Cardigan, 'It's crazy, I know, but if that's what the old man wants, off you go, old chap. Jolly good luck. Toodle pip and all that. I'll be tucked up in South America or somewhere by the time you get back.' Cardigan, being a good sport, does just as he's told, taking with him 673 cavalry, who are all convinced in their heart of hearts that Lord Lucan did it.

Straight into the Russian guns they hurtle. The result, twenty-five minutes later, is 113 dead, 134 wounded, 500 horses destroyed. But they get the organic carrot juice, I mean guns.

I, of course, blame Nolan. Having worked with a few Nolans in my time – I can think of one in particular – I know exactly what they're like. All airy-fairy, lah-di-dah, great presenters but useless when it comes to detail. Cardigan certainly gets all my sympathies. Lucan, of course, deserved to disappear.

As for the organic carrot juice, excuse me, I think I'm going to throw up.

Sebastopol today hardly seems worth the effort, let alone all the agony and loss of life. Once a heavily guarded, closed city, because the Russians didn't want the West to discover how they were going to conquer the world with an out-of-date, increasingly rusty fleet of decaying battleships, it's now as easy to get into as London, New York or any other city in the rush hour. And its out-of-date, increasingly rusty fleet of decaying battleships is no longer Russian. It's half Ukrainian and half Russian. The Russian half is in North Harbour, but only on a twenty-year lease. The Ukrainian half is in South

Harbour. And I'm sure you'll be pleased to hear that there's not a single nuclear warhead among them. As befits the country that is home to Chernobyl, the Ukraine, once the world's third-largest nuclear power, has renounced all nuclear weapons. Their stockpile of more than 2,000 strategic nuclear warheads they sent off to Russia for decommissioning and then destruction. We hope. We hope.

In spite of that, Sebastopol is still very much a military city, though a dead military city. I didn't have time to check, but one battle-scarred veteran told me that the town boasted over 1,000 military monuments, 600 to those who died during the Crimean War and 400 to those who died in the last war. And you can believe it. They're certainly everywhere. Almost completely destroyed during the Crimean War – it was bombarded non-stop for 349 days – Sebastopol was flattened again by the Germans in the Second World War. This time they were lucky. The siege lasted only 248 days. All that was left standing were seven buildings. So it's hardly surprising that wherever you turn there are reminders of wars and battles and death.

In the main street is the Black Sea Fleet Museum, which, to be honest, I found difficult to distinguish from the real thing. In the park there's a fantastic, huge, circular panorama based on the Crimea. Have a look at Prymorsky Bulvav. There's a memorial column there to Russian ships sunk in the harbour. On the edge of town is Jason's Redoubt, where Tolstoy was stationed as a second lieutenant in the midst of the fighting. 'Tolstoy, he writes like a German,' another old soldier told me. 'Because of all his long sentences.'

Today, rebuilt yet again, Sebastopol looks like any other new, faceless Russian town, all concrete blocks and no soul. To most Russians, and to many Ukrainians, however, it is still very much a holy city. For this is where it all began. Out on the peninsula is where St Cyril and St Methodius first

landed, bringing with them the Gospel and the Cyrillic alpha-
bet – or maybe, bearing in mind the new orthodoxy, it should
be the other way round – which, with the conversion of
Prince Volodymyr, Prince Vladimir to the Russians, led to
the foundation of the Kievan-Rus empire which gave us Peter
the Great, Catherine the even Greater, icons, Rasputin,
Communism, mass deportations, gulags, genocide, and, of
course, the Hungry Duck, for which we must be truly thankful.

Where it all ended, or rather, where it all started to come
apart, almost exactly 1,000 years later, was on the other side
of the country in Lviv, a wonderful, virtually untouched mediaeval city which, if there was any fairness in this world, would
be up there with Krakow, Prague, Salzburg and Luang
Prabang.

Just 85 kilometres from the Polish border, tucked away in
the foothills of the Carpathian Mountains, Lviv not only looks
like a mixture of everything – gothic, renaissance, baroque,
Rococo, art nouveau, with Greek gods the size of gorillas
holding up doorways – it has also been called everything:
Lempberg by the Lemps, Little Venice by the Hapsburgs,
Lwow by the Poles, Lvov by the Soviets, and now, of course,
Lviv by those Ukrainians who can speak Ukrainian. For centuries one of the major meeting points for traders from
everywhere, it has done deals in every language under the
sun: Italian, German, Polish, Russian, Hungarian, Czech,
Armenian, Yiddish and, of course, Ukrainian, although they
are still arguing over where to send the difference between the
invoiced price and the real price.

Today, largely because it is now almost inaccessible – at one
time you could get a train there direct from Paris, but no
longer – it's overlooked, ignored and isolated, which may or
may not be a good thing.

Go there today, or rather try to go there today, and it's like turning back the clock. The first time I managed it was by train from Krakow, around 200 kilometres away. It took me over twelve hours. The journey from Krakow to the border wasn't so bad: that was only about three hours. It was after that that the fun began. As one, we all had to get off the Polish train, lug everything along the platform, down the subway, up into the street, along the street to the Polish–Ukrainian ticket office/customs/emigration hall, wait hours on end for it to open and fight our way through it on to the platform and the waiting train. Talk about the Tokyo subway in the rush hour.

The train was already so jam-packed that there was no way even one more sack of flour could have been squeezed on board. There was no way I stood a chance of getting even a single square inch of space. I wandered as casually as I could along the platform to the only sleeper carriage, at the front of the train. The two Russian women prison officers in charge of it screamed at me and waved me back to the crammed carriages at the other end. Bursting at the seams as they were, somehow or other people were still fighting their way aboard. Back to the sleeper I went. Again I was yelled at. Back to the bulging carriages I returned. I've had plenty of experience fighting my way on to overcrowded trains – I have to do it most mornings at Victoria Station when I'm going to the office – but this was impossible. Back I went again to the sleeper. This time the camp commandant actually smiled at me.

'Dollars,' she whispered.

'Dollars,' I whispered back.

'Three dollars,' she smiled.

'Three dollars,' I grinned.

Three dollars. I'd have given her thirty if she'd asked me.

Within two seconds I was on the train, in a sleeping compartment with three Ukrainians, drinking vodka and sharing some lumps of red shoe-leather. I know it was unfair on the poor guys at the back, but they wanted the market economy. I didn't force it on them.

When the train finally trundled into Lempberg, Little Venice, Lwow, Lvov, Lviv at three o'clock in the morning, it was like arriving in a time-warp.

The station was 1920s Soviet massive. Huddled everywhere were bundles of old clothing, empty bottles of vodka and cardboard boxes. Outside it was 1820 pitch-black. What with Chernobyl up the road, electricity supplies are not exactly reliable. Neither is the water supply. The pipes are so old and corroded that less than 10 per cent of the water gets through.

We drove through cobbled streets, like something out of Tolstoy or Dostoevsky. I kept expecting a horse and carriage to come skidding out of one of the side streets.

Over the years, they say, Lempberg, Little Venice, or whatever they call it, has suffered thirty-four wars and fifty-three fires. If it has, it doesn't look like it. During the Second World War, however, it suffered grievously. Around 40 per cent of the population were Jews. They've all but disappeared. Most of them were taken back across the Polish border to Auschwitz. The Poles who were left were then either killed or deported by the Russians. But like Krakow, the city escaped serious bombing. As a result Lviv is Eastern Europe as it used to be, pre-McDonald's, pre-Coca-Cola, pre-tourists. In other words, empty roads, thick, black fumes and buildings crumbling into the dust.

Prospekt Svobody, Freedom Square, the main square-cum-boulevard-cum-city centre, is like a garden party run by the Russians. It's got everything, but it doesn't work. The Opera House at one end could be spectacular; instead it is closer to a run-down church hall. On either side are cheap, disintegrating shops and offices. At the far end it just seems to peter out into nothing.

In any other town in Europe, the old market square would be a showstopper because, it's the real thing. Here, would you believe, is still the Venetian Embassy. Over there is the house where Peter the Great slept on his tour of Europe. Further along is where Catherine the Great stayed while she was wheeling and dealing with the Poles. And have you noticed that every house has only three windows? That's because they once tried to tax people on the number of windows they had. And not a hamburger, a pair of Nikes or a copy of the *International Herald Tribune* in sight.

Across the way is the thirteenth-century Armenian Church, home to thousands of priceless icons dating back to the fourteenth century which are just rotting away. Above the Old Palace is a mini-Statue of Liberty and several lions. There are 435 statues of lions in Lviv. I know, because I saw every one of them. Apparently the son of the founder was called Liv, the Lion. Goodness knows what they would have done if he had been called Vlad the Impaler.

But for me the most important statue of all was that of Ivan Franko, a Ukrainian Zola. It was here, in the final years of the Soviet Union, that people, mostly dissidents newly released from detention, began making speeches demanding the release of political prisoners, the ending of party privileges and the dismantling of the KGB. At first they were virtually ignored. Then one or two sympathisers began to pay attention and before long, suddenly they were addressing crowds of 20,000, then 50,000 people. Then it was the usual. The police moved in, broke up the meetings, arrested the leaders and threatened everybody with everything under the sun. But it was too late. The spark had been lit. Demonstrations began breaking out in Kiev.

As if that wasn't amazing enough, St Peter and Paul's Church down the road announced it was no longer Russian Orthodox. It was going back to being Ukrainian

Autocephalous Orthodox, as it was in the 1930s. Just as towns all over the country began to follow the political lead set by Lviv, so churches all over the country began to follow the religious lead set by St Peter and Paul's.

If that's not more than enough claims to fame for one city, Lviv is also home to the first Wanda of the world, who is supposed to have done great things with the furs given her by her lover, Severin, on condition she insulted him, ridiculed him, humiliated him, walked all over him and generally treated him like dirt. On the other hand, of course, I suppose he could have been her husband. Either way, Wanda was the creation of Lviv's greatest living son, the man who made Ukraine what it is today.

Take a bow, Leopold von Sacher Masoch. Novelist. The man who invented masochism.

Tirana

OK, I can fix it.

For you, I can get CDs, cassettes, as many of the latest Microsoft Windows 2000 as you want, visas, passports – any kind of passports. Even official United Nations High Commission for Refugees documents, dated and stamped in Gnjilane in Kosovo, declaring you're a genuine Kosovo refugee, so you can apply for political asylum wherever you like in the world. Even certificates saying you've passed every examination that's ever been set at Tirana University.

I can get cars. Any type of car. Any make. The latest BMW 7 Series. A brand-new, sparkling Mercedes S500. Even a K-For Jeep NATO forces are using up the road in Kosovo. With or without bullet holes.

I can fix for you to bring your long-lost cousin, your aunt, your uncle, even your Filipino girlfriend, into the country. Without passports. Without visas. Without papers. Without anything.

Oh, I nearly forgot. I can also get you all the guns, drugs, liquid mercury and radioactive material you like to make any kind of infrared seeking weapon you like. Delivered wherever you like. Whenever you like.

All you've got to do is go see my friends in Albania, Byron's 'a shore unknown that all admire but many dread to view'. They'll fix everything

Yes, I know it's the poorest country in Europe. Over 60 per cent of the population are unemployed. Average incomes are less than nothing. Power and water supplies are more off than on. Prices are soaring. Inflation is knocking 50 per cent a year. There's not even enough food in the country to feed its own people.

Yes, I know they've only just rejoined the world. That they've been trampled on by the Italians and the Nazis. That for fifty years up to 1985 they were under the thumb of Enver – 'We Albanians will eat grass, we will never violate our Marxist-Leninist principles' – Hoxha, pronounced Hodger, who was not just your everyday Soviet tyrant. He used to order the entire population of the capital, Tirana, to stand in the streets in the pouring rain just so that he and his wife could drive around and watch them get wet. At least, that's what they say, although since his death there have been more and more reports that he didn't inconvenience himself by going out in the rain, not even to watch his loving subjects get wet. He is reputed to have had a surgically enhanced double do that kind of thing for him while he stayed at home in the dry.

Yes, I know they were the last Soviet satellite to collapse into their own dust; that they're all mixed up with the Balkans and Milosevic and Kosovo and all that; that Norman Wisdom is their big national hero, and that they tell jokes about boys having mothers who are Jewish, fathers who are Serbian and coming home from school and asking them whether they are Jewish or Serbian, and the parents asking why they want to know, and the boys saying there's another boy at school who is selling his bicycle and should they beat him down on the price or just steal it.

But these guys are not involved in that kind of thing. They're on their own. For, whisper it not, this is the world of the Albanian Mafia, the roughest, toughest, cruellest bunch of, er, good guys you'll ever come across anywhere in the world.

You don't believe me? Let me tell you, it's the Albanians who taught the Sicilians what it's all about. Albanians first arrived in Sicily on a deserted beach in the dead of night before forged passports were even thought of. Even today there are whole communities of them hidden away in the hills up in the top north-west corner of the island, still waiting for the lorries to arrive on the local bobby's night off to ship them to Palermo and then on to Bari, Turin, Calais and Finchley, where they can see out the rest of their days as technical advisers to Terry, Patsy and Sean Adams, who make the Kray brothers look like Sunday-school teachers. With them they brought not only pictures of their mamas but also their blood rites, together with the Besa, the strict oath of loyalty, and their favourite bedside reading, the *Kanun of Lek Dukagjini*, a bloodcurdling code of ethics which dates back as far as Roman times.

Other people have vendettas. An eye for an eye, a tooth for a tooth, if you don't take back what you said about my mother, I'll never talk to you again, that kind of thing. Not the Albanians. According to their *Kanun*, *gjak per gjak*, blood for blood, they must take practically two eyes and a leg for an eye, two arms and a leg for a tooth, and if that's how she feels about you we'll make certain she sticks with you for the rest of your life. What's more, there's no time limit. An Albanian vendetta is for ever. If you can't fix it in your short one score and ten and a half, it passes on to the next generation. And so on. And so on. And so on.

If you as much as think of looking at my wife I must kill you, your wife, your kids, your dog, your television, everything. If you kill my brother, I must kill your brother, his wife, his kids, their television, everything. You kill my dog, well, that's it, World War Three.

Up in the villages of the Prokletije Mountains in Albania, especially near the border with Montenegro and towards Kosovo, you will hear stories even today of how whole families as well as the dog have locked themselves into their homes and never set foot outside for ten, twenty, even thirty years, so terrified are they of the *Kanun of Lek*.

'So how many people are hiding in their homes frightened to go outside?' I asked one gnarled old veteran from Koplik, who refused to be parted from his double-barrelled shotgun. The only time, he told me, he had ever let it out of his sight was when his daughter got married. He had it painted white.

'Five thousand. Ten thousand. Maybe even fifteen thousand people,' he said.

'Do they know who they are hiding from?'

'Of course,' he grunted. 'Their next-door neighbours. The people across the street. The family down the road. These are small communities. Everybody knows everybody. That's why they have to hide away in their homes. They know who has sworn an oath to kill them.'

Others I spoke to put the figure as high as 50,000, even 60,000.

A businessman I met from Shkoder told me that in his village they had tried to stamp out the *Kanun*. They had organised reconciliation committees and amnesties. But in vain. The customs were so deeply ingrained in their culture that it was impossible to eliminate it.

Yet the *Kanun of Lek* is not all doom and gloom. According to the good book, women are a 'superfluity', if that's not too flattering an expression. A woman must have

no property, take no decisions, offer nothing but blind obedience to her gracious lord and master and at all times 'submit
to his domination'. If she dares even to think of 'scorning his
words', her husband is entitled to 'beat and bind' her. If that
doesn't do the trick, you can forget counselling. The poor,
downtrodden husband must 'cut off her hair, strip her naked,
expel her from the house in the presence of relatives and
drive her with a whip through the entire village'.

It is this happy mix of landing on deserted beaches in the
dead of night, drinking each other's blood and the gentle
guidance of the *Kanun* that has made the Albanian Mafia so
powerful, not only in Albania but also in the rest of the world.

Talk to a man in a black suit carrying a violin case outside
Milan Cathedral. He'll tell you that after a long, two-year strug-
gle, the Albanians have taken control of the local Mafia, itself
one of the roughest and toughest and cruellest in Italy. They
have grabbed the heroin business from the Turks. They are
moving into Germany, Switzerland and Greece in a big way.
Even the British National Criminal Intelligence Service, as up
to the minute as ever, say they have detected signs of Albanian
'organised criminal activity' in the UK. Like the occasional wife
being lashed and chased naked through Charlotte Street on a
Wednesday afternoon. If this is how our Albanian brothers
treat foreigners, you can imagine what goes on at home.

Officials in the Ministry of Defence in Tirana have been
caught importing shiploads of rice. So-called independent
accountants have been discovered fiddling the books not only
for private firms but for state-owned companies as well. The
secret internal police telephone switchboard – yes, they still
have such things in Albania – has been bugged. Even the
top-secret, closely guarded state treasury, hidden in deep
underground tunnels in Krraba, just outside Tirana, has been
broken into and all the state gold stolen. And guess what?
Not one of the guards saw a thing.

The government, government ministers and members of Parliament throw up their hands in horror. It's a blight on the country! they scream. It's a stain on the pure, unsullied reputation of Albania. But will they reassure an increasingly cynical electorate, underline their commitment to good, clean, honest, transparent government and take a stand once and for all against corruption by revealing the extent of their own financial assets and how they came by them? What do you think? A law forcing not only members of Parliament but also the prime minister, the speaker of the Parliament as well as key officials in the different ministries to reveal their financial assets came into effect in 1995, but it has not been implemented, even on a voluntary basis. And, while not wishing to prejudge any issues, I doubt if it ever will be this side of the last Albanian being landed on the last beach at five minutes to midnight on the last day.

On the other hand, credit where credit's due, they're ready and willing to do business.

If you are going to Tirana, stay at the Hotel Dajti. It's not your usual run-of-the mill international hotel; if anything, it's pretty downmarket. At one time it was supposed to have been the best in town, but now it's more like your typical Russian hotel. Big, long, echoing corridors. Lifts that never work. Carpets with holes in them the size of the Adriatic. The reception, or rather, the tables and chairs by the door, are always full of strange-looking men in black suits smoking thick Turkish cigarettes. The Dajti is named after the national park in the hillside behind the hotel, apparently famous for its wide range of trees and plants, many of which, judging by the gunge around the edge of my bathroom floor, have been incubated in the hotel.

But what the hell, it's not the worst hotel I've stayed in. And it's convenient. It's in the centre of town, on the main avenue designed, they say, by Mussolini's favourite architect.

If it was, it must have been an off-day. There's not a fancy wedding-cake design anywhere in sight.

Turn left out of the hotel, and in two minutes you're at the Palace of Culture, a sort of pyramid on Prozac. It used to contain the most comprehensive collection of Albania's most famous historical treasures ever gathered together under one roof. Enver Hoxha's ashtray. Enver Hoxha's favourite armchair. Enver Hoxha's used tube of toothpaste. Enver Hoxha's brief seventy-one volumes of autobiography. Enver Hoxha's umbrella. Unused. They've all been dumped now, but nevertheless it is still the one place in the city where you'll always find crowds of keen, eager, enthusiastic young people, skidding and skating and rolling down it on 3-litre plastic Pepsi Cola bottles. Apparently, it's the world's number one skateboard slope. Cheers, Enver. I promise I'll read your book one day.

Turn right out of the hotel, and in two minutes you're surrounded by policemen and soldiers carrying Kalashnikovs. Sorry, I mean you're in Skanderbeg Square. There used to be a giant statue of our Enver in the centre, but they tore it down. While it was raining, I hope. On the left is the National Bank the size of which, as always, is in inverse proportion to its nation's financial assets. Outside, facing the King Zog statue, you see where most of those financial assets have gone: all the legal illegal money-changers. Hundreds of them. Nearer the entrance are huddled the gold dealers, some practically smothered in the stuff. For a single gramme of 14-carat gold I was quoted US$9, compared with US$13.50 in the shops. When you consider that something like 5 kilos is traded openly every day, you'll get an idea of the amount of money changing hands on the streets of the poorest country in Europe every year: 1 gramme × US$9 × 5 kilos × 365 days = far more than the National Bank is ever likely to see outside a minister's bank account. Practically on its doorstep are the handful of legal illegal stockbrokers who buy and sell privatisation vouchers and try to make a buck on the Tirana stock exchange. Good luck to them.

At the top of the square, which is about the size of a month's illegal production of counterfeit US passports laid out side by side, is the Tirana International Hotel, reputed to be the best in the country. Most businessmen stay there. So that's another reason to avoid it.

By the side of the hotel, in the romantic-sounding Bulevardi Stalin, are the buses travelling backwards and forwards every day to Pristina in uranium-soaked Kosovo. Which surprised me. I thought that given all the problems it would be impossible to get in or out of Pristina, but you can get a bus there just as easily as you can from Victoria Station to Oxford Circus. No, that's not quite true. It's easier than that. The buses are always there when you want them. They're not your usual luxury coaches, I admit. They're more like, well, like the bus from Victoria Station to Oxford Circus. But they get you there. One morning I was all set to go to Pristina, or at least as far as I could get. They probably wouldn't have let me across the border, not being Albanian, but you never know what a forged Togolese passport and a US$20 bill can do. Then, suddenly, things changed. Shock, horror, I had to go and do some work. But next time I go to Tirana I'll do it. I'm determined. I am told it takes about six or seven hours, depending on, well, depending on what does or doesn't happen on the way. Most of the time, of course, you're in Albania, so even if my Togolese passport couldn't get me across the border at least I'd see a whole chunk of the northeast of the country.

On the other side of the square, the right-hand side, is some supposedly new faceless Soviet slab which reminds me of the inside of a Russian swimming pool. At the top corner, facing the Tirana International, is the opera house. At least, it's supposed to be an opera house, but from what I could gather it hasn't been in business since that silly woman threw herself off the top of the castle roof all those years ago.

All around, behind the square, is the real Tirana. Bare-brick blocks of flats with two, maybe three families to a room. Filthy hovels. Crumbling shops and offices. Across the street by the old hospital, round the patch of mud by the Palace of Congress, by the shops the Chinese have opened along Dibra Street, much to the annoyance of the locals, everywhere there is destitution. Everywhere there is poverty. Everywhere you can see people desperately struggling to survive.

Some money is coming in. Some help is getting through. There's a brand-new hospital built by the Greeks. The order of nuns founded by Mother Teresa, the most famous Albanian who ever lived, even though she was born in Skopje next door in Macedonia, is building another one. The Roma Moda has just taken delivery of the latest Italian fashions. *Grazie mille*, Donatella. It's just what people want in the poorest country in Europe.

In spite of everything, some businesses are booming. The Kastrati petrol stations, I couldn't help but notice, are always busy, for the good reason, I guess, that nobody wants to be caught short in the middle of nowhere. In Kevin Fast Food, however, everyone seemed to be leaping around as if they had been caught short. Almost every car parked by the side of the road had Shitet all over it which, I only discovered later, meant 'for sale'. The Virgin Travel Shop did not seem to be doing much business. Probably because, with a name like that, there must always be some doubt as to whether or not whatever ticket you get from them will go the whole way.

With a bit of luck you should get back to the hotel without seeing anybody gunned down or being embroiled in a shoot-out. There is so much violence in Albania that even MPs have shot each other, in an argument about, of all things, VAT. If your luck is out and you do go the way of the majority, I'd be very pleased to pass on any message to your nearest and dearest as well as to your family.

So, overall, the Hotel Dajti is not a bad place to stay. I like it because, it's well, Albanian. The bar is pretty rough. It's the only bar in the world I know where they close the doors to try to stop you from getting in. And when you are in they do everything they can to get you out again as soon as possible. The women who serve there are more like prison warders than anything else, but it's a laugh. The guys in the restaurant are even more of a laugh. One of them, an ageing French pop star lookalike, keeps telling me he has eighteen daughters and fifteen sons. Every time I go there I always shake him by the hand and offer to get him a chair. If you ever meet him, do the same. He'll show his appreciation in the traditional Albanian manner.

As for the food, it's not so hot. The usual, pretty tasteless, Russian hotel-style food. The wine? You've just got to try the Albanian wine. It's terrible. The white wine is unbelievable. How they got so many cats to sit on top of so many bottles for so long I shall never know. As for the red, I reckon there's something funny going on with that. They call it Kabernet, and on the label, it says it's 12 per cent proof. But I can drink the stuff all night long and not feel a thing, which is not what you expect from a Kabernet, especially one that is 12 per cent proof. Or at least, it's not what my liver expects. On the other hand – always think positive – I drink Albanian wine whenever I get the chance, because then I have to put away a couple of hefty slugs of Albanian Cognac to take away the taste.

To be honest, after the very first meal I had there I thought I was going to Puke. But there was yet another change of plan. Instead I got a call telling me I should go to Durres instead. I did what anybody would do in a country whose philosophy is 'When in doubt, wipe it out.' I agreed. Not that I was too worried. To go to Puke to visit some of its beautiful mediaeval electronics factories would have meant leaving at five in the morning. Going to Durres, way out on the coast, on the other hand, meant I could have dinner, spend the evening in the bar and leave after the prison warders had brought me my first drink. About five in the morning.

As for cabs, no problem. There are always plenty around first thing, because Albanians are used to getting up early. First, because Hoxha used to do his killing in the morning. By getting up earlier and earlier the poor Albanians thought they would be out of the way when his killers came to call. Second, because living in a Marxist-Leninist paradise they knew they had to be up early otherwise they wouldn't stand a chance of not getting a share of the loaf of bread when it was not delivered to the only baker's shop in the whole of Tirana. Which was closed anyway. As for the drivers, they're all very good. The one I always get is small, stocky, looks a bit like a retired hit-man and speaks terrible Italian. Which perfectly complements my own terrible Italian. We can spend days on end together driving all over the place, chatting away to each other, not understanding a word we're saying. A bit like talking to your accountant, only much more pleasant and nowhere near as expensive.

But I must warn you about Albanian roads. There aren't any. Enver, when he wasn't working on his autobiography, thought good roads would make it easier for the Russians, or even NATO, to invade his peace-loving little haven. So they're all potholes. If I was running the place, the first thing I'd do, well the second thing, after speaking to my advisers in Switzerland, would be to organise a National Albanian Pothole Filling Day. I'd hold it on a Sunday and ban all traffic. It would be inconvenient, but not nearly as inconvenient as all the potholes. I'd then insist that every family went to their nearest pothole and filled it in. The small ones a single family could look after; the big ones would probably take a whole street. To fetch the material to fill them in they could use wheelbarrows, or, for the big ones, donkeys, or even, I suppose, a horse and cart. At the end of the day, the roads would still be rough but they'd be a hell of a lot better than they are now.

So when you're ready to have every bone in your body shattered, you take the Kuga Konjressi i Permetit road, which runs down the side of the National Bank. Just beyond the bank you pass a mosque on your right, then a Catholic church on your left. Then, if you're quick, you can spot a spanking new Orthodox church tucked away up an alleyway behind a bar. There are some curly wrought-iron gates on the road, so you shouldn't miss it. For fifty years, while they stood in the rain, shut off from the rest of the world, they were shut off from everything else as well: books, films, art and, of course, every form of religion. 'The only religion in Albania is being Albanian,' said our Enver. Now, in addition to religion, they're rediscovering all sorts of things for themselves again: Madonna, Levi's three sizes too small, Swiss banks, body piercing, both inflicted and self-inflicted and, of course, how to grow a beard.

After the churches the scenery is nothing but one derelict, deserted factory after another, apart, of course, from the brewery and the Cognac distillery, which are in full working order – funny, that – until you hit open country. Well, I say open country. Open country in Albania is like the towns, except there are fewer buildings, fewer guns – I hope – and more rubbish. What buildings there are appear to be farm sheds. They're small and desperately overcrowded, and that's before any people have moved in. They're also mostly falling down. All around the farm sheds, or rather farmhouses, right up to their front doors, and you can bet your life inside as well, people are trying to grow everything they can to help feed themselves, plus anything they might be able to sell to make living just a little easier. There are also, wherever you look, chickens.

Even if the roads were anything more than a succession of potholes, there's no way you could get up to 17.35 let alone 19.5 kilometres an hour, because they are full of stony-faced men, women and boys on donkeys, ponies or horses, anything capable of carrying crippling sacks of everything. I even saw one pathetic bag of bones dragging to market a broken-down old cart containing three well-fed, healthy-looking cattle, presumably to conserve their hard-earned fat to get a better price for them. Every now and then you have to swerve for your life as an ancient, clapped-out tractor, the Pride of Belorussia 1923, comes chugging down the middle of the non-road, belching out thick, black smoke and ricocheting uncontrollably from one pothole to another. Well, if you lived in the middle of Albania, would you know where to get brake-linings for your Belorussian tractor, and if you did, would you have the money to buy them?

The villages are renowned for their huge, eager, strapping young girls. Or at least, they used to be. These girls, red scarves blowing in the wind, skirts billowing in the breeze, striding manfully over mountaintops followed by vast crowds of dewy-eyed peasants trying to catch them up, always formed the centrepiece of massive, heroic monuments and giant murals to our Enver. Not any more. What monuments are left are crumbling into the dust. What murals there are are covered in graffiti. Odd bits and pieces of statues have been used to line septic tanks. Now the villages are much like the countryside. Potholes, rubbish, more derelict buildings, but more dangerous than those in open country. Because inside them you're more likely to find a stash of arms, any number of hand grenades, a pile of bombs, and quite possibly the occasional gunman smashed out of his mind on hash.

But – whazawa! My back! – potholes apart, the thing that strikes you most about the Albanian countryside are the concrete bunkers or pillboxes. They're – phwa! Twazh! –

everywhere. Originally built after the Soviets were kindly invited to invade Czechoslovakia back in 1968, there are said to be over 300,000 of them scattered all over the country, one for every ten inhabitants. Some are morning-after-sized pillboxes. Others are huge, two-weeks-at-Club-Med-sized pillboxes. Some look as though they're in good condition; a good few of them have even been converted into homes or cowsheds.

Why don't they remove them? 'Just try,' said one businessman who'd just got back from Kosovo, where he told me he had a big printing business. 'They're the toughest things in the country. They're made of the best-quality concrete. They're reinforced with the best-quality steel. What's more, each one was individually tested. Twice. First, they put a goat in it and bombed it. If the goat survived, they tested it with a soldier inside it. If he survived it was passed fit for service. If he didn't, well, it wasn't, and they just got another soldier.'

Eventually, about 20 kilometres and three and a half weeks after leaving Tirana, the country opens out and you see a big hotel about halfway up a hillside on your left. At first you wonder what it is. A modern building, all fancy glass, in the middle of nowhere. But whatever you're after, this is the place to be. Ask for Sotir. Mention my name. He'll look after you.

The first time I went there I thought I was in some strange Mafia holiday camp. There were all these tall, pale, thin guys with long, greasy hair down to their shoulders, all dressed in black leather: black leather shirts, black leather ties, black leather suits, black leather boots, black leather overcoats, black leather gloves and the regulation two-day designer stubble. They were drinking Coca-Cola, whispering to each other, barking down mobile telephones or just staring vacantly out of the windows. The next time I went there they were with their families: wives who looked like blowsy young barmaids; bow-legged, hunched-up old mamas and 8-foot, 30-stone brothers who seemed to have a couple of NATO tanks tucked away in their armpits. And, of course, a million *bambini* running around, shrieking at the tops of their voices. Whatever they were doing, whether it was sitting in reception bored out of their minds with their families, wandering around outside laughing and joking into their mobile phones or even sitting down in the restaurant having plateful after plateful of spaghetti, the guys were still wearing their black leather shirts, black leather ties, black leather suits, black leather boots, black leather overcoats, black leather gloves and the regulation two-day designer stubble. And drinking Coca-Cola. It was weird.

As for the business, once I had passed on to everyone love and kisses from the family back home in, er, Palermo – well, what else was I supposed to do? – it was down to the details.

CDs, cassettes, the latest Windows 2000 or whatever, you can pretty well take away with you. If, however, you prefer to travel light, they can be delivered wherever you want, whenever you want. Gucci glasses, watches, pants or whatever; Hermès scarves, Hermès anything with horsey things on it; anything Louis Vuitton; Prada; Fendi; Salvatore Ferragamo; Dior; Chanel; whoever, they've got the lot. All guaranteed the very best, genuine, AA grade counterfeits. All direct from reputable world-class counterfeiters. Most of them in Shenzen, southern China, just across the way from Hong Kong. A few, the perfumes especially, from the Lebanon.

Visas, passports, virtually any kind of official document, they can fix. But it'll cost you. Three-month Greek visas are US$575; Italian visas US$1,000; British visas US$2,200 and US visas US$12,000. Passports? Greek, US$500; Italian, US$2,500. British are a touch more expensive at US$10,000 and US a whopping US$25,000. Payment on delivery, naturally. What do you want, charity? As for the quality, you've got no worries. They're as good as the originals, if not better. They buy the same equipment, the same papers, the same inks and the same anti-counterfeiting security devices. The documents are also produced by far more skilled and far more experienced designers and printers who are, of course, paid far more money to live and work in far more beautiful surroundings than High Wycombe, Buckinghamshire. After all, this is not some back-room, hole-in-the-corner operation. This is the real thing. It's also responsible for making more money than the real thing. Much more money.

One guy I once met in a bar somewhere or other told me that before he left his job in a bank and started working for a living, he did a trial run from Tirana to Vienna to test some passports he was negotiating to buy. He travelled on his own passport, which was genuine. He was stopped by Austrian customs, taken away and questioned for a couple of hours. The guys using the false passports got through without a hitch.

Drugs? That's a whole new department, what with Kosovo, just up the road, now virtually the European distribution centre for everything you could ever want: heroin, marijuana, hashish, whatever. One long black overcoat, when he wasn't trying to stop his kid from throwing bread rolls all over the restaurant, told me that everything was controlled by just four local families. Because they were locals, and because they were just four families, the whole thing was impregnable. Nobody could break into the net. A bit like the Adams family in north London. Before Tony Blair and Bill Clinton came along and liberated them, they had problems. The Serbs used to have an anti-narcotics squad which gave them a lot of aggro. Even during the war the Serbs were more interested in finding where the heroin was hidden than in beating up old ladies, because it meant money, big money. A kilogram of heroin in Belgrade was worth US$25,000. Ship it out to Britain, France or Germany, and it could be worth two or even three times as much.

Now, thanks to their friends, it was boom time. Shipments were up from two tons a month to 5 tons and still rising, with no risks involved. The Serbs had gone; the Kosovans who were after their business had moved on or were for one reason or another no longer around. There was no law and order in the area. The military were only interested in keeping the Serbs and Kosovans apart. They now had a free hand. They could do whatever they liked.

If I wanted to buy any heroin or whatever, it could be arranged. From Afghanistan, through the Caucasus, and now more and more often through Chechnya, it would come to Turkey. From Turkey it would find its way to Kosovo. From Kosovo, it could go by truck either through Germany, Belgium and France or through Hungary, Poland, Germany and Holland, or by boat to Italy, across Italy to Marseilles then up through France and across the Channel to Dover. They had friends in Barking in east London and Maida Vale in west London – the Lisi was a nice local Albanian restaurant. I should go in there for dinner. I'd meet some interesting people – who could make arrangements for the final drop from Dover.

But before we talked detail, they would need some character references to make sure I was a suitable person to do business with. No problem. So, while the administrators got to work, I continued to head west to the coast. More potholes. More donkeys. More men dragging their old cows along behind them.

Now the road drops down and you come to the worst road junction in the whole world. Everywhere there's mud. Not ordinary mud, but thick, gooey, squelchy mud. You drive across a narrow bridge, and if it's a dry day you come to this roundabout completely submerged in water. Thick, muddy, gooey, squelchy water. If it's a wet day all you can do is put on your wetsuit, switch on your oxygen supply and pray that your car is waterproof. Overhead are the struts of a road bridge that the Romans – or was it the Greeks? – first started building 2,000 years ago. This carries a road which apparently runs the length of the country, virtually linking Athens in the south with Titograd in Montenegro in the north. Out to the left on the beach is a big NATO military base which is supposed to be a supply depot for Kosovo.

This is decision time. Turn right and you head for Durres, known, of course, to us Greek scholars as Epidamnos. Epi: get in, get the car, get out; Damnos: otherwise you'll be condemned to twenty years in jail unless your brother is friendly with the local judge. The road is not so bad. The usual potholes, the usual mud, the usual three smashed-up old trucks trying to overtake each other on a hairpin bend built for one and a half bicycles. The usual Albanian object lesson in road safety.

The first thing you see as you drop down into Durres are a mass of tiny shacks and sheds and mini-bungalows. This is all your illegal housing. When things started hotting up in northern Albania and Kosovo, thousands of families fled here for safety. There was nowhere for them to live so they built their own houses. There was little the city fathers could do. There was no way they could object, knock down the houses and send them back, so they had to let them stay, under Durres, no doubt.

Further into town you begin to think Mediterranean. On a cool day it's hot, dusty and very sticky. On a hot day in the middle of summer, when temperatures can soar as high as 40 degrees Celsius, it's Africa.

Down at the port, whether it's a cool day or a hot day, the mercury is spurting out of the top of the one thermometer in town. But his is where it all happens. From Bari, from Brindisi, from Ancora, from Trieste, from Koper come ferries carrying all the cars and vans and trucks lifted from the car parks, backyards and front drives of Germany, Switzerland and Italy. Mercedes, Porsches, Audis, Peugeots, Volvos – whatever, they're unloaded as if it was the most normal thing in the world for huge ferries full of stolen cars to dock at a port and discharge their cargo into a world of black leather jackets. In fact so many stolen Mercedes have been unloaded here that Albania, the poorest country in Europe with the worst roads in Europe, actually has more Mercedes per head of population than any other country in Europe.

Occasionally, however, ships will sail in unannounced, armed crews will take over the entire port, port officials will look the other way and whole shiploads of special cars full of hi-tech schnozzle will be unloaded and driven into the countryside. What makes them special nobody has ever dared to ask. Or if they have, they haven't lived to tell the tale.

But don't think for a moment that the government stands idly by. Now and then they will pretend they're in charge and send in both their totally honest, upright and wholly reliable crack troops to impose some semblance of law and order on the place by making ships pay their parking fees, their offloading fees and, of course, for their round of drinks for the port officials. But it never lasts long, maybe five or ten minutes. Which is hardly surprising when the prime minister himself goes around bragging that it was in Durres during the Kosovo War, with vast quantities of NATO shipments of aid and supplies disappearing into thin air before they even hit the deck, that NATO's supreme military commander, Wesley Clark, admitted learning for the first time in his life the true meaning of the word *bakshish*.

So, rigorous official Albanian government anti-corruption crackdowns permitting, you want a 1997 Mercedes 300, with or without smoked-glass windows? It's here. A whole stack of them. A gleaming four-wheel-drive Toyota Land Cruiser? It's here. A silvery metallic-looking Porsche? It's here.

Talk to the dozy old port officials. If for some reason you can't find them, talk to the customs officers. If you can't find them – and the chances are you won't, because they will have had to borrow anything between US$5,000 and US$10,000 to pay to you-know-who to get the job in the first place, so the last thing they can afford to do is hang around all day talking to strangers: they've got to be out wheeling and dealing to make enough money to pay back the loan before they even think of working for a living – go and talk to the illiterate country policemen at the gates. They'll show you all the official papers for all the cars, the stamps, the pretty pictures, the thumbprints of every authority between here and Bino Automobile An + Verkauf, Sokoli, Kassel (tel: 57.81.66). All legal, they say. All above board. All legitimate.

Talk to Adem and Arben and Kujtim in the bar just down the hill from the old Roman amphitheatre, and they'll tell you that not only are all the cars and vans and trucks stolen, but all the official papers and stamps and pretty pictures and thumbprints are forged as well. Buy them a couple of glasses of cheap, white Albanian wine, which shows you how easily they can be bought, and they'll also tell you how they get the cars as well.

An insurance dodge, they say. Somebody in Germany or Switzerland or Italy, or wherever the steering wheel is on the wrong side, wants a new car but can't afford it. What they do is contact their friendly local Albanian fixer. The German butcher, the Swiss clockmaker or the Italian ice-cream man arranges to leave his car parked outside his butcher's shop, his masonic lodge or his mistress's apartment with the key in the ignition, and, because they are such innocents, copies of all the papers relating to the car in the glove compartment. The Albanian fixer arranges for the car or whatever to be lifted. It's put on a truck, and within a few hours, complete with a new set of papers, it's on a ferry. The butcher, the clockmaker and especially the ice-cream man, who doesn't want to be hurried, waits until the following day. He then calls the police and reports his car or whatever stolen, claims back the cost from the insurance company, does a deal with his local garage and collects a brand new car. QED. Everybody's happy. All that happens is that the following year the insurance premiums jump another couple of points, but they were going to do that anyway. So where's the harm?

Of course, sometimes the butchers and the clockmakers and the ice-cream men are so keen to do the deal that they will drive their own cars or vans or whatevers on to the ferry, or even the long way round through Austria, Hungary or Poland to Durres. They then call the police back home and say that their car has been stolen. They left it outside their house last night, and it wasn't there in the morning when they got home. Ah, the joys of the mobile telephone.

In the past, one hitch with this service so kindly provided by the Albanians was that if all the ferries arrived at the same time you could hardly move for stolen cars parked in the streets of Durres. Not only that, but whole fields on the out-skirts of town were full of them as well. Today they're more organised. They have created a lot of small, manageable car parks all over town, and such is Albanian efficiency that the ferries are unloaded within two minutes of docking and the cars can be evenly spread across Durres in moments.

Originally, of course, most of the cars were for Albanians. Under our Enver there was hardly a private car in the country. What cars there were were for the military, the police and, of course, the secret police. Although how long a secret policeman could remain a secret policeman while driving around in a car in a country where there were no cars would have been an interesting subject for discussion if the poor Albanians had been allowed to discuss anything at the time. Photographs taken then show huge boulevards, enormous squares, tiny back streets with not a car in sight. Not a pot-hole either, but that's another story. Now the streets are packed with stolen cars, trucks, coaches, even school buses, many of them still carrying their original number plates. Incidentally, if Herr Doktor is looking for his big black Mercedes, it nearly ran me down as I was trying to cross from the Mosque of Elhem Bay to take a look at the statue of the great Albanian hero Skanderbeg, who beat the Turks 25–0. In fact, so many stolen cars are there in the country – forget the official estimates, which put the figure as low as 90 per cent – that even government ministers have been found to own them.

Today, of course – the Albanians are nothing if not flexi-ble – most of these cars are turned round and either shipped out again by ferry back to where they came from, though not necessarily to the same owners, or driven north, east, south and west, potholes permitting, all over Europe.

Ask Toru. He's usually in one of the bars on the edge of town, close to the old Russian-built hotel which was looted way back in 1997 and has been disintergrating ever since. He can offer you two deals. Instead of bringing everything to Durres, he can ship it direct to the UK. There would have to be a halfway point for all the, how shall we say, administration. Alternatively, he can ship direct from Durres. Obviously, it's going to cost a bit more, but not much. Then, once the cars are in either Bari or Brindisi or Ancora or Trieste, two days and they'll be in London. Papers. Everything.

There is one thing, however, I should tell you. Naturally, the police, in spite of, er, everything, have to fight back. Or at least pretend to fight back. What they've come up with is a special security seal which is fixed directly to the number plate. Toru says not to worry. They've already got a lean on one of the top security officials in Berlin who has already promised them the formula. If he doesn't come across they know where his friend goes for her weekly keep-fit classes, if you understand me.

As for bringing in Auntie Whatever-her-name-is and all her friends from Bangladesh, not to mention that Filipina girl you keep on about, I'm afraid it's back to the worst roundabout in the world. Now, instead of turning right for Durres, you turn left, for Vlora, Greek for You'll need a vlora, vlora, vlora luck if you're going to reach Brindisi, let alone Calais, without the police spotting you.

At one time the most dangerous city in the most dangerous country in Europe, this is where the famous Albanian pyramid schemes were dreamed up and launched, and where they crashed with disastrous consequences for everyone. Apart, of course, from the organisers. Hardly anyone in the country wasn't affected in one way or another by them. Drivers I've met lost US$5,000, US$10,000, US$15,000. An office manager told me that his whole family, including his mother and father, had lost over US$30,000. A waiter lost US$40,000, his life savings. Well, he's a waiter now – at the time he had a wife, a car, a flat in Tirana, a house in the country. Now he's got nothing. His wife left him pretty soon after the crash, which is par for the course even in Albania, quickly followed by his car, his flat and finally the house. Now he is sharing a single room with three other people round the back of Tirana University.

Vlora, of course, is also where, largely as a result of the collapse of the pyramid schemes, the whole country began to fall apart. People who had lost everything went on the rampage, looting everything in sight. The army, not surprisingly, rather than fighting back, joined in. Over 3 million grenades and bombs, not to mention 700,000 rifles, were just lifted. You can bet your life that a fair number of them ended up in the hands of the Kosovo Liberation Front. Others were sold on to God knows who.

If you still want to go to Vlora, you turn left, past the NATO base on the right, and, I must warn you, along some of the worst roads my poor old back has had to suffer – and I was in a brand-new Mercedes. Well, I say, brand-new. It was brand-new when it left Oerlikonerstrasse, Zurich the day before. Without, I noticed, the special security seal on the number plate. I only hope it won't be too long before Frau Schmidt is able to return to her keep-fit classes.

Once through the Valley of the Shadow of Death by a Thousand Potholes, you come to Fier. Believe me, I know the meaning of Fier. It is home not only to an old, badly damaged, leaky oil refinery, but also to an old, badly damaged, leaky fertiliser plant, an old, badly damaged, leaky thermal-power plant and, just to stretch the white corpuscles to breaking point, an ever-swelling lake containing no less than 830 cubic metres of arsenic. Some experts say, no doubt with the professional's love of understatement, that in hazardous-waste terms it's equivalent to Hiroshima. Others, straining every fibre of their being not to be alarmist, reason that as it seeps through the soil it could eventually threaten not only the Adriatic but also the entire Mediterranean. Yet amazingly it has been there since 1972 and still nobody has done anything about it. So when you go to Fier, you take a deep breath and then wonder whether it's serious to spit up so much blood.

I tried to drown my sorrows in the appropriately named Bar Emigrante on the main street, but they wouldn't let me in even though I had all the correct papers. So much for the way they treat emigrants. Instead I decided I needed freedom from Fier itself, so I took a side tour. I headed 12 kilometres outside the city, about three and a half days by road, to the top of a hill looking down over the Adriatic and the old Roman city of Apollonia, which Julius Caesar declared a free city, although that certainly wasn't my impression, judging by the number of guides, both official and unofficial, and all the different rates they were charging. Official or unofficial, they all agreed it was the oldest archaeological site in the country. But I had the devil's own job trying to decide where the archaeology ended and the country began. The trick, I discovered after a while, was to look for something clean, bright and intact. That was the archaeology.

From beautiful Roman roads it was back to modern, twenty-first century . . . Bloodyhellwhyonearthcantthey . . . potholes . . . More men, women and donkeys, all well past their sell-by dates – Fatza. Wha. Tcha. Mind that— More kids selling mountains of carrots by the side of the . . . Mwa. Hazu. Vlaw . . . More roadside butchers with shrivelled-up, mangy-looking strips of meat hanging from metal clotheslines and, sitting underneath it, a couple of sheep patiently waiting their turn for the . . . Zarha. Wah. MybackmybackIthinkitsfinallygone . . . And car washes. I'll say one thing for the Albanians. They might have more stolen cars per head of population than any other country on earth, but they certainly look after them. About every three potholes there's somebody offering either a bucket and sponge, a mobile spray or the full drive-in car wash. So Herr Meister Heischer Beck of Silutie Strasse, Emerich. If you're worried about what's happened to your beautiful brand new Mercedes S500, don't. It's alive and well and being beautifully looked after in Cerkovinë, Albania.

Finally, having shattered a string of Albanian land-speed records by covering something like 45 kilometres in two and a half days, you come to Vlora.

Forget the bunch of heavily armed highway robbers who turned out to be policemen who were stopping every car and bus and truck entering or leaving the place.

'Problemo. Molto,' I said to my driver in our impeccable Italiano-speak. 'Illegal emigrantes looking for. Capisce?'

He shook his head.

'*Baksheesh*,' he grinned. 'Dollars. Capisce?'

Forget the Museum of Independence where the Albanians proclaimed their independence way back in 1912. If they'd known how it was going to turn out they probably wouldn't have bothered. Forget all the filthy, wrecked old police cars chugging around with 'Tattimore' plastered all over them. It just about summed them up.

Instead head straight for the port. The first thing that strikes you is that it must be one of the most perfect bays in the world. It's almost completely surrounded by beautiful green hills. There's a small entrance in and out to the Straits of Otranto, which link the Adriatic to the Ionian Sea. Across the way – you can almost see it on a clear day, speedboat fumes permitting – is Corfu. A couple of hours in the other direction and you're in Italy. It's no wonder that in the old days Khrushchev was so desperate to get Vlora as a secret hideaway for his nuclear submarines.

It's also, of course, perfect for, as they say, shipping merchandise in and out of Europe. By plane, by road, by train, across the lakes on the border with Macedonia, even across the mountains from Montenegro they come. Especially the Kurds, who have nicknamed the place Trampoline: their jumping-off point into Europe. Strange sense of humour, the Kurds. Once in Albania, they're collected by trucks and shipped into Vlora, where they are spirited away to safe apartments and houses. Sometimes for a couple of days. Sometimes a week. Sometimes longer. Depending on how many of them there are. Their minders are not going to run a special service just for a handful. They want a full load. Usually that's twenty minimum, thirty maximum, depending on size, weight and how much is on offer. Usually it's US$1,000 a throw. Sometimes as much as US$10,000. It's a market price. Then there's the weather. Bombing across the

Adriatic at up to 70 knots an hour in gale-force winds in the middle of the night, with no lights and no radar, in a rubber boat with four souped-up outboard motors is not the safest way to travel. While they cheerfully admit they might not lose too much sleep over mislaying one boatload they've got their reputation to protect like anyone else.

Then, of course, there are all the incidentals. Like the law. When these businessmen first set up their operation they had everything to themselves, but nothing lasts for ever. The Italians moved in and set up a big radar station just outside Vlora. The Financial Guardia, a special police force, set up a base on Sazan Island, just off the Karaburun Peninsula. The San Marco Battalion started patrolling the whole of the coast from Vlora to Durres at night. Agreements had to be worked out. The right people had to be found. Arrangements had to be made for the Italians to have some successes in preventing the flow of illegal immigrants, so a routine had to be established, the occasional boat discovered. Hence the price range. Now they reckon everything is in order. Some boats carry guarantees, others don't. Most, however, get through. Hence the ever-growing demand for the service.

If you want to make the necessary contacts, start off at the bar in the Bologna Hotel right by the harbour. This, incidentally, is where the intrepid gentlemen of the world's press hid away and kept their heads down and their notebooks out of sight as they wrote all their eyewitness accounts of the complete collapse of Albania. Have a couple of drinks there. Practise your Kurdish. Get yourself acclimatised. Then, just before you've had enough, come out, turn right and head for the Sun Bay Bar and Restaurant.

A warning: don't try and walk along the beach. They say it's perfect for holidaymakers, ideal for families and all that stuff, but forget it. It's not so much sand as earth. There's rubbish all over the place, including no end of burnt-out cars.

And as for what could be hidden underneath, it's best not to even think about it. Instead do what I do, stroll along the road.

At the Sun Bay Bar and Restaurant you'll soon forget all your troubles. Sit outside overlooking the water. A nice old lady will shuffle out and serve you. Ask her for a large Campari. Not with soda, but with mineral water, the way the Italians drink it. After a while, if you hit lucky, you'll meet Pirro. He's the guy you want to see. He'll fix everything.

Why go to the bar of the Hotel Bologna first? So that you're spotted, checked out, assessed and decisions can be made as to whether you're kept waiting five minutes, ten minutes or for ever. Don't you know anything?

After the deed is done, you can, of course, get the hell out of there as fast as the potholes will allow. Which I would not recommend. First because of the potholes. Don't forget there are 3.27 million of them between you and Tirana. Second, because it's bound to attract someone's attention that you've dragged yourself halfway across Europe for a five-minute meeting. What I do is have a couple more large Camparis at the Sun Bay, wander back to the Hotel Bologna for a large plate of their *spaghetti frutti del mare* and I forget how many beers. Don't bother with the local Albanian wine. It'll take away the taste of the *frutti del mare* and anything else you eat until your Auntie or whoever arrives in Chipping Sodbury. And don't, whatever you do, worry about sitting there by yourself staring forlornly at the ships unloading at the port. Instead ask any local how long it's going to be before they go for the big one and establish their own Greater Albania. That'll use up a couple of weeks.

The southerners will say no way. The south, they say, is different from the north. They have different dialects, different customs, different traditions. Their traditional dress is the two-piece suit. On traditional occasions they might wear the flat white fez, but that's usually only after a couple of bottles of stiff Albanian Cognac. Furthermore, if they mean yes they shake their heads, and if they mean no, they nod. Their Tosk dialect is the official language of the country, although in many ways they are more Greek than Albanian. So much so that they can stroll across the mountains into Greece in their hundreds of thousands, work there for a couple of years, then amble back home again without anybody noticing the difference. Those who don't fancy the walk across the mountains in the middle of winter can go to Italy instead. They catch a boat, either legally or illegally, work there for a couple of years, then catch the boat back. Again nobody notices the difference. Whereas the north, they say, is a different country. They have different dialects. They speak with funny accents. They have different customs. They wear suits that look as though they've come from Oxfam. On traditional occasions they wear little white skullcaps. They have different traditions. The big tradition, of course, being big families.

'In the north they always have eight children,' one southerner told me once in the Bologna. 'It is their custom. Two in case they die. Two to join the army. Two to go to work. Two to stay at home and look after them when they get old. It's no wonder the Serbs were frightened they were going to take over.'

The other big difference, according to the southerners, is that apparently, if the northerners mean yes they nod. If they mean no they shake their heads. Which, of course, might be one reason why they have so many children. Oh yes, and, the southerners say, the northerners have big noses.

The northerners meanwhile are all for a Greater Albania. First, they say, because the Albanians were all over not only present-day Albania but vast chunks of the surrounding countries as well before anybody else even knew they existed. The original Albanians, or if you prefer, the Albonoi, an

Illyrian tribe, arrived around 2000 BC. No doubt by way of Mercedes BC. Way before the Visigoths, the Huns, the Ostrogoths, the Slavs, the Bulgarians, the Normans and the Turks, all beaten by our great Albanian hero, Skanderbeg, in all twenty-five battles he fought against them. Not to mention the French, the Italians, the Austro-Hungarians and of course, Mussolini and Hitler. Secondly, because, they say, not only were the Albanians all over the place before anybody else arrived on the scene, they are still all over the place.

Look at the surrounding countries. Montenegro. The Turks might not have been able to conquer it, but the Albanians have. They're everywhere. In Cetinje, the old capital, which is about as Ruritanian as you can get, I've come across loads of Albanians. In Titograd, the new capital, it's the same story. In fact the whole of the big industrial complex at Niksic would probably have to shut down if it wasn't for the Albanians.

Serbia. Well, we all know what's happening to the Albanians in Serbia. There was no greater proof of the north-south divide in Albania than when, during the war first in Serbia and then during the war in Kosovo, over 500,000 Albanians fled both the Serbs and the NATO bombing. As one northerner told me: 'All the northern Albanians immediately took in two, maybe three whole families. Sometimes ten, sometimes fifteen, sometimes twenty extra people. We had to. They were Albanians. We are Albanians. We are the same. But in the south . . .'

Macedonia. You've only got to mention Albanians in Macedonia and everyone immediately shrieks Ohrid! Ohrid! Ohrid! Although what the pretty little lakeside resort on Lake Ohrid, way down in the south of the country, has got to do with it, I don't know. Whenever I go there, I come across more gypsies than Albanians. The first time I visited the place, the broken-down Yugo I was in needed urgent repairs. We pulled into a garage. The first question the mechanic asked me was nothing about the car, but whether I was Christian or a Muslim. Now, I know my name is Peter, but I didn't think it was worth denying anyone or anything for the sake of a sticky petrol pump. So I told him I was a Macedonian. He fixed the car for free.

Apart from the odd handful in various villages all over the country, most of the Albanians seem to be concentrated in Tetova, the former home of the big whirling dervish community, where the mayor once flew the Albanian flag and was sent to jail for his trouble; in Gostivar, where they are jostling the Turks for the honours, and in Debar on the shores of the artificial Lake Spiljsko. All the same, although nobody admits it, they make up about a third of the population.

Greece. Forget for a moment the fact that the Albanians came from Greece in the first place, and that the Albanians or, to be precise, the southern Albanians, the ones with the not quite so big noses, are kissing cousins to the Greeks. They've been tramping backwards and forwards across the mountains for hundreds of years, especially at Easter, which no self-respecting Greek would dream of celebrating without his stack of red-dyed eggs and a whole roast lamb, when they do a roaring trade smuggling lamb across the border. Once in Greece some stay Albanian. They speak Albanian, keep up their Albanian customs. They live like Albanians. Others become Greek. They change their names. Hoxha becomes Aristotle, Zogu becomes Plato, that kind of thing. Some even end up – honour of honours – playing for Greek football teams, winning gold medals for the Greek Olympic team, drinking Greek beer and in all respects being such a credit to the country that nobody bothers to ask them if they actually have any papers.

Now ask an Albanian politician whether he thinks Greater

Albania is a runner or not. He won't answer the question, of course – politicians never do. But he'll um and ah and say no without expressly saying no. Because it would mean upsetting the status quo, and most politicians are reluctant to do that. Because it couldn't be done voluntarily. Because it would cause enormous disruption, and so on. After all, much as the surrounding countries love their Albanian brothers, the last thing they want to do is surrender a vast chunk of land and revenues. And finally because – and this surprised me when I discussed the idea with Albanian politicians – they feel it would upset the great powers: the USA and Europe. The great powers had done a great deal for Albania, they said, and especially for the Albanians in Kosovo. Going for a Greater Albania they thought would be pushing their luck. In any case, they didn't have any money. They didn't have any leverage. I know it all sounds terribly nineteenth century, but that's what they said.

So, discussion over in the bar at the Bologna, if you're still in one piece there's only one thing left to do: put away as much booze as you can so you can forget the potholes and – *arrivederci*, Vlora – head back to Tirana.

Once you are back in Tirana, your deals done, your back pulverised, treat yourself to a couple more drinks, a meal or whatever you like at the Lady Diana Club. Everybody knows it. Don't ask me why, but in Albania, certainly, and throughout Eastern Europe in general, 'Lady Diana' seems to indicate an establishment offering a range of specialist services at very high prices. Again, just mention my name. They'll look after you and make sure you have a good time.

You might not make a million wheeling and dealing on your first visit to Albania, but you will eventually. It's just a case of Tirana boom delay.

Palermo

My friend, my friend, come in. Come in. Welcome to Palermo. Take off that silly *coppola*. They say they're the Mafia *birrittu*, or beret, but it's not true. It's all Hollywood. Don't listen to them. It makes you look like a *cafone*. So, *come sta?* Sit down, sit down. You're at home now. The mob's your uncle, as we say.

Now, what will you have? A glass of Strega? We always used to drink Strega in the old days, especially in the States. Here, though, we always used to drink champagne. You should have seen the champagne we used to get through. And the caviar as well. *Mamma mia*, we had mountains of it. Usually at the Hotel Villa Igeia overlooking the sea. Sometimes at the Hotel Zagarellas. Ah, those were the days. The Villa Igeia, let me tell you, was so exclusive that the number for reception was ex-directory.

Careful. Mind the board. We were just playing Tangentopoli. It's like Monopoly, except you don't make money buying and selling properties. You make money bribing everybody in sight so that you can become a town councillor or, better still, mayor and then really clean up, taking back-handers for all kinds of property deals. Very Italian. Goes on all the time. All over the place. Rome, Milan, Venice, Turin, Reggio Calabria, Mill Bavin, Brooklyn and, of course, here in Sicilia. So the more practice you can get, the better. Me? I don't have to practise. I'm perfect at it already.

No, don't tell me how cosy you think it is in here. I know from the outside it just looks like any other ordinary little house in an ordinary little street in an ordinary little town in Sicilia. But you can't be too careful nowadays. All my friends, especially my Moustache Petes, they are all pinched, all in the can – or in university, as we like to call it, because they'll learn more in there than they ever will outside. There are now so many in prison they say that VIP no longer stands for Very Important Person. It now stands for *Visitato In Prigione*. The doors you came through. You noticed? They're armour-plated. The very best US steel. Had them specially made. You'd need a nuclear *bomba* to get through them. Even then you probably still wouldn't get through. The windows are fake. *Illusione*. Outside in the street you think you're looking into a regular house, but of course you're not. The outside·is just the shell. What we're in now was all specially built inside the shell. Again, all specially made. All specially delivered. Couldn't have done it without the experience gained playing Tagentopoli.

You like paintings? Over there is Rembrandt's *Portrait of a Lady*. You recognise it? *Bene*. Next to it Bellini's *Portrait of a Young Man*. On the other wall is, guess what, Cézanne's double-sided watercolour. On one side is *Lakeside with a Lake*. On the other is *Sentry Between Two Rocks*. Got it from the National Gallery in Rome. It was ten days before they realised it was missing. I ask you, if they didn't know for ten days it was missing, it seems to me it might as well be here, where it is far more appreciated. It wouldn't take me ten seconds to know if it wasn't here.

The altar and all the holy pictures? They're the ones we use when we get the button or, as you say, for our initiation ceremonies. You know, when you cut your finger, let the blood drip on to one of the holy pictures then set fire to it and hold it in your hand while it burns, praying that your flesh may burn like the holy picture if you ever betray your *omertà*, your vow of loyalty. Something we picked up from the Albanians a long time ago. Maybe not as exciting as rolling your trousers up, wearing a leather apron and taking your funny Masonic vows, but much, much, more effective, I can assure you.

Yes, you're right. I've also got a special escape system. Just in case some young *babbo* decides he wants to do some free-lance work. It's upstairs. In two minutes I can be outta here and in a car on the other side of town. Good, eh? A tip I picked up from the Ndrangheta, our friends across the water in Calabria. I got them to do it. They've got all the contacts in the Balkans and Eastern Europe who make that kind of thing. Couldn't trust anyone here to do it for me. Not that I'll ever need to use the escape route, because the big, big thing about this house is that it's invisible. No, really. Nobody in the street ever sees it. Ask the local *polizìa* if it exists. They'll say they have no record of it. I don't even get any bills delivered. See what I mean? It's invisible. And if it's invisible, how can anyone know I'm here? It's the same if you leave your car parked outside. Within two seconds you won't see that, either.

Now, enough of that. You haven't come all this way to hear me going on about *la mia casa*. What you want me to tell you, I understand, is all the interesting places to go and visit in Sicilia. Not the historic places like the Palatine Chapel in Palermo, the Greek temples at Agrigento, the Greek theatre at Syracuse, that tiny Roman church in Yaormina, Mount Etna, Messina and all that Scylla and Charybdis business.

We've been invaded so many times – by the Phoenicians, the Carthaginians, the Greeks, the Romans, the Normans, the Muslims, the Spanish, the French and even the Italians – I reckon we've got too much to see. But that's only one old man's opinion.

What's far more interesting, I think, is our culture, all the things we've given the world, all the traditions we've created that have been copied far and wide. Murder. Torture. Terrorism. Kidnapping. *Pizzo*. Protection. Extortion. Gunrunning. Blackmail. Embezzlement. Racketeering. Fraud. Then there are all the businesses, big businesses, big, multinational, billion-dollar businesses, we've created. Tax evasion. Drugs. Piracy. Drugs. Money-laundering. Drugs. Stockmarket scams. Drugs. Fiddling the IMF and the World Bank, especially in Russia. Drugs. Security. Drugs. Insurance. Drugs. Computer piracy. Drugs. Credit cards. Drugs. Importing morphine from Turkey. Drugs. Not to mention all the incidentals: baby chicks, horses' heads, acid baths, concrete waistcoats, concrete coffins, stuffing your cheeks with Kleenex and going around mumbling, 'Who should you come to if not your godfather?' Dear Carlo, Carlo Gambino. How he used to love that. Said the whole thing was based on him. What a man. Forty years in the business, and never spent a day in jail. I was with him, you know, just before he died. Of a heart attack. In 1976.

Of course, I nearly forgot, one of our greatest developments: the numbers racket. You don't know the numbers racket? Go into any bar or restaurant in East Harlem and you'll see the numbers racket. They've got it off to perfection. It's a joy to behold. The other day I saw some report saying our turnover in the numbers racket alone is almost as big as Fiat's. About US$15 to US$20 billion a year. I don't know about that, but we're certainly doing very well. Very, very well. And I bet you we don't have half, one quarter, one

hundredth of the book-keepers and accountants and administrators Fiat has.

I don't know about you, but I don't think that's bad for a
little island the size of a plate of macaroni, steeped in *misèria*,
age-old poverty and destitution. We were so poor we even
missed out on Garibaldi's land reforms. Most people here
ended up owning less land after his reforms than before, while
somehow or other the rich landowners ended up with even
more than they had in the first place. Maybe that's why we've
been able to give the world so much.

OK, so you want to see the real Sicilia? Well, first you must
go to Corleone. Yes, I know it's the same name as the family
in . . . what's the name of that book? But it's a real town.
Well, village to you, I suppose. About 5,000 people. On the
side of a hill. Tiny little streets. Narrow alleyways. A little village square with a statue of St Francis of Assisi. A nice little
bar, the Leone d'Oro. Lots of old men sitting around remi-
niscing about the old days. Chicago, New York, weekends in
Newport, Rhode Island. The occasional police car. Driving
straight down the middle of the road. Not taking any notice
of what's going on. Old habits die hard. The village is surrounded by wide, open fields, trees – the Forest of Ficuzza
holds many a secret, I can tell you – and, conveniently
enough, a mass of deep, bottomless crevasses, although
they're not as deep or as bottomless as they used to be. It was
always known as the home of *i viddani*, the evil ones. It's
where the modern family, la Cosa Nostra, began.

I will tell you a story. Here, have another glass of Strega.
Or, if you prefer, some of this walnut liqueur. We make it
here. It's *molto bene*. What was I saying? Oh yes. The last war.
1943. The English, under your famous Lord Field Marshal
Montgomery, invaded the east coast. It took them five weeks
to fight their way up to Palermo, and they suffered heavy
casualties, some people say several thousand. Patton and the

US 7th Army invaded the west coast. They had no problems. They practically walked in. Within seven days they had swept through central and western Sicilia with the minimum of casualties. Patton, when he wasn't beating up men in hospital suffering from battle fatigue, went around saying it was because he mounted the biggest *blitzkrieg* in history. It was his leadership. It was the superior fighting skills of the Americans. Pah! The Americans were successful because Salvatore was with them. Salvatore Luciano. He was the *capo di tutti capi* of the American branch of the family. At the time he was serving up to fifty years in an American prison on ninety different counts of nothing. Extortion, prostitution, that kind of thing. But he did a deal. He told the Americans he wanted to help his old country, and they let him go, on condition he helped them win the battle.

Helped them win the battle? What 'Lucky' Luciano did was a stroke of genius. He told the Americans that before they invaded, they should tell everybody they were coming. What's more, they should drop flags with a big 'L' in the centre over the whole of the western part of the island. The 'L', he told them, stood for *libertà*, liberty. So the Americans produced millions of these flags and dropped them all over the area before the invasion began. What happened was unbelievable. Three quarters of the Italian army immediately turned and ran away. The Americans said it was because they knew what they had coming to them. Rubbish. It wasn't because they were scared of the Americans, but because they knew that 'L' did not stand for *libertà*, but for Luciano. Nobody wanted to be seen fighting against a man who was the boss of Murder Incorporated, who had ended all-out war between two opposing gangs by killing both their leaders, who had been responsible for forty murders, six attempted murders, forty robberies and over sixty extortion rackets, and who had been the *capo di tutti capi* of both the Sicilian Mafia and the

American Mafia. Another not inconsiderable factor was that they knew 20 to 25 per cent of the troops under Patton were Sicilian, and just itching to get their hands on the guys who had been going round raping their wives and daughters while they had been away fighting for the Americans.

Take Corleone. This American, Captain De Carlo, just drove in with some buddies and we all surrendered immediately. Why? Because he was also family. His cousin was Dr Michele Navarra, who was chief medical officer, the director of the hospital, the boss of the local Christian Democrats and, of course, chief book-keeper. In other words, Dr Navarra was also the *capomafia*, the head of the local family.

Being both the local *dottore* and the don was often very useful. Many's the time certain people were rushed to hospital after, shall we say, an incident, but unfortunately, in spite of all Dr Navarra's care and attention, did not survive. One particular case I remember concerned a ten-year-old shepherd boy. He saw something he shouldn't have seen in the woods outside the village one evening. Probably somebody or other being burned. He ran back to his mother, screaming hysterically. His mother rushed him to the hospital. Sadly, he never recovered. The following morning he was dead. A great shame. Nobody ever discovered what he saw in the woods that so terrified him.

Mamma mia, I often wonder if the Americans knew what they were doing. Dr Navarra, he was a great man. Everyone called him 'our father'. He was a good hunter, he played cards. He went to Captain De Carlo. He thanked him for liberating the island and finally bringing peace to everybody. Unfortunately, he told him, in the process, the Americans had wrecked our beautiful countryside and left all kinds of Jeeps and army vehicles and trucks and so on scattered all over the place. For a small fee, he told them, he would be only too pleased to collect them all together and restore the countryside to its original beauty. Of course De Carlo agreed. Within days Dr Navarra had restored enough vehicles to start regular bus services between all the villages. It was brilliant. It cost us nothing, and from then on it was not only a grand source of income, it also meant we always knew where everybody was going. The bus service grew and grew, and eventually it became the AST, the big bus company in Sicilia today.

Since then we've helped the American government on many occasions. Because we hated Mussolini far more than we hated the Americans we tracked down many Italian as well as German spies for them. Because we controlled the docks and the trades unions we helped them find many saboteurs. Then, in more recent times, in Latin America, in Asia, because we work closely with all the drugs barons or, as they call them today, narco-guerrillas, we were able to finger many local Communists. A healthy association. Mutual respect on both sides.

Incidentally, before I forget, did you see *Time* magazine? They recently hailed Luciano as one of the greatest 'business geniuses' of the century. What an honour for a poor boy from Corleone. Although knowing Lucky, he probably leaned on the judges. Did you see the photograph of him with his cousins? They're not his cousins. They're his *brugad*, his bodyguards. You can always tell. One of them is always holding a cigarette. That's because Lucky never liked being photographed with a cigarette. He probably didn't want anyone to think he'd support anything that was harmful to people's lives.

When you've seen the hospital, take a look at the local cemetery. It's just down from the *piazza*. In Sicilia most people visit their local cemetery maybe once or twice a week. Not to pay their respects to the dead, but to make certain that the money or the drugs or the guns and ammunition they've hidden in the family vaults are still there. But you have to be careful. Go too often and it attracts attention. A friend of mine, Pasquale, he went every morning because he used to keep all his cocaine supplies hidden in his mother's tomb. One morning he was arrested by police pretending to be cemetery workers. Somebody checked. They found out that his mother was still alive.

When I go there, I tell you what I do. I sit there and I think, how is it this small village in Sicilia became the head-quarters, the centre of one of the greatest money-making organisations in the world? The killings. The bombings. The torturing. The stealing. The extortion. That's all wrong, I know. But at the same time it takes organisation. It takes management. It takes strategy. It takes cunning. How come little Corleone has given the world first Dr Navarra, then Luciano Liggio and finally Salvo Riini, or Uncle Toto, as we all call him? Dr Navarra was good. But he was old-time. Luciano was good and new. But Salvo Riini, Toto, he's in a class of his own.

Go and have a look at his tiny little house in the Via Scorsone. His wife, Ninetta Bagarella, and his four children still live there today. Some people say that Ninetta is respon-sible for everything. She taught Toto to read. And the book she used to teach him to read was, can you imagine, Machiavelli's *The Prince*. After that there was no stopping him. He started by kidnapping practically everybody in sight. That made him a lot of money. Then he took over the other families in Palermo, San Giuseppe Iato, Trapani, Partinico, Mazara del Vallo and elsewhere. He tied up with the Camorra in Naples.

He is the man who made the family what it is today. When he took over we were still mediaeval, like the Albanese. He transformed us into a modern, up-to-date, worldwide, multi-national, billion-dollar operation, the greatest secret organisation in history. Before we were lots of different families. Now we have a structure, regional bosses, district bosses. He also, of course, took us into drugs. At first we all thought it was an interesting sideline. None of us realised it was going to become such a huge, worldwide money-making business. I doubt if even Toto did. Unfortunately, lots of people got in the way. They had to be iced. Over sixty people in Corleone itself, God rest their souls. But we would not be the fighting force we are today if it wasn't for Toto.

Mamma mia. I can remember him when he was our local butcher. A small man, but built like an ox. He never went to school. He didn't even speak good Italian. But he was lots of fun, a good cook. Once, I remember, he even cooked a fox casserole. It was very tasty, although not many people were happy with the idea of eating fox, even in Sicilia. If he liked you, he liked you. If he didn't, he could kill you with his bare hands. They say he either killed or had killed 800, 900 men, many of them rivals in the organisation, *capos*, many of them troublemakers, policemen, judges. I don't know if that's true but he certainly killed a lot of people. Once he showed me how he killed his first victim. It was a friend he was playing bowls with in Corleone. Toto was just nineteen. He did it the way he killed his sheep. You tie their hands and feet behind their back, tight. Then you tie the rope round their neck. As the muscles relax and expand the rope slackens then tightens, slackens and tightens, so that the victim kills himself. Doing it that way had another advantage, he told me. Afterwards it was easy to just pick up the body, throw it into the back of the car and then dispose of it. His son, incidentally, also killed his first victim when he was nineteen. A family tradition.

Toto was arrested. He went to college, but only for six years. He had influence even in those days. After he came out, he started butchering stolen cattle for Luciano Liggio. They had a secret abattoir in the woods at Ficuzza. Liggio was a gamekeeper on one of the big estates of Corleone. He knew everything and everybody. He was head of the Corleone family. He murdered the previous don in order to become the head of the whole family. But in the end, in spite of everything, he suffered the cruellest possible death anyone could imagine. He died in prison. I reckon he taught Toto all he knew.

In the late 1950s, early 1960s, we had another war. Over 150 people were burned. Dozens disappeared. Toto was arrested, but he was let off. When he went back to Corleone, however, he was again arrested. This time he was exiled to a small town near Bologna. But he never got there. He disappeared. For the next twenty-five years he was on the run. Or at least, that's what the police said. In fact, all the time he was living in Palermo. Then, suddenly, one day they picked him up. Who knows, maybe the envelope wasn't delivered on time. He was then the star in what they called the mega-trial.

A word of advice. If you're going to Corleone, don't go there looking like that. Blazers went out years ago. And get rid of that *coppola*. Don't forget you're going to a small farming village in the middle of nowhere. You've got to look like everybody else. You've got to be inconspicuous. Get yourself a three-piece Armani suit, a button-up white shirt, cufflinks, no tie. Wear a tie and you'll look like, how do they say? an associate, someone who hasn't made the grade. And the violin case. My friend, do you honestly believe. . . And whatever you do, promise me you won't go around kissing everybody in sight and doing that 'Here, share an olive with me' routine. Frankie always used to do that in America. When he was on his way up, when he first started his singing, we told him it was a sign of eternal friendship. He believed us. The schmuck. It was just a joke. But he kept on saying it for the rest of his life. Here-share-an-olive-with-me, Here-share-an-olive-with-me. I'm surprised he didn't have it set to music.

After Corleone, go to Palermo. Not by car, by bus. That will remind you of poor old Dr Navarra. In fact, while Dr Navarra was doing his little deal with the Americans, two of our other friends were doing even bigger deals, or their bits and pizzas, as we say. Vito Ciancimino teamed up with Salvo Lima. Vito was from Corleone. His father was my barber. Salvo became mayor of Palermo. Vito, he put in charge of public works. Between the two of them they ran the place. And how they ran it. In just four years they issued over 4,000 building permits, over 3,000 of them directly or indirectly to the family. We built cheap housing and expensive housing. We built estates. No expense was spared. At least, not when it came to sending in the bills. As for the buildings themselves, we built them as quickly and as cheaply as possible. Why not? That's why today Palermo has what I call a family feel to it.

One small stretch along the Viale della Libertà has all the expensive shops you can imagine: Armani, Versace, Louis Vuitton, Gucci. Here and there are some nice blocks of flats. On the Piazza Giuseppe Verdi is the Teatro Massimo, the new opera house, the second-largest opera house in the whole of Italy and one of the largest in Europe. It opened about twenty years late and is still hardly ever used. For some reason or other all the productions are staged at an open-air theatre on the edge of town where you can hardly hear what's going on because some Arab band across the street drowns out all the singing. But that doesn't matter. At least you can go to the opera without having to sit with your back to the door. The rest of Palermo is pure mediaeval. Tiny, twisting alley-ways. Houses falling down. Unlike most modern architects and builders, so good were we at fitting in with the existing environment that it's difficult to tell what we built after the war and what was built 500 years ago. Except that what was built 500 years ago is in better condition than what we built fifty years ago.

But that's not important. Salvo and Vito were pleased. Whenever they went anywhere they were greeted like, how you say, royalty. They would go into restaurants and people would stand and applaud. Some would even come up and kiss their hands. It was beautiful. Unfortunately Vito was later arrested and tried as a Mafioso, the first person in history to have that honour. They said he was worth over US$10 million, which I can tell you was a lie. He was worth much more than that.

Then, one day in Rome, Salvo met Giulio Andreotti. Andreotti had been a Cabinet minister in 1946 or 1947 when he was still in his twenties. They did a deal. If Giulio would back Salvo, Salvo would back Giulio, and deliver the votes. Within three years Giulio was prime minister. For ten, maybe fifteen years it lasted. Giulio in Rome; Salvo first mayor of Palermo, then a minister in the Italian government, and finally a member of the European Parliament. We were known as the friends, and we were. We were the friends of the government, the Christian Democrats. We were the friends of the Church. We were even the friends of the United States. We ran the whole show. We practically were the government.

In the beginning there was no food. There were riots. Communists were everywhere. Soldiers shot our people. Forty-four of them in one day in Palermo. Somebody had to take control. The politicians couldn't do it. The Communists had the organisation, but they couldn't get things done. The Christian Democrats could get things done, but they didn't have the organisation. We stepped in and took over.

Of course, one good turn deserves another, so it wasn't long before we got our *indipendènza*. Italy gave us, how you say, regional self-government. They sent us millions of dollars and let us decide how to spend the money. Some people, of course, wanted to spend it differently from the way we did, but we took care of them.

Two more friends, Nino and Ignazio Salvo – they were cousins, both sons of Mafia bosses – they also did a fantastic deal. They too went to the Americans at the end of the war. There was no way anyone could rebuild the country, they told them, unless there was a regular, secure source of income. In other words, taxes. The only way to raise them, they said, was to have a regular, organised, efficient tax-collection system. Because there was no such thing in existence, and because if the Americans tried to set up such a system it would have taken them years, and probably would never have worked anyway as they didn't understand Sicilia and the Sicilian way of doing things, Nino and Ignazio offered out of the kindness of their hearts and a sense of duty to their country, to collect the taxes on their behalf. And because they were eager to see their country rebuilt and taking its rightful place in the front row of the family of nations, they would charge only a meagre 10 per cent commission for the privilege of doing so. Furthermore, instead of hanging on to the money they collected for months and months before handing it over to the government, they would make it over on a daily basis. Less, of course, their modest commission.

At a stroke, everybody, but everybody, came within the grasp of the family. We now not only had a fabulous source of income but we knew everything about everybody's affairs. And, of course, somehow or other, money that should have been remitted overnight gradually took two days to transfer. Then three days. Then three weeks, then three months. Then it was delayed indefinitely. Who was going to complain? Who was also going to check the books? It wasn't long before Nino and Ignazio became not just the most powerful people in Sicilia but also probably the richest businessmen in the whole of Italia.

To understand all this, and the reason for all the big Mafia trials that are taking place at the moment, go and have a look at number 3 Piazza Vittorio Veneto, the house of Ignazio Salvo. This is where the famous kiss is alleged to have taken place. It was September 1987. Giulio Andreotti was supposed to be having lunch with all the local politicians at the Hotel Villa Igiea. But they say he cried off, dismissed his bodyguard and went by himself to Piazza Vittoria Veneto. He didn't go to the front door. He drove straight in through the base-ment garage, where he was met by Rabito, Salvo's driver. Rabito took him up by the secret lift to Salvo's apartment. They went down the hallway to the sitting room. On the sofa were Ignazio Salvo and Salvo Lima. Giulio joined them. Then Toto, at that time the head of the family, arrived. They all stood up. Ignazio kissed him. Salvo kissed him. Giulio kissed him. It's what we do all the time here in Sicily. It is our custom, our way of life. But not according to the police and the prosecution. They say that when the prime minister of Italy kisses the head of the family it is not a sign of courtesy or respect, but a sign of submission: the prime minister of Italy is a member of the family, and under the thumb of the family. Uncle Giulio, seven times prime minister, the doyen of the Christian Democratic establishment and the man who domi-nated Italian politics for fifty years was arrested and charged with being associated with us. Can you imagine? The prime minister of Italy. Arrested. For a courtesy.

But of course, he got off. He had to get off. The whole story was made up by Balduccio – his real name is Baldassare, but everyone calls him Balduccio – Di Maggio, Uncle Toto's driver, a real stand-up guy. He did a deal with the police. He confessed to killing twenty-three people, three of them while he was under police protection. But then, because he told them the story of the kiss and all about our *sistema del pot*, our organisation and structure, they let him off.

Once you've seen Ignazio's old house, go and have a look at the Hotel Villa Igeia where Giulio was staying when he is said to have slipped away for that meeting. It's on the edge of town. Overlooking the beach. It's a hotel to die for. And a number of people did, in various ways. We always used to have lunches and dinners and parties there. It was great fun.

Now if I go to the Villa Igeia, I don't talk to anyone. Everybody is on their mobile telephone. At first I didn't mind them, especially when we had endless power cuts and when the *carabinieri* started bugging all our lines. And, of course, when we were out on a contract, or getting a place ready, and had to communicate with each other, they were very, very useful. But it's gone too far. Today you can sit down and have lunch or dinner with someone and not talk to them at all, because they are for ever on their mobile phone. I had dinner last week at the Villa Igeia with an eager young American man who said he was doing a research project on farming in Sicilia in the eighteenth century. But he didn't speak to me once. He was on his mobile the whole time.

I didn't waste my time, though. I came up with what I thought was a fantastic mobile telephone scam. Tell me what you think. We have lots of difficulties with phone-tapping by the police. We've got our own code, Russian steel for machine-guns, pineapples for grenades, and so on, but it's still a problem. So why don't I lift hundreds of, say, English mobile telephones, get a friend at the local telephone exchange to check they are clean, and then hook them up to a string of different telephone lines here in Sicilia belonging to people or companies with big telephone bills or, better still, to people and addresses which don't exist? What do you think? That way we get a secure mobile phone network of our own paid for by other people. Good, eh? Bet you none of these so-called young Turks could come up with an idea like that.

Talking of hotels, there is also the Grand Hotel et des Palmes in Via Roma in the centre of town. That was a great place for parties too. It was Lucky's favourite hotel. Wagner wrote *Parsifal* there, and Renoir stayed there – he actually painted Wagner at the hotel. Today, however, it always seems to be empty. The plush red bar, which used to be famous for its *spumante* and crushed strawberries, and the restaurant. Last time I had lunch there, only three tables were occupied. It's a shame, especially after all the good times we've had there. They've also forgotten how to make a good Bloody Mary. No ice. Can you imagine? Call me an old-fashioned *consigliere* if you must, but I always like ice in my Bloody Mary.

Just round the corner from there, by the way, is Father Mario Frittitta's church. He is a Carmelite monk. He did us lots of favours. If somebody wanted to keep out of sight he would go and say mass for them in private. He has also performed secret marriages as well, somehow or other managing to keep the details from the authorities.

Bagheria. You must also go to Bagheria just outside Palermo. It's where all the rich traders and merchants used to build their summer villas. Full of glorious old baroque architecture, it used to be. It's also an old, old family stronghold, going back to the days of the Orchard Mafia of the nineteenth century. We had lots of parties and weddings and meetings at the Hotel Zagarello which the two Salvo cousins, Ignazio and Nino, built with money they stole from the Casa per il Mezzogiorno, the Southern Italy Development Fund. It was earmarked for other things, but they thought it would be put to much better use for building their own hotel in their own home. Not that they needed the money. Today it's a very downmarket beach hotel, all cheap paintings, plastic tables, dirty chairs and families sitting around the swimming pool moaning and arguing.

Bagheria is also famous for two other things: fantastic, unbelievable pastries and ice creams, the best in the world, and, unfortunately, for the Christmas massacre. For the very,

very best pastries, and especially the best *cannolo* Siciliano, go to the Bar Caravella. You wouldn't believe there could be so many kinds of pastry and ice cream. Some people say the best place to buy *cannolo* is in Piano degli Albanese, where they don't speak Italian like us. They speak Greek. Even the road signs are in Greek. It's good, I agree, especially the *cannolo* they serve in the ordinary-looking grocer's shop in the main street, but I prefer the *cannolo* from Bagheria. The sheep's cheese they make in Piano degli Albanese is another matter. That's the best in the whole of Italy.

As for the massacre, it was *stùpido*. These *pazzo*, crazy cokeheads. They drive into the centre of town and start shooting each other and everybody else as well. In the middle of town, in the middle of the day. Stùpido. Then Pina Bagarella, what does he do, the *cafone*? He leaves his fingerprints all over one of the cars. He was arrested. Taken to court. The Professor of Forensic Medicine at Palermo University was called in as an expert witness. He said the fingerprints were definitely Pina's. We tried to persuade him he'd made a mistake, but he wouldn't listen to us. So we had to burn him. It didn't make any difference, though. Pina was still sent to prison.

When you have finished in Bagheria, come back along the beach road and you'll pass the famous Spano fish restaurant. We had a big meeting there in 1957, I think it was, between all the big guys from the States and all the big guys here in Sicily. The American delegation, they thought they were the big earners. They were led by Giuseppe Bonanno. We all called him Joe Bananas. When he landed at Rome Airport on his way here, he got the red-carpet treatment. He was met by the Minister of Foreign Trade, Bernardo Mattarella. I always remember that. People said it was a fix. It wasn't. Both of them, Joe and Bernardo, came from di Golfo Castellammare, just outside Palermo. They were goombahs. The rest of his delegation, Rosario, Butch, Curly, were all big in the Fulton

Fish Market, construction, the garbage business. They told us they controlled over twenty different *capi*, or squads, with between 250 and 500 active soldiers. To them we were just zips.

Our delegation was led by another Giuseppe, Giuseppe Genco Russo. But it was Toto's thinking that was behind it all. Instead of two separate competing organisations, he envisioned a single, co-ordinated family that would dominate the world. The drugs business was just beginning to take off. It was not to be snorted at. He could see the potential. He could also see the fighting that would take place between different organisations trying to dominate the business. He thought that it was better for the two sides of the family to be together than apart. He also thought that if we were together we stood a much better chance of dominating the business than anybody else did.

Lunch, I remember, lasted over twelve hours. It was probably the single most powerful lunch in the annals of crime. But at the end of it nobody was going to give it the traditional response and shoot holes in it. We all accepted Toto's proposal, and the rest, as they say, is history.

Unfortunately, you can't go to the Spana any more for lunch or dinner. After the meeting was over it was bombed, to erase any evidence that the meeting ever took place. All that's left of it now are some twisted metal frames, the concrete floor and some down-and-outs who are using it as a kind of shelter. Last time I looked in there, for old times' sake, there were even syringes on the floor. Shocking. No respect for history. Joe Bonanno's organisation, I hear, is still going strong. It's now supposed to be the most dangerous Mafia organisation in the whole of the States after that of the Gambinos.

Talking of restaurants, I tell you another place you should go: the Charleston in Mondello, on the other side of

Palermo. This was Michele Sindona's favourite restaurant – he
went there whenever he was in town. You remember Michele
Sindona? He was the man who for a time was banker for the
Mafia as well as for the Vatican. He was everywhere: Sicilia,
Italy, Europe, America. In America they called him the best
businessman in the world. But it all came crashing down. It
was the biggest financial collapse in either Italy or in America.
It cost us, and probably the Vatican as well, billions of dollars.
Sindona was arrested, tried, found guilty. Then, the following
morning, he was found dead in his prison cell. He'd taken a
cyanide tablet. I often wonder how he got that cyanide tablet.

From time to time I still go to the Charleston, usually after
I've been to pay my respects to Salvo Lima. His villa is, or
rather was, just around the corner. When the *carabinieri* and
the lawyers and everybody else started moving in on us, when
even Giulio was arrested, Salvo was told to get them off our
backs. He didn't. Or he couldn't. Then, alas, one morning as
he was leaving his villa for the Centrale Palace Hotel, he was
shot. Poor Salvo. He did so much for the family. Seven times
mayor of Palermo, head of the Christian Democrats here in
Sicilia where, thanks to his leadership, they always got more
or less the whole vote, he was also a member of the European
Parliament for nearly fifteen years. But no matter who you
are, no matter what you've done, the family always comes
first. Or else.

As for the Charleston, the first time you go there I suppose
it's a bit of a shock. It's not like a normal restaurant. It's like,
how do you say? a seaside pier. Downstairs is usually receptions. Upstairs, looking out over the Bay of Mondello, with
all the lights twinkling in the distance and the stars, it can be
very romantic. But don't forget, however romantic it is,
always sit facing the door. It's also a good place to spot who's
fooling around and who, therefore, is, how shall I say,
approachable. All you have to do is look for the guys who are

falling over themselves to be attentive to their wives. They're the ones with a couple of *comares* hidden away somewhere, believe me.

Another thing. Always leave a big tip. Not because you want them to remember you, but because you want them to forget not only that you ever went there, but that you ever existed. Sindona dined there all the time when he was on the run from every police force in the world. Nobody ever recognised him. He even ate there once with Joe Gambino, the big Mafia boss from New York, one of the top five, when he was desperately trying to sort out his problems. But nobody remembered a thing.

Somewhere else you should go is Trapani, out on the west coast, which used to be run by Francesco. Francesco Milazzo. It smells of fish. There's a big tuna-fish operation there. They also handle all the salt collected from the big salt pans just south of the town. The salt is very good. Low in sodium chloride and high in magnesium. Or maybe it's low in magnesium and high in sodium chloride, I don't know. But everybody raves about it.

Walk up and down the main street, then up and down some of the side streets. See if anything occurs to you. When I went there for the first time a few years ago it struck me: banks. The town is full of banks. Big regional banks. There are six of them. Provincial banks? I counted at least thirty. In one of the little bars off the harbour, over a plate of *couscous di pesce*, somebody told me Trapani also has over 200 different savings organisations. Why? Because in the woods just outside the town in Alcamo some of our people had built the biggest heroin-processing plant in Europe. To get the merchandise out of the country they used the fishing boats, shipping it out to friends in Puglia or Calabria or even direct to Napoli. Everybody was in on it. Everybody was making money out of it. But nobody said a word. They made dopes of everyone.

Catania, way down in the south, was once known as Italy's wildest city. At one time there were over a hundred killings there every year. They were thinking of going for *The Guinness Book of Records*. Today it's quietened down a bit. That's because we're back in charge again. At one time we did a lot of business down there. They're experts on contraband. We needed their help when we first got into the drugs business. They helped us smuggle in the morphine base which we needed to refine heroin. We couldn't have done what we did without them.

Somewhere else you should go, especially if you're interested in the future, is Gela, where the Americans landed in 1943. It's also where Aeschylus, the tragic Greek poet, was killed when an eagle dropped a tortoise on his head. Which is why he's known as a tragic poet, I suppose. Just outside the town is one of our schools. Well, I say schools: it's where we take young boys and turn them into efficient killing machines. First we train them to be look-outs. Then decoys. Then to collect and dispose of weapons used in killings. And finally how to kill. Ask in the barber's shop. They'll tell you where it is.

What do you mean, you're more interested in what's happening today? Who's the new godfather? You know I can't tell you that. It's more than your life is worth. Well, all right then, seeing as you know my great friend in Scotland Yard, I'll tell you. But you'll have to swear that you won't repeat what I've said to another soul. If you do I might not be here the next time you come back to Sicilia. I might be coming to see you, in lots of little wooden boxes.

The first thing you must realise is that we're everywhere. As you drive out of Palermo, past the new prison, the Pagharelli, all that land is owned by one of the families, the Grecos. They control that area. The son, though, I notice, is now a famous Sicilian film-maker, Giorgio Castellani. I only hope his father, Michele, doesn't feel he's let them down. A bit further on you'll see flower shops. They are owned by another family, which controls all this area. Another area nearby is owned by the Graviano family. Giuseppe and Filippo are in prison, so it's being run by their sister, Nunzia, known as Picciridda, the baby.

Carry on until you get to Monreale, high above the Conca d'Ora. Forget the view. Take a look at the big cathedral and all its fancy mosaics, especially the one showing Eve being created from the rib of a very bored-looking Adam. Well, we used to run that as well. The Archbishop, Salvatore Cassisa, gave us lots of building contracts, almost as many as we got for rebuilding and refurbishing the big opera house, the Teatro Massimo – which, incidentally, has already taken longer to refurbish than it did to build in the first place. He also arranged for many of us to hide there. In the cathedral. In the cathedral grounds. Even on the cathedral's vineyards and estates. A truly holy man.

Somebody – I think it was some American *babbo* – once said there were over 200 different Mafia families in Sicily. How he found that out I don't know. But I suppose you mean the big league. Well, the first thing you must remember is that in Sicily the big three Mafia villages were always Corleone – you remember me telling you it was always known as the home of *i viddani*, the evil ones – Belmonte Messania and San Giuseppe Iato.

When you go to Corleone, stroll into the Leone d'Oro, slap a couple of million lira on the counter for a *cannolo*, casually ask if Bernardo Provinsanno is in town and see what happens. We all call him Binu the Tractor because he crushes anybody or anything that gets in his way. There were rumours a few years ago that he was dead. Don't believe it. He's very much alive. He is also very smart. He's been on the run for thirty years so he knows what it's all about. He probably started the rumours himself.

In Belmonte Messania stroll into a bar, any bar, and ask where Benedetto Spera lives. Nobody ever knows. I guarantee you. But I can tell you where he lives. Just out of town, on the hillside overlooking the valley, is a group of maybe ten big houses, all completely surrounded by tall iron railings and big, big gates. All the houses are floodlit. There are also a lot of aerials all over the place. That's where he lives.

As for San Giuseppe Iato, ask there for Balduccio. No, no, I'm kidding. Ask for Balduccio and you'll be run out of town. He is the one, don't forget, who caused us all the problems with his stories about Uncle Giulio and the kiss. He also shopped Toto. Took the police to the block of flats where he was living in Palermo. And all because – the usual story – of a girl. He wanted the same girl as Giovanni Brusca, another member of the family. As if there are not enough *comares* for everybody. And the crazy thing was he was already married. Toto decided to get rid of him, and that's when he did the deal with the police. He got them to arrest him crossing the road in the middle of Palermo so it looked as if they had just hit lucky. Then he turned big-time *pentito*. Didn't do him any good, though. The others then kidnapped his son, killed him and threw the body in an acid bath. Poor kid. But Di Maggio wasn't just a problem for us, he was also a problem for the authorities. He took their money, said *molte grazie* and went back to his old ways, this time as the big chief of San Giuseppe Iato, because he had either eliminated or shopped all the competition.

Well, now I've told you about Di Maggio, let me tell you about our two arch-enemies, the two lawyers who were determined to crush us, Giovanni Falcone and Paolo Borsellino. They kept changing the law, making it more and more difficult for us to hide. They started paying our people to break their solemn vows and tell them what was going on. They were behind the so-called maxi-trials in which hundreds of our *amici* were rounded up including, of course, Toto himself.

What good did it do them? Falcone was blown up on his way home from the airport, along with his wife, Francesca, and three bodyguards. You can see where. There's a sign by the road. It was Giovanni Brusca who did it. Paolo Borsellino they got when he went visiting his mother in the Via d'Amelio. Every Sunday he went to see her. Everybody kept telling him it was too dangerous, but he wouldn't listen. You know what Italians are like with their mothers. Especially the men. So one Sunday he goes calling. Parked outside the block of flats where his mother lived was a car packed with explosives. He rang the bell to her flat and that was it. It was Enzio Scarantino who did it. He also turned *pentito*. He was the chief prosecution witness at the trial.

After all the work they did, all the risks they took, all they've got is the airport named after them. Not one airport each, like J.F.K. or Charles de Gaulle or John Wayne in Orange County. They have to share. It hardly seems fair.

Not that they are the only ones who had to be eliminated. At one time hundreds and hundreds of people were being iced every year, but not any more. Not that the killings have stopped. Now we make our killings on Wall Street, in London, in Rome. Even in Moscow. What we do is simple. First of all we get ourselves some tame brokers. Next we get a tame company. Then we get the tame brokers to push shares in the tame company. Often you can push the shares up 50, 60 maybe even 70 per cent in a few weeks. Then you sell and run. Simple. But very, very, very profitable. And, above all, safe. Trouble is, you can't do it too often, too fast, in the same market. You've got to move around.

Another, much bigger scheme I'm working on at the moment is recycling Bolivian government bonds. Around US$500 million, which we bought with some of our drugs profits. What I want to do is use them to invest in some of these go-ahead companies in Eastern Europe. It's a bit complicated, but there's no reason why it shouldn't work. It always has in the past. Whatever kind of killing we make, they'll never break us. No way. Today we are bigger than many countries. We are richer than many countries. We are more powerful than many countries. We have more resources, more weapons, more power. That's why I have to smile whenever I go to the Teatro di Verdura to see the open-air opera – my favourite is *Orfeo all' Inferno*: I identify with that more than with most other operas – and I drive past that huge police and military complex facing the sea. All that, I think. All those people. All that money. All that technology. Just to try to understand what is really a simple family business. It's crazy.

Take their present campaign. They can't beat us head on, so they're trying to persuade us to become *pentiti* and inform on each other. Will they win? Of course not. Because we're now telling everyone to forget the *omertà*, our code of silence, and become *pentiti*, because if everyone is a *pentito* nobody is a *pentito*. And obviously every *pentito* costs the government money. Big money, cash. Plus everything that goes with it: new names, new identities, new homes, crêches and schools for the children. And constant protection, naturally. Even though many of the *pentiti* are multimillionaires and have more than enough money to pay for everything themselves. In fact many *pentiti* live better, more lavish lives now than they ever did before – at the taxpayers' expense. Buscetta, for example. He was one of the first of our so-called double-agent *pentiti*. He was discovered on a Mediterranean cruise with his Brazilian wife, Cristina De Almeya Guimares. Everything, as you say, hit the fan.

Then they have to follow up what they are told. That means more police, more investigators, more lawyers, more bodyguards, more equipment, more buildings, more prisons, more guards, more protection for the guards and their families and friends. On top of that, there is no way they can ever check whether or not everything they've been told is true; whether the *pentiti* actually committed the crimes they say they committed. Then there is the biggest problem of all: the Di Maggio factor. Someone confesses. You bury him in money. You guarantee him immunity. Then he goes back to doing what he was doing before, only worse. So far there are over 5,000 *pentiti* and, thanks to us, more and more are signing up every day. Sooner or later the government will run out of money, especially as it is now trying to be a proper government, not like the governments we had in the past run by Uncle Giulio, which just printed money to get out of trouble.

How do we know they'll go on and on paying more and more people to become informers? Because that's what the public wants. That's why we pay so much money to different organisations and different people so that they will continue to congratulate the government, tell them they're doing a good job and to keep at it. We even spend a fortune making certain that wherever you look there is some graffiti or other praising the government for their campaign against the Mafia. The last thing we want is for them to stop spending money fighting us and giving us far more money than they give our victims. It would ruin everything. It could upset the whole balance of Italian society as we know it.

Whenever anyone turns against us, the police say they will protect them for life. They will find them a new home, a new identity. Plastic surgeons will even change the way they look. Well, if the police can change people's identities and the way they look, so can we. We have far more resources at our disposal and far more expertise. We also have more plastic surgeons prepared to work for us than the police do because, don't forget, one way or another, over the years we've been the source of an enormous amount of business for plastic surgeons all over the world. Bearing that in mind, ask yourself one question: if our leader, Toto, really was locked up in the Ucciardone, the enormous concrete nuclear bunker down by the waterfront which, incidentally, our people built to withstand even missile attacks, would we really let him stay there? Of course not. The reason we have not bombed the place to kingdom come to get him out is simple. He's not there. The man the police say is Toto is a lookalike. Or at least, he is now. The real Toto, the real *capo di tutti capi*, is alive and well and living in Palermo, just like he was before.

You're smiling. You don't believe me. Come on. Think about it. You know it's possible. For us, everything is possible. Just think of the alternative. If we hadn't lifted Toto, according to our code of honour we would have needed to eliminate the whole of his family as well as all his old associates. And that hasn't happened, has it? They're all still living in Corleone. His wife even writes to the newspapers saying her son is a good boy just like every other nineteen-year-old, and he didn't mean to kill his best friend like that. It was all the fault of the programmes they put on television nowadays.

Still not convinced? All right, then. Before we have lunch, some *frutti di mare* with a bottle of *vino locale*, if you'd like to come next door, I'll introduce you to a friend of ours . . .

Tegucigalpa

I only hope that Jorge and Tomás and Mañuel and José, and my driver, Julio César, and everybody else I met in Honduras, is alive and well and still knocking back the tequilas.

I was there just a week before Hurricane Mitch, or El Monstro, as they called it, roared in and all but destroyed the place, leaving more than 60 per cent of it in ruins, most of the country under water, 2 million people, of a total population of 6.3 million, homeless and setting back development ten, maybe twenty, perhaps as much as fifty years. With 80 per cent of the population already living below the poverty line, and Honduras already seriously in debt – in good years 40 per cent of its budget goes on debt repayments – even that still sounds wildly optimistic to me.

It was raining at the time. There were also high winds. But nowhere near as bad, of course, as the hurricane, which they reckon was the worst storm in the west for over 200 years. Everybody kept saying it was going to get worse, but I don't think anybody expected it to get that much worse.

I'm no expert on hurricanes – I slept through the one that

hit the south of England in 1987 – and once, for my sins, I
was forced to sit out Hurricane Irene in the Turks and
Caicos – but anyone could see why, when they were hit by the
real thing, they hardly stood a chance. Virtually the entire
country is sweeping, lush, green, unexplored mountains;
deep, lush, green, unexplored valleys, with long, unbroken,
deep, lush, green – no, that's not right, but you get the drift –
strips of sand, especially along its northern coast, around
Mosquitia, where strangely, the beach is littered with hundreds of tiny watertight plastic bags containing some kind of
white powder which seems to put a bit of a zip in the air.

Even the capital, Tegucigalpa, which started life as a camp
for silver miners whose only entertainment was trying to
goose a galpa – they were obviously very successful, because
there hasn't been one around for a long time – is at the
bottom of a huge valley surrounded almost entirely by mountains. A bit like La Paz without the snow. In one tiny area are
the hotels, the main square, the government buildings, shops
and offices. At least I think they are there. There were so
many gun-toting security guards around that I could hardly
see them, although lots of them were swathed in miles of
sticky tape. The guns, that is. And outside one doughnut
shop I couldn't help but notice that the local neighbourhood
guachimán was sporting a rusty old machete. Whether they're
toting a rusty old M16 or a rusty old machete, they're still
highly dangerous. Shoot first, ask questions later seems to be
their motto. Unfortunately, most of them, I gathered, have a
tendency to shoot the people they are supposed to be protecting. Apparently, as a result of all the nervous tension,
most of them spend a great deal of time asleep on the job.
Wake them up suddenly to complain that you're paying them
for doing nothing, and they think they're being attacked and
will shoot the living daylights out of you.

As for the rest of Tegucigalpa, it was nothing but shacks,

many of which looked as though they were held together by miles of sticky tape as well.

So when the hurricane stormed in, with the country already saturated by weeks and weeks of wet weather, the rain had nowhere to go but straight down the sides of the mountains and straight into the valleys, carrying everything, eroded soil, loose rocks, trees, before it. People spoke of a 'wall of water' destroying not only buildings but whole streets in a matter of seconds, and burying everything in thick, brown mud. It was not just inches, but feet deep, in many cases reaching halfway up ground-floor windows and in some places even up to the first- and second-floor windows. It was only the guys in the centre of town, in the big houses in and around Las Lomas Guijarro, the only ones with any kind of drainage, who stood a chance. As for the rest, there was nothing they could do.

As soon as I heard about the hurricane – I was back in Miami by then, doing the rounds in Coral Gables, not to mention the occasional midnight flit to Coconut Grove – I tried to check whether everyone was safe, but it was impossible to find out. Telephone calls and faxes were useless because, of course, the lines were all down.

One news report I saw showed San Pedro Sula, the big, industrial capital. It was just a sea of water. A village, they called it, which shows you how much you can rely on trained professional American journalists for accuracy. When I was there, it was a hustling, bustling city with a population of around 600,000, the second-largest in the country. A big main square, a cathedral almost as old as San Pedro himself, back streets that made you feel as if you'd stepped back into nineteenth-century Spain and a million horses and carts clogging up the roads, not for giving rides to tourists, but for real, hard, solid, bone-shaking, knackering slog. Except for outside the swish Arab-Honduran Club, which you could hardly get near for Mercs. You have to admit, that's some village.

I went there for a couple of drinks and, of course, to look at the textile industry which has sprung up in the area over the last ten or fifteen years and turned San Pedro Sula into Central America's fastest-growing city. From nothing they've built no fewer than eleven huge industrial estates housing more than 150 factories and employing over 75,000 people. Most of them, it must be said, are sweatshops. Lured by cheap labour, cheap operating costs and cheap everything else, foreign companies, mostly from South Korea, have moved there to finish clothes designed and made elsewhere so that they can then ship them duty-free to the US.

But that night the city was completely submerged. Not a horse was in sight. Over 250 public buildings, including the giant Inmude Sports Complex, were being made over, they said, for accommodation for the survivors, or what they called the *damnificados*. Which probably meant 500 public buildings and half a dozen sports stadia. As for all the factories and processing plants, they're not expected to be back in operation again until whenever. How the US will manage without its cheap supply of cargo, or whatever they call it, I shudder to think.

Other news and television reports described Tegucigalpa as 'completely ruined with no external communications'. Of the city's eighty-eight districts, fifteen had been completely destroyed and fifty severely damaged, although how they could tell the difference amazes me. I don't think I've ever been any-where that so closely resembled the inside of a dustbin. Take, for example, the area around Parque Central. Even the locals tell you it's noisy, polluted and foul-smelling, although whether that was because it is near City Hall they didn't say. To me it looked like the morning after one hell of a party. Amid all the rubbish there were drunks everywhere. Not just your usual sad, guilty-looking drunks, but your genuine, rip-roaring 'Let's have another bottle of tequila' drunks. It was crawling with beggars and cripples. The steps of San Miguel looked more like the stairs to hell than the stairs to a cathedral. And, especially in the heat of the sun, there was an awful stench, caused, I was assured by a local banker who had obviously not learned his English from a Berlitz course, 'by so many people in the dark of the night, oblivious, stripped of all earthly possessions, discarding perhaps in an unconscious but supremely liberating act of defiance their only disposable assets: the fruits of their bowels'.

As for the rest of the country: it was now nothing but mud, mud and still more mud. As if the hurricane wasn't bad enough, they also had to cope with flash floods some miles wide, which roared into rivers making them ten, fifty, a hundred times their normal size. Some rivers were so swollen that they even changed course, wreaking still more havoc.

When I was there I didn't just stick to the big towns. I went everywhere: across country, through the mountains, up into the cloud forests. Out to the border with Guatemala. Instead of taking the plane from San Pedro Sula to Tegucigalpa like your typical intrepid traveller in search of adventure, I went by road so that I could stop off at the towns and villages on the way.

I saw some pretty swish *haciendas* about the size of Buckingham Palace and some pretty smart *rancheros* on some fabulous horses. At the same time I saw women doing what little washing they had in mountain streams. I saw barefoot kids carrying huge stacks of wood on their backs. I saw pigs wallowing in the mud outside people's homes, or rather shacks, horses wandering aimlessly through towns, cattle blocking the traffic for hours on end. Or maybe it just seemed like hours on end. I travelled along country tracks as well as on some pretty decent roads. I also experienced – vroom – the crazy speed – vroom – at which Hondurans drive – in spite of all the local carpenters – vroom – working away by the side of the road finishing off coffins and polishing them up ready for their next – yaargh – customer.

On the other hand I discovered Santa Lucia, a wonderful old Spanish mining town tucked away in the pine forests in the middle of nowhere, which I put high on my list of top ten favourite villages in the world to disappear to if I ever suspect they're on to me and I'm about to get the knock on the door at three o'clock in the morning. So I reckon I've done enough hairpin bends and frayed old rope bridges over fast-flowing streams to have a pretty good idea of what happened to them and what the place looked like after Hurricane Mitch had done its worst.

I also think I know why the Hondurans were so badly hit. Their statue of Christ standing on top of one of the hills overlooking Tegucigalpa is nowhere near as big as the one in Rio, so clearly they didn't get the same level of protection. You can scoff, but when was the last time Rio was hit by a hurricane? The design is also a bit off. To me it looks as if He is balancing precariously on one foot which came as a bit of a shock. I thought Christ spent all his time in the temple, not at ballet class, although judging by some of the priests you see nowadays, especially in the States, I may be wrong.

At first, I will admit I had all the wrong vibes about Honduras – and it was nothing to do with the rain or Hurricane Mitch hovering on the doorstep. It was just that, not exactly being a tree-hugger, I didn't fancy the idea of a landscape of trees, trees and nothing but trees. Apart from all the pollution they pump into the atmosphere – you don't believe me? OK, tree-huggers, take a deep breath. What's that blue haze they keep on about whenever two or three trees are gathered together on a hillside? – Costa Rica put me off trees for life. Although to be fair to Honduras, it does have a different approach. In order to prevent all the broken-down Mayan cars and trucks and buses from being infected by the pollution being pumped out by the trees, they've put up not just giant but double-enormous-giant billboards all over the

country. In towns. By the roadsides. Halfway up hillsides.
On the very tops of the hills themselves. The one that must be
the all-time winner of the Honduras National Environment
Award is a giant Coca-Cola bottle about the size of the Statue
of Liberty. To build all the double-enormous-giant billboards
to protect all the cars and trucks and buses, they had to chop
down all the trees that were creating the pollution in the first
place. The result is that today there are hardly any left. But at
least the hoardings are safe.

I didn't reckon much to all this eco-tourism business,
either. With all due respect to whoever, what's it to me if
their butterflies are as big as birds, the birds as big as 747s
and the dragonflies so huge they have to flap their wings
rather than whirr them around, or that they've got about a
million different species of birds, half a million white-tailed
deer and fifty-seven spider monkeys? Whatever main road,
side road, country lane or track through the forest you take,
I guarantee you a couple of tons of isoprene – in other
words, tree smog – to a one-way ticket to Virginia's Blue
Ridge Mountains that within minutes you'll be swerving
round, stepping over or ploughing straight through the
middle of a dead dog, cat, white-tailed sheep, spider goat,
horse, crocodile or something. Honestly, some days driving
around Honduras it's like some zoological version of the
Battle of the Somme. In one village outside Teguc, as we
locals call it, I came across one old man who told me his dog
had been run over so many times it now had three legs, one
ear, one eye, liver problems, a bad back and mange. It
answered to the name of Lucky.

Honduras also boasts the most bizarre form of eco-tourism
I've ever come across. Every year a bunch of German vets
descends on the place, scalpels at the ready, with the sole purpose of going around neutering every cat and dog they can
find in order to protect what they say is a rare form of wildlife:

the unbelievably named wish-a-willy. Which, to the uniniti-
ated, is some kind of rare iguana found only in Honduras.

What's more, to tell you the truth, I didn't fancy traipsing
round even more Mayan ruins, or staggering up and down still
more Mayan staircases, even if they were at the southernmost
spot of the once so-called great Egyptian, oops I mean Mayan
empire. As in the Egyptians mayan got here and started the
whole thing, because there's no other sensible explanation for
the size and shape of their damned temples, or they mayan not.

And last but not least, I didn't particularly relish the
prospect of being shot, kidnapped or delivered home in a
box. Bit by bit. There are plenty of people I can think of
who might well be in favour of it, and who would be only too
willing to put up the readies, but I didn't see why I should go
out of my way to satisfy their requirements.

But guess what, I was wrong. Honduras is a great place.
Providing you ignore the hammocks you see everywhere you
turn. Hanging between trees. Outside people's homes. Inside
courtyards. On the verandas of cafés, bars and restaurants.
Strung up along the side of the road. In fact, I would say it's
the hammock capital of the world. There must be one hammock for every pair of trees in the country.

Far more exciting are the *rancheros* riding around all over
the place, and all the horses and cattle. And, especially to an
old Africa hand like me, it's the third-most corrupt country in
the world. So as far as I'm concerned, it's the best place in
Central America.

Guatemala is OK. But it's a bit rough – and a bit dangerous. Guatemala City, the bit around the airport, is great fun
and the countryside is fantastic. It's the bit in between that
worries me. Well, maybe apart from Antigua.

El Salvador is too nice. When it had an enormous civil
war, by the following morning they had cleaned everything
up. It's also too serious, too hard-working.

Nicaragua is nothing but evangelists. Your aggressive, shirt-sleeved, Bible-thumping types. Dear God, if I ever have to go to Nicaragua again, please save me from meeting another hot-gospel evangelist.

Costa Rica is all rope sandals and trees and trees and still more trees. It's so eco-this and eco-that you're frightened to breathe.

Panama is not as much fun as it used to be in the days of old Pineapple Face. But for laughs there's nothing better than hitting the tequila and trying to get a passing American to explain why it was right for the US to arbitrarily, against every international law in the book, invade sovereign, independent Panama to seize Pineapple Face, but wrong for the Russians to invade Chechnya.

And as for Belize, well, it's been nice talking to you, but I've got to be going . . .

The second-largest country in the region, depending on whether or not you include all the lakes in Nicaragua as Nicaragua, Honduras started off rough and has just got rougher. First came a breakaway bunch of failed Egyptian architects disguised as Mayans. Then Columbus in 1502. Then the generals. After they broke away, first from Spain and then from the Federation of Central America, it was 1982 before they had such a thing as a civilian government.

Today, like so many other countries, it should be OK. It is rich in mineral resources: gold, silver, copper, lead, zinc, coal, antimony and iron. But even before Hurricane Mitch arrived on the scene, it was one big mess.

The politicians, as far as I could discover, are as dedicated as ever to maintaining all the traditional values and standards befitting the third-most corrupt nation in the world. Even I couldn't help noticing that their Congress building is on stilts, which must be their way of proclaiming to the world their determination to remain permanently above the daily hustle of trying to make a living like the rest of us. It also presumably means that if the floods hit the centre of town, the odd politician who by chance might be in there and not whooping it up in Miami will be safe. But no. Wrong again. I was told it was only on stilts because to build a building on stilts is more expensive than building it on the ground. And the higher the costs, the more room there was for . . . Wait a minute. Is that the phone ringing?

As for the police, they're the same as all the fast-asleep gun-toting security guards in town, except that they seem to have bigger pockets. Even so, you can't help but like them. A quick smile, a shake of the hand, 50,000 lempiras, about US$3, to the police social fund, and they're yours. Of course, it's better to remove the body or put the jewels in your pocket first, but if you should forget, it doesn't matter. They're very understanding.

With the economy in such a desperate state it's good to know that they are also very conscious of the considerable amount of time, let alone money, it takes to bring people to court. As a result, if you're rich they don't even bother to go looking for you. If you're poor, they just lock you up without worrying about such trivialities as trying to prove whether you're guilty or not, and throw away the key. Four years, would you believe, is the average length of time somebody can be in jail on suspicion without ever coming anywhere near a court, never mind justice.

The courts themselves are another laugh. For a fee, judges' secretaries will let you know in advance when they're going to issue an *órdenes de captura*, so that you've got time to make the necessary arrangements. They'll also, for a further fee, arrange to lose your case files, so that if you should by the slightest chance actually appear in court, there will be no paperwork and you'll be back ploughing through your traditional lunch of *arroz, frijoles, huevo, plátano frito y queso* – rice, beans, egg, fried plantain and cheese – before you can say long live Amnesty International. If all that fails, however, a quick call to your local *matones a sueldo*, or hitman, will do the trick. Not that you would necessarily want the judge taken out. That's too subtle. Get him to go for the wife or daughter instead.

It's not as if there's not much crime about. One guy I met just outside San Pedro Sula – he had a beautiful factory surrounded by immaculate lawns in the middle of nowhere – told me he always carried a pistol. 'How often do you use it?' I asked.

'About once, maybe twice a year.'

'Does it work?'

'Sure,' he said. 'They never come back again.'

Another businessman, seventy years old but in good shape, told me that the previous evening he'd been carjacked as he was driving home. The thieves pulled him out of the driver's seat and pushed him into the back of the car, but as they were fiddling with the automatic gears, he escaped.

In Tegucigalpa I even met a group of Russians from Novosibirsk, Siberia's answer to St Louis, Missouri. It owes its existence to the railways. They were wheeling and dealing: buying from the Koreans, the Chinese and the Japanese, and selling on to middlemen throughout Central America. But they reckoned things were now becoming too dangerous and were planning to move to Moscow which, they said, was safer.

And if that's not enough to make you think twice, when I checked into the Hotel St Martin I was handed a card which boldly announced: 'Dear Guest. The management reserves the right to admit those persons whom we consider detrimental to your safety and to the hotel's prestige.'

If the police are an easy touch, you should see the customs and immigration officers. They're never there. I've never even seen one. I've just strolled in and out of the place a number of times. No queuing up. No silly questions. No packing and unpacking my bag. I still don't have any Honduran stamps in my dog-eared old passport. Wonderful country.

It's the government officials and civil servants, however, who take the biscuit. Well, actually, they take far more than the biscuit, if you get my drift. Goodness me, they won't even say *buenos días* unless they see the colour of a US$10 bill. Or a bigger one, depending on how civil they are. I forget the number of businessmen and companies I talked to in San Pedro Sula who told me that they wanted to invest in the country, but after years of filling in forms and going to meetings which never took place, they'd given up. One guy I met, an American, but we shouldn't hold that against him, used to be a computer engineer with NASA. He wanted to open up a big, international computer-repair operation. He told me he had spent not only all his investment funds but his life savings as well, doing the rounds. He got nowhere. You can see him playing the saxophone three evenings a week in a bar down the road from the central *plaza*.

Call me easily led, but I decided that while I might be for Honduras, Honduras was not for me. Judging by everything I had been told – and this was before the hurricane, don't forget – it wasn't likely to be, either, in my lifetime or anyone else's.

Seeing as I'd done San Pedro Sula, discovered that Rancho Manacal was nowhere near as much fun as it sounded, had my fill of the *merengue*, not to mention the *cumbia* and the *punta*, and was being threatened with some tickets to a play about some environmental do-gooder, I decided there was no alternative but to head for the hills and take in the misnamed Mayan ruins way out in the jungle jungle, as opposed to the urban jungle, at Copan, as in a cop an' his silence will only cost you US$10. I also decided to go by cab, because I'd heard that so many buses and trucks were being held up and people were being forced to hand over every penny they possessed for next to no reason at all. At first I thought that, having once worked for a merchant bank, it might be interesting to meet some overseas colleagues, but in the end, remembering what my own colleagues had been like, I decided against it.

What should, however, have been a quick swing took me ages. Partly because of all the dead bodies on the road. See, I was telling you the truth. Partly because of all the deserted villages, or rather deserted village squares, we pulled into. And partly because, don't ask me how, I fell in with what seemed to be an illegal emigrants' reunion in some roadside bar in a politically incorrect place called Portillo. These were all Hondurans who had by various means got into the States without any papers, found a job, taught their employers enough Spanish to say *favor de limpiar el excusado* (please clean the toilet), *tiene que limitar las llamadas* (Goddamn it, I told you to stop using that phone) and *usted está despedido* (OK, you're fired), stayed there for a while but, one way or another, were eventually rumbled and thrown out.

One guy, a tiny man about 5 foot going on 4 foot 6 with a thick, bushy moustache, told me he got through Guatemala and Mexico easily enough without any papers. At Veracruz in Mexico, he was taken to someone he called a *patero* who looked after him, made a fuss of him and showed him a safe place to cross the border. He also told him friends would meet him on the other side and take him to Houston, Texas. The cost: US$600.

When he got to the banks of the river, there were six or seven others there also waiting to cross. They stripped off, bundled up their clothes and plunged into the water, holding their belongings above their heads to keep them dry. The river was only about 30 feet wide at that point, but there was a strong current. One of the men couldn't swim, so the *pateros* folded him into a big car inner tube and dragged him over.

On the other side, the little guy was out and dressed, met by the friends as promised, dashed across a golf course and was on his way within seconds. First stop was Brownsville,

Texas, which I would have thought would have been enough
to make anybody want to go home – all I can remember of it
is mountains of burned-out rubber tyres and garbage all over
the place – but apparently not a Honduran. From Houston
he made for Rosewood, Georgia, where within days he got a
job as a cleaner. The fee due to the mysterious middlemen
was another US$500 which, when you think that the Chinese
and others have to pay anything up to US$35,000, is not a
bad deal. On the other hand, of course, it gives you an idea of
where Hondurans stand, or rather crawl, in the illegal pecking
order. So how long did it take him to pay the money back, no
doubt another factor in the equation?

'About three months,' he said.

'So how come you're back in Honduras?' I had to ask him.

'I got caught,' he grinned, 'driving car. Without licence.
They send me back. But it was good time. I was there three
years.'

It was the same story with the others. One was a *ranchero*
complete with boots and hat; the other wore a jacket, which
must have meant he was an important something or other.
Both made it, both had a great time while it lasted and made
and saved a lot of money. But they too got caught and were
sent back.

'OK,' the *ranchero* said to me after I forget how many cof-
fees. 'I'll tell you immigration joke. Honduran man on
bicycle. He has two sacks on his shoulder. He cycles up to
border. US policeman stops him.

'"What have you got in the sacks?" he says.

'"Sand," says Honduran man.

'"OK," says US policeman.

'He cycles across border.

'Next week, same Honduran man cycles up to border with
two sacks on his shoulder. US policeman stops him.

'"What have you got in sacks?"

'"Sand," says Honduran man.

'This goes on week after week after week. Finally, US policeman says to Honduran, "OK. I won't arrest you. Tell me what are you smuggling across border?"'

'Honduran man says, "Bicycles."'

'Good joke. Yes?'

'Yes,' I said. 'Good joke.'

I'm more than convinced that, apart from being politically incorrect, Portillo is shifty, totally unreliable and not to be trusted in any way at all. And what with all the coffee I had to drink, I found Portillo left a bitter taste in my mouth.

Once I finally got to Copan, home of such legendary Mayan or maybe not kings such as Sun-Eyed Blue-Green Quetzal Macaw, Smoke Monkey and Mat Head, I couldn't for the life of me see why people go on about it not being as impressive as the jungle pyramids at Tikal in Guatemala, or as cleverly constructed as the temples at the mother-in-law of all ruins at Chichen Itza in Mexico. In fact, to tell you the truth, I couldn't see a thing. The whole area was blocked off by a bunch of local Indians holding some big demo demanding a 50 per cent slice of all the ticket sales and other revenue generated by the site.

'Mayans. We are brothers. We want half. Government have other half,' one guy who I'd swear was related to Mat Head told me.

All around the site, which must be the size of ten or twelve polo fields, other Indians were acting out the role of good companions. To each other, not to me. They had pitched tents and were cooking meals, drinking beer, walking up and down with sticks or calling out to me what I imagined could only be cheery greetings of solidarity. Stuck outside a Mayan ruin surrounded by hundreds of Indians, there was only one thing to do: head for the nearest bar.

At first the police wouldn't let us through a barrier they'd set up to keep the demonstrators at bay. But once again the open hand of friendship did the trick, and within ten minutes I was ambling around the main square of the nearby town, Copan Ruinas – surprise, surprise – your standard, Spanish-issue, small Latin American town which looked as though it had been living off the backs of tourists since the first Egyptians arrived in the area about a million years ago with plans for what they no doubt called a more accessible pyra-mid. Cobbled streets. Small leafy squares. Tiny houses. Enormous churches. Bijou restaurants. And plenty of bars and blokes all dressed as instructed by Central Casting in black pants, white shirts and panama hats.

Instead of just plunging into the first bar I came across, as is my wont, I thought, Copan being Copan, I should go for a Mayan pub crawl. I don't mean the kind of pub crawl during which you keep saying to yourself, I mayan I may not have another one. I mean going for the same number of bars as there were temples at the site I couldn't see because Mat Head and his friends were blocking the way. For the same reason I felt I should choose the bars with the most steps out-side them. The Mayans, as all we Egyptian scholars know, built all their temples at the top of piles of steps to make it dif-ficult for the in-laws to come calling every week.

Top of the stairway to my Mayan heaven was the Hotel Marina Copan: eleven steps outside, four inside, and another four to get into the dining room. A total of 11 plus 4 plus 4. Who said the Mayans were not mathematical? Another inci-dental plus in its favour was that the pool had a bar right beside it. Not that I'm in any way interested in pools, or whatever it is that goes inside them. To the Mayans, the stuff signified burst bladders. Which, when you think of it, is prob-ably not far from the truth.

Next came the Hotel Acropolis Maya which also had eleven steps outside it, but none inside. And worse still, no bar.

Number three was the Hotel California. Even though it had

four and a half steps outside, a sign saying Tres Locos and a bar surfaced with coins from all around the world – all the ones from Belize were mine – it was not, frankly, anything like your real Mayan bar. It was just that by now it was getting hot, I was getting thirstier and thirstier and my driver had a thing going with Juanita, who served behind the bar. So it all seemed like a good idea at the time. Suitably refreshed, and because I got the distinct impression that my driver had important business to discuss with Juanita, and definitely not business of a mayan may not basis, I made, as they say, my excuses and left.

For some reason it occurred to me that going for bars with a lot of steps outside them was perhaps not such a good plan. After all, any one of them could move at any second, and then where would I be? Swathed in bandages, looking like one of their Egyptian forebears with one leg in the air in the local Mayan hospital, being treated by Mat Head's grown-up brother. On the basis that Copan was a long way from Eastbourne General – not that you'd be guaranteed any medical attention even if you were able to drag yourself there – from then on I decided I'd switch to non-Mayan bars.

I staggered down past, would you believe, the Copan Net, the local website shop, past Lavanderia, the local book exchange, and into this scruffy hole in the wall with just one, unreconstructed Mayan step. It was like something out of a linguine Western. Not quite as basic as your spaghetti Western: a touch more fashionable, with guys toting rifles and wearing heavy bulletproof jackets, cowboy hats and fancy jeans with pistols strapped to their thighs. There I would have quite happily stayed until the next wave of Egyptians arrived, but duty called.

I was wandering back to the main square where – sorry about this, Rupert – the church clock stands at ten to four when I spotted the most non-Mayan bar of all, a bar with no steps whatsoever. No wonder. Inside I discovered that it was actually being run by two Dutch girls, cousins, one of whom, would you believe, was the daughter of a guy I used to know years ago in s'Hertogenbosch, Den Bosch to you, in North Brabant in Holland. Which just goes to show how careful you have to be, even high in the mountains of Central America, because you never know who you're going to bump into. Or, rather, whose daughter you're going to bump into. Anyway, after a traditional Honduran meal of Dutch cheese, bread and a couple of cans of Heineken, taken in the open under a sign nailed to a tree which said: 'No Armas', with parrots to the left of me, a string of hammocks to the right of me – see what I mean about hammocks – we ended this convivial occasion in the Dutch manner: I paid the bill and left, hoping like hell that the next time I was in North Brabant I wouldn't bump into any Honduran girls who might recognise me.

Was it worth the hassle? Going to Copan, I mean. All I would say is, if you're ever stuck in San Pedro Sula and you've got a bit of time to spare, try out the local Garifuna and Honduran dishes at Café Mariano, or even the Super Donuts bar opposite the cathedral. Unless, of course, you're looking for a girl from North Brabant.

What amazes me is why the Hondurans don't ditch the Mayans altogether. After all, the stories about the Egyptians don't do them any good, and wherever you go in Central America you can't help but bump into one Mayan ruin or another. Instead they could concentrate on resurrecting some of their other, earlier tribes and try turning them into a cult. The Tawahka, for example. Of all the tribes in old Honduras, they're the only one never investigated and the only one whose tribal areas have never been subjected to any kind of archaeological research, let alone digs. Were the Tawahka concentrated on the banks of the Patuca River, or were they all over the place? Was the Rio Cuyamel Tawahka, Lenca or even Pipil? Were the Tawahka humble farmers and fishermen, or were they a gang of robbers? I think we should be told.

Or, better still, what about the Pech? Their big hero, Kao Kamasa, travelled to the end of the world to prove that it was held up like their traditional *tapesco*. In other words, like a four-poster waterbed. Apparently, every three days, four giants arrive to change the posts because, being water, they rot very quickly. Now if that hasn't got potential, I don't know what has. You can imagine the display now, can't you? A huge, four-poster bed, completely surrounded by water, four huge giants, and oh yes, I nearly forgot. Mermaids. They look after the fish. I tell you, it would knock all your Mayan ruins for six. Or seven. Or twenty-three. Or however many steps it is they have leading up to their temples.

I'm not saying I didn't enjoy myself. I didn't get shot. I didn't get kidnapped. And I wasn't – sorry to disappoint you – delivered home in a box, even though there are supposed to be gangs on every street corner run by such colourful characters as the Doctor and Angel of Death, who at one time was a trusted member of the security force responsible for guarding presidential candidates. Nevertheless, while I was there there were goodness knows how many robberies, including one involving a group of Italian tourists whose bus was held up by one of the local gangs. Now you see why I got a cab to take me to Copan.

Then there were all the murders – a local television reporter was shot seven times in the head – not to mention the kidnappings. The exact figures I scribbled in the back of a Michelin Guide, but it was stolen. According to the Committee for the Defence of Human Rights in Honduras, no fewer than 10,170 people throughout the country were killed by firearms between January 1994 and June 1998. On top of that, 12,150 received gunshot wounds, some minor, some serious. Those figures I know are correct, because I wrote them down on the inside cover of Dervla Murphy's book *Cameron with Egbert*. And while people are only too eager to steal Michelin Guides, nobody ever seems to want to steal books by Dervla Murphy. Not even the poorest peasants in Honduras. Funny, that.

But whatever you do, don't run away with the idea that Honduras is some kind of lawless black hole at the' mercy of whoever has the biggest gun and a direct line to the local police chief. In spite of the fact that many known gang leaders, criminals and hitmen, or *matones a sueldo*, as they call them in Honduran Spanish, are alive and well and living there because the police, for some reason or other, cannot get a search warrant to enter the premises they are hiding in to arrest them, the long, unsleeping arm of the Honduran police force does have its successes. During my visit, for example, they successfully recaptured a witch who had escaped from prison. But it has to be said that even then it was a close-run thing. At first the police didn't recognise her. As one of them told the local press, 'We didn't think it was her. By now we thought she would have been transformed into a bunch of green bananas.'

But if you think the police are inefficient, you should see the courts. Again while I was in the country, the San Pedro Sula Court of Appeal sentenced Crisanto Alfredo Alvarado to fifteen years' hard labour. The right thing to do, you're probably saying. Sets an example to others. Tough on crime, tough on the . . . Except he was dead. He was the murder victim. The murderer they let off.

Before I left Miami I tried to contact everyone again. Still no luck. No telephone lines. No fax lines. No nothing.

Back in London I had another go. I rang Jorge. Nothing. Tomás. Nothing. Mañuel and José. Nothing. My driver, Julio César. The phone rang. Somebody answered it. It was his wife. Everybody, she told me, was safe. 'The Honduran people, we're very religious. We pray to God every day,' she told me. 'Because we know nobody else will help us.'

If Julio César's wife says it, you've just got to believe it.

Belize City

If only Belize, the one English-speaking country in Central America – it's about the size of Wales, which, of course, is not English-speaking, but what the hell – would put a bit of effort into it and capitalise on their enormous weaknesses, I reckon they could easily become an award-winning tourist destination. For the worst tours. For the worst tour guides. For the worst hotels. For the worst bars and clubs and restaurants. You think I'm joking? Listen, one restaurant I tried served cows' foot soup followed by jam tarts, which, if nothing else, must be some kind of tribute to the British influence. Either that or the chef was moonlighting from British Airways, Kitchen Division. Food for first-class passengers. Only.

In fact, Belize City deserves a prize for the worst everything under the sun. It's as if an enormous radioactive cloud of Mogadon has enveloped the whole country and they've settled down for a big 1,000-year sleep-in and nothing, but nothing, is going to disturb them. Certainly not visitors or, dare I say it, tourists. One bar I went to actually sported a big sign saying, 'Conserve Energy. Be Apathetic.' And apathetic

they are. Not to mention all the other positive virtues stimu-
lated by 180 years of British colonial rule, such as
indifference, reluctance, unwillingness, sloth, far be it from
me, not in a million years and if you think all I've got to do all
day is . . . and so on.

Calling Belize City Belize City was obviously some kind of
British public-school joke. It's not even big enough to be
called Belize Village. About all it's got is a church, a handful
of grubby, clapboard houses, a couple of weed-infested dirt
tracks, a main street where you'd be hard pressed to buy a bag
of nuts, let alone a johnny cake, a bridge built by the Chinese
and . . . and . . . and that's about it.

I've been to a million places that are as small, if not smaller,
as run-down and seedy, if not more run-down and seedy,
like, say, Siem Reap, Ouagadougou or South Central, Los
Angeles where, as it happens, many Belizeans live, or rather
drag out their existence. But at least they've got a bit of a
buzz about them. People walk around with their eyes open.
More than two bicycles a day trundle down the main street.
Not in Belize Village. About the only thing it's big on is
boredom and waiting and zzzzz. Which is odd, seeing as the
country was once the centre of the Egyptians' great Mayan
empire, which stretched across the whole of Central America.
It is still about 65 per cent rainforest, mangrove swamps and
zzzzz and it has over 500, or is it 5 million, different species
of birds zzzzz and a barrier reef teeming with fish, driftwood
and plastic bottles second in size to the Great Barrier Zzzzz in
zzzzz.

In order to maintain this unparalleled zzzzz where the
whole world and its camcorder can snuggle up to Mother
Nature and then walk all over it, the government, in its
wisdom, has decided to create a whole string of artificial
nature reserves, limit hotels to forty rooms and stop guests
from zzzzz no matter how zzzzz they are. Call the prime

minister's office to try to fix a meeting to discuss the plans of theirs that are about to shake the world and you get one of those recorded messages telling you to press 1 for the prime minister. You press one and what do you get? Zzzzz. It's said that the place is so dull and lifeless that even the dead commit suicide out of boredom.

On my first trip there, for example, I waited longer for my cab to arrive at the airport than the flights took from London to Miami and Miami to Belize. And I'd already booked it way in advance. We then slowly chugged our way from the airport up to a roundabout.

'So where are we now?' I asked the driver in my usual, interested, oh-isn't-it-exciting-to-be-alive way.

'Belize City,' he grunted.

We turned down a street straight out of *Heart of Darkness* and crawled along by the corrugated-iron roofs until we came to a church opposite what could have been a museum.

'What church is that?' I asked, ever the mildly interested visitor.

'A church,' he grunted.

I didn't bother to inquire about the museum-like building.

On we went until we came to the St George Hotel. 'A good hotel?' I wondered. 'Or is it . . . ?'

'It's a hotel.'

If I hadn't been in town to tie up another top-secret multi-million-dollar arms agreement, which I'm sworn not to reveal to anybody, not even my accountant – what am I saying? Especially not my accountant – I'd have turned round there and then and headed back to the airport. But, dedicated as I am, and especially as I don't know any other way of making a living, I stuck it out.

What do they think about it in Belize? Do they think they're indifferent, surly, boring, bad-mannered? Well, to be honest, they don't care. Either it's all above their conch shells or they're just not interested. As far as I can gather, the only thing they're bothered about is getting that award for being the worst country in the world for any kind of visitor. Which, if they succeed, will, I'm convinced, be a complete and utter disaster. Because as far as I'm concerned, the only good thing about the place is the almost total absence of services and facilities for visitors.

The following morning, having bored myself even more by checking out no fewer than fifty-four pirated US cable channels on the hotel's television set, ever the optimist, I got another cab, another driver and decided to give Belize Village another whirl. Having done the Worst Tour in the World tour, this time I decided on the Worst Tour Guide in the World Tour. It was exactly the same.

'So which church . . . ?'

'It's a church.'

One. Two. Three. Four.

'A good . . . ?'

'It's a hotel.'

One. Two. Three. Four. Five.

Back at the hotel, I did, for a split second – no, I tell a lie, it wasn't as long as that – think of going on their world famous greasy-spoon tour of the capital's finest restaurant, but as I didn't fancy any more conch fritters I decided the only exciting thing to do was some work.

In another taxi I headed off to see some wheeler-dealer on the edge of town who claimed he'd bought all the cement production from next-door Honduras. We chugged across the Chinese bridge, along some more weed-infested dirt tracks to a fancy-looking little bungalow. After that it was the usual round of excitement: a long wait to see some government official who had long ago outlived his uselessness; a long wait to see some guy at the bank; a long wait to see some lawyer; a long wait to see some so-called local fixer who told me he could make certain I would never ever again have to wait a long time to see anyone in Belize. Some hope.

That evening in desperation, I got yet another cab. I asked the driver to take me to the best bar in town. We ended up hundreds of miles away somewhere in the middle of the jungle outside a collapsing wooden shack called Obsession. It was closed.

'But it's closed,' I sighed, as one does after a ten-hour drive through tropical rainforests for a drink that doesn't exist.

'I know,' the driver muttered.

'But in that case why—'

'You didn't ask me if it was open. You only said . . .'

One. Two. Three. Four. Five. Six.

The next morning, you'd better Belize it, I was out of there. Wherever I stay in the world, I like to leave a room as I found it. So I took out all the lightbulbs, scattered cockroaches all over the floor and blocked up the toilet. I had a ticket. I had a cab. I got to the airport, or rather the airshed, two hours ahead of . . . No plane. It was cancelled.

What to do? I ruled out suicide as an option, although at one stage it was touch and go. That was when the cab driver who took me to the airport said he couldn't take me back because he wasn't an airport taxi, he was a town taxi.

'So where are the airport taxis, then?'

'There aren't any.'

'Why not?'

'Because the plane's been cancelled.'

'So how do I . . . ?'

He then turned tail and drove back to town. Empty.

I, the guest of their wonderful country, the visitor, was left to stand by the side of the road and thumb a lift.

By now, of course, I was out of my mind. I also wanted out of Belize Village as soon and as fast as possible. I wondered whether to take a trip up-country to one of the islands, but when I saw the rickety old quay and the leaky old boat, I decided to give it a miss. For another split second I also wondered whether to head up-country to some jungle resort or other, say hello to the howler monkeys, go around tapping tapirs on the head, no matter how shy they were, swap stories with a couple of wild boars and overtake a jaguar. Apart from the friends of the chairman, Belize is supposed to have more jaguars than anywhere else in the world. But I remembered the advice once given to me by an old African guide as we were trudging through somewhere or other in deepest Zaïre: 'If you look up, close your mouth. The monkeys. They are not house-trained.'

I considered popping in to see Francis Ford Coppola, who is said to love the naturalness of the country so much that, deep in the hills, he's built a private retreat for fifty friends that is not so much eco-friendly as pure Hollywood. All bamboo poles, tropical hardwood floors, Guatemalan rugs and Filipino fittings with a wood-burning pizza oven imported from Rome, an airstrip, a fleet of Land Rovers, landscaping that makes the fabulous Swat Valley up near the Hindu Kush look like a football pitch and his own Napa Valley wines. Which, I suppose, proves trees grow on money, especially in rainforests in Belize.

Then, of course, it occurred to me. So concerned is the Belize government about the environment and protecting it from hordes of so-called eco-tourists, or rather ego-tourists – 'I want to see the giant tortoises on the Galapagos Islands, and even if it means destroying half their breeding grounds to build an airport, I'm going to see them' – that they've rented out vast chunks of it to overseas military to blast each other to bits. Up near the border with Guatemala there is also supposed to be a secret training camp for the British and American military where, no doubt in exchange for them looking the other way on the odd occasion, the Belize government lets them shoot the hell out of the vast stretches of forest. It might be fun, I thought, given the alternatives, to drop in on them and see what kind of a dog soup they had made of the place.

I had the perfect cover story. At least, if I was pushed, I had some kind of cover story. Years ago I vaguely knew the Belize consul in Birmingham. He was a church organist and a bit of a John Betjeman when it came to things ecclesiastical. For some reason he always dressed in black jacket, wing collar, striped pants and bowler hat. He must have thought it made him look like some high-class lawyer. To me he looked like a wine waiter. Either way, he was born in Belize while his father was stationed there with the army, and he told me to go and look the place up if I was ever in the area. Well, to be more accurate he boomed at me to go and look the place up. He was one of those guys who speak to everyone as if they're addressing a public meeting. The last I heard of him he was going to every diplomatic reception he could find, handing out advice to the Foreign Office on everything under the old colonial sun and waiting to be summoned back to the old country to be hailed as some kind of long-lost chief and given the reins of power.

But in the end I didn't bother. Partly because I couldn't find anybody who knew in which part of the jungle they were playing with their Harrier jump jets or shooting up at that particular moment. And partly because of the incident with the Obsession. The last thing I wanted was to drag myself through miles of jungle and across vast tracts of rainforest to find the place closed.

Back at the hotel, where the room was so small the cockroaches had to walk sideways to get in, someone suggested I went out to Barton Creek, where the Mennonites, distant relations of the Amish, have dispensed with electricity, computers and even, I was told, such modern luxuries as zips for their eighteenth-century technology and were supplying the whole country with chickens and eggs and lettuces and all that kind of unhealthy stuff. But I'd already come across them in West Virginia, and they hadn't exactly seemed a bundle of laughs. And I don't care what you think of me, there was no way I was going on anything called 'tubing through caves', no matter how sacred they were to the Mayans and how many heads I would see stuck on top of stalagmites. In spite of what they tell you, it's no fast-track way to heaven.

Instead, ever the workaholic, I decided to head for the country's new capital, Belmopan, to check out some government reports. Created to replace Belize Village should it ever be destroyed by a hurricane, every building in Belmopan is designed in the shape and style of a Mayan temple, an exciting, revolutionary synthesis of old and new, a groundbreaking attempt at the new architecture. That's what they tell you. Don't you believe it. It's a dump. Nothing but a handful of scruffy building blocks scattered haphazardly around a few rough old fields.

The intention may have been there, but if so, it certainly hasn't worked. Most of the buildings look a darned sight older than the Mayan temples they are supposed to be based on. That includes the ones way out in Xunantunich, which, if the Belizeans were not their typical Belizean selves, they would promote as the Machu Picchu of Central America. As for what goes on inside the buildings, somehow they don't seem to have grasped the point of spending millions building a new capital in case the old one is destroyed by a hurricane.

Again and again the few officials who were behind their desks informed me that documents I was looking for were still back in Belize Village.

'But I thought they would be here. This is the new capital.'

'Yes,' I kept being told, 'but it takes a long time to photocopy everything and send . . .'

'You mean you are photocopying everything?'

'Yes, of course.'

'But why? Why don't you just get them to send the originals all here? After all, this is . . .'

'Oh, no. The originals must remain in the Central Registry in Belize City. That's where they are supposed to be.'

'But why not move the whole Central Registry to Belmopan? That would solve all the problems. It would also save money.'

'That's not possible.'

'Why?'

'Because it was decreed that the Central Registry should remain in Belize City.'

At one meeting with some guys at the Finance Ministry I got so mad I told them where they could put their narco-dollars. I said I would go to the Central Bank myself and get the information direct.

'In that case,' they all grinned at me. 'You'll have to go to Belize City. The Central Bank didn't want to move, either.'

I ask you. A capital city without a central bank.

Could things get worse? Oh yes, they could. Having got to mildly exciting, do-anything Belmopan, I couldn't get back. No taxi would take me, not even the gloriously named Rivas Fumigation and Taxi Service. Something or other about agreements. Too punch drunk to even try to fight back, I made for the bus station which, like all bus stations and markets throughout the country, seemed to have been colonised by Guatemalans selling sacks of vegetables. In fact, as far as I could see, the only people who did any work in Belize were the poor Guatemalans. Wherever there was a patch of dirt, they were growing vegetables on it. Wherever two or three people ambled together, they were there selling something. No doubt because they needed the business, but also because, as far as they're concerned, Belize belongs to them. Look at a

Guatemalan atlas and you'll see that Guatemala and Belize appear as one country. Why? The British mucked it up. Way back in 1859, when neither place was anything but provision trees, pimento palms and devil's-gut cactus, keel-billed toucans, scaly-throated leaf-tossers, red-eyed tree frogs, opossums and thousands of different bats and beetles, in other words, pretty much as it is today, Britain promised to build a road linking Belize City and Guatemala City. And the nation that makes such a big play about its word being its bond and all that stuff welshed on the deal. We never built the road. So, say the Guatemalans, quite rightly, if you welshed on the deal, the deal is invalid. Guatemala and Belize are one country. Olé.

Talk about trudging through the rainforest to stay in a typical native hut with all mod cons and a US$25,000 natural thatch roof, some of these so-called adventurers should try a bus ride from Belmopan to Belize Village. It is a far, far more rewarding experience than fighting off orange-breasted eagles and clambering up Ben's Bluff in the Cockscomb Basin Jaguar Sanctuary to look at a bunch of trees. It's also a unique opportunity to ask yourself yet again why, oh why it is, in a country made up of Mayans, plus slaves from Jamaica, black Garifunas from St Vincent, Mestizos from Mexico, Syrians, East Indians, Lebanese and, of course, Chinese, that the British influence so obviously predominates in dealings with visitors?

Was I sad to be back in the worst village in the world? Prepare yourself. This is going to come as a shock. No, I was not. Not because it had changed in any way at all – there's no hope of that ever happening – but because I found out that the following day was going to be party time. They were going to celebrate Christopher Columbus Day.

I must tell you, I've never understood the fuss people make about Christopher Columbus, to give him the name he never had when he was alive. I mean, wasn't he the guy who turned up completely uninvited, discovered a string of places that had already been discovered and then, yelling, 'Ho! Ho! Indios!', proceeded to show his gratitude by destroying everything in sight, raping, torturing and killing anything that moved, infecting the whole area with a load of glorious diseases that had never before been known in these countries, stealing everything worth stealing and then high-tailing it out of there as fast as his little sails could carry him?

Maybe I'm getting soft. But isn't a Christopher Columbus Day a bit like asking Eastern Europe to celebrate an Adolf Hitler or even a Joseph Stalin Day? OK, I agree that maybe Chris the Colon, to give him the name he was no doubt called when he was alive, is not quite at their level. But for all that, he was still pretty much in their league. Yet here, and throughout the Caribbean, they are actually proud of the man who took away their land, their culture, their dignity and repaid them with horrifying cruelty and every kind of rapacious illness you can think of.

On Grand Turk in the Turks and Caicos, where Columbus is reputed to have landed for the first time, they've put up a big brass plaque on the beach. Here, it says, on Grand Turk was the first landing of Christopher Colombus, on 12 October 1492. He called the place Guanahand, which is olde-worlde Spanish for your olde days are numbered, sunshine. The locals called him and his bloodthirsty gang of Rioja louts the 'people from the sky'. They then gave them food and drink with, Columbus said afterwards, 'marvellous love', which, I'm sure you don't need me to tell you, has nothing to do with luncheon vouchers.

When I was on Grand Turk– I'd just been to the local museum, where they make a big fuss about one of our Chris's ships, the *Pinta*, which didn't even get as far as the island: it sank off the Molasses Reef – one of the locals, an old boy, sidled up to me. He said he was ninety-six years old, the second-oldest man on Grand Turk, and had no fewer than fifty-three grandchildren.

'Dat Christopher Columbus.' He waved his finger at me. 'Dat great man. He take dat big clipper and he doggone circumcise the world.'

Which I have to say brought tears to my eyes. Actually, it still does, now I come to think of it.

In Santo Domingo in the Dominican Republic it's even worse. There, in the middle of an enormous, beautifully landscaped park, they've gone as far as to build a huge, eight-storey block of what looks like jazzy council flats in the shape of a huge, hollowed-out cross. Inside the cross is a kind of mini-shopping-mall-cum-courtyard full of art galleries and displays, all paying tribute to Chris the Colon and 'the courage of those who discovered and explored the New World'. Gee whizz, they've even got the anchor from his flagship, the *Santa Maria*.

In the centre there is a virtual shrine to the man, watched over by soldiers standing with their heads bowed, as if they were on guard duty for the Pope himself. On the outside there are vast panels with a series of quotations from famous Dominicans such as Isaiah, Aristotle and Seneca praising a man they all obviously knew well. The most important panel of all states simply: '*Gran Almirante del Oceano, Gobernador General de las Islas y Continente de Asia y de Ambas Indias, Capitán General de la Mar, Membro de la Corte Réal Debajo de Rey y la Reina*.' In other words, all praise to the Great Exploiter.

Even more absurd, in Puerto Rico I discovered on a trip to the big Intel plant there that they're planning to put up a 660-ton statue of Chris the Colon that will be bigger even than the Statue of Liberty. The only two redeeming features of the project, as far as I could gather, are that it has been designed by Zurab Tsereteli, the Georgian sculptor who is currently president of the Russian Academy of Arts, and who is responsible for the fifteen-storey statue of Peter the Great in Moscow, and that it is actually being built in, of all places, St Petersburg and then being shipped over bit by bit. Assuming that the Russians are serious about it and not using it as a scam to ship out drugs or more IMF dollars that we have so generously given them, they'll never even get halfway to finishing it. It will never be built and it will never be shipped over. For which we must all be truly thankful. Although why the Russians, of all people, should have thought it was up to them to champion someone like our Chris the Colon, Lenin only knows. Unless, of course, it's the usual Russian trick: they are designing it and building it and shipping it over and hoping the Puerto Ricans will pay the bill. I wouldn't put it past them. Clever guys, the Russkies.

On top of all the plaques and funny-shaped buildings and huge statues, the entire area the Colon claims to have discovered also goes in for shows and pageants and parades and stamps and coins and days off and, of course, an infinite number of different T-shirts.

Goodness me. If only I was one of those rough, tough New York lawyers I'd be drawing up massive claims for compensation. For illegal infringement of national sovereignty. For total disregard of human rights. For wanton brutality. For rape. For pillage. For looting. For killing nine-tenths of the population. For reducing a happy, innocent, and in some ways incredibly sophisticated people to slavery and disease.

If you think I'm exaggerating, listen to what one of their own guys, Bartolomé de las Casas, has to say about it in his catchily entitled *Brief Relation of the Destruction of the Indies.*

They came with their Horsemen well armed with Sword and Launce, making most cruel havocks and slaughters . . . Overrunning Cities and Villages, where they spared no sex nor age; neither would their cruelty pity Women with childe, whose bellies they would rip up, taking out the Infant to hew it in pieces. They would often lay wagers who should with most dexterity either cleave or cut a man in the middle . . . The children they would take by the feet and dash their innocent heads against the rocks, and when they were fallen into the water, with a strange and cruel derision they would call on them to swim . . . They erected certains Gallowses . . . upon every one of which they would hang thirteen persons, blasphemously affirming that they did it in honour of our Redeemer and his Apostles, and then putting fire under them, they burnt the poor wretches alive. Those whom their pity did think to spare, they would send away with their hands half cut off, and so hanging by the skin.

Instead of having Christopher Columbus Days and all that nonsense, I'd give the whole Caribbean a massive Colonic irrigation up what is known in the business as its tradesmen's entrance. Instead of having Christopher Columbus Days, I'd be calling for ABC Days – Anything But Columbus Days – all over Latin America. No shows. No pageants. No parades. No souvenirs. No stamps. No coins. Most of all, no T-shirts. Well, maybe no dry T-shirts.

Then there's the question of compensation. I'd be demanding billions from the Spanish government. Surely, in all justice, they should come across with at least some readies to pay for the horrifying cruelty inflicted on so many people, for the destruction of their culture, for the theft of their lands and so many of their precious natural resources and, of course, for the rapacious diseases they left behind. Look at what the Indians have got from the Americans. Look at what the Aborigines have got from the Australians.

Finally, there is the question of an apology. On the 500th anniversary of Chris the Colon's first trip to the States, Bill Clinton, then the US president, apologised on behalf of white America to black Americans for slavery, although I noticed he still saw fit to ignore the promise Lincoln made during the Civil War that if any freed slaves fought on his side they would be entitled free, gratis and for nothing, to a small parcel of land and a donkey. Some say the problem is the practicalities of the thing. For a start there aren't 30 million donkeys to go round. And it would play hell with the streets of Harlem, let alone downtown Atlanta. I don't know about you, but to me that's all typical lawyers' shilly-shallying. What a president says, a president should do. You've only got to look at Clinton to see the high standards of honesty and truthfulness and moral integrity that the Americans uphold.

So with the Chris the Colon matter sorted out and the compensation billions rolling in, let's look at how much we Brits can hit the Normans for. Not to mention the Vikings. Not to mention all those GIs for what they did during the Second World War.

So how did Belize Village celebrate Chris the Colon Day? In the way you would have expected. With indifference, with reluctance, with unwillingness, sloth, far be it from me, not in a million years and if you think all I've got to do all day is . . . What else? To be honest it was difficult to tell the difference between this and any other day. The place was deserted. There was nobody around. There were hardly any cars in the streets. The bar in the hotel was closed, or rather, there was nothing on the plank of wood on top of that pile of wooden boxes in the corner of that space by the door when I staggered down there at lunchtime. There was no barman, no customers, nobody.

Call me a glutton for punishment, but I decided to try another tour. This time I got a taxi in the length of time it usually takes to clear customs in Miami. Which was just as well, because I fancied a night-time tour.

Up to the roundabout we chugged.

'So where are we now?' I asked in my best, desperate-to-be-interested voice, ever hopeful that things would somehow improve.

'By the roundabout,' grunted the driver, obviously another graduate of the British Airways Charm School.

Along Heart of Darkness High Street we spluttered until we came to a bank.

'What bank is that?'

'It's got the name there,' mumbled my ever-helpful driver.

Up a bit further to a church.

'So what church is that?'

'A church.'

'Yes, but—'

'A church.'

'Yes, of course. Thank you very much.'

Opposite, this time I noticed, was what used to be the governor's mansion. It was now a museum.

'So what's that?' I inquired hesitantly.

'Museum.'

'Yes, but what—'

'Museum. That's all. Museum.'

Up to a wreck of a building we trundled.

'This used to be the hospital. But it was moved because the place was dangerous.'

The driver was actually saying something to me?

'Where was it moved to?'

'To the new site.'

'But where . . . ?'

Oh, what the hell.

We shuddered to a stop by a beautifully preserved light-house.

'This is a lighthouse,' announced my oh-so-informative guide.

On we went to the St George Hotel.

'A good hotel?' I wondered yet again.

'A hotel.'

I went in. It brought joy to my soul. For there, for all to marvel at, was the full extent of British influence after all those years of imperial rule. The doorman was wearing a highly blanco-ed pith helmet. Inside, in the bar – where else? – was an actual Brit doing his duty. He was on the phone trying to buy up all the cement production from next-door, Honduras. In a corner were two Americans earnestly discussing ways in which to bring much-needed foreign investment to the country. They were planning to sell off huge tracts of land to overseas industrial countries at half the market price.

'Half the market price!' I said. 'But how can you do that?'

'Because it's underwater half the year,' they hollered. 'But don't tell them. That'll ruin it for them.'

Back to my hotel we chugged. Again, there was not a living soul about. Whether this was Belize Village being Belize Village, or whether it was a form of protest against Christopher Columbus Day, I couldn't tell you. There was nobody to ask. Not even any Chinese meandering backwards and forwards across their bridge. In any case, why should they celebrate? I'm not exactly up on Chris the Colon and his Voyages of Aggression, 1492–8, but as far as I'm aware he no more set foot in Belize than he did in Intercourse, Pennsylvania. Partly because he'd heard what a bundle of laughs the place was, even in those days, and partly because, however hard he tried, he couldn't find what in those days they called a safe passage – today, I gather it has a totally different meaning. Whenever one of his ships got anywhere close to the shore, the barrier reef ripped it to pieces. So why on earth should Belize celebrate, or even attempt to celebrate, anything whatsoever to do with Chris the Colon in the first place?

If there is one man they should well and truly celebrate, it's a Portuguese sailor called Baron Bliss, the only man in the whole history of the world who, as far as I can tell – I'm still waiting for the photocopies to be sent from Belize Village to Belmopan and then on to me – who . . . who actually . . . who actually liked Belize. In fact he liked it so much that he never ever went there, presumably on the age-old basis that since everything looks good from a distance, it's a shame to ruin it all by getting up close. Instead he sailed up and down the coast for years on end, gazing at the shore wistfully. Then, when he died, he left Belize all his money, which, even to this day, they are still using to finance various good works.

'It's a funny old *mondo*,' as one conquistador said to the other while they burned down another village and started slaughtering a couple of hundred more innocent people in the name of civilisation.

Machu Picchu

I know it's not the thing to say, but I don't reckon the Incas. Everyone says they were great guys, gentle and civilised. And they go on about how they invented something absurd like over 9,253 different types of *turmas de tierra*, the Spanish for testicles of the earth, in other words, potatoes. Which I'm sure you'll remember the next time you handle one. A potato, that is. Can you imagine? Over 9,253 different types of potato. Or whatever. As if that qualified them for anything other than being honorary Irishmen. And, of course, about how they were wiped out by the horrible, wicked, nasty Spanish.

But I don't buy it. To me the Incas were stupid. It's no wonder they disappeared, because everything they did was wrong.

Take Machu Picchu, which is supposed to be their crowning glory, the achievement that puts them up there with the ancient Egyptians, the Greeks, the Romans and the apprentices who designed and built Milton Keynes. There it is, astride a small ridge, either 1,500, 15,000 or 15 million feet up in the Andes, depending on which guidebook you look at. Behind it, Huayna Picchu, their very own Sugar Loaf Mountain. Behind that even more hills and mountains. But, I ask you, who builds a major tourist attraction like that in the middle of nowhere, a million miles and a four-hour rickety train journey from the nearest town? Not even the Windsors were as stupid as that, and they've done plenty of stupid things in their time. But at least give them credit for building Windsor Castle close to an airport to make it easy for tourists to get in and out of.

To get to Machu Picchu from Cuzco, the old Inca capital and the longest-inhabited city in either North or South America, takes nearly a whole day. You have to set your llama clock at five. It is still pitch-black. By six o'clock you're at the station fighting to get on a train built for midgets. And all this to im-peru-ve your knowledge of the Incas.

As it's getting light the train is zig-zagging its way backwards and forwards out of Cuzco's deep valley. Zig. The train trundles along within two inches of mile after mile of corrugated-iron shacks. Already pigs and dogs and children, in that order, are running backwards and forwards across the line in front of the train. Zag. It judders to a halt. The guard – or is it the driver, or does the same guy do both jobs? – jumps off, throws a lever and the train switches on to another track, which takes us further up the side of the valley past vast piles of rubbish, stacks of oil drums and all this gungy, black stuff flowing all over the place. Zig. The train judders to a halt again. The guard and driver, or is it the driver and guard, gets out and does his stuff. We switch on to an even higher track. This time I can't see a thing. Every one of the 10,327 Japanese tourists on the train is leaning out of the window photographing something or other that moved. Zag. And so it goes on. Backwards and forwards. Backwards and forwards. Higher still and higher until we're eventually out of the valley and on to the Altiplano, mile after mile after mile of warm, desolate, wide, open greenery, full of nothing but emptiness, the odd peasant keeping his eye on his sheep and the occasional llama or hummingbird.

Now and then we trundle into tiny villages where time has stood still since the arrival of Sky Television and *Neighbours*. Every time we stop we're besieged by a thousand Indian women of all shapes and ages and sizes selling all kinds of food and snacks they've cooked specially for the train. They're wearing their traditional Andean costumes with those enormous petticoats which, Ché Guevara charmingly informs us in his book on South America, in what to me is the most memorable phrase in the continent's literature, are nothing but 'veritable tents of excrement'. Thanks a lot for that useful information, Ché. I knew you were an expert on undercover activities in Latin America, but I didn't think you went that far. Enjoy your breakfast.

As if that is not enough local atmosphere to be getting on with, we are also hotly pursued by every child in the country under seven years old, every single one of them selling every kind of genuine Inca knick-knack you can think of: Inca necklaces, Inca bracelets, Inca shawls made of genuine Inca alpaca wool, Inca Coca-Cola, Inca home-made cakes. Excuse me if I sit down for a moment. I suddenly feel as though I'm Inca for a nervous breakdown.

On and on we go. Along by the Urubamba, which is at first a stream, then a river and finally a raging, thundering tributary of the Amazon. Through gorges thick with Inca ruins until slowly we wind down to the upper fringes of the Amazonian rainforest. Which is your real jungle. Enormous trees, thick vegetation, impenetrable undergrowth. The kind of stuff you have to hack your way through to get any decision taken by head office. Finally, after the time it takes for a single e-coli 0157 bacteria to become a raging plague, we crawl into Grand Central Station, Machu Picchu, where I sit down and weep. Because everybody getting off the train is, I can't help but notice, not only wrapped up to the nines in their khaki combat trousers, their whoopy-do I'm-an-explorer anoraks, which must be designed and made for the congenitally insane – how else can you explain why on each pocket there are instructions telling you exactly what you can put in them? – their woolly hats, their trekking boots and their trekking gloves. As if that is not enough to almost make me turn round and head straight back for Cuzco, they are also laden down with everything from sunblock, lip balm and gallons of insect-repellent to great, big, woolly towels, biodegradable soap and sleeping bags. Not to mention little plastic water bottles, Steiner 8×50 binoculars, complete with vegetarian beanbag stock rest, flashlights, walkie-talkies and, of course, the inevitable Swiss army knives. As if, for all the world, they are expecting to spend six months in the Andes and then end up by eating each other. There are also a whole tribe of Americans of the back-to-front baseball-cap-wearing classes. Me? I'm doing it the Mallory way. I'm in my usual Sunday morning gear: sports jacket, collar and tie, a pair of old cords, my old black shoes. No anorak. No boots. And definitely no Swiss army knife. Well, if Mallory could climb Everest wearing a sports jacket, a good pair of cords and a decent pair of shoes, why make all this fuss about a couple of thousand feet?

So how do we get from the station to Machu Picchu? Do we have to scale the sheer cliff face of the mountain with the aid of our Casio PRT 40E compass watch? Do we have to hack our way through the jungle using only a £25.95 dry-feet heater for removing moisture from our ski boots? Do we have to risk our lives battling through raging, merciless currents with only our Mulberry pewter and leather hip flask, £65, available from all good adventure shops everywhere?

No, we don't. We have to queue up for the bus. The bus is driven by some raving Inca throwback with a bad haircut who seems convinced that in order to avenge his people, it is now his turn to hurl people off the side of the mountain. As a result we scream round corners like a bat out of hell. We skid to within inches of the edge. And, then, of course, we get stuck. In some enormous Inca bog. On the corner of a crazy, Inca hairpin bend. Halfway up the side of this Inca mountain.

Immediately all the whoopy-do-I'm-an-explorer anoraks start squealing and panicking – there are no instructions on their jackets telling them what to do in cases of emergency – and complaining that, having paid the fare, they're not going to walk anywhere for anyone. All the trekking boots and trekking gloves start leaping around, shouting at the driver, demanding he calls the AA and asking for the telephone number of the local branch of the RAF mountain rescue team. All the sunblock and lip balms and insect-repellents form a crocodile so that they can trudge back down the mountain before they get eaten alive by butterflies. I may be wrong, but I swear one or two Indiana Jones lookalikes were talking about lunch and eyeing up some of the more portly members of the party somewhat suspiciously.

I stay put. I settle back in the empty bus while the demented Inca driver revs and revs and revs his Inca bus into a deeper and deeper Inca hole. When his battery is finally flat and the bus is exhausted I get off and – you'd be proud of me – stroll casually up the rest of the mountain in my sports jacket, my collar and tie, my pair of old cords and my old black walking shoes. No anorak. No boots. No Swiss army knife. And definitely no sunblock and lip balm.

Machu Picchu itself, when I finally get there is, I admit, impressive. There is an impressive self-service, open-air restaurant, an impressive hotel and a string of impressive shops, not to mention an impressive cloakroom where you can check in your anorak and your Swiss army knife and your sunblock and lip balm if you find they are just too heavy to carry. Oh yes, I nearly forgot. The Inca ruins. Well, they look like a cross between Pompeii and the *Marie Celeste*.

The location is spectacular. Hiram Bingham, the Yale professor who discovered Machu Picchu in 1911, waxed lyrical about 'the sublimity of its surroundings, the marvel of its site, the character and the mystery of its construction'. The Western hemisphere, he said, 'holds nothing comparable'. I don't think I'd go quite that far. But then, Yale professors always go over the top. Either way, it's better than, say, Yale on a wet Wednesday afternoon.

Strolling around it is a bit like strolling around Sissinghurst, or any one of a thousand National Trust gardens or areas of natural beauty, on a Sunday afternoon, except that you've got to keep stepping over all these New Age Incas in their pigtails and long coats and funny hats lying around trying to strike up some kind of meaningful relationship with the odd stone or rock because they think the Incas were descended from a bunch of little green men who landed at the bottom of Lake Titicaca in a flying saucer. If *The X Files* came here they would have enough material for an entire new series.

I latch on to a guide who looks as though he's had a plastic surgery accident. He seems to be obsessed with 'protuberances'. Whether or not this has anything to do with the fact that one Inca king had over 300 sons, I couldn't tell you.

We start with the grand-sounding Terrace Caretakers' Houses on the lower south-east corner. They are just your basic, simple worker's cottage. 'This year the girl who was going to clean the protuberance has more money for buying meat. They have a bull for doing the work. They kill the bull also. They say, your father can die. Don't be stupid. But once in their life they are important. Yes?'

'Er, yes,' I mumble.

At the Watchman's Hut I can see the whole site. On one side is the city proper. On the other is the workers' quarters. Behind me is the cemetery. Along the terraces to the north-west is the original entrance. All the guide can talk about are the protuberances on the stairway, on the terrace, on the old entrance to the site.

He leans towards me. 'I give to you secret,' he says. 'We are mixed. Not blended. The past is in front. The future is behind. We have hopes and spectation. The dead will be alive and the alive dead.' I don't care what any deconstructionist might say, but to me that was proof positive that one week-end, instead of hobnobbing with the Bloomsbury set without a word to Viv, old Possum must have whizzed off for a quick fling in Cuzco.

We go into the Temple of the Sun, the only circular build-ing. Now the guide is going on about the Inca Tomb below, where they used to keep the mummies, and about how far north of the temple the famous Inca ceremonial area is. At least, I think he is. What he actually says is: 'I tell you, it is rainfall. But it is not rain all the time. You get clouds. It opens like a curtain. I tell you all the possibilities. We all to observe the protuberances.'

I did my best to observe them. Honest.

It's the same story at the Temple of Three Windows, the Principal Temple and the Sacristy, which contains one stone with no fewer than thirty-two corners. 'Everything happens in five hundred years: five hundred years Incas, five hundred years Spanish. Then, in 1983, we have terrible rain. The rain makes lot of wet lands. The wet lands make crops. The crops make babies. So everything every five hundred years. Yes?'

Well, no actually. Old Possum was easier to understand than this poncho honcho.

At the Temple of Intihuantana, however, he is struck

dumb. Is it because it's the most sacred place in all of Machu Picchu? No, it's because in the centre is the biggest protuberance in the whole place: a sculptured rock which gradually becomes a pillar of grey granite. A number of questions puzzle me, though. First of all, what is it? Machu Picchu, I mean, not the protuberance. I know what the protuberance looks like. Is it a fortress? But if it was meant to be a fortress, why didn't the Incas use it as one and stay there and protect themselves from the Spaniards? Some kind of religious centre? But if it was some kind of religious centre, where are the religious buildings? Where are the religious remains? Where are the collecting plates? The only thing that makes sense to me is that it is some kind of high-society country club. Look at the facts. Ten times as many female skeletons have been discovered there as male skeletons. Come on, let's be honest, any place in the middle of nowhere in which women outnumber men by ten to one can only be one of two things. And the other thing is not some kind of fortress or religious centre. It might also explain why the Incas didn't have any strength left to fight the Spaniards.

As for the Incas themselves, they were pretty dumb. They couldn't write, so they had no written language. They had no wheels. Everything was carried by men or llamas. They couldn't add up, let alone try their hand at complicated things like subtraction, multiplication and whatever the other one is. They had no clock. The only way they could tell the time was by watching the shadow of the big rock and the shadow of the little rock, and when they were in a straight line it was time to go and have a drink. They couldn't handle such complicated pieces of technology as a hammer and chisel. The only way they could build was by chipping away at an old block with a bit of harder stone. They couldn't do a simple thing like mix cement with water. Instead they were forced to chip away at the old blocks so finely that they fitted together tightly without the need for any mortar. Apart from cultivating their earth-bound testicles, they were lousy farmers. They didn't even know how to cut the wool off their llamas. Instead, I ask you, they killed them, then cut the wool off.

As for being fierce, brave and noble warriors, I don't see that either. Admittedly they weren't exactly a bunch of wishy-washy liberals. For generations the Andes had echoed to the pitter-patter of their tiny feats. They had conquered the surrounding tribes and assimilated them into their empire. They put Inca garrisons all over the place. They forced everybody to speak Quecha. When the Chancas marched on Cuzco they fought them off, even though there were more of them and they had superior power. The Inca chief even took on the Chanca chief hand to hand and killed him. Under Pachacute they mopped up all their old rivals. They conquered the mountains around Cuzco. They subdued the area around Lake Titicaca. They pushed as far north as Colombia and almost as far south as Santiago in Chile. They also developed their own social structure. At the top was the king and all the royal families. Below them were the upper classes. Below them the lower classes. Everybody was expected to pay their taxes, get a job, get married, go home on time and watch *Coronation Street*.

But when it came to the big one, they crumbled. Just like that. The great Manco Inca II simply handed over Cuzco, with all its massive battlements and impenetrable defences, to the Spanish. Why? Why didn't he stay and fight? Why didn't the Incas hot-foot it back to Machu Picchu, if it was indeed a fortress and not some high-society country club for the big boys, and wage guerrilla war against them? Instead Manco is said to have sat down and wept. Now, does that sound like a rough, tough, majestic Inca warlord? Is that the kind of guy Mel Gibson would want to play in a film, painted face or not?

And what about Atahualpa? He had 40,000 warriors at his beck and call. Forty thousand. And in ten minutes they were wiped out, by how many Spaniards? By 170, that's how many.

In the left-hand corner, the Spanish soldiers, led by Francisco Pizarro. In the right-hand corner Atahualpa, with twenty times as many. The Spaniards grab him. The Incas just stand there. With their grand protuberance gone, there is nobody to tell them what to do. They are impotent. The Spaniards just wipe them out, like a bunch of non-executives in a boardroom row. Not content with that, the Spanish then demand a ransom. The few remaining Incas hand over no less than 6,092 kilograms of gold and 11 tons of silver, worth around US$100 million at today's prices. Pizarro just grabs the money and murders Atahualpa anyway. Do the Incas go bananas? No, they turn and run. The Spaniards give chase. But after a couple of metres they give up. What's the point? They've now got so much gold and silver they don't know what to do with it. In the end, they ship the gold back to Seville and use the silver for horseshoes. Which to me is completely shocking. If I was there, I'd have sent the silver to Seville and given the horses golden shoes. I mean, are they your best friend or are they not your best friend?

No Inca, or rather, nobody remotely related to an Inca, has ever claimed the money, or even an apology, from the Spaniards. Not to mention all the interest that has been stacking up all these years. Yet if what the Spaniards did wasn't tantamount to breaking solemn and binding international agreements, let alone outright theft, I don't know what is. The United Nations, the European Court of Justice, the arbitration panel of the International Chamber of Commerce, not to mention every single Native American, Aborigine and Maori in the world would all come down on the side of the Incas. The judges wouldn't even have to have a heavy, three-hour lunch to think about it. They'd go straight for it.

About the only thing the Incas could do was fiddle with bits of string, get bombed out of their tiny minds and eat, drink and sleep potatoes. Which is obviously why they're known as honorary Irishmen. If, of course, there is anything honourable about fiddling with bits of string, getting bombed out of your mind and eating, drinking and sleeping potatoes.

The bits of string were their only form of measurement. Which probably accounts for the fact that practically every single Inca building is made up of stones and rocks and boulders of a thousand different shapes and sizes, like some giant Irish drystone wall.

As for hitting the booze, did they hit the booze. According to various accounts they hold the Guinness blue riband for being the boozers extraordinary of Latin America. Go to an Inca party and you'll be drinking for days on end. A Spaniard who went to one in 1833 said they drank so much – the women as well as the men – that 'two wide drains ran with urine throughout the city, as abundantly as a flowing spring'. Which, even for non-Rotarians, is some drinking.

Which goes some way to explaining why – eat your heart out, Sir Walter Raleigh – potatoes were not just the centre of their world, they *were* their world. They needed them first to make the booze – leave potatoes in the cold and they turn to alcohol – second to soak it up afterwards. As a result, the Incas planted nothing but potatoes, potatoes and still more potatoes. In their gardens. In their backyards. In the valleys. Halfway up the side of a mountain. On the mountaintops themselves. They even planted an ornamental garden decorated with potatoes. In gold. They also ate only potatoes. In fact you can bet your life that if the odd Inca politician was found dead in his flat wearing a plastic mac, there would be two potatoes around somewhere.

Even today, they're obsessed with potatoes. If a girl wants to get married the first thing she has to prove – feminists, put down your cigars and look the other way – is that she can peel a potato. If she can she's OK, if not, she's out. Babies are brought up on *arracacha* potatoes, which apparently look like white carrots and contain the correct amount of starch or whatever it is that babies need. Teenagers, when they're not high on drugs, survive on *achiva* potatoes, from which noodles are produced. Everybody else survives on *oca* potatoes, which are used instead of wheat flour in making bread. Blokes even swan around looking like Louis XVI with potato flowers in their buttonholes. It's no wonder the Incas had their chips as far as the Spaniards were concerned. They were probably so stuffed full of potatoes they could hardly move off their couches, let alone ask for arbitration.

Some people maintain that the Incas were great architects and town planners. But I don't see that, either. They didn't know how to cut stone. Give or take the occasional trapezoidal gateway, they didn't actually design or build anything of their own. What they built they copied from previous Andean peoples. And their techniques were not exactly advanced.

As for their being town planners, I think the less said about that the better. Take Cuzco, their crowning achievement, the Mecca of the Inca empire. It is supposed to be laid out in the shape of a puma, which was some kind of Inca god. The eye is Sacsayhuaman, the great imperial Inca fortress, which at one time sported a giant central tower. Alongside it is a man-made cliff face, composed of so many huge stones you cannot possibly believe they were moved there all those hundreds of years ago. The feet were different imperial Inca palaces and imperial Inca temples. The tail was another imperial Inca something or other. And why they built the entertainment area and the sewage works alongside each other I have no idea.

In any event, Cuzco was a complete and utter disaster. Originally it was intended to be the hub, the centre of the empire, with a vast network of roads radiating from it, reaching down to Chile in the south and as far north as Colombia. If there were any problems, troops covering around 150 miles a day, Roman-style, could be on the move immediately. But instead of being an effective means of quickly stamping out the slightest hint of trouble, the road system became a series of daggers pointing straight at their poor Inca hearts. It was equally useful to anyone who wanted to attack them, especially as they had forgotten to build any defences to protect them should the need arise.

Who says so? The great South American revolutionary and undercover expert Ché Guevara. So there.

Yet as you fly into Cuzco, it does look impressive. Set as it is in a deep bowl of green hills, you can see why the Incas called it Quechua, the navel of the world. What they would have called it had it been on a long, fairly thick protuberance, I shudder to think. To the Conquistadors, however, when they stumbled across it 'at the hour of high mass' on 15 November 1533, it was 'the greatest and finest city ever seen in this country or anywhere in the Indies'. The biggest city on the whole continent, with over 125,000 people, it was so beautiful and had so many fine buildings they thought it would be remarkable even in Spain. Which, for the Spanish, is saying something.

To me, though, it's more like the Katmandu of the western hemisphere. Except that the air is crisper. Everything looks clean and sparkling. And the views of the mountains, some of them covered with glaciers, which almost surround it are truly breathtaking. The trouble is, it's just a mass of genuine, authentic Inca ice-cream shops, Inca kola shops, Inca petrol and diesel stations, Inca pizzerias and Inca snack bars selling Inca bread and butter and Inca jam sandwiches. There is even an Inca pub. About the only places not calling themselves Inca this or Inca that are the genuine Inca remains, a travel agency called United Mice and the old Koricancha, the Temple of the Sun, the most elaborate temple ever built by the Incas, which is now called the Church of Santo Domingo. Once it had altars to the moon, to thunder and to the rainbow. It was covered in 700 gold panels, each weighing 5 pounds. Today they're all gone. But, against all the odds, the church, with its Inca foundations, is still there. It was first destroyed by an earthquake in 1650. It was rebuilt but flattened a second time by another earthquake in 1950. It is now in the course of being rebuilt yet again. Go and see it if you have the chance. But if I were you, I'd give it a miss in 2250, just in case.

One street, Hatruntumiyoq, the Street of Enormous Stones, is, surprise, surprise, more or less one huge Inca stone after another. One of them has no fewer than twelve different angles. How do I know it so well? Because – I cannot tell a lie – it's the logo on the bottles of local Cuzquena beer. In another street, Arcquipa, the Inca stones are virtually two storeys high.

To church-crawlers, the cathedral is famous the world over. Not because it is full to overflowing with heavily ornate silver altars, intricate wood carvings and a mass of other decorations, but because it boasts an enormous painting of the Last Supper showing Christ and the Apostles digging into chilli peppers, roast guinea pig and gallons of maize beer.

The central square, the Plaza de Armas, is colonial Spain surrounded by arcades, or ambulacra, as we used to call them at school. But there is nowhere to walk because all day and for most of the night every square inch is taken up with the wreckage of once-proud Indian races squatting on the ground hustling Inca chewing gum, Inca packets of cigarettes and Inca colour film, or just staring vacantly into Inca nothing. All around them are thousands of babies training for a lifetime of sucking up to tourists.

For some enlightenment I went and stood in the eye of the puma, but all that happened was that I was besieged by a hundred Inca photographers all trying to take Inca photographs of me so that they could paste them on Inca postcards and sell them to me for a couple of million Inca dollars before I left their Inca town.

As for Lima, the City of Kings – King Edwards – it's so bad you could be forgiven for thinking that the Incas designed and built that too. In fact it's the ideal place to take the wife, especially if she keeps complaining that all you do as you travel the world is roast in the sunshine, meet fun people and drink champagne. Once she's seen Lima, a city of colour – the colour is grey – I guarantee she will believe only two of the three. For even though it has incredible beaches to the south and even more fantastic restaurants to the north, the sun never shines in Lima. At least, it never has whenever I've been there. The rain never rains, either, and it's never, ever really dark. Just grey. Because from morning till late at night, it's almost totally covered by a blanket of thick, damp, dusty, clammy, mist or fog. It's so bad that people travel halfway round the world to see it, much as people travel halfway round the world to see the Northern Lights, because they cannot imagine such a thing is possible.

The reason for this is that the entire length of the coast is arid desert, nothing but vast areas of black, yellow and red sand dunes that rise to 50 metres so that when the wind blows, it blows everything straight on to Lima and straight up your nose. It's such a problem that smoking in public is absolutely, totally against the law. Which is probably just as well, because you just wouldn't be able to walk if the air were any thicker. The only place you'll find anything approaching fresh air and a totally clean environment is inside the most important building in the whole city: the earthquake-proof potato gene bank housed deep in the International Potato Centre.

Between 1980 and 1995 the country was practically out of bounds, not because nobody could find it, but because you could hardly go anywhere without being bombed or attacked or shot at, either by the government or by a bunch of Maoist guerrillas called the Shining Path. Around 250,000 people were killed. Those who could left. Those who couldn't, or wouldn't, stayed, kept their heads down, ate potatoes and prayed. One local businessman told me that in those days he had to wait even longer than usual to be served in his local bank because there was invariably a government tank in the queue in front of him. If the government didn't like what you were doing they just sent in a tank. Now, of course, it's worse. They send in IMF officials.

In 1990, from nowhere, Alberto Fujimori arrived on the scene and got himself elected president. An agronomy professor of Japanese descent – he's known locally as Chinito, little Chinaman – he was so obscure even he didn't know who he was. Since then, however, he's changed everything. The violence has gone. The economy is booming. Year after year, Peru has the fastest-growing economy in the whole of Latin America. But he's not been without his problems, the biggest one of all, of course, being his wife. The last time I was there she was making a pathetic attempt to become the Princess Di of Latin America by moaning and complaining about her husband and going on four-day hunger strikes. Or was it just another attack of bulimia?

As for Lima, it started out with all the advantages. It wasn't designed by the Incas but by Francisco Pizarro, the Spanish conqueror in 1535 and the world's greatest town planner. He simply sketched out the layout of the place in the sand while chatting away to his buddies on the banks of the River Rimae.

'Thirteen streets down here,' he said, drawing the lines in the sand. 'And seven crossing the lot of them. Now, who did you say won the bullfight back in Seville last Friday afternoon?'

Under first Napoleon and then Louis XIV, Lima was the golden, glamorous centre of Latin America. It was recognised for its architecture. It was a major trading centre. Even today, unlike other cities in South America such as Buenos Aires, Santiago, Bogotá or Quito, it still has its old colonial centre. Admittedly it's a bit seedy and run-down. Admittedly it has armed guards on almost every corner. Admittedly there are battered old tanks guarding buildings that have already been bombed to smithereens by terrorists, presumably on the basis that in Peru lightning often strikes in the same place twice. Either that or the tanks are even older than they look, have broken down altogether and have simply been abandoned by the army because it's cheaper to leave them where they are than to try to repair them and take them home.

Its treasures are still there, too. The Plaza de Armas, the seat of government; the Plaza San Martin, the real historic centre; the Church of San Francisco, the oldest monastery in South America, with its catacombs containing the remains of over 70,000 people; its library, with over 6,000 scrolls; its several paintings by Van Dyck and Rubens; the Church of Santo Domingo; Polvos Azules, the black market, and, of course, way out on the edge of the city, the two-in-one museum: the Museo de Oro, the gold museum downstairs in the vaults, and upstairs the Museo de Armas, which is packed with everything anybody could possibly need for hacking, butchering or plain putting another human being to death. Not as good as the Wallace Collection, one of my favourite London museums, but still worth a quick visit between meetings.

The more I wander round Lima, the more I'm convinced that, like Cuzco, it is based, Inca-style, on the local fauna, in this case on one of those enormous Peruvian blue-backed tarantulas the size of a dinner plate with legs coming at you from all directions.

The brains are the Place San Martin where, if you're lucky,

you might get yourself checkmated. The square is full of chess tables and everybody is waiting for a game. Go to Miraflores, and you're only likely to get yourself mated. As for Place San Martin, there you stand a fair chance at least of coming back with your life, if not your wallet and all those credit cards. Providing, of course, you hide them in your shoes.

The ears are Barranco, where you can't hear yourself think for the music blasting out of all the bars, restaurants and whatever you call those places where girls hang out who are about the same age as the chairman's niece, the one who always comes to see him on Friday afternoons when his wife is away visiting her mother.

The pouch with all the money would be Monterrico, which is so full of luxury homes you almost forget you're in the land of the Incas.

The empty belly would be either San Juan de Miraflores, which is really empty, or Villa El Salvador, which started out as your usual Peru-style slum but has now turned itself into a model for the rest of South America. When it was first established, over twenty-five years ago, the government gave every *pobladore* a patch of sand and told them to get on with it. Today, they are organised, pleasant and nothing like you'd imagine. They have running water and electricity. Various families have formed themselves into groups. Different groups have formed themselves into sectors. And each sector has its own kitchen, its own community centre, its own hospital and, even more important, its own radio and television station.

The hooves are, of course, the Monterrico Polo Club, a beautiful, lovingly cared-for green oasis at the foot of a bare, dusty hill crowned with satellite, or more likely television dishes.

And, psst. To see cockfighting, go to Mamacona or Sandia. But don't say I sent you.

The Incas might get all the publicity, but there were plenty of other tribes around at the time who were a million times better. Like the Sican, the Chimu, the Nazcas, the Vicus, the Cupisniques, the Chavins, the Huaris and the Recuays. Or the Paracas, who were famous for their sophisticated weavings. Or the Mochicas, who made advanced ceramics. Or the Tiwanaku, who made massive carvings of the Wankas, who have since spread throughout the world and now hold most of the senior positions in government, industry and commerce. They all had their traditions, they all built great cities, they all fought desperate battles, but for some reason, not, surely, because their names are more difficult to pronounce than 'Inca', they don't get the same coverage.

Take the Moches. From about AD 100 up to about AD 700 they were number one. They also, like the Egyptians, built a string of huge, impressive pyramids where they buried their lords and masters surrounded by all the usual business: gold, silver, copper and jewellery adorned with lapis lazuli, turquoise and conch shell inlays. One burial chamber also contained three young women, two men, a boy, a guardian, a watchman, two llamas, a dog and twenty pieces of pottery. Another, for a forty-five-year-old chief, had only a llama and a young woman, or should that be a young woman and a llama.

Or what about the Chachapoyas, or Cloud People, who worshipped the Condor as a god? Some say that because they had blue eyes, blond hair and fair skin, they were descendants of a mysterious band of Vikings who somehow managed to sail up the Amazon in their longboats in the tenth or eleventh century, liked what they saw and decided to stay. Whatever their origins, the Chachapoyas' empire covered an area far greater than that of the Incas. It also lasted six times longer. They built massive self-contained walled cities high in the Andes, each ruled by a council of elders. Below that was an established social structure. They built roads and intricate irrigation systems. And, the biggest thing in their favour, they didn't grow potatoes. Instead they cultivated bananas, yuccas and papaya. They also had great herds of llamas.

Then there are the Cium. Naimlap, the first of the great sealords of Lambayeque, arrived out of nowhere at the head of a fleet of rafts and proceeded to build the Temple of Chot. Then, in order to turn himself into a god, he had himself locked up inside it for the rest of his life. Which is, I think, a wonderful example to anybody who thinks they're a god. But then he tried to remove the sacred statue of Chot and the priests and military – surprise, surprise – turned against him. He was bound hand and foot and unceremoniously thrown into the sea. Which was probably a darned sight better fate than being sent to the House of Lords, reformed or not.

But the really clever guys, the ones who, as far as I'm concerned, deserve the Inca crown far more than the Incas do, are the Aymaras.

First, because they are still with us. The vice-president of next-door Bolivia is an Aymara, the first pure-blooded genuine native South American to hold such a high position on the whole continent, which by definition means the Aymara have something the Incas never had: the ability to survive. They still have their own language, their own culture and their own radio station which discusses common, everyday Aymara matters. When I tuned into it an Aymara psychologist was talking about what you do if you discover that your friendly old Aymara uncle has just raped your sweet, innocent eighteen-year-old Aymara niece. El Alto, the Aymara city way up in the clouds, is also the fastest-growing city in Latin America.

Second, they were doers. They didn't just plant potatoes and run away. They planted corn, cocoa, squash and a wide range of fruits. They didn't only breed sheep and cattle and llamas and alpacas, they made a fuss of them, too. They even

sang to them, especially when they had just been born. Years
ago we used to keep cattle and many's the time I've pulled
out a calf, scraped off all the afterbirth, stood it up on its
wobbly legs, pushed it on to its mother and got out of the
way quick before I was lashed by its tail whizzing backwards
and forwards. But sing to it? Never. But for the Aymaras it
was a couple of choruses of, 'Where have you come from
across distant trails to our farm? Thank you for arriving', in
Aymara, of course, and zap, within no time at all they had a
Smithfield champion on their hands. Or on their feet, if they
were anything like the cattle we had.

Third, they were dealers. The Incas built their enormous
road system and then wondered what to do with it. The
Aymaras, on the other hand, used every highway and byway
they could find to wheel and deal and hustle and trade. As a
result they maintained and developed their contacts with the
outside world, made money and expanded their economy.

Fourth, they were engineers and scientists and technolo-
gists without whose inventions and developments we couldn't
even buy a tin of beans today. Controlling the weather? Easy.
As soon as you see black clouds gathering in the distance, you
sound your *phututus* and bang your *bombo*. For those of you
not too familiar with the wonders of Aymara technology, you
blow like hell down your hunting horn and thump like mad
on your drum made out of tree trunks – what else? And hey
presto, the clouds have gone, disappeared. Growing the
biggest crops? No problem. Plant wherever you see a skunk
digging in the dirt like a pig. And if the *thola* bush blooms
early, plant early; if it blooms late, plant late. Catching the
biggest fish? A piece of cake. Watch for a shudder in the
totora reeds. It means one of those big 25-pound *arrobas* is
moving in for a bit of shut-eye. Be out there first thing the
following morning and – zonk – you've got him. Calculating
the number of days to your next holiday? Simple. They

divided the year up into thirteen months and each month into twenty-eight days, with New Year's Day on 21 June, the mid-summer solstice. Far more logical than our present system.

And if all that fails have a word with Pachamama, or Mother Earth. 'Please give me food to survive. Take care of the animals my children will need in the future. Give me what I need for today. The rest is sacred.'

But a word of advice. Slip her some alcohol first. Then, the following morning, some cocoa. It's the way to handle most women, and according to the Aymara, who know more about this kind of thing than I do, it also does the trick with Pachamama.

Which Aymara invention couldn't we do without today? Their system for calculating the number of days the sun shines, the size of their crop or the number of fish they've caught: their row of thick and thin lines of different lengths and colours. Because that's the concept behind our system of barcodes, which affects everybody going about their normal lives, buying newspapers, champagne and buckets of caviar, every day of the year everywhere in the world. They made one mistake: they didn't patent the idea.

But in spite of that momentary lapse, you must admit that the Aymaras have to be the good guys. The Incas were just a bunch of drunks with an easy-to-pronounce publicity-seekers' name. It's not even as if it's their real name. Inca means emperor. Calling the lot of them Incas is like calling Americans queens, if you see what I mean.

Your honour, I rest my case.

City of London

Holy Father.

Gratias for your exemplum simillime expressum, or should I say holy orders, which I've just received. At first, if I may say so, I thought it was a load of old papal bull. But the more I think about it, the more sensible it seems. After all, as they say, pax vobiscum, which, if memory serves me correctly, means retaliate first.

Now, as to the question you ask me: with Tony Blair and his ever-growing family elbowing out more and more lifelong Catholics on Sunday mornings, or whenever he sees a photographer hanging around a church door; with more and more people changing sides and with the almost imminent collapse of the Church of England, yes, of course it makes sense to start planning now which churches the bastards – sorry, Your Popeship, I got carried away – I mean which churches we graciously lent the civil authorities we should now start planning to take back under our control when the time is right. After all, absens laeres non erit, if you're not there, you don't deserve to inherit it.

It strikes me that there are two ways to do this. We could do unto them as they did unto us. In other words, shaft the hell out of them. Or we could adopt the cool, calm, intellectual approach.

I know from all your preachings and writing, and the unique position of respect in which you are held throughout the world, that you may well disagree with me, but I would recommend the cool, calm, intellectual approach. My proposal, therefore, is as follows: to divide the country into priorities, starting with the City of London.

Primus, because it not only has more churches to the square mile than anywhere else in England, it also has more churches than many of the great centres of Christianity such as Krakow, Warsaw, Poznan, Gdansk and, I dare say, East Pomerania. Originally there were no fewer than XCVII churches in the City of London. Some were tiny, like St Katherine Cree or St Vedast. Others were huge, monastic foundations, like St Bartholomew's or St Helen's. Come the Great Fire of London, which took place about the same time as you managed to finally get rid of the Swedes who had carved up over a third of the Polish population, LXII were left in various states of disrepair. An ordinary, jobbing architect – had he been one of us he would, of course, have been one of the greatest architects who ever lived – Sir Christopher Wren, then set about remodelling, redesigning and rebuilding them. This is what is known as the Wrennaissance, although, of course, the Europeans spell it differently on purpose and make out it means something else entirely. Then came the Victorians. They were so mad about not only Newman but Manning and, of course, Manley Hopkins coming over to our side that they deliberately demolished another XIX of them. Hitler damaged and razed many more – IX of them on the night of 29 December 1940. Others were destroyed by accident, as well as by terrorists, which may or may not have been preferable to being redesigned and rebuilt by Lord Rogers. Today there are XXXVIII left, not to mention X church towers.

Secundus, because the Church of England hardly seems to want them any more. Even though they contain one of the most fantastic art collections this side of Malopolska – carvings by Grinling Gibbons, stained glass by William Morris and Burne-Jones, statues by Epstein and Moore, cups and saucers by Woolworth's – most of them are locked and barred and bolted most of the time. Some of them even on Sundays. Which makes me wonder if, having replaced the Ten Commandments with Five Proposals, Three Suggestions and Two If You Feel Like Its, and taken religion out of our lives from Monday to Saturday, the Church of England isn't now turning Seventh Day Absentist and taking religion out of Sunday as well. When you want to visit some of their churches they don't even know how to get in them themselves. Call Church House, and they haven't the faintest idea what you're talking about. Call the Diocese of London, useless. Call the Council of Churches and you get an answering machine. It's almost enough to make you go happy-clappy. Almost.

Tertius, because the City of London was also, of course, home to a whole mass of Catholic martyrs, such as Thomas More, John Fisher and, of course, Roberto Calvi who, you may recall, was found hanging under Blackfriars Bridge.

Quartus, because, and I hardly know how to admit this, but in the heart of one of the major cities, one of the richest cities in the world, we're seriously under-represented. All we've got is St Mary Moorfield, a tiny, scruffy Corinthian chapel built in 1820 which doesn't look as though a thing has been done to it since. The priest who runs it is young and very eager. Some people I know criticise his sermons. They say they're too boring and predictable, although personally, at the end of them I always experience this tremendous sense of awakening.

As far as the costs of all this are concerned, I wouldn't worry. Judging by the merchandising skills and techniques you have developed on your world tours, I reckon we'd cover them in a matter of weeks. Out would go all those dust-covered old leaflets and booklets trying to explain what makes the Church of England tick, and in would come the usual exciting range of Pope T-shirts, Pope watches and the ever-popular Pope-on-a-Rope. I think we'd also try *audentes fortuna juvat*, the Pope ring – fake gold ring with plastic lips, modelled on your very own Popeship's, which kiss you back when you kiss them; the Pope fans with a picture of yourself on them and the slogan 'I am a fan of the Pope', and, of course, the bestseller of all time, the Pope's Let Us Spray Together lawn-sprinkler, which, as you know, is shaped like yourself, arms outstretched, and which spins round and round squirting water out of the hands. I tell you, we'd need a good few Popemobiles to shift all the cash.

So *laborare et orare*, as they say. Let's get down to business, or rather, the chapter and verse.

THE CITY OF LONDON

Every church I have now visited on your behalf. Some are old faithfuls, like St Mary Abchurch, St Magnus the Martyr and St Martin, Ludgate. Some are quite smart, like St Vedast. Some are depressing, like St Nicholas, Cole Abbey, which may be the home of the Free Church of Scotland but is only too pleased to welcome all denominations – £5 notes, £10 notes, £20 notes and especially £50 notes. Some are places to dodge into out of the rain, of which, thanks to St Swithun, we have plenty in this country. Some are just short-cuts, like St Andrew-by-the-Wardrobe or the most famous place of all for short-cuts in the City, Bevis Marks, the old Spanish-Portuguese synagogue for Sephardic Jews which was built in

1701 and still has all its original woodwork and candelabra, probably because they feel they've never been offered a good enough price for them.

For some reason, I don't know why, I always started my visits at 1538, which may or may not be significant, so I'm afraid I cannot tell you if anyone ever visits the churches. I can only give you a general indication of the buildings themselves.

Here, then, for better or worse, is my selection of City of London churches or, I suppose you could say, my pope pourri of City of London Churches.

The Our Lady of Krakow Category

These are the top of the range, the ones we should go for. No hesitation. No doubts. No excuses.

St Peter-upon-Cornhill
This is practically yours already.

On the church gate there is a carving of St Peter with the keys. On top of the spire is a weathervane, again shaped like the keys of St Peter. So they certainly know which way the wind is blowing. This was the first church built in London. It's also on the highest point of the City, almost the very spot where London was founded by the Romans. Four big pluses nobody can argue against.

On the other hand, it'll break your heart. Here we have virtually 2,000 years of history. The church was founded in the year 179. For 400 years, until St Augustine turned up in Canterbury, it was the Metropolitan and Chiefe Church of the Kingdome. The rector took precedence in all City processions in mediaeval times. Admittedly most of it was destroyed in the Great Fire and largely rebuilt by Wren, but it has occupied the same site for the best part of 2,000 years.

What do you see when you go inside? A mess. An unholy, Anglican mess. There are no pews, no chairs. Where other churches have discreet church notices, usually so small you can hardly see them, let alone read them, they have a big, garish sign warning you that if you spill anything on the already heavily stained carpet you must wipe it up immediately. Which makes the mind boggle. And what do we find behind the chancel screen, one of only two ever designed by Wren, to provide some extra privacy for people going to communion? A pub football slot machine.

See what I mean about the Church of England not being interested in their churches? Now if that doesn't deserve to come home, nothing does.

St Bartholomew the Great, Cloth Fair

This is for real. It's old, old, old. It was founded in 1123 by the jester to Henry I, Laffaminit Rahere, who went on to become a prebendary of St Paul's and later an Augustinian canon, as opposed to an Anglican blunderbuss, so there's no doubt about who it really belongs to. It's also built like a church. A rock-solid Norman church, or even cathedral, to last to the end of time. It survived the Great Fire. It survived a Zeppelin attack in 1916. It also survived the Second World War.

Stand outside in West Smithfield, with St Bart's Hospital on your right, and you wouldn't know it was there. Next door to Johnson's Wine Bar is the top of a Tudor-style house. Go through the archway underneath and you're in twelfth-century London. Henry I gave all this land, then known as Smoothfield because of all the PR consultancies based in the area at the time, to Rahere. On it he built the church as well as, of course, St Bart's Hospital, which many people claim was far more modern and up-to-date when it was first built than it is now.

Inside the church you suddenly realise that heaven is more than eating foie gras to the sound of trumpets. You can imagine monks shuffling in and out at all hours of the day and night. You can hear crusaders clanking in and out, paying their respects before setting out for death and glory in the Holy Lands. As for decoration, there isn't any. Well, hardly any. The whole place is practically burned black with age.

To the left of the high altar is Rahere, plastered in make-up but without even the flicker of a smile on his face. Up on the right-hand wall is the prior's spy hole, or rather window. From there he could watch everything: how much money people were giving to the shrine of Rahere and what on earth are those two doing in the back row? Behind the high altar is the Lady Chapel. During the nineteenth century this was turned into a printers' workshop. One of the workers – sorry, I mean one of the printers – was Benjamin Franklin.

For a church built by a court jester it's low on jokes, although I did spot one. Just below the prior's window is a crossbow or bolt piercing a wine barrel or tun. The name of the prior who came up with the spy window idea was Bolton. Get it? Oh well, never mind.

St Bartholomew the Less, St Bartholomew's Hospital

If you're going for St Bartholomew the Great, you've got to go for St Bartholomew the Less as well. They're part of the same package. In fact, from the odd painting I've seen of poor old St Bartholomew himself, I don't see why he should be labelled the Less. If anything he should have been called the Much More To Do Than Any Of The Others if for no other reason than he's stuck right in the middle of the hospital, where he obviously gets more business than the other St Bartholomews, who are stuck on busy high roads, on housing estates or in country villages where they are to all intents and purposes ignored from one day to the next. It's no wonder his poor little church looks old and worn and in need of a long deserved rest.

Built originally in the twelfth century, it has more than done its duty. If anything, I feel guilty popping in there, perhaps after a hearty breakfast at the Fox and Anchor round the corner, where they serve fabulous black pudding, or on the way to a big meeting behind a couple of sacks of potatoes in Smithfield itself. It's a bit like waking up a nice, kind, elderly gentleman in an egg-stained suit and thick woolly cardigan. On the other hand, I bet St Bartholomew would enjoy the black pudding at the Fox and Anchor.

St Helen Bishopsgate, Great St Helens

To some people, this is one of the biggest and most interesting of all the City churches. To others, it's the Westminster Abbey of the City because it is so overloaded with monuments and memorials.

To me, though, it's an Essex girl of a church. First because St Helen was an Essex girl, the first and last ever to be considered a saint. Born in Colchester when it was a big Roman garrison town, she was the mother of Constantine, the holy Roman emperor. Second, it's far more impressive on the outside than it is inside. From the street, tucked away behind Bishopsgate, it looks like a mediaeval municipal swimming baths. Inside, what little it has seems to be disappearing every time I go in there. First it was the choir stalls, then the communion table. Then the floor tiles. Then the total-immersion baptistery. See what I mean about a mediaeval municipal swimming baths? I'm frightened to go in there any more in case there is nothing left at all.

My favourite memorial, if it's still there, of course, is the one to Captain Martin Bond, just above the nuns' squint, the secret slots in the wall which enabled the nuns in the convent next door to watch and take part in the services held in the

church. It shows the good captain, haberdasher and commander of the City's Own, resting outside his tent at Tilbury
in 1588, the year of the Spanish Armada. With him are his
guards and a groom looking after his horse. Another three
and we would have had an apocalypse.

Temple Church, Temple

In theory, Temple Church of St Mary should be a stunner.
It's circular like the Holy Sepulchre in Jerusalem. It was
founded in 1185 by the Order of Knights Templars who protected pilgrims in the Holy Land. It's in the Temple.

But it isn't. It's like a very bad lawyer's compromise. Not
to mention a lawyer's very bad compromise.

First, it's not really circular, although somehow it looks it.
It's more oblong with a blob on the end.

Second, it's neither one thing nor another. Look this way
and it's Norman. Look the other way and it's Gothic.

Third, it's not actually a Knights Templars' church, even
though it was consecrated by Patriarch Heraclius of Jerusalem
in 1185. There are a couple of effigies of knights on the floor
in the blob at the back of the church, but that's all. There
should be banners and flags and coats of arms all over the
place. Instead it looks like a very nice, very pleasant parish
church with some fancy stained-glass windows.

As for being in the Temple, you would have thought it was
their local parish church. But it isn't. It's what's known as a
Royal Peculiar. Not that it's the only one around, although
the only other Royal Peculiar I can think of at the moment is
Westminster Abbey. You might have better luck.

St Mary Abchurch, Abchurch Lane

Now this is a beautiful little church, about as 100 per cent pure
Wren as you'll get. Any purer and you feel it would inhibit the
earth. The pale red seventeenth-century brick exterior. The

lantern-shaped tower. The lead-covered obelisk spire. Tucked away in a small, cobbled yard, on a sunny day, it's almost Castel Gandolfo. Some people say Abchurch has something to do with the church of the Abbas, some primitive, heathen, musical Nordic race, but I doubt it. The Abbas that I have heard are not musical.

Inside, almost floating over everything, is a fabulous dome. In the centre, Jehovah is spelled out in Hebrew. All around the edge are decorations symbolising traditional Christian virtues such as Charity so long as it doesn't cost me anything, Neighbourliness so long as they don't come from anywhere east of Tunbridge Wells, and what on earth happened to Prudence? I must give her a call some time. The oval windows, some say, were painted by Britain's own Michelangelo, Sir James Thornhill, who also painted the dome of St Paul's. Others maintain that they were painted by a local parishioner, William Snow, for the princely sum of £170 which, in today's terms, would take a good few whist drives and summer fêtes to raise. Either way, anybody who knows anything about domes will tell you that it shouldn't be there. Apparently because of its size – it is over 40 feet across – there should be flying buttresses to support it, but it just rests on four plain brick walls. Which is a tribute either to Wren, yet again, or to the power of prayer. I know which I think it is.

As if that's not too much for a single church, there's the woodwork. This is about as 100 per cent pure Grinling Gibbons as you'll get. There's hardly a splinter out of place. The huge, limewood panels behind the altar, topped by four gilded urns, are the largest he designed and made for any church in the City. What's more, all his receipts are still in the parish records. But ask them how much they took last Sunday and they have no idea. The fact there isn't a splinter out of place is even more remarkable, bearing in mind that the whole thing was blown to bits during the last war and took over five years to put together again. The pulpit, by William Grey, is decorated with fruit and flowers which, I'm told, can open and close a number of times during the course of an average Sunday sermon. The door cases, the font cover and rails, the royal arms are all by William Emmett. I also like the memorial to the gloriously named Sir Patience Ward, lord mayor of London in 1680, although what all those little boys have to do with the lord mayor I have no idea.

The trouble is, because it's such a pretty little church, it's always full of people. Organ recitals, receptions, readings, tea parties . . . almost every time I've been there are crowds of people milling around at the back with cups of tea and plates of cake for all the world as if they were filling in time before the Last Judgement. But you could soon change that. Hand it over to the Poor Clares. They'll soon drive everybody out.

There's only one drawback. There are now pews on only three sides of the church. On the south side there's nothing. In the old days, the pews on this side used to have dog kennels built in underneath them, so that people could bring their pets with them to church. Otherwise, sermons being what they were, they wouldn't be fed for two or three days. Should this get out if – sorry, I mean when – we take over, we are in danger of being inundated with a lot of silly demands from the animals-are-better-than-people brigade to have them restored. There is only one thing worse than the animals-are-better-than-us mob, and that's their dogs. Hounds of heaven they are not.

St Vedast, Foster Lane

There is no real reason for including St Vedast in the priority hit list except that I like it. Sorry. From the outside it's not much to look at – well, apart from the steeple, which is supposed to be the most subtle and the most baroque of all Wren's steeples –

but to see it properly you've got to be on top of a London bus heading down Cheapside, turning left into Cannon Street at six o'clock in the morning in the middle of June. Inside, though, it's a tiny jewel of a thing, about the size of your average cathedral choir stalls. It's light. It's clean-cut. The floor is black and white. The ceiling is white with silver and gold. It's straightforward. It's to the point. There aren't even the urns and vases you usually see scattered around any building Wren has had anything to do with. What is there seems to have come from everywhere else. The grand, seventeenth-century carved organ case is from St Bartholomew-by-Exchange. The carved font and font cover is from St Anne and St Agnes. The fancy pulpit is from All Hallows. The altar panels and communion rail are from St Christopher-le-Stocks-and-Shares, the stockbrokers' church. The communion table and royal arms are from St Matthew, Friday Street.

You could almost hand it straight over to the Maronites. It's almost the right size for them. In fact, it could probably take them all with room to spare. They, too, seem to take bits and pieces from everywhere – a bit of Arabic here, a bit of Latin there, a bit of Aramaic for good measure – so I'm sure they'd both be very happy.

OK, those are the ones we should go for first. No negotiation. No haggling. No due consideration. Straight in. Grab them by the throat. In, of course, a suitably humble manner.

Now the next batch, which I've named after the second-most important place of pilgrimage in Poland.

The Our Lady of Czestochowa Category

These are the ones we go for after a little bit of haggling, just to prove we haven't forgotten the bit about the meek inheriting whatever it was we're more than entitled to have in any case.

St Martin-within-Ludgate, Ludgate Hill

I'm sorry, I don't know why, but it was years before I made it to St Martin-within-Ludgate, which, seeing as it is dedicated to St Martin of Tours, should, if nothing else, make it the City church for the travel industry. It was probably because it's halfway up Ludgate Hill. If I was in a mad rush, it was so easy to pass it by. If I had the odd moment to spare it always lost out to its much bigger brother at the top of the hill. When I did finally visit it, it was more than worth it. In fact, if anything, I felt guilty for having overlooked it for so long.

It's a wonderful church. In many ways, once inside, you wouldn't think you were even in England, let alone the boring old City of London. It's old. Some say it was founded in 677, which is about the last time the travel industry was run by saints. It's dark. Perhaps because of the barrel-vaulted shape of the ceiling, perhaps because they botched the lighting. Either way, about the only source of light is the seventeenth-century chandelier from St Vincent in the Caribbean, which I've never really thought of as a great centre for chandelier-making. For making the stuff that makes you want to swing from them, maybe, but not the chandeliers themselves. It's shaped like a Greek cross, rather a stubby cross, but a cross all the same. The pillars are a touch Corinthian, too, and there's also a Greek inscription on the font at the back of the church. For generations there have been arguments over why it is there and what it means. But it's obvious. Being where it is, it is nothing more than a tribute to the skills of the City, which can make even the simplest statement sound totally Greek to any sensible person. Some people, most of them admittedly wholly unaware of the world around them, in other words stockbrokers, translate it as 'Wash my sins not just my face.' Don't you believe it. It actually means 'If this damn prospectus doesn't raise the £100 million I'm looking for I'm not only going to drown myself but I'm taking you lot with me.' I should know. What little youth I had I spent marching across Persia with Xenophon and his merry bunch of killers.

Wrenovated by the great C.W. more or less as a sideline while he was building St Paul's, today St Martin's remains much as it was then. There's even a tiny two-door lobby at the entrance. They say it's to block out the noise of any ox cart that may be passing, although I reckon it's to stop the noise made by the scratchy old soprano who always seems to be there practising at the piano from ever reaching the outside. Otherwise there'd be panic the length and breadth of the City.

Viewed from halfway down Fleet Street, the spire is supposed to cut the dome of St Paul's exactly in half. Yet no matter how many times I tried, I've never managed to see it. Probably because I'm either rushing to lunch or, I suppose, staggering back afterwards. All the same, the guys at St Martin's need shaking up. They boast that the church will prosper and 'will surely outlive us all into the second millennium AD'.

Excuse me, I may be wrong, but I thought we'd already finished with the second millennium and were now into the third.

St Dunstan-in-the-West, Fleet Street

St Dunstan's is a bit like St Martin's. For years I lurched backwards and forwards past it without ever going in. When I did, it was a revelation. For this is where East meets West, or maybe West meets East.

From the outside it looks as though it is going to be another one of your run-of-the-mill churches. A dull, flat-looking brick façade. A square, stone-faced tower. Except that, to the right there is a fancy-looking clock which has Gog and Magog hammering away every fifteen minutes. Apparently, it was the first public clock in London to have a minute hand. Up until then everybody was on time.

Inside, however, it's a stunner. You don't know where you are or where to look. First, as befits John Donne, who kept on about the round earth's imagined corners and was rector here from 1624 to 1631, it is circular, with chapels all the way round the walls. The pews in the centre form a circle as well. Although, of course, they have more than four corners between them. Next, right between the eyes – wham – you are struck by icons all over the place. And not your imitation, namby-pamby icons, either. They're the real thing. Then, of course, you see Orthodox crosses. Because for – take a deep breath – St Dunstan's is not only High Anglican, it is also home to the Romanian Orthodox Church in London. Although, to add my two leis' worth, I would say it's more Orthodox than High Anglican.

In one of the side chapels about halfway round, squeezed between the icons, which may or may not be significant, you'll find something truly astonishing: a monument to Hobson Judkin Esq., the Honest Solicitor. As far as I'm aware this is the only monument ever displayed anywhere in the known universe to an honest solicitor. Which must mean something. Especially as the Law Society is round the corner in Chancery Lane.

I am putting St Dunstan's in the Our Lady of Czestochowa category rather than in the Our Lady of Krakow category because I thought, being half Orthodox and half Anglican, you might feel you already had it in your cassock pocket. The statue over the vestry porch, by the way, is of Elizabeth I. It's supposed to be the oldest public statue of an English monarch. I thought you might also like to add it to your other scalps.

St Olave, Hart Street

St Olave's, I always think, is a bit of a cross between St Martin's and St Dunstan's. It's nice and old like St Martin's and it has got all the foreign connections of St Dunstan's. Except that in this case they're Scandinavian rather than Eastern European. It was also Samuel Pepys' parish church when he was living nearby in Seething Lane with his wife, Elizabeth. Or should that be when he was living in a nearby lane with his seething wife Elizabeth?

What I don't understand is how come St Olave is St Olave. As far as I can gather from studying the old Khronicles, Olave, or rather Olaf, *sigurd syr* at an early age. He *ringarike* when he was twelve with the Vikings. After a great deal of *harald groenske* he *tryggveson* to *aasta* and ended up coming to the aid of King Ethelred, who was not at all ready to fight the Danes. On the north of the Thames, close to the site of the Tower of London, was our unready Ethelred. On the south were the Danes. Between them was a single bridge. On to the bridge came the Danes, all fired up to rush Ethelred, overwhelm his troops and storm across our green and pleasant land, raping and pillaging as they went. Suddenly, below the bridge, appeared good King Olave, or rather Olaf, and his merry men. They tied cables round the supports and then turned and rowed like mad in the opposite direction to bring down the bridge, the Danes and any hopes they had of raping and pillaging their way up the A1. Like something out of a Seamus Heaney translation, he remained here for three years, until the death of King Ethelred, who you can bet wasn't ready for that, either. Then, when King Canute took over, he turned with the tide and fled back to Norway where, once he had regaled his fellow countrymen with stories of England and the English way of doing things, they all promptly converted to Christianity. For this he was made a saint.

As for the church, which escaped the Great Fire, it could almost be the same as it was in the days of St Olave with a touch – if that's the right word – of Samuel Pepys about it. By all accounts, Pepys found it very comfortable. So comfortable

that he regularly fell asleep during the sermons. So comfortable was it, in fact, and so boring the sermons, that he is still
sleeping there. He is buried beneath the high altar, along
with his wife. So too, incidentally, is Mary Ramsay, who is said
to have brought the Great Plague to London.

If you visit St Olave's don't go in by the side door in Hart
Street. Enter through the tiny churchyard in Seething Lane.
There, above the gateway, is an arch decorated with skulls and
crossbones. Hence Dickens' description of the church as St
Ghastly Grim, though I always thought he was referring to his
mother-in-law.

Inside it's smaller than you'd imagine, but somehow
homely. Everything seems to be on top of everything else.
There's a wonderful lifelike monument to Mrs Pepys which,
even today, still has her glaring at the Navy Office pew in the
South Gallery where, when he wasn't fast asleep, our Sam
used to do what we all do: complain about the number of collections.

St Magnus the Martyr, Lower Thames Street

Goodness me. St Magnus has got it all. I almost feel as
though I should wear stained-glass spectacles whenever I go
there.

One of the oldest churches in the City, it was originally
built around 1066 and pulled down and enlarged to its present size around 1235. So important was it, even in those
days, that in 1250 Pope Innocent IV decreed that it should be
the general meeting place for all the local clergy. Shortly afterwards the popes became the church's very own patrons and
directly appointed no fewer than five rectors to the parish.

Today it's the short-cut to London Bridge. Come along
Lower Thames Street . . . I'll say that again because of the
noise of the traffic. COME ALONG LOWER THAMES
STREET, and St Magnus is on your left. Just past it are the

stairs up to London Bridge. Then it's over the bridge, into the station and off and away to wherever. Or you could just go straight home. Whenever I get the chance, I pop in there on the way. I don't know why, but something inside me makes me identify with martyrs.

I like the way the tower is right over the top of the entrance. I'm no expert, but I can't recall any other church quite like it. Normally a tower is part of the church. Occasionally it is stuck out on its own. In this case, though, it's slap-bang over the space outside the entrance like a giant, fancy umbrella. And fancy it is, too, with its lanterns and domes and little spires and a clock. Apparently, this was Wren's way of welcoming people to London. Nowadays, of course, all we get are a posse of City of London policemen stopping any scruffy-looking car or truck they feel like stopping in order to cause a traffic jam a mile long.

Inside, St Magnus takes your breath away. It's rich. It's lush. It's beautifully decorated. It's also very bright. The altar is magnificent: the wood panelling fills practically the whole of the end wall and Moses and his PR man, Aaron, are stationed on either side. At the top is an almost life-sized crucifixion. All very baroque. In front of the altar are some fancy Sussex wrought-iron rails. Apparently T.S. Eliot used to pop in here from time to time and raved about the 'inexplicable splendour' of the pillars. Who am I to disagree?

It's also terribly High Church. So High Church, in fact, that I reckon on bingo nights the vicar calls out the numbers in Latin so that the ordinary, common old Protestants can't win. Like St Dunstan's I didn't put it on the Our Lady of Krakow list because I thought that, seeing as it was once being sponsored by the popes, you might as good as have this one in your pocket as well. Besides, it's difficult to tell whether it's one of ours already or not.

All Hallows-by-the-Tower, Byward Street

This one is more or less in the bag already, too. It has a high altar; a Lady Chapel, which remains much the same as it was when it was built in 1489; a Chapel of St Francis of Assisi and a Chapel of St Clare. It's also got some beautiful silver gilt communion plate, including a fantastic sixteenth-century Spanish silver crucifix.

Founded in 675 by the Abbey of Barking, All Hallows is where the bodies of Thomas More and John Fisher were brought after they had been beheaded down the road in the Tower of London. Which is another reason for grabbing it, sorry, I mean reconsidering its reallocation in the light of the prevailing circumstances.

Like St Magnus, it's in good shape. I don't manage to get there very often – it's at the wrong end of the City from all the banks and brokers I'm forced to deal with – but with its slight touch of Gothic, nave, aisles and tunnel-vaulted roof, whenever I do, I feel at home. Also there whenever I pop in, whether by accident or design, is the oldest man I've ever seen in my life. He's got a long white beard almost down to his waist and a rough old coat tied round the middle with a bit of old string.

There are some drawbacks to All Hallows, however. The present vicar seems to have lost his head a bit. Or if he hasn't, he should. There are exhibitions all over the place. The south aisle is effectively used as a parish hall with, God help us, dinners and socials and even cabarets being held there. But we can soon sort that out.

St James Garlickhythe, Garlick Hill

I would also have included St James Garlickhythe in the Our Lady of Krakow category, but I thought it might create a big stink. First, because it's the parish church of garlic-eaters. Garlick, garlic; hythe, you have nothing to hide. Second, the organ is dripping with oxblood. Third, there's been a dead body hidden away in a cupboard in the vestry for over 400 years. They say it's now a mummy, which, if that's true, is even more remarkable. But what they don't tell you is how it became a mummy, and in a church, as well, or, more importantly, how it got there in the first place. I have my own theories. But I don't believe any vicar of such a stunning church would ever terrify young men so much that they would resort to hiding in a cupboard to avoid him. Not even the Irish Christian Brothers are as bad as that.

If that's not mysterious enough, listen to this. The church survives for nearly 300 years, through two world wars and Mrs Thatcher, and then what happens? Suddenly, for no reason at all, a giant crane smashes down on top of it, crashing through the side wall, destroying the rose window, shattering the chandelier into smithereens and reducing the pews to matchsticks. Now what do you reckon? Was the crane driver a long-lost relative of the poor man in the cupboard? I know what I think.

That apart, it's still one of my favourites, probably because in many ways it looks more like a swish, upmarket college library than a church. The floor is black and white marble. The carpets are red. The wood is all dark and sombre. But it's all surprisingly light and cheerful. The only problem is the ceiling. It's all soft, billowy, chocolate-box clouds. So open a book, look up and in three seconds you're doing a Sam Pepys. Still, it would make a perfect library for all those books you've been banning all these years. People would have access to them, but because of the atmosphere they'd be fast asleep before they read anything even slightly out of line.

St Andrew, Holborn Viaduct

St Andrew's, the biggest of all Wren's City churches, I used to know fairly well. It's almost opposite where the old *Mirror* building used to be. Round the corner was a pub everyone

called the Stab in the Back because that's where *Mirror* journalists used to gather to celebrate each other's downfall,
although from what I could gather they didn't do too badly.
One guy I knew was fired by the *Mirror* but so hopeless was
their administration before, during and after Robert
Maxwell's reign that for years he continued to draw his
expenses, which, naturally, were far, far higher than his salary
had been. St Andrew's was a good place to go to either prepare for or recover from a session in the Stab. Especially as he
is the patron saint of Scotland.

But there is nothing mean about the church. It's big. Some
say it's more like a basilica or a cathedral than a church. It's
also in superb condition. But it's best known for being the
organists' church. Part of the organ case was given by Handel
to Bloomsbury Foundling Hospital for Abandoned Children,
and then given to, or more likely lifted for, St Andrew's,
which kills all those jokes about Handel's organ. Although
what puzzles me is why would Handel give part of an organ
case to a children's hospital in the first place.

'Mr Handel. We're collecting for this Bloomsbury thing. I
wonder whether you would like to give something to help the
children?'

'Go away. Can't you see I'm writing "The Hallelujah
Chorus"?'

'What, for the greater glory of God?'

'No. Because my wife has just left me.'

'Well, I was wondering whether you would . . .'

'Certainly. Here, take part of my organ case.'

It doesn't make sense, does it? Well, it doesn't to me.

There's also a fascinating stone slab on the outside north
wall. Lots of little figures pushing back their tombs and climbing out of their graves. Some say it's of the Last Judgement.
Don't believe a word of it. It's old *Mirror* journalists still
coming back from the dead to claim their expenses.

St Botolph Bishopsgate, Bishopsgate

In the old days it used to be the downstairs bar at the Great Eastern Hotel. Now, if I've got time to kill waiting for a train out of Liverpool Street Station, it's St Botolph's. Not because I'm getting particularly old and decrepit, although of course I am, but because the Great Eastern has gone so far downhill that I'd rather go anywhere than there.

I'm sure at one time St Botolph's must have been a nice little church. It had what it called a zoo out the back, although today it would probably be called a Children's Chapel or some such thing. It even had its own tennis court.

Since then, however, it has been revamped so many times that it has lost its soul. It's still being restored even now, having been affected by the big IRA bomb that virtually destroyed the old NatWest Tower. It wasn't as badly hit as that, but the cost of the work is still around the £1 million mark.

Inside it's all white and gold and brown and blue. Corinthian columns run the length of the church. There is a glass dome over the nave. Remind me never to visit it during a red alert. There is also so much Victoriana – screens and paintings and leadwork and carving – that any day now I'm expecting to bump into William Morris in there.

In the old days this was one of the richest churches in the City. Who knows, with a bit of the right management, it could be again. Hence the reason for putting it on the Our Lady of Czestochowa list. A suggestion, though. Let them raise the £1 million before we move in.

All Hallows, London Wall

I always think this is a funny little church. It survived the Great Fire, but it was rebuilt almost 100 years later by George Dance the Younger, who was only twenty-four at the time, at a cost of £3,000. It was badly bombed during the war and rebuilt again in the 1960s. To look at it you wonder how it is still there. It could so easily have been knocked down to make way for the widening of London Wall, for an office block or even for a footpath.

Years ago I got involved in some church restoration programme and had to go there from time to time. As a result I was able to shuffle around behind the scenes. It was pure Trollope, if there is such a thing.

The church itself is simple, restrained, spare, chaste, although I suppose that's the case with all churches. Well, real churches, anyway. The barrel-vaulted white and gold ceiling somehow seems to sparkle. Maybe it's because it is lit on either side by big, semi-circular windows. The only thing that seems out of place is the large oil painting behind the altar. But as that is the work of the architect's brother . . .

OK. We've dealt with the ones we want and the ones we go for after a little bit of haggling. Now the next group.

The Our Lady of Gdansk Category

These are the churches we want, but if they argue about it, we can let them keep them.

St Margaret, Lothbury

In many ways I like St Margaret's. The brass candelabra, the rich, dark woodwork, the white and gold walls. But it's a bit of a car-boot sale of a church. Like St Vedast, everything it's got seems to have come from somewhere else. The communion rail is from St Olave, Jewry. Half the church plate is from St Stephen, Coleman Street. The altar screens are from St Christopher-le-Stocks-and-Shares, named after the patron saint of stockbrokers, which was demolished in 1781 to pay for an IPO that went wrong. You know what IPO stands for? Outside the City people think it is Initial Public Offering.

Insiders, however, know that it means It's Probably Overpriced.

Every time I nip into St Margaret's to get out of the rain it looks more like a boardroom presentation than a church. There are screens in front of the altar. There are loudspeakers all over the place. There is a piano tinkling away in the background.

Disgraceful.

St Edmund King and Martyr, Lombard Street

This is an early morning in the middle of winter type of church. The faithful handful in the dark, wooden pews. A few flickering candles in the distance. Shadows on the walls. Great lumps of plaster everywhere. It's like the churches you find in the back streets of Spain and Italy.

But whenever I've visited it any time between May and October it has always seemed to be full of WI-type women lounging back in the pews, eating sandwiches and sipping away at flasks of weak tea.

All the same, I reckon it's worth checking out. It has a nice, distinctive exterior, a clock with a crown on top, Victorian stained-glass windows and a monument to Charles Melville Hays, who died on the *Titanic* rather than meet Leonardo Di Caprio.

St Anne and St Agnes, Gresham Street

Somebody should do something about St Anne and St Agnes, because it's one of the craziest, mixed-up churches I think I've ever seen.

First, it doesn't know whether it is St Anne or St Agnes, or both. And if it's both, why bracket St Anne with St Agnes? St Anne was the mother of Our Lady, the grandmother of Christ. St Agnes was a thirteen-year-old girl martyred in Rome around AD 300. What on earth could they possibly have in common?

To make matters worse, and don't ask me why, St Anne is the patron saint of the Bridget Joneses of this world. On St Anne's Day unmarried women desperate for a husband are advised to search for the biggest pea pod they can find. If it contains nine peas they are supposed to put it on the mat by the front door with a note saying, 'Come in. You've only got to mind your peas, not your queues.' The first sucker, sorry I mean guy, through the door becomes the woman's poor, unfortunate husband.

Like St Martin Ludgate and St Mary-at-Hill, which we'll come to later, it's built in the shape of a Greek cross. It looks Greek. It feels Greek. But it's Lutheran. And it's not just Lutheran Lutheran, it's Estonian Lutheran, Latvian Lutheran, Ethiopian Lutheran and even Swahili Lutheran.

All the same, it's the most unLutheran Lutheran unGreek Greek Bridget Jones of a church I've seen. It's also the most unWren Wren church you could imagine. It is full of stained-glass windows. The plasterwork is much too simple. The font is a copy. The pulpit has lost its sounding board. The altar screen has been rearranged. Instead of being behind the altar, the paintings of Moses and Aaron are now hanging on the east wall. The altar rails are modern and nothing like the originals. The floor is parquet. Yet it maintains it is authentic Wren. Looks more like twentieth-century Wren to me.

But the thing that terrified me most was on the bookstall at the back. The only book of its kind I've ever seen. On any bookstall. In any church. Anywhere in the world. *Every Woman's Guide to Cystitis.*

Somebody's got to do something about it before it's too late. How about a gang of Polish miners to flatten the place?

St Botolph, Aldgate

St Botolph's is what it is. A great, big, dark, forbidding lump of a church. Over 1,000 years of history behind it.

Redesigned in the middle of the eighteenth century by George Dance the Elder, who also designed the Mansion House, the official home of the lord mayor of London. Redesigned again towards the end of the nineteenth century by J.F. Bentley, the architect of Westminster Cathedral where, you will recall, you stopped the show on your visit when, halfway down the nave, you paused during the official entry procession, bent down, picked up a holy picture one of the women in the congregation had dropped on the floor and gave it back to her.

On the east wall there is a copy of Rubens' *Descent from the Cross*. There is lots of eighteenth-century ironwork, including the elegant altar rails. Carvings on the organ case are by Grinling Gibbons. It's got a fine peal of eight bells and, they say, the oldest church organ in London, if not in the country.

The trouble is, it's desperate to be flip and up to date. The panels behind the high altar are dye and wax batiks which, on a good biretta day, are striking and original, but on a bad biretta day look like a high-school painting competition. If that doesn't put you off, there are always strange-looking paintings around the walls which look exactly like a high-school painting competition. There are also lots of happy-clappy things going on all the time.

If that's all there was to it, I'd say ditch them. But downstairs in the crypt they look after tramps and down-and-outs and all kinds of social failures, such as accountants and merchant bankers. Knowing how much my family care for me, I shall probably end up there one day. So for that reason if for no other, it would be nice if it were one of ours. But I'm not racing down the street begging anyone for it.

St Katherine Cree, Leadenhall Street

Grabbing this back should cause some fireworks. Oops, done it again, sorry. I should have said, reaffirming the fundamental blah-blah of the centuries-old commitment should cause some fireworks. Not that I think St Katherine would mind. After all, she had to put up with far worse things.

Properly restored, decorated and generally tidied up, this could be up there with St Mary Abchurch and St Vedast. It's a nice little church, the last to be built in the City in the Gothic style and, the experts will tell you, the most important built in the City between Inigo Jones and Christopher Wren. Corinthian columns divide the nave from the two aisles. Above them are elaborately decorated arches. There is a solid Jacobean pulpit and lots of plaques and memorials. Purcell and Handel used to play the organ here. So did Wesley, although my guess is he more thrashed it than played it. Hans Holbein was a parishioner. It also has a stunning, sparkling stained-glass window, of St Katherine, obviously.

But someone needs to light the blue touchpaper because at the moment it looks, and worse, feels, more like a church hall than a church. It's a mess. It's scruffy, it's dirty, and the row of ramshackle offices they've built on either side of the two aisles and the outside wall is unbelievable. And whenever I go in there, nobody ever seems to be doing anything. They're clearly all holy unemployed.

The laugh is that it's the headquarters of the City Churches Development Group, which is supposed to make churches more attractive and welcoming to visitors. It must have poor St Katherine spinning in her grave.

OK. We've done the ones we want, no argument, and the ones we want after perhaps a little argument. Now for the ones we want, but hell, I mean heaven, if they want to keep them, they can keep them, and the ones we definitely don't want, so if we get them we'll hand them straight over to somebody else. These I've divided into two: the Marie Curie list and the Gomulka list.

The Marie Curie list

Like Marie Curie, who the French claim was French, whereas all honest people know she was Polish – she was born at Ul. Freta No 16, Warsaw – these are churches we're not going to fight over. If anybody else says they belong to them, it's OK by us.

St Mary-at-Hill, Lovat Lane

If St James Garlickhythe is like a library, St Mary-at-Hill is like one of those old-fashioned banking halls you stumble across in some tiny high street in the middle of Scotland. Huge. Metal chairs all over the place, and not a banker anywhere in sight.

It's also practically impossible to find. I've known people tramp up and down Lovat Lane for hours on end trying to find the entrance. Then, when they finally stumble across it, like all banks it's closed.

It is said that at one time St Mary-at-Hill had one of the most gorgeous interiors in the City. Presumably some UK banking director then came along, decided it would cause too much fuss and bother to close it as it stood and instead removed all the fittings so that customers would stay away and he could then close it at a later date without anyone saying a word.

St Andrew Undershaft, St Mary Axe

Poor St Andrew. He's certainly been undershafted, if not well and truly shafted. In the architectural sense of the word, of course.

In theory this could be a pleasant little church. It is pre-Fire of London, which is in itself very unusual. The woodwork is late seventeenth century. Since then the Victorians have had a go at it. So also have the old London

County Council, judging by the wooden roof of the nave. But it's still got a nice feel to it. John Stow, the historian who wrote the sixteenth-century *Survey of London*, is tucked away, complete with real quill pen in his hand, in the top left-hand corner. There is also a brass plaque to Hans Holbein the Younger, court painter to Henry VIII, who produced the famous Thomas More portrait which hangs in the royal library in Windsor Castle. He lived in the parish before dying of the plague in 1543.

But shock, horror, today it's a mere church hall to St Helen's Bishopsgate round the corner. Instead of the tiled floor, there's a tatty red carpet. Instead of gloriously carved wooden pews, there are battered metal chairs and crude wooden partitions. Distracting the eye from the seventeenth-century stained-glass royal portraits and the rich roof bosses of Henry VIII's Tudor rose and Catherine of Aragon's pomegranates are dog-eared notes about meetings that nobody is ever going to attend. As for poor John Stow, I practically had to clamber over massive stainless steel ovens, keep-warm compartments and baskets of fruit to get to him. I'm surprised he hasn't broken his quill pen into tiny pieces, thrown them all over the floor and stormed off to St Mary Abchurch. I would if I were him.

St Michael, Cornhill

Another church crying out to be saved. The trouble is, it's got too much competition. The Jamaica Inn is just down one side. The George and Vulture is round the corner. Both famous if not legendary City watering holes, a bit like the Café Krokodyl or the gloriously named Il Fukiera in the Stare Miasto in Warsaw. Then there's Bengal Court. Don't you remember Bengal Court? It was once a famous coaching inn and features in *Pickwick Papers*.

Another Wren original, St Michael's has been altered and

rebuilt so many times that it now just looks as if they decided enough was enough and threw in the towel, which, in many ways, is a shame.

From the outside it is quite imposing. It has a grand Gothic porch and a Gothic tower with tall pepperpot spiked pinnacles. To me it has a touch of the Scottish about it. Maybe it's the Portland stone.

Inside it looks as if it's being run by a Scottish parish council. It needs not only a good clean but a good lick of paint as well. The paint is peeling off the walls. There are also great chunks of plaster all over the place. Some people call it Victorian Gothic. That's being charitable. It's more workhouse Victorian. For a real Victorian church, go and have a look at All Saints, Margaret Street, which isn't in the City, I know, but it's fabulous. St Michael, Cornhill, no, thank you.

St Sepulchre-without-Newgate, Holborn Viaduct

You're right, there is no St Sepulchre. Well, you should know. After all, you've created more saints than all your predecessors put together. This, the biggest parish church in the City, was originally dedicated to St Edmund the Martyr King of East Anglia, because, as I think one of your forerunners put it when he raised him up, he deserved it for having to live in East Anglia and put up with Delia Smith going on about boiling an egg and how great Norwich City Football Club is. But of course, St Edmund the Martyr King of East Anglia was too complicated for the Fenners. Instead they decided to call it St Edmund and the Holy Sepulchre, after the Holy Sepulchre in Jerusalem, although how that came into the equation I have no idea. Probably a side-effect of all those eggs.

After a while – some say it took as long as two or three minutes – even this became too complicated for them so they abbreviated it, against all the rules and regulations, not to mention historical and church accuracy, to St Sepulchre, which, let's face it, is like calling St Paul's St Cathedral, St Peter's Basilica St Basilica or even, I suppose, St Anselm's Parish Church St Parish Church. But there was no changing their minds. I often used to think they needn't have bothered because for a long time the church was always closed. Probably to keep out St Delia and her eggs. But now it's fully open and back in business. For a few hours a week.

Inside, it's not particularly stunning, although it is noteworthy for being the musicians' church. Here, in the St Stephen Harding's chapel, is where Henry Wood learned to play the organ and was appointed assistant organist at fourteen. His ashes lie under the window which shows him as a young boy seated at his organ, and also as the great Sir Henry conducting a Promenade Concert at the Queen's Hall. In other parts of the church you can find Dame Nellie Melba, the composer John Ireland and Walter Carroll, who invented all those special Christmas hymns. All the blue carpets, various kneelers and one of the altar frontals were donated in memory of St Malcolm Sargent. The cushion on the organ seat made a marked impression on Handel, Mendelssohn and the two Wesleys, father and son, or to be precise, Handel, Mendelssohn and the two Wesleys, father and son, made a marked impression on the cushion on the organ seat.

Even if music is not your scene and you prefer Walt Disney, this is the church for you, too. Remember Princess Pocahontas? She saved the life of and then married Captain John Smith, who went on to become president of the Council of Virginia, admiral of New England and an all-round good bloke. He died in 1631 in a house across the street and is buried in the church.

But that's not the reason I'm suggesting we reconsider its possible reallocation. Over the road is the Old Bailey which, of course, is built on the site of the old Newgate Prison. For almost 300 years St Sepulchre's looked after the prisoners, especially the condemned prisoners. The great tenor bell was also rung on the morning of executions to ensure that they had the best possible send-off.

All the same, we could take it over and rename it St Pocahontas. It's no more absurd than calling it St Sepulchre's. It would also bring in more people. Especially with the film soundtrack playing in the background. Conducted by Sir Henry, with Handel on the organ and Dame Nellie whipping them up in the aisles. It would also drown out St Delia.

Shall I check it out?

In this Marie Curie section I've also included a number of key churches which play a vital role in the modern life of the City and are appreciated every day by thousands of people, and which, if they were to close, would cause considerable upset and hardship to many lives. These are the churches that provide valuable short-cuts to and from work or a shelter in bad weather. First the short-cuts.

St Andrew-by-the-Wardrobe, Queen Victoria Street

To praise or not to praise. St Andrew-by-the-Wardrobe, Wren's last City church, was Shakespeare's local whenever he was in town. There's a memorial to him tucked away in the west gallery. But for all that, I always think it's somewhat plain, straightforward and perhaps a little uninspiring. Not that I hold anything against it; on the contrary, it's one of my favourites. It's a quick short-cut if you're racing up from Blackfriars Station towards St Paul's.

It was also useful in the days when John Addey, the old-time PR wheeler-dealer, was in his prime just around the corner in Wardrobe Chambers. He was the original spin-doctor. His powers of influence were such that he could wine and dine at all the top tables and then stagger off to *Private*

Eye lunches, spill the beans and, more importantly, get away with it. It was widely held that this was because of the gallons of champagne that flowed around him wherever he went. In fact so many people used to spend so much time after long sessions with him in his office recovering in St Andrew's-by-the-Wardrobe that for a time there was a move to have it renamed St Andrew's-by-the-Drinks-Cabinet. Actually, the reason why Addey was so successful as a PR man was that he was born on 15 August, the Feast of the Assumption.

Where does the Wardrobe come in? The church is just down the road from the Royal College of Arms. This is where they used to store all the ceremonial robes in the old days.

St Mary Aldermary, Queen Victoria Street

This church is sometimes called the 'Older Mary', and you can see why. There is a certain heaviness about the place. It's a bit dull and a bit stolid. The organ, on the left of the sanctuary, is a solid block of an instrument, although the pipes are so fussily decorated that the first time I saw them, for a moment I thought they were a row of fancy gilt books. The benches are all very heavy. The panelling reinforces the built-in, you're-totally-surrounded effect. It is supposed to have been destroyed in the Great Fire and rebuilt later by Wren, but to me – and I know nothing – it doesn't look Wren. It's a bit Gothic, and heavily mediaeval. All those wooden screens and decorations.

It's a good short-cut if you're racing from Mansion House to Cheapside.

Now the port-in-a-storm churches.

St Mary-le-Bow, Cheapside

You've forgotten your Auntie Ella. Your weasel and stoat is soaking. The Andy Cain is running down your bushel and peck. You're Dr Crippen. It's taters. The battle cruisers are not yet open. You're boracic. There's only one thing to do. Forget your South Sea Bubbles, pull up your almond rocks and go take a butcher's at St Mary-le-Bow.

OK, from the outside it's looks all belt and braces. But inside – don't worry, you don't need a bat and wicket to get through the Rory O'More – it's quite partridge and pheasant. Lots of Harry Randalls and april showers. There's also a good mix. Bubble and squeaks and Barnaby Rudges in their fancy whistles and flutes. Garden gates. Ginger beers. Even, you can bet your life, the odd Jerry O'Gorman. You won't be a Glasgow Ranger for long.

St Mary's, would you Adam and Eve it, is the David Hockney, or Cockney church, which is why they're big on twin pulpit conversations: in one they speak English, in the other David Hockney. At first I couldn't make up my mind about twin pulpit discussions or sermons, but St Mary's converted me. Whenever I hear them, I always feel twice as pleased when they're over.

Many people rave about St Mary's. Not me. Apart from the steeple and its dragon weathervane, there doesn't seem to be much to it, although I must admit I've never been in the crypt. I'm told it's better than the church. I'll let you know if I'm ever allowed down the apples and pears.

Incidentally, shouldn't it be St Mary-la-Belle?

St Clement, Eastcheap

From Bow Bells to the nursery-rhyme church, although you'd never believe this was it. First because you hardly notice it. Somehow it just seems to merge into the other walls and buildings at the junction of Clement Lane and Eastcheap. In fact, I reckon if you stopped a hundred people racing down Clement Lane or Eastcheap for the tube, or across the bridge to London Bridge Station, ninety-nine of them wouldn't know there was a church there. Second, apart from a minor reference on the noticeboard outside, there's no other indication of its claim to fame. Which is crazy, because when you think about it, probably more people have heard of this church than any other in the City.

Go inside it and you're dazzled. It's a well-kept courtroom. There are plain cream walls, a flat ceiling with a huge, oblong plaster panel of all kinds of exotic fruit. Then, staring you in the eyes, is not the altar but this enormous carved pulpit with a fantastic carved canopy which seems to swoop out and cover half the church. If ever a high-court bench was specially designed and built for Judge Jeffreys, this would be it. I can just see him sitting there, black cap on his head, merrily condemning another bunch of would-be rebels to their deaths.

As for the rest of the church, the panels behind the altar look to me like rejects from a Greek Orthodox church. They sparkle. They glitter. They're sugary. But not sugary enough. Overall, I wouldn't say it was quite a lemon. But it's not a rich, juicy orange, either.

St Bride, Fleet Street

The journalists' church? The cathedral of the old newspaper-ridden Fleet Street? A haven for hacks? Come on. It's much too nice and pleasant. Much too neat and tidy. The number of times I've been in there I've yet to see one cigarette end stubbed out on a statue, one crumpled beer can tossed casually in the aisle, one hat flung on top of a candlestick. In spite of all the jokes about Christ being surrounded not by evangelists but by reporters, the whole idea of journalists and churches doesn't work. It's like talking about bookies and churches. Or, God help us, accountants and churches, although, come to think of it, the guy who took the thirty pieces of silver must have been an accountant.

I used to go in there a lot when I worked for a while for an advertising agency just around the corner. As I remember, the weekly expenses run up by some of the directors came to more than Wren spent building the thing in the first place.

Don't forget the spire. It's the original wedding-cake design, and the highest ever built by C.W. One of the original parishioners, appropriately called Mr Rich, is said to have earned himself another fortune by making wedding cakes that looked exactly like it. It's probably not true. But what do you expect of a journalists' church?

St Mary Woolnoth, Lombard Street

This church should be the patron saint of wage slaves. One of its vicars, John Newton, started off as a slave-trader and then, when he saw which way the apple was falling, changed sides, became a fierce abolitionist and even lectured William Wilberforce on the need to fight the good fight.

Outside, maybe because it's black and grimy, it looks a bit forbidding. Like a cross between a mortuary and a coroner's court. Inside it's all pillars. I bet you could fall asleep there during a sermon and nobody would notice.

All the same, it's a good place to skip into when it's pouring with rain, Bank Underground Station is full to overflowing and you've got a meeting in Lombard Street in twenty minutes.

St Botolph, Aldersgate Street

I don't know why, but I was disappointed when I finally managed to get into St Botolph's. From the street, squeezed between Postman's Park and the enormous London Museum roundabout, it looks quite exciting: a Venetian window, a couple of columns, a black board celebrating its eighteenth-century ceiling.

The interior is certainly eighteenth century. Including some old verger wandering around doing nothing. The

Venetian window was deep and sombre. The galleries were dark and serious. The ceiling, however, was quite splendid.

Maybe it was disappointing because, having tried to get into it so many times and, in spite of the blackboard telling me otherwise, found the doors locked, when I eventually made it there was no way it could live up to my expectations. I'll try it again on another occasion and see if I feel the same. Perhaps when it's raining.

The Gomulka List

Like Gomulka, these are churches we'd perhaps prefer not to have anything to do with. But if, in the long term, we feel it could possibly be in our interests to take them on, we might consider it.

St Nicholas, Cole Abbey, Queen Victoria Street

It might sound nice. St Nicholas: Christmas. Cole: a roaring fire. But believe me, you'll freeze to death in here before you get through even the first decade of the rosary. It's been run by the Free Church of Scotland – the Wee Frees – for so long and they've spent so little on heating the place that there are icicles hanging off the walls. How they can sit through services that last anything up to two hours and include a full one-hour sermon, goodness only knows. Maybe they can't. Maybe they're just frozen solid.

Talk to the huddled figure in three overcoats in the corner and, if you can understand his accent, he'll tell ye that, och aye, they've nothing to do with Christmas or roaring fires, Cole Abbey means cold harbour. Once upon a time, when St Nicholas was a wee lad no higher than yer sporran, this was where they had a cold harbour and the area was packed with fishermen. Which I'm afraid I don't buy. Because if Cole Abbey is a corruption of cold harbour in this part of the country, why isn't it everywhere else there is a cold harbour?

On the other hand, it could be because of all the fishermen that today the church looks so gutted.

St Giles-without-Cripplegate

Now, I know this used to be Thomas More's local. The problem is that these days it's in the middle of the Barbican, which to all intents and purposes is a bit like being stuck in the middle of limbo. There are loads of signs pointing to it. Maps show it as bang in the centre of the development. But for the life of me I could never find it. One morning, heading for a meeting at the top of Wood Street, I glanced up and, surprise, surprise, there it was. After the meeting I popped back for a quick look.

First things first. It's a Norman church as opposed to a Wren church. It's firm, squat, four-square. It's also a parish church. You've only got to look at the church tower to see that. If anything was designed by a parish council, it's the tower. The bottom section is stone. The top section is brick.

The whole church has been too well restored. It's so restored it's squeaky clean. There's hardly a patch of dust or a cobweb to be seen. Yet it has stood here for nearly 1,000 years. Somehow that doesn't feel right. It should be dank and dark and eerie. And much easier to find.

St Giles himself is another worry. He was crippled at the gate of his cave by one of the locals. There was a group of them out hunting deer. This guy took a shot at the deer, it moved and the arrow hit St Giles. Everyone agreed it was an accident. The King of the Goths apologised to St Giles personally and even built a monastery for him to make up for it. St Giles forgave everybody concerned. But you know the fuss they make about this kind of thing nowadays. If we took it over the place would be surrounded by the animal-rights brigade before you could kick the Presbytery cat. Believe me, it's not worth the bother.

St Lawrence Jewry, Gresham Street

St Lawrence Jewry is not worth the effort, either.

You'd imagine that the very own church of the Corporation of the City of London would be something grand, sturdy, almost spectacular. The City of London is, after all, steeped in tradition. It is chock-a-block with spectacular guild halls. Whatever it does is all pageant and ceremonial. But you'd be wrong.

The location, I admit, is grand. It's straight across the courtyard from the Guild Hall itself. Mind you, if I had had anything to do with it I would have put the entrance, not just a side wall, facing the Guild Hall, but obviously greater minds than mine thought otherwise.

Inside, however, it's pretty much boring, nondescript, local government. It is spacious, though – at one time there used to be a gallery, but that's no longer there now.

Designed by Wren, and no doubt a committee of 1,000 chairmen, or rather chairpersons, it has been renovated so much that it has lost all its style and atmosphere, the last restoration being fifty years ago, as a result of damage caused during the last war by what signs outside the church describe as the 'King's enemies'. The altar and altarpiece are squeezed up against the wall. The stained-glass windows are straightforward. The pews and the woodwork are all very practical.

Nevertheless, the last time I was there it was full – of part-time soldiers and a bunch of over-eager women journalists. But that was because some crazy people were about to abseil down the front of the church tower.

God knows how they got any committee chairman to agree to that.

St Margaret Patten's

St Margaret's is good for the soul. No, not because 'pattens' was the name given to the wooden platform shoes people used to wear to keep their feet or their decent shoes out of the mud, but because it tests your patience to breaking point.

If you're out in the street you're on the side of the goat. If you're in the church you're on the . . . well, at least you're not on the side of the goat. The goat, of course, is the one that belongs to the flowersellers outside. More often than not it is tied to the railing, munching all the greenery they can't or don't want to sell. On occasions, however, it has been known to take more than a passing interest in my right trouser leg. Although so far, I'm pleased to say, it's escaped without any real damage. The goat, I mean.

Inside is where the real problem begins. St Margaret Patten's makes me seriously wonder whether I am fit to enter a religious building. I have to say, with all the humility I can artificially muster, that judging by everybody else I came across here, I most definitely am not. Because in a back room they run, would you believe, keep-fit classes. Not spiritual keep-fit classes, physical ones. So, another world church first: you stand more chance of being knocked down by a health freak than by a gaggle of old ladies hobbling around on zimmer frames.

As for the reception area for the gym, in other words the church itself, it's more skipping rope than personal trainer. Cheap, downmarket, but still perfectly capable of doing the job.

The best thing is the benches. Look at the churchwardens' pews at the back under the gallery. See the C.W. monogram? Some say it stands for Christopher Wren. That this is where the great Christopher Wren went to church, and that this was his very own personal and private pew. Others argue that C.W. stands for churchwardens. This is where the churchwardens

stood, sat, knelt and fell asleep during the sermons. Me? I
agree with them. There's no way good old Christopher
Wren would insist on his own pew. And if he did, there's no
way he would insist on such a grand, imposing design.
Churchwardens are another matter. Most of those I've come
across are not only pompous beyond belief but they spell it
out in capital letters. They are far more likely to insist on
their own box than any great architect.

St Margaret Patten's also has a fantastic lead-covered spire.
At 200 feet, it's the tallest ever built by C.W. I've never seen
it myself. I'm always too busy keeping an eye on that damn
goat.

St Michael Paternoster Royal, College Hill

This is said to have been the parish church of Dick
Whittington, four times mayor of London, but better known
as Dick, head of London, the poor, pathetic slave of a walking, talking, domineering, kinky cat which strode around on
its hind legs wearing tights and a pair of black leather boots.
If it was, he'll be turning in his grave. It's not that there is
anything wrong with the modern stained-glass window
depicting him and his damned flea-infested feline, it's just
that it should be in a modern church.

St Michael's, one of the last churches to be rebuilt according to the good Sir Christopher's designs, should have been
left alone. Instead it's a real cat's dinner. The tower and the
west end have been converted into offices. Not, unfortunately, for the Corporation of the City of London, which
wouldn't have been so bad. If you enter the church from
College Hill you don't come into the church at all. You come
unwittingly into a room they call – surprise, surprise. –
Whittington Hall, which I'm sure is not what our Dick
intended. The altar panels, the pulpit and the lectern are all
seventeenth century and should be dark, rich, red, warm

wood. But they're as light as a cat's whatever. The ceiling is too deep a blue. The east window is far too bright. The pews keep slipping and sliding over the marble floor, probably because of Dick Whittington's damn cat.

I'm sorry. The answer is no. I know, it breaks my heart too, especially as Paternoster Lane is so called because it was once the centre of the London rosary-making industry and the 'Royal' in its name comes from La Reole, a once famous wine centre near Bordeaux. But it's just not worth it.

St Benet, Queen Victoria Street

Forget St Benet. I've tried to get in there a hundred times without success. It's the Metropolitan Welsh Church of the City and Diocese of London, so I can only assume they think that they're six times more perfect than the rest of us and only need to open on Sundays. Either that or they're all out playing rugby the whole time.

Dutch Church, Austin Friars

Ditto the Dutch Church. You can never get in there, either. Which, I reckon, proves they only built it to try to ensure that, having bought Barings, they would turn it round and it would start to make money as quickly as possible.

St Stephen, Walbrook

Gee whizz, this was a surprise. A shock, even. It is supposed to be Wren's major City church, his masterpiece, its dome the first of its kind in England.

It certainly took my breath away. It's like a showcase for Danish furniture. It's big. It's wide, or rather, circular. It's bright. And it's spacious. The altar in the centre was sculpted by Henry Moore from a single block from the same quarry just outside Rome used by Michelangelo. All around are the flash Danish-looking benches.

At the back, by the door, is something everybody can identify with: the original telephone used by Chad Varah when he set up the Samaritans. But don't bother to ring the number, Mansion House 9000, now – you'll be dead before they answer it.

Why do I think we should turn it down? Because everybody will think that, as it has everything going for it, it will be top of our hit list. So let's surprise them.

St Paul's Cathedral

The same applies to St Paul's, the Church of England's great pride and joy, the largest and most famous church in the City. I tell you, if we also say no to St Paul's, it'll just kill them. If they cause any trouble, you can always get Lech and the boys out of retirement to come and carve them up ad majorem Dei gloriam as they say in *Lock, Stock and Two Smoking Candles.* Why not give it a whirl? Every left-footer in the country will, I guarantee, give you a kneeling ovation.

Well, there it is, your Popeship. The end of my first Roman, as opposed to Chinese, Takeaway. The others, covering the rest of the country, I'll let you have as soon as possible.

Yours, Speculator Tectus OOVII